"ELLINGTON UPTOWN"

Duke Ellington, James P. Johnson, & the Birth of Concert Jazz

John Howland

The University of Michigan Press ⒝ Ann Arbor

Copyright © by the University of Michigan 2009
All rights reserved
Published in the United States of America by
The University of Michigan Press
Manufactured in the United States of America
♾ Printed on acid-free paper

2012   2011   2010   2009   4   3   2   1

A CIP catalog record for this book is available from the British Library.

Library of Congress Cataloging-in-Publication Data

Howland, John Louis.
    "Ellington uptown" : Duke Ellington, James P. Johnson, and the birth of
concert jazz / John Howland.
        p.   cm. — (Jazz perspectives)
    Includes bibliographical references and index.
    ISBN-13: 978-0-472-11605-8 (cloth : alk. paper)
    ISBN-10: 0-472-11605-3 (cloth : alk. paper)
    ISBN-13: 978-0-472-03316-4 (pbk. : alk. paper)
    ISBN-10: 0-472-03316-6 (pbk. : alk. paper)
    1. Ellington, Duke, 1899–1974—Criticism and interpretation.   2. Johnson,
James P. (James Price), 1894–1955—Criticism and interpretation.   3. Big band
music—New York (State)—New York—History and criticism.   4. Jazz—History
and criticism.   I. Title.

ML3518.H68   2009
781.65'3—dc22   2008032105

For Agneta, Oskar, & Nils

CONTENTS

𝄢 ACKNOWLEDGMENTS

To my family and parents: you have my deepest gratitude for your support and patience throughout the long journey of researching and writing this book. I could not have done this project without your help. I am also especially grateful to the Jazz Perspectives series editor, my friend and colleague, Lewis Porter, as well as to my general editor at the University of Michigan Press, Chris Hebert. Thank you, Lewis and Chris, for your faith and help in developing this project. Stephen Hinton, Thomas Grey, and Scott Bukatman were each crucial to the inception and early development of key materials in this book during my dissertation work at Stanford University. I likewise owe a debt of gratitude to Howard Pollack, who has been extremely generous in his time, support, and friendship, and in offering thoughtful advice from very early on in my research on the subject of concert jazz. A good number of other scholars have provided great encouragement, generously read portions of this book, and given professional support that has been invaluable over the last several years. These friends and supporters include David Ake, Richard Crawford, John Hasse, Jeff Magee, Henry Martin, Brian Priestley, Christopher Reynolds, and Walter van de Leur. I also received generous and thoughtful input from the expert reviewers who read the manuscript for the University of Michigan Press.

For their input on research that has previously appeared in preliminary forms in essays for *American Music*, the *Annual Review of Jazz Studies*, and the *Musical Quarterly*, I would like to thank Ellie Hisama, Evan Spring, and Irene Zedlacher, as well as the reviewers who provided input on my work for these publications. I am grateful to the publishers of these earlier essays for their permission to reprint.

I am especially grateful to Barry Glover Sr., and Barry Glover Jr.—*thank you* for your friendship and generosity in sharing your family's rich inheritance of James P. Johnson's scores and other career memorabilia. I also would like to express my gratitude to Donald Shirley, who offered his rich memories of working with Duke Ellington. For their invaluable assistance in providing and locating other material, I would like to express my sincere gratitude to Aurora Perez, Richard Koprowski, and Barbra Sawkwa of the Stanford Archive of Recorded Sound; Lance Bowling; Marin Alsop; Sylvia Kennick Brown and the staff of the Williams College Archives and Special Collections; Annie Kuebler; John Hasse; the past and present staff of the Archives Center of the Smithsonian Institution's National Museum of American History; the past and present staff at the Institute of Jazz Studies; Gert-Jan Blom; and Atro "Wade" Mikkola. I am further grateful to Jim Nadel for both the course we taught together on Duke Ellington and the subsequent Ellington projects that we worked on for the Stanford Jazz Workshop. These experiences were the inspiration for this book. I am also indebted to both Maurice Peress for sharing his deep knowledge of Ellington and numerous score materials, and Louis Bellson and his fabulous orchestra for allowing me to work with them on several performances of reconstructed Ellington scores. Last, I would like to thank several granting bodies that have supported research that helped in the development of this book, including the Lloyd Hibberd Publication Endowment Fund of the American Musicological Society, the Whiting Foundation, Stanford University, the Institute of Jazz Studies, the University of California at Davis, and Rutgers University at Newark.

Symphonic jazz of the 1920s exerted a significant influence on a wide variety of American musical traditions well into the 1950s. Despite its broad legacy, this idiom is now often remembered merely as a minor footnote in most modern-day histories of American music. The term *symphonic jazz* is still regularly applied to the idiom's best-known concert work, George Gershwin's *Rhapsody in Blue*, which was premiered with much fanfare by the dance band leader Paul Whiteman at his "First Experiment in Modern Music" concert at New York's Aeolian Hall in 1924. Beyond this famous composition, modern concert performers and orchestras occasionally revive a small repertory of jazz- and ragtime-inspired concert works from this era. This repertory includes compositions by such celebrated composers as Aaron Copland, Paul Hindemith, Darius Milhaud, and Igor Stravinsky, as well as works by lesser-known figures like George Antheil, Louis Gruenberg, and John Alden Carpenter. Beyond this small body of well-pedigreed concert music, symphonic jazz had a far more profound cultural impact in a wide variety of sophisticated popular music arranging and hybrid orchestral traditions of the 1920s to 1950s.

In the 1920s and 1930s, the foremost exponents of symphonic jazz in the form of dance band arranging and popular concert works were Paul Whiteman and his chief arranger, Ferde Grofé. Whitemanesque symphonic jazz was a stylistically heterogeneous idiom that referenced jazz, syncopated popular music from Tin Pan Alley to Broadway, African American music, and the "light" classics. The *jazz* component of symphonic jazz paralleled 1920s journalistic uses of the term as both an adjective and verb to imply a mildly irreverent interbreeding of white and black and high and low music. The *symphonic* characterization referenced the music's heightened theatricality, its comparatively complex multithematic formal structures, and especially its "sophisticated" introductions, interludes, and codas, its unexpected modulations and dramatic cadenzas, and its emphasis on orchestrational and stylistic variety. The hybrid symphonic jazz sound developed an unusual cultural breadth that spanned the concert hall, jazz and dance bands, radio orchestras, Tin Pan Alley, Broadway musical theater, the variety prologue shows of the deluxe movie palaces, and certain genres of film music of the late 1920s and 1930s. In each of these contexts, the proponents of symphonic jazz sought to endow contemporary popular music with an aura of glamour and elevated cultural refinement.

The rich programmatic themes associated with symphonic jazz concert works primarily centered on a glamorous urban lifestyle and American metropolitan mythology that was widely represented in contemporary media portrayals of both white and black New York. Such topics are readily reflected in the titles and descriptive programs of works like Louis Alter's *Manhattan Suite* (1928) and *Side Street in Gotham* (1938), Vernon Duke's *New York Nocturne* and *Lake Shore Drive* (both 1939), and Ferde Grofé's *Metropolis* (1928) and *Broadway at Night* (1924; copyrighted 1944).[1] These Tin Pan Alley–published scores, as well as related counterparts with more highbrow pedigrees, celebrated the idea of the metropolitan environment as a jazzy "city symphony." Such metropolitan rhapsodies sought to evoke themes such as the mythological aspects of the skyscraper and the glorification of the modern machine, as well as the omnipresent noise and hectic ambiance of the modern urban milieu. By the end of the 1920s, this interest in jazz-derived musical modernism had largely gone out of fashion and given way to new aesthetic concerns in contemporary art music circles. In popular culture, though, these themes and hybrid jazz-classical stylistic affectations continued to have important cultural relevance for at least another two decades. During the 1930s and 1940s, most contemporary critics damned this miscegenation of concert hall culture, entertainment intent, jazz, dance band arranging, Tin Pan Alley tunes, and quasi-symphonic instrumentation as mongrel, middlebrow culture for the masses. Despite long-standing traditions of cross-fertilization and cultural hybridization in all strata of American musical life, this anti-middlebrow criticism resonates with contemporary concerns for policing the cultural boundaries between art and entertainment and between "high" and "popular" cultures. Such class-hierarchy and mixed-culture discourses are central to understanding the meaning, intent, and reception of symphonic jazz. For that reason, these vibrant middle-culture topics form an important secondary focus in this book.

In its ambition to marry classical prestige, lush symphonic-style textures, jazz orchestration, and contemporary popular music, symphonic jazz was intimately tied to American preoccupations with class and race. There were great disparities between the cultural profiles of white and black creative contributions to this musical trend, however. For both black and white advocates of African American cultural advancement in the mid-1920s, the lack of a black leader in jazz-inspired concert music was troubling. As evidence, consider Paul Whiteman's professional scrapbooks, which include five copies of a nationally circulated essay from July 1927 by the celebrated (white) critic H. L. Mencken.[2] This essay provides a frank and racially confrontational critique of the complex relations between the New Negro literary movement, African American entertainers and musicians, and the new symphonic jazz vogue. Writing at the height of the Harlem Renaissance in art and literature, Mencken suggests that the newly fashionable white "acceptance of the educated Negro leaves him exposed to the same criteria of judgment that apply to everyone else." Mencken notes that the educated African American author, artist, or composer has

> hitherto . . . derived very considerable advantages from the fact that he was an outcast; it seemed a marvel if he made himself heard of at all. But hereafter he will have to produce the goods or shut up.

So far . . . his accomplishments have been very modest. Even in those fields wherein his opportunities . . . have been precisely equal to the white man's, he has done little of solid value. I point, for example, to the field of music. It may be, as they say, that the Negroes invented ragtime, and jazz after it, but certainly it would be absurd to say that they have surpassed or even equaled the whites in writing the new music. The best jazz of today is not composed by black men but by Jews—and I mean best in every sense. *Why did the Negro composers wait for George Gershwin to do his "Rhapsody in Blue"? Why, indeed, did they wait for Paul Whiteman to make jazz a serious matter?*[3]

The spiritual is another musical form that the Negroes are supposed to have invented. . . . [L]et us admit that theory. But where is the Negro composer who is writing spirituals today—I mean good ones? If he exists he is not heard of. Certainly there is plenty of opportunity here—and it has been permitted to go to waste. The spiritual, [for instance] . . . , could be considerably improved. It might be developed into something resembling a cantata. It might be given instrumental support. But no Negro composer has ever made any serious effort to work out its possibilities. It remains naïve and crude like hoe cakes.

Mencken's ruminations on black concert music are focused on the cultural terrain of 1920s Tin Pan Alley "jazz," Harlem entertainment (the black peers of Gershwin and Whiteman), and symphonic jazz concert works instead of the classical music tradition per se. Mencken suggests that Whitemanesque concert works represent a white realization of the cultural potential inherent in black musical traditions. (Mencken's comment about Jewish jazz is partly a reference to the syncopated popular music of such high-profile Jewish musicians as George Gershwin, the clarinetist Ted Lewis, and Irving Berlin.)[4] Mencken implies that the cultural imperative of symphonic jazz concert works actually lies in the project of African Americans accomplishing this goal from *within* black popular music. His complaint is that African American talent has squandered its rich musical traditions on derivative entertainment rather than follow the more sophisticated models of popular music produced by their white New York entertainment peers.

While Mencken's opinions on black concert music may at a superficial level resonate with the New Negro hope for producing extended concert music forms from black folk idioms, they diverge from that musical agenda by principally locating the realization of this goal within the creative talent of contemporary black popular music (from Harlem cabarets, musical revues, etc.). Moreover, through his comments on "serious" jazz, Mencken also seemingly advocates that a black concert music tradition—whether performed by symphonic, jazz, dance, or hybrid orchestras—be built through the "improvement" and expansion of the aesthetic and formal foundations of jazz, blues, and spirituals idioms of contemporary black urban entertainment, rather than through the appropriation of rural black "folk jazz," or other folk music sources. This particular viewpoint was at odds with the high-culture, classically biased musical aspirations of elder New Negro leaders like James Weldon Johnson who sought a high-culture symphonic elevation of African American *folk* music (as opposed to contemporary popular music). Mencken did not, however, see any Harlem musical figures that paralleled either the literary accomplishments of James Weldon Johnson or the musical sophistication of Paul Whiteman. While there is some validity to Mencken's comment on Whiteman, this period opinion suffers from cultural, racial, and commercial near-sightedness. Whiteman merely represented the prominent tip of the symphonic jazz iceberg, and July 1927 marked a moment in which concert-style symphonic jazz was just beginning to have widespread national impact. Over the remainder of the decade and into the early 1930s, this trend gained far greater clarity and cultural dissemination, and a good number of white *and black* contributors emerged.

From roughly 1910 to the 1940s, the symphonic jazz vogue intersected in a number of ways with the world of Harlem, and African American, entertainment. In the larger arena of popular culture, most of these activities were overshadowed by the dominant white symphonic jazz entertainments of the day and the bona fide jazz tradition itself. Nevertheless, the critical reception of Duke Ellington's music in the 1930s and 1940s reveals a gradual shift in the ideological basis of symphonic jazz away from its Whitemanesque roots in (white) New York entertainment toward the hope of a "serious" concert work idiom based on the elevation of "authentic," African American hot jazz. While Ellington's high-profile concert jazz activities of this period offered a major African American redefinition of symphonic jazz, so did the lesser-known extended compositions of Ellington's early musical mentor, James P. Johnson. Johnson was known chiefly as a successful Broadway composer of the 1920s, a popular songwriter, and the father and main exponent of Harlem stride piano. After 1930, Johnson turned his artistic aspirations toward the composition of racially expressive, jazz-based concert music. From the late 1920s to the 1940s, he created a large and varied body of symphonic jazz-oriented instrumental and choral concert works for forces that ranged from solo piano, to string quartet, to large hybrid orchestral ensembles.

Both Ellington and Johnson pursued richly diverse professional careers that spanned musical theater, cabaret and nightclub revues, jazz, and dance bands. They both worked as Harlem jook joint and rent party pianists, and both shared an ambition to compose jazz-based concert works. Such multifaceted careers were not without precedent in the world of Harlem entertainment. For the purposes of this book, the central circle of the Harlem entertainment community from 1910 through the 1940s includes the older generation of Will Marion Cook, Will Vodery, W. C. Handy, and James Reese Europe; the middle generation of James P. Johnson, William Grant Still (as a popular music arranger), Willie "The Lion" Smith, and Charles Luckeyeth Roberts; and the younger generation of Duke Ellington and Fats Waller. Older figures such as Cook, Europe, Will Vodery, and Handy were the generation of black musicians who initially broke New York entertainment's racial barriers in the first two decades of the century. The cross-racial respect and relative financial success of these senior musicians positioned them as role models for aspiring young black musicians in the 1920s. The subsequent symphonic jazz ambitions of Johnson and Ellington were an outgrowth of the musical activities and cultural aspirations of Cook and Europe in the second decade of the century. Most notably, though, there were great aesthetic differences between the cultural agenda of this circle and the musical aspirations espoused by the leaders of the Harlem Renaissance in art and literature.

This book examines the African American contributions to the symphonic jazz vogue of the 1920s through 1940s. This subject is centrally explored through the concert jazz compositions of two of Harlem's most famous musicians, Duke Ellington and James P. Johnson. This project is not intended to be a comprehensive overview of

Ellington's and Johnson's efforts in extended composition. Rather, it explores both the ideas and formal models that these composers employed and how these works relate to broader social and cultural concerns among the multigenerational Harlem entertainment circle. By focusing on Ellington and Johnson, this study illuminates the little-discussed world of a truly hybrid compositional tradition that has been lost in the cultural gap between the venerated "art music" canons of authentic jazz (where these works are seen as too "pretentious," "classical," or "symphonic") and classical music (where these works are seen as too "entertaining" or not "serious" enough). This study further aims to contextualize the black symphonic jazz tradition by exploring its deeply enmeshed relations with this era's heated and divisive debates on cultural hierarchies, musical hierarchies, racial uplift, race relations, the marketplace, and other aspects of American society.

This study reveals that despite their shared artistic origins and their mutual rhapsodizing on the subject of Harlem, Johnson and Ellington ultimately arrived at two different but equal versions of "serious" concert jazz. While Ellington's "symphonic" vision remained true to his lifelong career in big band jazz, Johnson's more outwardly symphonic compositions display an equally faithful, rich, and unique musical portrait of Harlem's dynamic cultural heritage. Though each artistic vision owed a great debt to the vernacular concert work aspirations of the older generation of Harlem musicians, Johnson's "serious" compositions are ultimately more closely aligned with the musical theater roots of these elder composers than with the rich orchestral jazz tradition that was so central to Ellington's compositional voice. Regardless, with their shared cultural ambition and their mutual social pride, as well as their shared histories in the Harlem entertainment renaissance, the vibrant musical tapestries of Johnson's and Ellington's concert works embody the quintessential artistic expressions of the collective hopes, passions, and humanity of Harlem's celebrated community of entertainers.

The first chapter of the book introduces the historical, contextual, and formal issues of the Harlem-based concert jazz tradition. It specifically explores the connections between the black entertainment pioneers Will Marion Cook, Will Vodery, and James Reese Europe, on the one hand, and the younger generation of Johnson, Ellington, and their 1920s Harlem musical peers, on the other.

The second chapter concerns the history of Johnson's 1927 composition *Yamekraw: A Negro Rhapsody.* Johnson's rhapsody is used to illustrate the legacy of the symphonic jazz idiom as it existed beyond the George Gershwin–Paul Whiteman circle. By examining appropriations of this work—particularly its transformation into a 1930 Vitaphone film short of the same name—I explore the unique cultural breadth of this musical idiom.

Chapter 3 examines the interrelation between Johnson's and Ellington's concert jazz ideals and traditions of arranging for production numbers in all-black stage, floor show, and film entertainments of the 1920s and 1930s. This chapter involves source studies from Johnson's musical theater works, Ellington's little-documented musical contributions to the floor shows of the Cotton Club, Ellington's score for the 1935 film short *Symphony in Black,* and several of Johnson's concert jazz works that derive from earlier stage production numbers.

Chapter 4 explores the complex relationship between Whitemanesque and Ellingtonian concert jazz. This chapter involves both historical and formal studies of Ellington's early extended works, from the 1926 *Rhapsody Jr.* to the 1943 *Black, Brown and Beige (BB&B).* This chapter reveals the relation of these works to an important compositional model that Ellington adapted from 1920s symphonic jazz concert works. *BB&B* simultaneously represents both Ellington's transcendence of this model and the apotheosis of his unique adaptations of—and expansions on—the formal model of the Whitemanesque symphonic jazz tradition.

Chapter 5 broadly considers Johnson's post-*Yamekraw* concert works and the difficulties that he faced in finding an audience for these projects. This chapter involves source studies of a wealth of long unknown Johnson archival materials, including scores and compositional sketches, correspondence, scrapbooks, and other primary materials. The history of Johnson's 1932 *Harlem Symphony* receives central consideration.

The final chapter considers the histories of both Ellington's Carnegie Hall concert series of the 1940s, and the extended compositions that were featured in each of these concerts. Of these works, the 1943 *New World A-Comin'* and the 1950 *Harlem* will receive special attention. Particular attention will be given to the idea of the "symphonic Ellington," the formal and programmatic ideas behind his mature vision for concert jazz.

The book concludes with a critical discussion of the differences between Johnson's and Ellington's visions for concert jazz, as well as a consideration of the larger legacy of Ellington's concert jazz. This final chapter revisits a number of themes from previous chapters, including the relation of Johnson's and Ellington's compositions to midcentury Afro-modernist aesthetics and Ellington's role in defining the idea of "jazz composition."

Last, I would like to underscore two aspirations that have motivated this book. The first is my hope that the music discussed in these pages will be heard, both in new performances and by making older recordings available. As my book demonstrates, this music is a vital expression of African American musical art, and symphonic jazz in general defines a rich musical legacy that should be known and appreciated for its uniquely American desire to combine art and entertainment, black and white, and high, middle, and low cultural expressions. The second aspiration is that this project will foster a renewed public interest in the career and widely diverse musical output of James P. Johnson, an early jazz giant who left a major musical legacy beyond his central role in this quintessential American art form. Johnson's concert works, popular songs, and musical theater productions demonstrate his impressive contributions to American music of the twentieth century. The rich history, beauty, and broad accessibility of his concert works in particular should underscore the relevance of this music to modern musicians who hope to speak more broadly to America's multicultural audiences.

one   𝄢   FROM *CLORINDY* TO CARNEGIE HALL

The Harlem Entertainment Community

*I*n early 1950, the NBC Symphony conductor Arturo Toscanini commissioned a series of compositions for the radio orchestra that were to be broadcast and recorded as a suite entitled *Portrait of New York*. Duke Ellington was asked to musically depict the community of Harlem, his longtime home in Manhattan. (Six composers were scheduled to be engaged for the project. Beyond Ellington, Skitch Henderson, Vernon Duke, Sigmund Romberg, and Don Gillis had committed to the project, and the organizers were "angling for either Leonard Bernstein or Aaron Copland" as the sixth contributor.) In response, Ellington wrote his masterly concert work, the *Harlem Suite* (which is also commonly known as *A Tone Parallel to Harlem* or just *Harlem*). This highly personal image of Harlem as a diverse, multifaceted community stands apart from the typical media caricatures of this neighborhood as either an overcrowded slum or as a morally and racially transgressive haven for nightclub life. *Harlem*'s descriptive program vibrantly juxtaposes pious church scenes and a nightclub floor show, a street parade and a funeral, and depictions of both 125th Street (Harlem's commercial heart) and the community's Spanish neighborhood. In some versions of the program, portions of the work are said to commemorate Harlem's celebrities, including the boxer Jack Johnson, the dancer Bill "Bojangles" Robinson, the comedian Bert Williams, and the musician and entertainer Thomas "Fats" Waller. The work also purportedly includes musical evocations of the great variety of people who can be seen in Harlem—from "cats shucking and stiffing" on a street corner, to the "chic" ladies who parade the latest fashions down the neighborhood's streets. Nearly all versions of the program reinforce the idea that Harlem has always had "more churches than cabarets." The closing episodes of the work are said to depict Harlem's increasing demands for racial equality and civil rights. In sum, for Ellington, Harlem represented a microcosm of African American experience. While Ellington saw this community as the greatest evidence of the rich potential of black American culture, he knew that the Harlem entertainment tradition from which his career grew was founded on a complicated social relation between African American artistic traditions and a restrictive and often misconceived white reception of this art.

James P. Johnson held a similarly strong interest in celebrating Harlem's African American community and Harlem entertainment. These interests are realized in subtle ways across all of his concert works. In a composition like *Harlem Symphony* (1932), for example, these topics form an overriding programmatic narrative. Here, Johnson constructed his own musical tour of Harlem's diverse highlights across four movements, which are titled "Subway Journey," "Harlem Love Song," "Night Club Life," and "Baptist Mission." Similar slice-of-Harlem-life programs lie at the heart of two of his unperformed ballet suites, *Manhattan Street Scene* and *Sefronia's Dream: Negro Fantasy* (both undated), and his jazz-based opera, *The Dreamy Kid* (ca. 1942).

In both Ellington's and Johnson's concert works of the 1930s and 1940s, such portraits typically represent idealized, nostalgic images of a Harlem that had already begun to vanish following the onset of the Depression and the Harlem race riots in 1935 and 1943. These later events were not the origins of Harlem's decline, however. Despite the great civic pride expressed in New Negro literature and the programs of these later concert works by Ellington and Johnson, the decline of Harlem into an impoverished, crime-ridden black ghetto had begun early in the 1920s, in near parallel with the rise of the neighborhood's brief but bright cultural renaissance. As a result of the Great Migration, from 1920 to 1930, New York City's black population expanded 115 percent, from 152,467 to 327,706, with the vast majority of these residents living in the roughly two square miles of Harlem's traditional boundaries.[1] This largely impoverished mass of humanity suffered under the unscrupulous practices of landlords who charged them on average nearly twice the rent that lower-class white families paid elsewhere in New York for similar tenement accommodations. This combustible mix of overcrowding, poverty, and racial ghettoization gave birth to an irreversible pattern of urban decay, crime, and other social ills.

Harlem's smoldering social tensions came to a head in 1935, when a false rumor circulated that the police had killed a young African American boy who had been caught shoplifting on 125th Street. This rumor led to a widely publicized race riot that left three men dead and hundreds of stores looted. This social catastrophe marked a clear end to the New Negro renaissance in art and literature and the beginning of the end for Harlem's entertainment boom. As Alain Locke recollected in 1936, "The Harlem riot of March 19 and 20, 1935 . . . [was] variously diagnosed as a depression spasm, [or] a Ghetto mutiny . . . [I]t etched on the public mind another Harlem than the bright surface Harlem of the night clubs, cabaret tours and arty magazines, a Harlem that the social worker knew all along." For Locke, this event "brought the first vivid realization of the actual predicament of the mass life in Harlem." He saw this event as a call for Harlem's more privileged citizens to rise to social action:

> No emerging élite—artistic, professional or mercantile—can suspend itself in thin air over the abyss of a mass of unemployed stranded in an over-expensive, disease- and crime-ridden slum. It is easier to dally over black Bohemia or revel in the hardy survivals of Negro art and culture than to contemplate this dark Harlem of semi-starvation, mass exploitation, and seething unrest. But turn we must. For there is no cure or saving magic in poetry and art, . . . or in international prestige and interracial recognition . . . Today instead of applause and publicity, Harlem needs constructive social care, fundamental community development and planning, and above all statesman-like civic handling.[2]

The race riots of early August 1943 were again sparked by hearsay and confrontations with the white police force. According to one *New York Times* report, the riots began after "Private Robert Bandy, the 26-year-old Negro soldier" was "charged with attacking a white policeman who was arresting a Negro woman in a Harlem hotel."[3] This event led to rumors that the police had killed a black soldier who was protecting his mother. According to the *New York Times*, this story sparked the ensuing riot in which "five [people] were killed, 500 injured and 500 arrested," and there was "property damage estimated at $5,000,000."[4]

Harlem's cross-racial entertainment business died altogether after the 1943 riot, and the neighborhood's fortunes continued to decline until its rock-bottom lows in the 1970s and 1980s. That Ellington composed *Black, Brown and Beige* and *New World A-Comin'*—his two earliest "tone parallels" to Harlem—within roughly a year following the 1943 race riots underscores his steadfast optimism and pride in what Harlem had once represented to his generation.

The early careers of Johnson and Ellington are central to the story of the entertainment renaissance in Jazz Age Harlem. This chapter will explore Ellington's and Johnson's relations to the history and cultural mythologies of Harlem entertainment across the 1920s and 1930s. Each personal history will be followed up to a brief account of the premiere performances of their first major concert works at Carnegie Hall, the celebrated New York performance space that has long been portrayed as America's most venerated shrine to musical art (despite the fact that artists could rent the hall for privately promoted performance events). In their day, Johnson's and Ellington's Carnegie performances carried great cultural significance to the African American and jazz communities, as each composer prominently featured concert works that proudly celebrated the art of Harlem's popular music traditions.

In his autobiography's discussion of his early days in Harlem, Duke Ellington remarks that in the era of World War I and early 1920s "Harlem had its own rich, special folklore, totally unrelated to the South or anywhere else." He also sadly observes that this rich urban folklore is "gone now, but it was tremendous then."[5] Throughout his career, Ellington viewed the diversity and richness of Harlem's black culture as unique, and he continually sought to celebrate and portray this world in his music. The origins of Ellington's fascination with this "folklore" can be found in an earlier passage from his autobiography, where Ellington notes that in his youth in Washington, D.C.,

> it was New York that filled our imagination. We were awed by the never-ending roll of great talents there, talents in so many fields, in society music and blues, in vaudeville and songwriting, in jazz and theatre, in dancing and comedy. . . .
>
> Harlem, to our minds, did indeed have the world's most glamorous atmosphere. We had to go there.[6]

At the heart of this folklore are Harlem's famous nightclubs, ballrooms, and theaters. These sites include such establishments as Leroy's (aka Leroy Wilkins's) Restaurant, Barron's (aka Barron Wilkins's) Exclusive Club, Connie's Inn, Small's Paradise, the Lafayette Theatre, the Apollo Theatre, and many other smaller venues.[7] This was the heart of Harlem to the young Ellington in the early 1920s, and the rich urban folklore that accumulated around this entertainment community is central to images that Ellington and Johnson depicted in their concert works. As such, it is vital to understand the biographical connections of these two musicians to this community.

13 THE FIRST ENTERTAINMENT RENAISSANCE OF BLACK MANHATTAN, 1898–1921

James Weldon Johnson notably titled his landmark account of African American history in New York *Black Manhattan*. At the time of its publication in 1930, most Americans associated Harlem with black life in New York. Johnson's title, though, implies broader historical perspectives on the ever-shifting tides of New York real estate. In an earlier 1925 essay, "The Making of Harlem," Johnson wrote that "Negro Harlem is practically a development of the past decade." In this article, he briefly sketches the history of key black New York neighborhoods up to the 1890s, when "the center of [the] colored population had shifted to the upper Twenties and lower Thirties west of Sixth Avenue." He then notes that there was yet another geographic shift in the black population a decade later up to the area around West Fifty-third Street. On this latter relocation, Johnson remarks that this second period

> deserves some special mention because it ushered in a [n]ew phase
> of life among colored New Yorkers. Three rather well appointed
> hotels were opened in the street and they quickly became the cen-
> ters of a sort of fashionable [African American] life that hitherto
> had not existed. . . . One of these hotels, The Marshall, became
> famous as the headquarters of Negro talent. There gathered the
> actors, the musicians, the composers, the writers, the singers,
> dancers and vaudevillians. There one went to get a close-up of
> [Bert] Williams and [George] Walker, [Bob] Cole and [Rosamond]
> Johnson, Ernest Hogan, Will Marion Cook, Jim Europe, Aida
> Overton, and of others equally and less known. . . . The first . . .
> jazz band ever heard in New York, or, perhaps anywhere, was orga-
> nized at The Marshall . . . and . . . called The Memphis Students.
> Jim Europe was a member of that band, and out of it grew the
> famous Clef Club, of which he was the noted leader, and which for
> a long time monopolized the business of "entertaining" private
> [white society] parties and furnishing music for the [n]ew dance
> craze.[8]

In this passage, Johnson identifies the historical nucleus of an ever-expanding social group that came to dominate New York's black musical theater and entertainment circles up to the early 1940s.

The musical theater scholar Thomas Riis has noted that the early twentieth-century black musical theater tradition grew out of conflations of several key nineteenth-century American traditions in entertainment. Nineteenth-century African American folk music and dance traditions were a major cornerstone. Equally important were the cross-racial refractions of these traditions in blackface minstrelsy, by both white and black actors.[9] Beyond minstrelsy, early twentieth-century variety theater owed significant debts to the imported operettas that were popular on American stages from the 1870s to the 1890s, the spectacle or extravaganza (which subordinated narrative coherence for elaborate stage tableaux, scenic effects, and rich dance-oriented numbers), and burlesque theater (that featured both girl-oriented acts and other entertainment). In this broader theatrical context, the 1890s saw the rise of the revue, which Riis characterizes as "a topical variety show in which a group of performers work in several different sketches and roles."[10] The all-black musicals and musical revues that Johnson and his peers produced at the turn of the century moved black entertainment away from the demeaning legacy of minstrelsy, but Johnson himself credits the all-black *Creole Show* of 1890 (produced by a white impresario) as the "first successful departure" from "strict minstrelsy."[11] Johnson stresses the production's influential use of top comedic talent, "smart and up-to-date" material, and its innovative use of "a chorus of the sixteen most beautiful colored girls" in the "glorified" manner that Florenz Ziegfeld's *Follies* revues were later renowned for.

The entertainers who gathered at the Marshall Hotel at 127–129 West Fifty-third Street (between Sixth and Seventh avenues) represent a key circle of musicians and other creative talent who became black pioneers in Broadway musical theater, in the nascent recording industry, and in the dance band industry of the second decade of the century. The West Indian–born Bert Williams and his partner George Walker had formed a nationally popular vaudeville team from 1893. In late 1897, a young black composer and violinist, Will Marion Cook, had approached Williams and Walker with the idea of mounting a full-scale, all-black musical comedy, which he called *Clorindy, or, The Origin of the Cakewalk*. Born in 1869, Cook's training in music was initially directed toward a career as a concert violinist. In fact, from 1888 to 1890, Cook had studied in Berlin with Joseph Joachim, the leading European violinist of the era and an intimate colleague of Johannes Brahms. Realizing the bleak prospects of establishing a career as a black concert violinist, Cook upon his return to the States focused his energies on composing. In 1895, Cook studied composition at the National Conservatory of Music in New York, a tenure that included a brief period of study with the Czech composer Antonín Dvořák, who was then residing in New York. Whether he acted under the impetus of Dvořák's call for American composers to explore their own music heritage or was more influenced by the burgeoning success of contemporary black musical theater, Cook ultimately focused his efforts on composing in characteristically African American idioms. This development in turn led to his employment in black theater and his association with the celebrated black poet Paul

Laurence Dunbar, who wrote the lyrics and book for *Clorindy*. Cook's hour-long musical opened (without Williams and Walker, who had other contractual obligations) on July 5, 1898, at the Casino Theatre Roof Garden in New York (Broadway at Thirty-ninth Street). This all-black musical comedy sparked an African American entertainment renaissance in New York. From 1900, Williams and Walker were production partners with Cook. Their theater company produced a string of all-black musical theater hits, including *Sons of Ham* (1900), *In Dahomey* (1902), *Abyssinia* (1906), and *Bandanna Land* (1907). Another key member of this creative team was Will Vodery, who shared duties as musical director, composer, and arranger with Cook on all of the Williams and Walker musicals. In tandem with these successes, Williams's popularity extended beyond color lines, as he became the best-selling black recording artist before 1920[12] and a central performer in the long-running *Ziegfeld Follies* revues on Broadway. Vodery followed Williams to work in the *Follies*, and he became the most celebrated black arranger on Broadway during the first two decades of the twentieth century.

The successes of Williams, Walker, Cook, and Vodery were not isolated. In particular, the brothers James Weldon and J. Rosamond Johnson, along with the performer Bob Cole and the conductor James Reese Europe, mounted serious competition to Williams and Walker. From 1897 to 1910, Williams, Walker, Dunbar, Cook, the Johnson brothers, Cole, the vaudeville star and songwriter Ernest Hogan, and their larger circle "constituted a core group of black writers, musicians, and vaudeville stars who together would create the new-all-black musicals that Americanized Broadway, moving the Great White Way from waltz to ragtime."[13] As this initial vogue for all-black musical theater waned shortly after 1910, however, James Weldon Johnson turned his increasingly high-culture ambitions to writing. By the 1920s, he had become the most prominent voice in the New Negro movement in Harlem.

As Johnson indicated, the Marshall Hotel circle gave birth to an important orchestral ensemble, the Memphis Students, which was also known at various times as the Nashville Students and the Tennessee Students. (None of the members was from Memphis, Nashville, or Tennessee, and none was a student.) The Memphis Students were an all-black, variety entertainment act founded by Ernest Hogan with the help of Will Marion Cook (as musical director). By 1905, Hogan was famous as a comedian, songwriter, and vaudeville star. As a composer, he was most famous—or infamous—for "All Coons Look Alike to Me" (1895), which sparked the pre–World War I vogue for "coon songs." Like Cook, Hogan found great racial pride in reclaiming black-influenced, dialect-based popular song. Their relation to musical dialect—meaning both the lyrical setting and race-based musical idioms—is related to the conception of "double-consciousness" voiced in the previous decade by W. E. B. DuBois.[14] For Cook and Hogan, potentially derogatory elements could be tempered to work as both contributions to contemporary popular entertainment trends and black-written celebrations of African American heritage, speech, and physical traits. On numerous occasions, Cook spoke about the "unbleached" idioms (to paraphrase DuBois) that he believed best represented the authentic, modern, African American musical aesthetic. He promoted these musical idioms in all of his musical theater and variety entertainment ventures, including the Memphis Students.

The Memphis Students officially premiered at Proctor's Twenty-Third Street Theatre in the spring of 1905. The group involved roughly twenty members, and showcased performers who performed multiple entertainment roles. Johnson claimed that the group was the first "jazz band," and the ensemble purportedly employed a jazz-oriented instrumentation of "banjos, saxophones, clarinets and trap drums." In *Black Manhattan*, Johnson repeats this claim and expands his account of the group's ensemble to "banjos, mandolins, guitars, saxophones, and drums in combination. . . . There was also a violin, a couple of brass instruments, and a double bass."[15] These latter claims—from 1930—partly imply that the orchestra was an early incarnation of a Paul Whiteman–style hybrid big band. This said, no contemporary sources verify Johnson's anachronistic descriptions. According to Reid Badger, James Reese Europe's biographer,

> the Students seem to have consisted of . . . predominantly . . . mandolins, harp guitars, and banjos (with perhaps three celli added for good measure). All of these, with the exception, possibly, of the celli, are plucked or strummed and . . . would provide [a] strongly rhythmical effect . . . [for] the kind of syncopated music that Will Marion Cook was then composing.[16]

Evidence suggests that the musico-theatrical design of the Memphis Students was akin to the minstrelsy-burlesque theatrical hybrid offered by the *Creole Show* fifteen years earlier. In both cases, the emerging vaudeville aesthetic and transformations of minstrelsy-derived traditions were central to the presentations of these projects.

The year 1905 brought two other turning points in the history of black Manhattan. A new subway line had opened along Lenox Avenue in 1903 but had not sparked the real estate boom that many white developers had projected for the neighborhoods north of Central Park. On Christmas Eve of 1905, there was a well-publicized murder in an apartment building at 31 West 133rd Street, which scared off most of the building's tenants. Reacting to this bad publicity and the depression in the neighborhood's housing market, the building's manager began working with a young, African American realtor, Philip A. Payton Jr., to repopulate the apartments with reliable black tenants willing to pay higher rents than the "lower grades of foreign white people" that had previously occupied the complex.[17] This was the catalyst for the black migration to Harlem that James Weldon Johnson had noted.

The second important event that fed the Harlem entertainment renaissance was the founding of Gotham & Attucks Music Company, a black-run publishing firm, on July 15, 1905.[18] This event marks the birth of the first African American publishing house in Tin Pan Alley proper (which was then located on Twenty-eighth Street between Fifth Avenue and Broadway), as the new firm relocated to 42 West Twenty-eighth Street. Led by the songwriter-entrepreneur Cecil Mack, the company's top-tier talent pool included Cook, Europe, Alex Rogers, Bert Williams, Jesse Shipp, William Tyers, J. Tim Brymn, Henry Creamer, J. Leubrie Hill, and Ford Dabney. A variety of black-owned publishing companies rose in its wake. The most important were the companies of Pace & Handy, Perry Bradford, and Clarence Williams, all of which set up shop in the Gaiety Theater Building at 1547 Broadway (at Forty-sixth Avenue), a site that in the early 1920s became the epicenter for black Tin Pan Alley (which had moved to Midtown by that point).

In 1908, the Marshall Hotel circle formalized their professional relationships by establishing a black entertainers organization that they called the Frogs (after Aristophanes' comedy). The organization soon purchased a clubhouse in Harlem on West 132nd Street. According to

Badger, their first organized event was a "mid-summer costume and novelty dance" at the Manhattan Casino on 155th Street and Eighth Avenue, in northernmost Harlem.[19]

In 1910, a second important black professional organization was formed: the Clef Club. With James Reese Europe as the first president, it quickly became the premiere New York social club, booking agency, and trade union for black musicians. As the conductor Maurice Peress has suggested, "If there ever was a Moses of African American music, one who single-handedly led black musicians and their music into the land of respect, professionalism, and pride, it was James Reese Europe."[20] While the club did include some trained musicians who specialized in standard string instruments (violin, viola, cello, and double bass), as Badger notes, the greater majority "were players of instruments then associated with American minstrelsy and European and Mediterranean folk music: banjos, mandolins, bandoris (a cross between the banjo and mandolin), and harp guitars."[21] The group also included percussionists, but no brass or woodwind players. This unusual, motley group of "legitimate" musicians and nonreading musicians (who played by ear) created ensembles that emphasized percussion-driven, plucked, and strummed textures. Six and a half weeks after the founding of the Club, on May 27, 1910, Europe premiered a one-hundred-member orchestra with ten pianos in a thirty-minute performance that was part of a larger evening's variety program and dance at the Manhattan Casino. Later that year, the Clef Club established its headquarters at 134 West Fifty-third Street, just down the street from the Marshall Hotel.

Europe and the Clef Club were at the forefront of a social dancing craze that ran from roughly 1913 to 1919. During this period came the first wave of a white interest in refined interpretations of African American ragtime dances. This phenomenon was shaped by Vernon and Irene Castle, the famous white dance couple that was backed by Europe's Society Orchestra from late 1913. In near tandem, new dance halls opened all over the city, and hotels hired orchestras catering to the new public interest. There was a related interest among liberal socialites in hiring black orchestras for private dance parties. These developments meant growing opportunities for black musicians, and a high-profile organization like the Clef Club guaranteed performance quality and brand prestige.

The Clef Club spawned most of New York's important black bandleaders of the second decade of the century, including those of key members such as J. Tim Brymn, William Tyers, and Dan Kildare.[22] Will Marion Cook also ran internationally renowned syncopated orchestras in the years before 1920. Though the period of World War I saw fewer African American productions on Broadway, these black syncopated orchestras maintained a major presence of black performers in white entertainment traditions. As such, they carried cross-racial class and cultural prestige. In some ways, this air of sophistication had more to do with an attention to details in presentation than their actual musical repertory. This quality closely relates to the era's emerging "glorified" entertainment aesthetic. In this context, *class* and *high class* are not synonyms for *highbrow* and *art*. Rather, these terms—including the idea of "glorified" entertainment—denote an aura of elegant, exclusive, and expensive entertainment. These cultural tensions are most readily recognizable in the large ensembles of the Clef Club in second decade of the century. In specific, Europe gained great press coverage for his famous Clef Club Symphony Orchestra concerts at Carnegie Hall in 1912, 1913, and 1914. These events were renowned for their massive ensembles of a 125-plus performers. The immense hybrid "symphony" orchestras of these concerts featured upwards of fourteen pianists and an army of guitars, banjos, mandolins, strings, percussion, and a sizable chorus performing a decidedly nonclassical, variety-oriented repertory. These prestigious, cross-racial events were prefaced by similarly large ensembles at the Clef Club's semiannual dances. An ad in the black newspaper *New York Age* notes that for their November 9, 1911, "mélange and dancefest" performance, the "Clef Club Symphony Orchestra" of "150 musicians" will include "50 mandolins, 20 violins, 30 harp-guitars, 10 cellos, 1 saxaphone [*sic*], 10 banjos, 2 organs, 10 pianos, 5 flutes, 5 bass-violins, 5 clarinets, 3 tympani and drums."[23] One such orchestra can be seen in a photo from the May 11, 1911, Clef Club "Dancefest" at the Manhattan Casino.[24] Here, the hybrid ensemble is organized in front of the stage proscenium in a symphony-style, semicircular configuration, with each member clad in the symphonic garb of black tuxedo. On stage, a second tuxedoed orchestra is set behind a semicircular row of performers—some with banjos—who seem to be presenting an African American blackface minstrelsy show. This show-within-a-show minstrelsy troupe is clad in white pants, nineteenth-century-style black coats with tails, and large, floppy bow ties. The 1911 advertisement notes an added attraction of "a select coterie of [Clef Club] members in a merry, mirthful, miniature cabaret show," with a "cabaret orchestra" under the direction of William Tyers. As Badger notes, the May 1911 Manhattan Casino concert interleaved performances by the "Celebrated Clef Club Symphony Orchestra" with various "song, dance, and comedy routines drawn from 'Ye Olde Fashion Minstrel' tradition."[25] Keep in mind that this event was for friends and families of the Clef Club members themselves, and though this event was open to the community, the audience was likely almost entirely black New Yorkers—as underscored by the placement of this advertisement in an African American newspaper. This "mighty merry musical mélange" was in fact the variety revue that formed the evening's entertainment. In sum, such Clef Club "symphonic" ventures juxtaposed contemporary popular entertainment with social markers of both "highbrow" ensembles (symphonic-style proportions, "highbrow" performance venues, and concert-style presentations), and upper-class society (formal wear, an elite social club of professional businessmen, etc.).

A number of important changes in the black dance band business took place from mid-1913 to 1917. In the fall of 1913, a division began to emerge in the inner circles of the Clef Club. According to Badger, several Clef Club members accused Europe of placing his own ambitions ahead of the interests of the organization. Shortly thereafter, Europe began his formal association with the Castles, thereby raising his international business profile. At the end of December 1913, Europe, Cook, Tyers, and other key members of the Clef Club broke off to found the Tempo Club, a second black booking agency and trade union that provided direct competition to the Clef Club. As before, Europe was elected the first president. He held this position from 1914 to 1916, when he became the leader of the famed Hellfighters Band of the all-black 369th U.S. Infantry Regiment (from 1916 to 1919). The founding of the Tempo Club marks an important geographical shift in New York's black entertainment world. Whereas the Clef Club was based on 53rd Street, the Tempo Club was founded up in the heart of Harlem on West 136th Street.

Just after World War I and into the early 1920s, the young Rudolf Fisher was part of a privileged black social circle that reveled in what he called "the real Negro cabarets" of Harlem. His friends included the celebrated black college football stars Fritz Pollard and Paul Robeson (who would soon begin a stage career), the songwriting team of Henry Creamer and Turner Layton, the comedian Bert Williams, and others.[26] From 1922 to 1927, Fisher was a graduate student in medicine in Washington, D.C. After completing his studies, he returned to Harlem. Fisher's 1927 *American Mercury* article, "The Caucasian Storms Harlem," chronicles the "jolt" he experienced upon visiting his old Harlem haunts after a five-year absence. As he tells it, he "wandered about in a daze from nightclub to nightclub." He "tried the Nest [Club], Small's [Paradise], Connie's Inn, the Capitol [Palace], Happy's [aka "Happy" Rhone's Orchestra Club], and the Cotton Club. . . . [M]y old crowd was not to be found in any of them. The best of Harlem's black cabarets have changed their names and turned white." He found himself wondering if "this was Harlem at all."[27] Fisher's essay specifically ponders the nagging question of why "Negro stock is going up, and everybody's buying."[28] He notes one obvious explanation in the success of the influential all-black Broadway musical *Shuffle Along* in 1921, which may have encouraged whites to seek "this stuff out on its native soil."[29] While he does consider the phenomenon of high-society, cross-race and cross-class "slumming" as an integral factor in the white invasion of Harlem entertainment, he also observes "an active and participating interest" in many of the white patrons, and most significantly he notes their "spellbound" interest in black popular music and "that endemic Negroism, the Charleston" dance. He even suggests that "maybe these Nordics . . . are at last learning to speak our language."[30]

Fisher's extended essay examines broad trends that contributed to Harlem's cross-racial entertainment boom of the 1920s and early 1930s. Fisher points to Harlem's cabaret scene, *Shuffle Along*'s landmark reintroduction of black entertainment on Broadway stages, and the era's Charleston-fueled dance craze as the primary catalysts for black Manhattan's "Nordic" epidemic. Despite the continued contributions of Cook's and Vodery's generation, the engine for each of these emergent trends lay in a younger circle of black musicians and entertainers, many of whom had recently followed the same siren call to Harlem that drew the young Duke Ellington in 1924. As a venerated pianist, celebrated composer of popular song and stage, and the author of the generation-defining "Charleston," James P. Johnson's rise to fame in this postwar entertainment boom provides an exemplary model of the rise and contributions of this dynamic creative generation.

Near the end of his life, Johnson was interviewed extensively about his career for articles that were published in 1959 and 1960.[31] Born in 1894, Johnson grew up in New Brunswick, New Jersey. His mother was a recently transplanted Virginian, and through her Johnson was exposed to the music of traditional southern cotillion, set, and square dances, and the music and dances of the black southern church traditions. By 1902, at the age of eight, Johnson's family had moved to Jersey City, where he first heard syncopated piano derived from ragtime. By 1908, his family had moved to the Hell's Kitchen neighborhood of Manhattan. Now typically called Clinton, this neighborhood extends roughly from Fortieth to Fifty-ninth streets, bounded by the Hudson River and Fifth Avenue. Until fairly recently, Hell's Kitchen had always been an ethnically mixed neighborhood for migrants, immigrants, and blue-collar workers, many of them longshoreman. It was at this point that Johnson first heard "real ragtime," including midwestern and eastern piano styles. He recalled his first exposure to classical music during this prewar period by way of New York Symphony concerts. Around 1913–14, Johnson received formal piano lessons from an Italian music teacher named Bruno Giannini, improving his fingering and performing works by Johann Sebastian Bach. A "Certificate of Award" in the Johnson estate indicates that at some point in 1920–21, Johnson had pursued piano studies at the Conservatory of Musical Art in New York.[32] Despite these formal studies, his most extensive musical education came from his elder ragtime pianist acquaintances.

During his teenage years in New York, Johnson met a string of regional and nationally touring ragtime pianists. While still a teenager he found his way into a number of important early Harlem nightclubs to hear music, among them Barron Wilkins' Club. The wide repertory of these pianists ranged from various regional ragtime schools, to more traditional cotillion dance tunes, to stomps, drags, and set dances, to Tin Pan Alley and vaudeville popular songs and novelties, to faux Indian-type parlor instrumentals, to medleys and arrangements of light classics and nineteenth-century classical warhorses. As he built his career as a pianist, Johnson found employment in small cabarets from Manhattan to Coney Island, accompanimental work in dancing schools, and background work and vaudeville/variety prologue accompaniment in movie houses. His most extensive employment was as a cabaret and dance hall pianist in the Jungles, a rough black neighborhood in Hell's Kitchen. In these years, Johnson began to earn his considerable reputation as a pianist in black Manhattan's competitive piano circles, and he gained the respect and friendship of top older performers such as Luckey Roberts and Willie "The Lion" Smith. By the summer of 1914, Johnson had also met Eubie Blake, another key eastern black ragtime pianist and the future composer of the score to *Shuffle Along.*

With Johnson, Roberts, and Smith at its center, an elite circle of black New York pianists developed a unique ragtime style that came to be known as stride piano. By the early 1920s, Johnson was the acknowledged father and chief exponent of this influential jazz idiom. According to jazz lore, Johnson's 1918 and 1921 piano rolls of *Carolina Shout* laid the stylistic foundations for a generation of pianists—including Duke Ellington—who learned the work note-for-note from these rolls. His Okeh solo piano recording of this work in 1921 is a primary document for the definitive sound of Harlem stride piano.

By the time of World War I, Johnson also aspired to become a composer of popular songs and ragtime instrumentals. For a young black composer like Johnson, the most glamorous publishing firm was Gotham-Attucks. Johnson recalled that "all the great colored musicians had gathered around the firm—Bert Williams, George Walker, Scott Joplin, Will Marion Cook, Joe Jordan, Tim Brymm."[33] Johnson suggests that he began to circulate among this group around 1914, but his introduction to this circle had to have occurred somewhat earlier, since Gotham-Attucks was bought out and closed in 1911.[34] Despite these early professional connections, Johnson published his first songs somewhat later, in 1917.[35]

James P. Johnson's inclusion of Joe Jordan and Tim Brymm on his list of "great colored musicians" brings into view another important facet of influence in this circle of musicians. In the middle of the second decade of the century, when Johnson began to pursue both publishing and performing work, Jordan and Brymm were celebrated as composers, conductors, and arrangers. Both were key members in the Clef Club. When asked in an interview, "What was considered to be the best Negro band in New York in 1917?" Johnson responded:

> Ford Dabney had the best Negro band in New York at that time. It played the [after-theater *Midnight Frolic* revue at the] Ziegfeld Roof [i.e., the New Amsterdam Theatre's roof garden restaurant] and was made up of sixteen musicians who played straight Broadway music, pops and show tunes. . . .
> One of Dabney's men, Allie Ross, a pianist and violinist, was one of our early ambitious musicians. He wanted to be a leader of ability and studied theory and harmony with E. Aldema Jackson, a Juilliard graduate . . .
> Allie later became a conductor for [the white Broadway impresario] Lew Leslie . . . and later trained Fletcher Henderson's first orchestra, that opened at Club Alabam on Broadway.
> Allie was . . . was one of the first to recognize my talent [as a composer], and one of his ambitions was to transcribe some of my piano pieces for chamber orchestra; but he never got around to it.[36]

As Johnson's comments show, Harlem's entertainment circles fostered vital mentor-apprentice relationships between these two generations of musicians. Here and elsewhere, Johnson credits accomplished senior figures in this circle for inspiring his desire to become a "serious musician" and his ambitions as a composer for Tin Pan Alley, the stage, and the concert hall.

Johnson played numerous "gigs and fast calls" with Clef Club orchestras from 1915 to 1918. (By "fast calls" he likely meant last-minute calls to fill in for a single performance.) He recalled Europe's organizational savvy and the "fine sound" of the Clef Club's "concerts with a 110 piece orchestra and 10 pianos on stage."[37] At roughly the same time, Johnson had his first opportunities to lead small bands in theater productions, and he contributed small amounts of interpolated music to the same productions. During this period he first made the acquaintance of the vaudeville team of Flournoy Miller and Aubrey Lyles.

New York's black entertainment community suffered several major business setbacks from 1917 to the months following World War I. First, the arrival of the Original Dixieland Jazz Band (ODJB) in New York in 1917 marked the first national wave of white interest in jazz-related music (as distinct from ragtime). Following the New York success of the ODJB, this new style was quickly disseminated across the country by newly formed white jazz orchestras that sought to emulate this hot New Orleans–style jazz (often as raucous novelty music). At about the same time, regional white dance bands were forming that embraced this new interest in jazz-style music but distanced themselves from the ODJB's rough-edged performance style and vaudeville hokum. These outfits included, for example, the orchestras of Paul Specht, Isham Jones, George Olsen, Vincent Lopez, and—in 1918—Paul Whiteman. These so-called sweet-style orchestras sought to refashion this new white jazz as a more subdued and musically diversified idiom for use in hotels, cabarets, and theaters. In Whiteman's case, he had at least one model in the band led by Art Hickman at San Francisco's Fairmont Hotel from 1914. An important turning point in the racial makeup of New York's music scene occurred in 1919 when the Hickman ensemble displaced the black orchestra of Ford Dabney at Florenz Ziegfeld's roof garden restaurant.

In his reminiscences of the "real Negro cabarets" of the years prior to the early 1920s, Rudolf Fisher provides a detailed account of Harlem establishments he frequented, including Edmund's Cellar, a "honky-tonk, occupying the cellar of a saloon" on Fifth Avenue at 130th Street. He describes this establishment as "the social center of . . . Negro Harlem's kitchen."[38] Fisher also mentions Barron's Club, run by Barron D. Wilkins. At the turn of the 1920s, Barron's was one of the first large nightclubs in Harlem, and was located at 2259 Seventh Avenue (now Adam Clayton Powell Jr. Boulevard) at 134th Street. However, as Fisher notes, despite this establishment's top-tier black performers, Barron's "simply wasn't a Negro cabaret; it was a cabaret run by Negroes for whites. It wasn't even on the lists of those who lived in Harlem—they'd no more think of going there than of going to the [all-white] Winter Roof Garden" in Times Square.[39]

Both Barron's and Edmund's were pioneer "black and tan" cabarets (establishments that allowed mixed-race audiences) that had moved to Harlem in 1915 from locations in the black midtown neighborhood in Hell's Kitchen, where James P. Johnson was performing during the war era. According to the Cotton Club historian Jim Haskins, "Following the 1910 victory of black heavyweight boxer Jack Johnson over 'Great White Hope' Jim Jeffries, . . . outraged whites rioted, smashing, among other establishments in the 'Negro Section,' the rathskellers [i.e., cellar-situated cabarets and bars]. Rather than reopen at their old locations, many rathskeller owners chose to relocate in the fast-growing [black] residential area of Harlem." Haskins adds that "only one or two of these transplanted nightspots were owned by blacks; the rest were owned by Irish." These latter Irish-run establishments included Edmund's, though as Haskins notes (and Fisher affirms), "The clientele of these nightspots was chiefly black," even though "it was not uncommon to find . . . a group of whites . . . [s]lumming."[40] As black populations and black entertainment venues moved uptown, so did their entertainers. The entertainers that performed at Barron Wilkins's Harlem establishment offer an ideal example of the birth of Harlem nightlife.

The midtown African American nightclubs and dancehalls in the first decade of the century relied upon black piano talent for solo entertainment and as the primary accompaniment for singing acts. This entertainment model was relocated to the early black nightclubs in Harlem. For example, the ragtime pianist Luckey Roberts—who later became a close friend and mentor for both Ellington and Johnson—was the first regular house pianist at Barron's. Barron's featured a host of celebrated black pianists who laid the foundations for Harlem stride piano before the war. This piano circle included both Johnson and Willie "The Lion" Smith. As with club entertainment in the "Jungles," these musicians performed solo piano, sometimes also sang, and were sometimes accompanied by a drummer, violin, or other popular secondary instrument. Quite commonly, these pianists (or small duo or trio backing ensembles) also accompanied such entertainers as the blues and vaudeville singers Mamie Smith and Mattie Hite, both of whom had performed at Barron's prior to the Harlem blues diva vogue of the early 1920s.

As Harlem's premiere piano accompanist during this period, Johnson was also central to the early 1920s blues craze. Until a few years before 1920, New York musicians generally were not interested in the blues. For upwardly aspiring black New York musicians in particular, this idiom represented a rural southern past that they often sought to distance themselves from. With the nearly simultaneous arrival in New York of the jazz craze precipitated by the Original Dixieland Jazz Band (January 1917) and the arrival of W. C. Handy's Memphis Blues Band and the opening of the New York offices of his Pace-Handy music company (also 1917), blues slowly made inroads on both the Harlem pianists and the more conservative Clef Club musicians. The August 1920 recording of Mamie Smith and Her Jazz Hounds singing Perry Bradford's "Crazy Blues" was the first commercially successful black jazz record, a release that launched both the race record industry and the early 1920s craze for blues-oriented popular songs.[41] With the phenomenal success of "Crazy Blues," the blues became a regular repertory staple of the Harlem piano ticklers. The urban, race-record "classic" blues recordings of the early and middle 1920s document the gradual assimilation of the blues idiom and aesthetics into the musical language of many pianists of the Harlem stride school. This circle was dominated by middle-class or northern-bred pianists, individuals whose musical development had generally involved little firsthand exposure to rustic southern black forms such as work songs and blues. There were, however, some transplanted southerners in this circle who were familiar with these music idioms, such as Clarence Williams and Perry Bradford, two of the biggest Harlem blues entrepreneurs of the 1920s.[42] Johnson performed with many of the recording groups of Williams and Bradford, and he likewise became the first-call recording and vaudeville accompanist for several of the top blues divas of the day, including Bessie Smith.

1.3 HARLEM IN THE JAZZ AGE: NIGHTCLUBS AND BIG BAND JAZZ

Even though the celebrated Clef Club orchestras entertained white and black New Yorkers up through the mid-1920s, Harlem's new nightclubs did not originally adapt the larger orchestral traditions of the Clef Club to their growing floor shows. While these large Clef Club bands still performed for top white restaurant, hotel, and society dances, as well as for stages and theaters, nightclub employment was far less prestigious in the caste system that had developed among New York's black musicians. The trumpeter Rex Stewart, who was just beginning to build his career as a musician in the mid-1920s, described this milieu in terms of four distinct ranks of musicians. Stewart notes that at mid-decade the first tier was still occupied by the Clef Club musicians, with "burlesque musicians"—meaning the ensembles and performers that found extended employment on the national vaudeville circuits—falling into the second tier of the "select fraternity" of black musicians. Stewart believed that during this era— around roughly 1924—he still occupied the lowest professional tier of musicians who worked "the small clubs, neighborhood joints, the Penny-a-dance halls." According to Stewart, the next tier up was occupied by the "bands of over ten pieces," the "newest members" of the "fraternity" of top-rank black musicians. These orchestras included recently formed large ensembles in New York and Chicago. "In my opinion," Stewart states, "the Chicago counterpart of Fletcher Henderson was Doc Cook. The opposite of Chicago's Dave Peyton and Erskine Tate would be New York's Sam Wooding and Billy Fowler. There weren't many bands of over ten pieces around during those days, but what few there were really had little to do with the rank and file such as us."[43] This list of bands is telling in that it subdivides this new generation of large ensembles between refined ballroom and cabaret-nightclub dance bands, on the one hand, and theater-stage orchestras, on the other hand.

Peyton and Tate directed popular black movie theater orchestras. From 1919 to 1928, the violinist-bandleader Erskine Tate led the house orchestra at Chicago's Vendome Theater, the most celebrated black movie house in the city. While Tate's group started out as a five-piece band, it gradually expanded to an orchestra of ten-plus musicians by the mid-1920s. In both size and repertory, these large, black movie palace ensembles resembled the hybrid symphonic jazz orchestra model seen in Paul Whiteman's band. (By early 1924, Whiteman's recording and dance orchestra had grown to fourteen or fifteen musicians. It included two trumpets, two trombones, three to four reeds with doubling abilities, two violins, two pianists, banjo, tuba, and drums.) Despite their pretensions of sophistication, most Whiteman-style orchestras adhered to the era's dominant model of variety entertainment. This hybrid, jazzy orchestral model was introduced in the pit orchestras of several Broadway shows in 1922 and 1923. By 1923–24, a small number of deluxe movie theaters began to adopt this orchestra model as well, both for film underscoring and for new, variety-entertainment-based prologue stage entertainments. This is the orchestral model that Erskine Tate expanded upon in Chicago. Most notably, as a black bandleader, Tate merged this refined but "jazzy" orchestra format with black improvised jazz after he hired the young cornetist Louis Armstrong in December 1925. Armstrong's improvised solos quickly became a popular feature in the orchestra's performances. Tate's Vendome orchestra was renowned for its stylistic versatility, from classical music to hot-style jazz—a repertory that closely reflected the capabilities of the Whiteman orchestra.[44] The black bandleader-pianist and *Chicago Defender* columnist Dave Peyton led the pit orchestra at Chicago's Regal Theatre, which opened in 1928 and quickly became the Vendome's primary competition in African American deluxe movie houses.

In many respects, these black theater orchestras were also updated versions of the syncopated orchestras of the Clef Club. A key difference, however, lay in the older Clef Club musicians' disdain for improvisation, despite jazz-oriented improvisation's central part in black (and white) popular music in the early 1920s. The conservative attitude of the older Clef Club musicians reflects the larger middle-class reaction to jazz, readily seen in most contemporary critical accounts. The elder circle's emphases on the musical skill of sight-reading and adherence to orchestrations written by trained arrangers reflects the emerging New Negro ideology, which called upon black professionals, including professional musicians, to aspire to self-control, dignified presentation, education, and an industrious work ethic. This ideology devalued jazz improvisation, which was regularly described as "faking it" and "playing by feeling" rather than a musical skill. That said, these new movie house orchestras struck a unique balance between these two musical worlds, albeit in accordance with the general public reception of symphonic jazz as a culturally elevated and sophisticated refinement of the crudities of true jazz.

Rex Stewart equated these Chicago theater orchestras with the New York ensembles of Sam Wooding and Billy Fowler. Neither of these bandleaders' careers was strictly tied to theater orchestra work. There is little documentation on the orchestras that were led by Fowler. While he played baritone saxophone in Fletcher Henderson's studio orchestra (Henderson's Dance Orchestra), which recorded on the Black Swan label from 1921 to 1923, Fowler subsequently ran a nonjazz society dance orchestra and theater orchestra in the mid-1920s. Sam Wooding's career as a bandleader in the 1920s is far better documented, and illustrates the important connection of stage and theater orchestras to the new, large dance band and nightclub-cabaret orchestras that were formed by Fletcher Henderson, Doc Cook, and others.

Following the arrival of the first jazz craze via the white Original Dixieland Jazz Band, and increasingly after the war, Harlem cabarets and nightclubs began to feature small band-oriented ensembles in addition to the aforementioned piano performers. In time, these bands were backing ever more elaborate nightclub floor shows. The initial large bands of Wooding, Henderson, and Cook were tied to these developments. Wooding's ensemble, for example, was central to the rise of the floor show traditions. Wooding and His Society Syncopaters were notably hired as the house band at Barron's in the early 1920s, and this prominent engagement was followed by similar work for the Nest nightclub and Club Alabam (in Times Square). Because of its simultaneous success in vaudeville and the Club Alabam, Wooding's orchestra was chosen to back a new stage revue, *Chocolate Kiddies*, featuring songs by the young Duke Ellington. This production was organized to capitalize on the European success of two earlier nightclub revues, the 1922 *Plantation Revue* (aka *From Dover to Dixie*) and the 1922–23 *Plantation Days* (with music by James P. Johnson), which had both success on Broadway and lucrative European tours. These trends illustrate the fluid boundaries that had developed between nightclub and stage entertainments in the early 1920s. These revues also reflect the growing white and black public interest in a new wave of all-black musical theater projects. The roots of this trend are found in the landmark all-black musical, *Shuffle Along*.

In the summer of 1920, the black stage duo of Flournoy Miller and Aubrey Lyles began to plan a new all-black Broadway production. They joined forces with the pianist Eubie Blake and his vaudeville singing partner, Noble Sissle, and sought out the services of the arranger Will Vodery, among other talent. The partnership of Miller, Lyles, Sissle, and Blake led to the hit *Shuffle Along* in 1921. *Shuffle Along* was the catalyst for a new wave of black musicals that played Broadway during the 1920s and early 1930s. It sparked an immediate wave of imitators, including an equally successful 1923 Miller and Lyles show called *Runnin' Wild*, with music by James P. Johnson and lyrics by Cecil Mack. The popularity of Johnson's hit dance number from this production, "The Charleston," sparked the dance vogue that defined the 1920s. With this show, Johnson moved to the center of black Broadway. He continued his stage partnership with Miller until the late 1940s, and together Johnson and Miller produced such major hits as the 1928 Miller and Lyles show *Keep Shufflin'* (as well as a good number of lackluster productions).

Harlem's musical revue tradition was also a product of the burgeoning nightclub scene. Indeed, many stage productions first originated as floor shows before transitioning to larger Broadway venues. In many respects, these new Harlem revues aspired to be just as lavish as their Broadway counterparts. This ambition translated into an interest in hiring larger orchestras, though usually without the expensive addition of a string section (thereby settling on a proto-big-band instrumentation). In some respects, these trends were also influenced by the highly popular *Shuffle Along* orchestra, which Eubie Blake regularly hired out—outside of the show—for dance and stage engagements.

The mixed aesthetic concerns that intersected in the transition from small improvisation-oriented bands to the newer, arrangement-oriented big bands in black-performed cabaret and nightclub entertainments in the mid-1920s can be seen in the careers of Johnson and Ellington. In his autobiography, the New Orleans saxophonist and clarinetist Sidney Bechet recounts his early professional associations with Johnson and Ellington at the Hollywood Club in mid-1920s New York. This venue, located on West Forty-ninth Street between Seventh Avenue and Broadway (in the heart of Times Square), featured black musical talent for an upscale, white audience. In the summer of 1924, Johnson was leading a band at this venue. The group included both Bechet and the saxophonist Benny Carter. Bechet recalls that there were significant tensions between his New Orleans improvisational ideals for ensemble jazz and what he disparagingly calls Johnson's preference for "orchestrational Jazz," "Concert Jazz," and

"Fancy-Arrangement Jazz." These latter characterizations underscore the rising prominence of orchestral arrangements in these contexts. Bechet notes that "James P. was trying to make it almost like one of those big swing bands—hit parade stuff. He was all for making these big arrangements, adding musicaners [sic], adding instruments."[45] Bechet thought that his personal contribution was to add a "New Orleans . . . foundation in the numbers" that Johnson arranged by "ad libbing and giving my improvisation," but "there was trouble because of the attention I was getting, because people wanted [to hear] New Orleans" improvised jazz. As a result of his conflicts with the "fancy-arrangement jazz" ideals of Johnson and the management, Bechet was ultimately fired. (Though Bechet paints himself in a favorable light, readers should bear in mind that he was notoriously difficult to work with. His commentary likely does not give a thorough account of the reasons for his own dismissal.)

At the Hollywood Club, Johnson was filling in for the resident house band, the Washingtonians, a five-piece group led by the banjoist Elmer Snowden. This group notably included the young Duke Ellington and three future Ellington orchestra musicians. The Washingtonians began their tenure at the club in September 1923. At some point after Johnson's work at the club, Bechet briefly joined the Washingtonians. This association occurred after Elmer Snowden had left the group (in February 1924), and after the venue had changed its name to the Kentucky Club (in the summer of 1924) and Ellington had assumed control of the band. In his autobiography, Ellington characterizes the club as "a rendezvous for all the big [white] stars and musicians on Broadway after they got through working. Paul Whiteman came often, and he always showed his appreciation by laying a big fifty-dollar bill on us."[46]

Ellington's reference to Whiteman and the top-tier entertainment clientele of the club underscores important factors that informed the aesthetic interests of the new, enlarged black orchestras of the day. From roughly 1922 to 1925, the smaller black cabaret and ballroom orchestras in Chicago and New York were gradually replaced by the newer "bands of over ten pieces" that Stewart recalled. The Harmon's Dreamland Ballroom orchestra of the Chicago pianist-arranger Doc Cook (aka Charles L. Cooke) had upwards of sixteen musicians. This all-black ensemble held residence at this prestigious white ballroom from 1922 to 1927, employing many famous jazz sidemen, including cornetist Freddie Keppard, clarinetist Jimmie Noone, and guitarist-banjoist Johnny St. Cyr. As Stewart implies, an apt New York counterpart to Cook's orchestra could be found in the bands of the pianist-arranger Fletcher Henderson. While he had already led studio orchestras of various sizes for Black Swan Records, Henderson organized a ten-piece band in 1923 for the Club Alabam, another Times Square establishment (on Forty-fourth Street at Broadway) that provided black musical entertainment for white audiences. With the help of the Clef Club violinist-conductor Allie Ross and the arranger-saxophonist Don Redman, the new Henderson orchestra provided music for the club's new twice-nightly floor shows as well as dancing. Connie's Inn—which opened in June 1923—also introduced floor shows, first with a relatively small group led by the clarinetist Wilbur Sweatman, but this small band was quickly replaced with the large ensemble of the violinist Leroy Smith. Smith was one of a number of rising black bandleaders of the day who were striving to win fame by adopting the dance-band formulas of Whiteman. As the jazz scholar Jeffrey Magee has pointed out, Henderson was similarly positioned as a "Paul Whiteman of the Race."[47]

Despite their initial relation to sweet, Whiteman-style dance music, over the next several years Henderson and Redman gave birth to authentic big band jazz. In specific, with the ten- to eleven-man Henderson orchestra of the mid-1920s, the two men developed a highly influential model for integrating sophisticated, jazz-derived arrangements with improvised jazz (a project that greatly benefited from Louis Armstrong's celebrated tenure with the band). The evolution of the Henderson band happened not at the Club Alabam but at the Roseland Ballroom (on Broadway between Fifty-first and Fifty-second streets). During their tenure at the Roseland, from July 1924 to 1931, this Times Square emporium was one of the most important dance halls in New York. As Magee has observed, "Ballrooms such as the Roseland occupied a social middle ground between the high society hotels and restaurants and the lower-class cabarets and taxi-dance halls. But in its category, Roseland stood out."[48] By the later 1920s, however, increasingly sophisticated nightclubs raised the social status of work in such venues. The premiere Harlem nightclub of this latter era was the Cotton Club, which featured Ellington's orchestra in lavish, sophisticated floor shows that were said to rival the expense and spectacle of top Broadway entertainments.

⓵⓷ DUKE ELLINGTON: FROM *CAROLINA SHOUT* TO CARNEGIE HALL

Born in 1899, Duke Ellington was five years younger than Johnson. Unlike Johnson, Ellington was born into a stable, middle-class household, with regular exposure to the high-minded ambitions of Washington's proud middle- and upper-class black social circles. Like Johnson, Ellington had short periods of rudimentary formal (i.e., classical) music training in his youth. Like Johnson, however, the education with the greatest impact on his growth as a musician came from the lessons he learned—directly and by observation—from more accomplished ragtime pianists. The Ellington biographer Mark Tucker has made persuasive arguments about the major role that Washington's black music community played in the career and artistic outlook of Duke Ellington.[49] Tucker identifies major influences in the city's long tradition of black historical pageants, its professional musicians who contributed to Ellington's early musical education and endeavors as band leader, and the "Washington pattern" of professional black composer-bandleaders. As Tucker explains, this pattern involved the pursuit of multifaceted careers as bandleaders, performers, composers, and songwriters, the acquisition of a professional demeanor that commanded cross-racial respect, and the active promotion of "black vernacular idioms"—specifically "syncopated jazz, ragtime, show tunes, Negro folk songs, arrangements of spirituals"—in original compositions. Tucker points to Will Marion Cook, James Reese Europe, and Ford Dabney as the three most important potential career models for the young Ellington. Both Cook and Dabney were natives of D.C. Though he was born in Mobile, Alabama, Europe too had important youthful ties to Washington, where he spent his teenage years. This said, the careers of Cook, Europe, and Dabney were built and centered in New York. In Tucker's research, as in Ellington's youthful reflections on Harlem already cited, we see that Harlem entertainment was a fluid world, in which most working musicians based themselves in New York while touring nationally, with special emphasis on such major black cultural hubs as Washington, D.C. It was through his exposure to these touring circuits that the young Ellington gained firsthand knowledge of the celebrated musicians of early 1920s Harlem entertainment.

Ellington's rite of passage into James P. Johnson's world came about after a friend dared the youthful Ellington to play his rendition of *Carolina Shout* for Johnson. The Ellington biographer John Hasse has suggested that this legendary encounter occurred on November 25, 1921, when Johnson was in D.C. as part of a "large jazz revue at the Convention Center."[50] Through similar local encounters, Ellington was gradually exposed to other key Harlem musicians and entertainers. While there is no proof Ellington saw the well-publicized D.C. performances of the ensembles of Europe, Cook, and Dabney in the years leading up to the early 1920s, his appreciation for these "great talents" is clearly expressed in his autobiography. This source also provides evidence of the impact of similar Harlem outfits, such as the Whiteman-style band of Harlem's Leroy Smith.[51]

From around 1917 to 1918, Ellington was organizing his own small bands for local D.C. engagements. By 1923, he had finally made it to New York. On this first trip, Ellington and his longtime drummer friend Sonny Greer had been hired as musicians for the vaudevillian-clarinetist Wilbur Sweatman's engagement at Harlem's Lafayette Theatre. During and after their short stint with Sweatman, Greer and Ellington began to move in Harlem's musical circles, particularly Johnson's piano circles. Ellington was also introduced to players who would join his first New York bands, including the trumpeter James "Bubber" Miley (who was with blues singer Mamie Smith's band at that time) and the trombonist Joe "Tricky Sam" Nanton. After their money and gigs ran out, Greer and Ellington headed back to Washington. By the summer of 1923, however, they had returned with the band of banjoist Elmer Snowden. After several minor fiascos and a spot of good luck, the nascent band landed a prime spot at Barron Wilkins' Exclusive Club up in Harlem. Snowden's group cultivated a sweet dance band style similar to that of the club's previous house orchestra, Sam Wooding's ensemble. The Harlem nightclub scene was booming in the summer of 1923. A number of nightclubs, like the newly opened Connie's Inn, began to introduce elaborate floor shows. While Ellington largely played for dancers at

Wilkins's club, he had the opportunity to work as a rehearsal pianist for the Connie's Inn revues, where he began to learn "first-hand about the musical structure of revues," as Tucker has noted.[52] By late in the summer of 1923, Ellington was partnered with the lyricist Jo Trent in a new songwriting venture.

By the fall of 1923, Snowden's orchestra had relocated to the Hollywood Club. Within a short time, Ellington had assumed control of the band and the club's name had changed to the Kentucky Club. The Washingtonians, as they were called, had shifted to a more distinctly "hot" sound with new additions such as "Bubber" Miley on trumpet. Ellington's first songs with Trent were published in the fall of 1923, and they had contributed several number to the aforementioned *Chocolate Kiddies* revue. At this point, Ellington had built influential friendships with several senior Harlem musicians, including Will Marion Cook and the songwriter-publisher Maceo Pinkard. Pinkard's business influence helped place the orchestra with the Victor Record Company. By the fall of 1923, the Washingtonians had also entered the nascent media of radio through local broadcasts of live performances at the club. The Washingtonians likewise began to pursue local vaudeville work. Over the next several years, the band expanded to seven members and underwent key personnel changes.

In middle to late 1926, Ellington began his professional association with Irving Mills, a well-connected white music publisher, impresario, and talent manager. Mills was a part owner, along with his brother Jack, in both the Mills Music talent agency and the successful Tin Pan Alley publishing house of Jack Mills, Inc. Mills began his formal managerial role with the Washingtonians during the latter part of 1926.[53] It is in this period that Ellington began to find his unique compositional voice in such early arrangements as "East St. Louis Toodle-Oo," "Birmingham Breakdown," and "The Creeper." He also wrote his first tentative "extended" composition, the Whitemanesque "Rhapsody Jr.," which was copyrighted by Jack Mills in October 1926.

During 1926–27, beyond continued work at the Kentucky Club and in smaller engagements, the band pursued regional tours for dances and vaudeville appearances. In October 1927, it had joined the Lafayette Theater's *Jazzmania* revue, performing both on stage and in the pit. This engagement led to other small stage revue appearances during that fall. Nevertheless, it was the *Jazzmania* performance that caught the attention of the songwriter Jimmy McHugh. While McHugh had formerly worked for Mills Music, in late 1927 he was busy developing a new revue at the celebrated Cotton Club in Harlem. At the encouragement of McHugh, Ellington and his orchestra were brought into the new revue. With the Cotton Club engagement, the Ellington orchestra had moved to the center of Harlem entertainment. For these revues, Ellington's band contributed both arrangements of songs by the club's celebrated white composing staff as well as his own distinctive compositions as background music for select numbers in the revues. The band likewise provided music for dancing. This latter area of work was soon broadcast nationally, adding to the band's considerable fame. The Cotton Club floor shows were elaborate affairs meant to rival the lavish and glamorous Ziegfeld *Follies* revues on Broadway. Despite the club's highly restrictive entrance policies for black patrons, the Cotton Club performers became major celebrities in the Harlem community. Ellington's Cotton Club employment was the catalyst for his long career. It soon led to national and international tours, work in Broadway and Hollywood musicals, and many other opportunities.

Mills astutely sought to advance Ellington's career by raising him rung-by-rung up a ladder of prestigious accomplishments, all with an eye to maintaining the dignified persona that Ellington had long cultivated. To paraphrase a famous catch phrase of the Cotton Club, Ellington and Mills promoted the bandleader as "the aristocrat of Harlem." Much of the band's cross-racial success was likely engineered by Mills and Ellington together. In the early 1930s, however, there were still significant limitations in the market for aspiring black composers and bandleaders. The most successful white bandleader of the day was Paul Whiteman. By 1931, with the Whiteman model in mind, Mills had encouraged Ellington to write a jazz "rhapsody." This led to *Creole Rhapsody*, Ellington's first true "extended" jazz composition.[54] Ellington's interest in concert jazz was progressively realized through a diverse series of extended compositions, including *Reminiscing in Tempo* in 1935, his score to the film short *Symphony in Black* (Paramount) in 1935, the two-part recording of *Diminuendo and Crescendo in Blue* in 1937, and several lesser-known score commissions (*Bird of Paradise*, *American Lullaby*, and *Blue Belles of Harlem*) from Robbins Music and Paul Whiteman in the 1930s. However, these early experiments in composition pale when compared to the scale and intellectual breadth that Ellington brought to his *Black, Brown and Beige*, a symphonic-length work that Ellington premiered at his orchestra's Carnegie Hall debut concert on January 23, 1943. While this event is a landmark in the cultural achievements of the Harlem entertainment circle, it was preceded by several other celebrated Carnegie Hall events that featured Harlem talent, including James Reese Europe's Clef Club orchestra appearances in the second decade of the century and an usual 1928 concert organized by W. C. Handy that featured the premiere of James P. Johnson's first major concert work. The background of this latter event, which forms the subject of chapter 2, underscores important cross-generational artistic exchanges that greatly influenced the concert jazz ambitions of Ellington and Johnson.

𝄢 THE QUESTION OF ROLE MODELS

The difficulties in measuring connections between the musical activities and cultural aspirations of the older Harlem entertainment generation—Will Marion Cook, Will Vodery, W. C. Handy, James Reese Europe, and so on—and the jazz-based concert works of Ellington and Johnson can be illustrated through considerations of Vodery's and Cook's relations to these younger musicians. While Will Vodery's training lay in classical music, his career was made in the commercial world of musical theater. During his work with the Williams and Walker musical theater company, Vodery was also active in the Clef Club and a member of the James Reese Europe circle.[55] Most importantly, from 1913 to 1932, Vodery was a central arranger for the Ziegfeld *Follies*. In the 1920s he performed similar functions for other white Broadway productions, such as the George White Scandals of 1922 (in which he notably arranged George Gershwin's one-act "Opera à la Afro-American," *Blue Monday*), as well as Lew Leslie's *Blackbirds* revue in 1927.

His professional accomplishments and talents made Vodery a highly regarded mentor to the generation of black musicians that matured in the 1920s. Ellington, for instance, claimed that Vodery gave him "valuable lectures in orchestration" during their joint work in

Ziegfeld's *Show Girl* in 1928 (Ellington even credited Vodery with se-curing the job for his band). In an interview in 1943, Ellington re-called Vodery's professional prestige in the 1920s, and commented that Vodery "was a strong influence on me. His chromatic tendencies penetrated my ear, and are largely responsible for the way I think music, even today."[56] In an oddly symbolic connection, in the spring of 1938, the Ellington orchestra was featured in a Cotton Club show that was advertised as "The Ziegfeld *Follies* of the Colored Race." The show's musical supervisor and arranger was Vodery, and the revue was notably held at the relocated downtown Cotton Club, a venue that occupied the site of the Palais Royal, the establishment at which Paul Whiteman first rose to fame in the early 1920s.[57]

Despite such tempting evidence of the relation between Vodery and Ellington, there is, as Tucker notes, a "disjunction between . . . [Vodery's] legendary reputation and . . . [his] quotidian output."[58] After careful consideration of Vodery's manuscript and commercial arrangements, Tucker observes that the scores "do not reveal the vaunted abilities for which the arranger became legendary." Though he finds competent craftsmanship, Tucker is struck by their lack of "bold harmonic gestures, novel instrumental effects, or other signs of an extraordinary musical personality." While he does find select in-stances of what Ellington called Vodery's "chromatic tendencies," Tucker observes that these "intermittently modern" passages seem to nod "in the direction of Paul Whiteman's 'symphonic' jazz."[59] This disjunction between Ellington's high praise of Vodery and his rather commonplace extant scores forms the central thread in Tucker's quest to understand Vodery. (Despite Tucker's impressive research, certain preconceived hopes for finding the roots of Ellington's innovations in instrumentation, harmony, and chromaticism cloud Tucker's judg-ment in contextualizing and assessing the relative merits of a pre-1925 commercial arranger. For example, beyond Tucker's curious faulting of Vodery's instrumental doublings in a stock arrangement—cross-scoring, that is, the doubling of instrumental parts, was central to selling a commercial arrangement to a variety of ensembles—no real consideration is given to comparing Vodery's extant work with the stock-in-trade craftsmanship and generic formulas of the musical theater and Tin Pan Alley arranging of his day.)

Tucker locates a solution to the discrepancy between Ellington's innovations and Vodery's work in the larger question of how Vodery's Harlem peers likely measured his stature. Tucker suggests that "for the African American writers and musicians who knew him, Vodery symbolized power and achievement" through his unparalleled success on white Broadway and his associations with top-tier celebrities, musicians, and producers.[60] Tucker observes that later jazz critics who were not personally familiar with Vodery or his work (citing Barry Ulanov, Gunther Schuller, and James Lincoln Collier, for instance) positioned this senior Harlem musician "as a conduit" who had transmitted "'classical' and 'modern' musical ideas to an impressionable Duke Ellington."[61] Tucker's astute study of Vodery thus provides a warning against reading too much into the statements by Ellington and his peers on their relations with this older generation of New York's black musical leaders. While this lesson seems particularly appropriate for the specific question that Tucker sought to answer—whether Vodery was "a conduit transmitting 'classical' and 'modern' musical ideas to . . . Ellington"—the issue of whether this older generation provided inspiration and encouragement for the greater compositional ambitions of Ellington, Johnson, and their peers is not answered.

While there is little comparable evidence of such direct associations between Ellington's concert works and the encouragement of Cook and Vodery, Ellington nevertheless pointed to both individuals as seminal figures in his professional development and in his desire to compose concert works. For instance, in Richard Boyer's essay "The Hot Bach" (1944), Ellington famously responded that in his early years in New York he received most of his formative compositional instruction "riding around Central Park in a taxi" with Will Marion Cook. He explained that "he and I would get in a taxi and ride around Central Park and he'd give me lectures in music. . . . He was a brief but strong influence. . . . Some of the things he used to tell me I never got a chance to use until years later, when I wrote the tone poem, *Black, Brown, and Beige.*"[62] In his 1973 autobiography, he similarly described this experience as a key influence on his mature compositional methods, and claimed that this period "was one of the best semesters I ever had in music."[63] In both sources, Ellington proudly recounted the story of how Cook left behind his aspirations as a concert violinist and art music composer in favor of a career in Harlem entertainment. This story clearly held a personal significance for Ellington, and his attachment to it reveals the manner in which he had positioned Cook as a professional role model. To paraphrase Tucker's comments on Vodery, to Ellington, Cook represented the "cream of New York's black musical" talent, and his rich career was an attractive symbol of professional "power and achievement." Cook also represented a black musician who had achieved great cross-racial respect and celebrity by conquering the hitherto all-white world of Broadway after racial prejudice had proven to be an insurmountable impediment to his original career goals as a concert artist. This latter point provides further reinforcement for Tucker's aforementioned hypothesis on the Ellington-Vodery connection. However, Tucker's quite valid thesis was based on the study of compositional evidence rather than professional inspiration per se.

Evidence of the type of professional encouragement that Cook was renowned for can be seen in a 1936 letter from Cook to James P. Johnson, who was at that time at the peak of his efforts to establish himself as a composer of concert works:

> My dear Jimmy:
>   . . . I was delighted to hear of your study and works. Keep it up! Sooner or later, you're sure to go to the top. Strive for originality of themes, forms and development of ideas. Of course there is little new to be done as regards harmony. Debussy seems to have set the whole world mad on [the] whole tone scale and every composer tries to be more modern, more dissonant than his predecessor. Your rhythms are magnificent and are your own. Don't try to be anybody else. Don't even be influenced by *anybody*—no matter how great, how popular. I trust you are making enough to look after wife and children and yourself properly. . . .
>   That you have cut the drinking and the worthless friends makes me very proud of you.
>   I wish I could do something to help along your present ambitions; but I am just a sick and discouraged old man and just manage to eke out an existence.
>   I am sure, however, that you will win out gloriously in the end. With your talent, and now that you have acquired technique—you can't fail.
>   But you must be original!

Why just to earn some easy money, don't you write a beautiful light but worthy song. . . . Maybe you . . . could hit upon something that might make some money and cause you to be in the public eye. It all helps. I mean something both classy and light. . . .

If you keep up the good work—and the good behavior—there's nothing else for you—*but success.*

I'm very proud of you. Dad.

> Sincerely
> Dad Cook.
> Will Marion Cook[64]

Though Johnson's original letter to Cook is lost, it is clear that he greatly valued Cook's encouragement, even though Cook no longer held the same cultural stature that he had enjoyed in the first two decades of the century. In this letter, Cook equally emphasizes the importance of Johnson's persistence at his aspirations in concert music and his continued attention to the Tin Pan Alley imperative of being "in the money" by writing that next song hit that could keep Johnson "in the public eye." While his comments on Johnson's compositional ambitions are all very general, he notably plays down the importance of writing fashionably "modern" or "dissonant" music. He similarly states that "there is little new to be done with regards to harmony." Instead, Cook's advice for Johnson broadly stresses the need for "originality of themes, forms and development of ideas." Despite these seemingly generic classical formal concerns, however, the one trait that Cook specifically praises in Johnson's music is that his "rhythms are magnificent and . . . [his] own." The term *rhythms* is obviously a reference to the jazz-based idiomatic language of Johnson's concert works, and this stylistic foundation is a central attribute that Cook encourages Johnson to retain. Beyond these direct musical concerns, however, what comes through in this letter is Cook's sincere warmth, and his concern for Johnson's professional ambitions and personal well-being. On the latter point, the professional model of a Clef Club–era musician can be seen in Cook's great praise for Johnson's efforts to give up the hard-drinking, Jazz Age lifestyle that he was known for in the 1920s. Cook's relation to Johnson as a musical, professional, and personal mentor—a relationship that clearly held in the Ellington-Cook context as well—is appropriately reflected in the letter's last line: "I'm very proud of you. Dad." (Cook's nickname among the younger generation was "Dad.")

This intimate, mentor-like relation between these generational groups in Harlem entertainment was greatly facilitated by their overlapping careers and projects. Throughout the 1920s and early 1930s, Johnson and Ellington were routinely working side by side with older, established entertainment figures like Vodery, Rosamond Johnson, and Flournoy Miller. These encounters were endemic to musical theater productions and nightclub floor shows, environments that required diverse collaborative teams. The intersections of these theatrical traditions, the cultural aspirations of Cook's and Europe's generation, 1920s symphonic jazz arranging, and Harlem jazz form the central roots of the later concert jazz works of Ellington and Johnson. The key historical moment when all these threads meet can be found in the history of James P. Johnson's first concert work. In 1927, Noble Sissle, Perry Bradford, and other Harlem entertainment peers began to encourage James P. Johnson's ambitions to compose concert works. The result was his *Yamekraw: A Negro Rhapsody. Yamekraw* was premiered by W. C. Handy at Carnegie Hall in 1928 in a "jazz" orchestral arrangement by William Grant Still at a concert that was directly indebted to earlier Carnegie Hall performances by James Reese Europe in the war years. While this later concert purported to trace the "evolution of Negro music," its larger purpose was to celebrate the cultural achievements of the Harlem entertainment community, which had risen from the dank rathskellers of Manhattan's rough Jungles neighborhood, to new life in Harlem, to the bright lights of Broadway stages, and had finally arrived at Carnegie Hall. In both its rich compositional and programmatic designs, as well as its role as a centerpiece for this concert, Johnson's *Yamekraw* represents a microcosm of this community celebration.

two   𝄐   JAZZ RHAPSODIES IN BLACK AND WHITE

James P. Johnson's *Yamekraw*

*A*s a hybrid style employed in popular music arranging and diverse concert works, symphonic jazz developed an unusual cultural breadth that spanned the concert hall, jazz and dance bands, radio orchestras, Tin Pan Alley, Broadway, and Hollywood. This broad cultural presence and the programmatic associations of the idiom positioned symphonic jazz as a rich reflection of overlapping contemporary views on race and class politics, modernity, and the relations of art and entertainment. Such cultural interchanges permeate the multifaceted history of the idiom's best-known work, Gershwin's *Rhapsody in Blue*. Paul Whiteman used the final theme of this work as the signature piece for his orchestra in concerts, film appearances, and on his radio programs for twenty-five years. Gershwin himself used the composition in a similar manner in his two 1934 CBS radio shows.[1] In musical theater it was used as a production number for *George White's Scandals* of 1926,[2] and the Broadway impresario Lew Leslie had the rhapsody arranged as a choral number for both his *Blackbirds* revues of 1933 and 1939, and for the 1931–32 and 1941 editions of his *Rhapsody in Black* revues.[3] *Rhapsody in Blue* was also used as a prologue ballet entertainment at Radio City Music Hall from 1933 to 1937.[4] Hollywood equally had an interest in this work. For instance, Fox Studios hired Gershwin to compose music for their 1931 film *Delicious* in part because of the studio's desire to construct a film sequence around a Gershwinesque "New York Rhapsody" in the spirit of *Rhapsody in Blue*. At nearly the same time, Universal paid the unprecedented sum of fifty thousand dollars for *Rhapsody in Blue*'s use as an extravagantly staged production number in Paul Whiteman's 1930 film *King of Jazz*. These high-profile commercial appropriations of *Rhapsody in Blue* helped to turn the work's themes into well-known musical signs in contemporary popular culture. A similar history of entertainment appropriations and cross-cultural resonance is seen in James P. Johnson's 1927 piano solo *Yamekraw: A Negro Rhapsody*.

Johnson's *Yamekraw* represents a unique African American parallel—and musical response—to Gershwin's *Rhapsody in Blue*. Though initially composed for solo piano, *Yamekraw* was premiered at Carnegie Hall in 1928 in a "jazz" orchestral arrangement at a concert organized by W. C. Handy. At this event, *Yamekraw* was presented as the centerpiece of a program that intended to trace the "evolution of Negro music."[5] This composition was thus positioned as an overt attempt to employ "authentic" black popular music in a concert-length work. In contrast to both 1920s Whiteman-influenced symphonic jazz concert works and the more traditional symphonic compositions of such Harlem peers as Florence Price or William Grant Still, *Yamekraw* celebrates contemporary African American *popular* music in its blues- and song-based episodic formal structure, and in its direct relations to various race records and black musical-theater songs of the 1920s.

From the late 1920s to the mid-1940s, *Yamekraw* was one of the most important works to emerge from the popular culture vogue for concert jazz. Like Gershwin's *Rhapsody*, *Yamekraw* was performed by top radio orchestras of the late 1920s and 1930s. In a pattern akin to the musical theater appropriations of Gershwin's *Rhapsody*, Johnson derived a number of songs from *Yamekraw*'s themes for use in his musicals of 1928 to 1930. *Yamekraw* additionally formed the basis for two 1930s film shorts by Warner Bros. and Pathé studios, and was featured as an orchestral overture for performances by the American Negro Ballet in Harlem in 1938 and for the eight-month run of Orson Welles's legendary WPA-sponsored "Voodoo" *Macbeth* in 1939.

This chapter examines the history of Johnson's *Yamekraw* from its origins as a 1927 piano solo, to its 1928 transformation into an orchestral rhapsody, to its ultimate adaptation into a quasi-folk opera in the 1930 Vitaphone film short. This historical overview will explore the cultural and conceptual background, formal design, performance history, and film adaptation of this jazz rhapsody. *Yamekraw*'s history brings to light the diverse cultural meanings of symphonic jazz as it existed beyond the high-profile activities of Whiteman, Ferde Grofé, and Gershwin.

𝄢 THE CULTURAL BACKGROUND OF *YAMEKRAW:*
A RHAPSODY IN BLACK AND WHITE

There are four extant texts that record discrete moments in the performance history of *Yamekraw* during Johnson's lifetime. These texts include *(a)* the original piano solo score published in 1927 by Perry Bradford; *(b)* the orchestral arrangement by William Grant Still that was commissioned by W. C. Handy for his April 27, 1928, Carnegie Hall concert (and subsequently published by Alfred Music); *(c)* the 1930 Vitaphone musical film short derived from the Still arrangement; and *(d)* the 1944 solo piano recording Johnson made of the work for Moses Asch that was later released on Folkways Records in 1962.[6] This composition's complex web of cultural associations can be traced in part through the histories of these extant texts and in the work's intermusical relations.

As a jazz-based concert work of the late 1920s, *Yamekraw* was undoubtedly received by many people as a product of the Whiteman-inspired symphonic jazz vogue. Johnson's *Yamekraw* is related to this idiom, but it represents a new African American perspective on symphonic jazz. *Yamekraw* was promoted as a racially "authentic" attempt to employ black popular music and jazz in a concert-length work. The work was also positioned—first by Bradford and then by W. C. Handy—as a pointed response to the success of Gershwin's *Rhapsody in Blue*. Bradford's advertising to the 1927 piano score, for instance, begins with the following foreword:

> *Yamekraw* [is] a genuine Negro treatise on spiritual, syncopated and "blue" melodies by JAMES P. JOHNSON, expressing the religious

fervor and happy moods of the natives of Yamekraw, a Negro settlement situated on the outskirts of Savannah, Georgia.

This is not a Rhapsody in Blue, but a Rhapsody in Black and White. (Black Notes on White Paper.) We hope it will meet your approval.[7]

Despite the professed neutrality of the work as being merely "black notes on white paper," the "Rhapsody in Blue" versus "Rhapsody in Black and White" promotional construct underscores the publisher's claims of racial authenticity in the initial description of this work as a "genuine Negro treatise." The characterization of the composition as a "treatise" further reinforces the implication that Johnson was an artistic authority providing a mediated explanation of these "folk expressions" for the outsider—more specifically, for the type of *white* outsider that Tin Pan Alley commonly targeted as "lovers of Negro music." It seems plausible to assume that Bradford's company sensed that this white market group of the 1920s would have interpreted Gershwin's *Rhapsody in Blue* as an example of "authentic" jazz or as an authoritative interpretation of black musical idioms. These promotional claims for racial authenticity and the attempt to position Johnson as an inside authority on "Negro folk idioms" are echoed in a 1928 Bradford advertisement that described *Yamekraw* as "a Rhapsody in 'Blues,' 'Jazz' and 'Spirituals' characterizing the real American syncopation as in the life of the Composer."[8]

While the exact racial and class audience to whom Bradford was originally marketing *Yamekraw* is open for interpretation, the score's program implies that this target market was a mixed public rather than solely the race market at which Bradford's own blues were aimed (in both his recordings and in his publishing firm's song catalog). The phenomenon of 1920s race records is important to bear in mind when considering Bradford. He personally established this segregated market through his management of Mamie Smith's historic 1920 recording of "Crazy Blues," famous as the first commercially successful black jazz recording.

Though the development of a commercial music market in the early 1920s created specifically for black audiences has long been acknowledged in jazz histories, this topic has been critically addressed almost entirely in terms of recordings. Even with reference to this medium, however, critical commentary has often been made without any basis in market data to back up the frequently made claim that the white market was largely oblivious of race catalog titles. In the early 1920s, records were still thought of as a means to encourage sales of sheet music. However, few scholars have examined the relation between race-record marketing and the published sheet music for many race-record songs. A possible clue to this relation is suggested in the sheet music for Bradford's race record from August 1920, "It's Right Here for You (If You Don't Get It—Tain't No Fault o' Mine)." This Bradford song was published as sheet music with a cover displaying the image of the white vaudeville singer Sophie Tucker alongside a larger image of a dapper white couple in evening dress, top hat, and tails.[9] This image suggests that a certain part of this "race" market was the white Harlem entertainment audiences that sought titillation from such racial transgressions. It is still unclear how successful this cross-race marketing was. Nevertheless, this revisionist view of the race record phenomenon is supported in the race catalog advertisements of such companies as Black Swan/Pace Phonograph Corp., Okeh Records, and Perry Bradford Music in such trade organs as the *Talking Machine Journal*. A 1923 Okeh advertisement claimed, for instance, that "the growing tendency on the part of white people to hear their favorite 'blues' sung or played by famous colored 'blues' artists . . . has made the Negro record field more fertile than ever before."[10]

I raise the issue of race-based marketing here to emphasize two main points. First, it is quite likely that the publishing of *Yamekraw* through Bradford's firm may have had little effect among white consumers who may have confused *Rhapsody in Blue* with "real" jazz. This argument is based on the supposition that the white Harlem entertainment enthusiasts who bought racially marketed sheet music could likely distinguish between Tin Pan Alley "jazz" and Harlem jazz. Second, *Yamekraw* is racially and socially coded through Johnson's various melodic borrowings from Bradford's blues catalog and other sources—compositions that were directly tied to the race market. This work is thereby constructed in a manner that would be received in one way by a specific group of African American insiders (and possibly a small circle of white "lovers of Negro music"), and merely heard as generic blues or jazz by most white audiences and middle-class blacks who commonly shunned the blues and race records because this music was too "low class" or "too black."

Despite the marketing of *Yamekraw* to a narrow, race records market, the score of *Yamekraw* ultimately found a wide, multiracial audience when the Still orchestral arrangement was licensed to the Tin Pan Alley firm of Alfred Music. In order to meet the needs of a broader market, the work was promoted as "the greatest orchestra novelty in years." This shift from "artistic treatise" to "novelty" indicates that the newly whitened audience for the score likely consisted of the same market group that was targeted by novelty ragtime and Whitemanesque symphonic jazz. This interpretation is further reinforced by the published arrangement's note that "*Yamekraw* . . . has already been played in manuscript form by such leading orchestras as: Nat Shilkret's Victor Recording Orchestra, Don Voorhees' Columbia Orchestra, Jimmie Johnson's 'Keep Shufflin' Orchestra, and by W. C. Handy at his concert at Carnegie Hall."[11] This short list of ensembles reveals the cross-racial appeal of the score. Shilkret and Voorhees, for example, were major white promoters of symphonic jazz in the 1920s. Johnson himself also recalled having heard performances of his rhapsody on Willard Robison's *Deep River Hour,* a popular national radio show for "lovers of Negro music" featuring the orchestra of Robison (a white singer-pianist once associated with Whiteman) performing a repertory of spirituals and blues, many of which were richly arranged in the symphonic jazz idiom.[12]

Yamekraw's promotion and marketing were also closely intertwined with the problematic definition of "jazz" in the 1920s. In this era, *jazz* was a catchall term that simultaneously referenced the syncopated music of Tin Pan Alley, Broadway, "sweet" dance bands, symphonic jazz orchestras, and "hot" jazz (black or white). This inclusive definition of jazz was part of a variety entertainment culture that regularly encouraged stylistic confluences.[13] Similarly, 1920s journalists also regularly used *jazz* as both an adjective and a verb to characterize an irreverent, playful mingling of white and black, and high and low, cultural phenomena. This is the central meaning of "jazz" in the symphonic jazz vogue. For example, most of the "sweet" ensembles regularly employed "hot" soloists after the phenomenal impact of Louis Armstrong (with Fletcher Henderson) and Bix Beiderbecke (with his Wolverines, and later with Whiteman) in the mid-1920s. Many of the large orchestras, hot or sweet, likewise included a broad diversity of music styles in their performing repertories. These variety-based dance orchestras were a great concern for later jazz critics who thought that the journalism of the 1920s was far too inclusive about what constituted jazz. John Szwed has made a useful distinction between the core jazz tradition and a parallel "jazz"—or jazz-in-quotes—tradition.[14] This latter tradition stands for the broad, popular-culture boundaries of the authentic jazz tradition. The term thus represents a wide range of music that is typically excluded from the "official version of jazz history" that Scott DeVeaux has identified[15] (i.e., "jazz" represents the family of "jazzy," syncopated popular music that extends from Tin Pan Alley and symphonic jazz, to stage and film musicals, to Hollywood's "jazzy" film underscoring practices, and so forth). Post-1930 jazz critics ultimately divorced authentic jazz from this messy "jazz" context in their quest to define a stylistically pure tradition. Despite its great cultural value, the "official version of jazz history" has shortchanged our present-day understanding of the larger cultural context in which jazz functioned in its first decades. What the later exclusionist narrative of jazz has marginalized are the extensive interchanges between the world of jazz and its syncopated relations in American popular music. I am not arguing for an inclusion of this latter music in the jazz canon, but it is clear that this music ("jazz") is a vital part of the contextual history of jazz. This multifaceted "jazz" culture is likewise central to understanding both *Yamekraw* and *Rhapsody in Blue*.

A similar critical problem lies in the fact that for much of the twentieth century, critics and music historians perpetuated a narrative dichotomy between "high" and "popular" cultures. While this dichotomy was indeed quite prominent in interwar America, this critical mind-set has subsequently marginalized a great deal of cross-fertilization that occurred between all strata of American musical life, and most notably in the mildly irreverent intent of the symphonic jazz idiom's intermarriage of the concert hall and dance band. These cultural hierarchy issues and the 1920s white discovery of black culture were both part of a larger historical shift toward cultural "mongrelization," as historian Ann Douglas has termed it.[16] This said, white manifestations of the symphonic jazz idiom rarely emulate African American musical aesthetics accurately. Instead, black jazz aesthetics are filtered through the stylistic interpretations of Tin Pan Alley, Broadway, and Hollywood, rather than directly emerging from composers within the jazz tradition. The social tensions of these ideological class divisions and cultural hybridizations likewise permeated Harlem's intellectual and entertainment communities in the 1920s.

When considering the contextual background of *Yamekraw*, a critical distinction must be made between the Harlem Renaissance in art and literature in the 1920s and the contemporaneous renaissance in Harlem's popular music and musical theater. The contemporary white entertainment trade of the era did not distinguish between these two parallel trends. However, in the creative lives of many authors, artists, and composers, there was relatively little interaction between these groups from the early 1920s to at least the mid-1930s. As jazz orchestra leader Cab Calloway once noted, "The two worlds . . . rarely crossed. We were working hard on our thing and they were working hard on theirs."[17] A slightly different perspective on the relationship between these artistic and commercial circles can be seen in the recollections of the pianist-composer Eubie Blake, who was a personal acquaintance of such celebrated New Negro authors as Langston Hughes and James Weldon Johnson. In a 1973 interview, the historian Nathan Huggins persistently questioned Blake about his relationships with New Negro writers and artists. Blake continually redirected the conversation back to the subject of Harlem popular entertainment. His avoidance of this line of questioning ultimately led Huggins to pose a question suggesting that, from Blake's perspective, "music . . . was at the center of the Harlem Renaissance." In his response, Blake affirmed that from his personal experience, "music and entertainment" *was* the Harlem Renaissance. In his view, "show business" formed the very heart of what he called the "heat wave" of interest in this community in the 1920s, when "white people were coming up to Harlem to hear this music."[18] The comments of Blake and Calloway obviously run contrary to many post-1930 critical definitions of the Harlem Renaissance.

What I am calling for is a more socially nuanced consideration of the relations between Harlem's entertainment community and the more high-culture New Negro movement in arts and literature. This is by no means a new critical argument. For example, the African American music scholar Samuel A. Floyd Jr. has noted that in the

1920s "two cultural universes existed [in Harlem music]: one based on the values of the jook, in the form of rent parties, cabarets, and after-hour joints; the other, on those of the concert hall, the art gallery, and the composer's studio."[19] Several key historians of black musical theater have reinforced Eubie Blake's views on the cultural divisions between the "show business" circle and the New Negro movement. John Graziano, for example, observes that "the relationship of the black musical to the philosophical underpinnings of the Harlem Renaissance [in arts and literature] is a tenuous one." Graziano adds that while "black musical theater flourished during the years of the Harlem Renaissance, it was treated with grudging respect by the cultural leaders of the movement" because "the books, music, and lyrics of black musicals did not project the appropriate intellectual image of the 'New Negro.'"[20] Likewise, Allan Woll observes that "the world of the New Negro and the world of the [black] Broadway musical tended to remain separate." Woll further notes that "many leaders of the new cultural movement frowned upon the impressions of black life that the new musical comedies gave to white audiences."[21] Academic studies on black cultural activities in the 1920s and early 1930s could benefit from greater attention to nuances in individual perspectives, class status, and generational and professional concerns among this boom in creative activity, as well as to the social obstacles between these two camps. I stress this separation of artistic worlds not to underscore any lack of cross-fertilization between these two communities, but to emphasize the fundamental aesthetic differences that divided these worlds and their respective projects of cultural elevation.

For New Negro leaders, a central cultural problem with Harlem entertainment was its uneasy mix of traits that both celebrated racial pride and perpetuated racial stereotypes for white entertainment. These stereotypes were manifest through a restrictive body of theatrical narratives that centered around Deep South black plantation and religious themes, exotic "Jungleland" scenarios, or black-themed rural (South) versus urban (North) narratives. Alain Locke called this Harlem theatrical tradition a "transposed plantation formula."[22] These theatrical sources provided the aesthetic and programmatic roots for both Johnson's *Yamekraw* and its filmic transformation.

By the 1920s, there was a widening divide between popular entertainment and the ascendant New Negro renaissance in art and literature, and Will Marion Cook was even openly critical of both Negro-tarian patrons like Carl Van Vechten and the celebrated accomplishments of Harlem Renaissance authors like W. E. B. DuBois and James Weldon Johnson. This shift is displayed in a letter that Cook wrote to Carl Van Vechten in 1927, via the editor of the *New York News*.[23] In this document, Cook implies that Van Vechten and his Negrotarian peers had helped to perpetuate a "habit of weak [inter-racial] imitation" in Harlem's arts. Cook argues that Harlem's artists, authors, and composers must develop a "pride in things Negroid." Cook's vision of musical "Art"—which involved the celebration of contemporary black *popular* music—differed significantly from the high-culture musical hopes of DuBois and Johnson, who promoted the symphonic elevation of black "folk" music traditions.

In his 1936 book *The Negro and His Music*, Alain Locke creates a useful but awkward account of the 1920s and 1930s black musical landscape in terms of jazz, symphonic jazz, and commercial and classical music. (These divisions are partly derived from a mix of borrowings from two conflicting traditions of "jazz" criticism. Locke does not distinguish between the post-1930 critical definition based on black musical aesthetics and improvisation, and the more inclusive 1920s definition focused on the white syncopated music of George Gershwin, Paul Whiteman, and Tin Pan Alley.) Locke suggests that in the 1920s and 1930s there were hierarchical layers of black musical activity. The first he terms "cheap low-browed jazz," a "mass of mediocrity" that "is manufactured for passing popular consumption."[24] The second category he terms "worthwhile jazz." This bipartite category is said to include both "jazz classics" and "classical" or "super" jazz. Locke defines two primary fields of excellence in "jazz classics." The first is found in his ideal of the jazz virtuoso, a concept he identifies with Louis Armstrong. The second area of "jazz classics" is the field of "jazz composition," with Duke Ellington as Locke's exemplary model. Locke further explains that this latter category includes arranger-composers working in a "typically racial or 'pure' [black] style" (such as the jazz orchestra arranging of Don Redman, Sy Oliver, and Benny Carter).[25] Locke additionally views Ellington as the most promising candidate for his ideal of "classical jazz," a third layer of African American musical activity that he describes as "a type of music that successfully transposes the elements of . . . jazz idioms . . . [to] more sophisticated . . . musical forms."[26] The significance of this latter distinction is made clear when Locke identifies a "romantic school" of black composers who write in nonracial "straight classical forms" (such as Florence Price) or who follow Antonín Dvořák's call for employing "racial [folk] idioms" as the basis for a black symphonic tradition. Locke thus distinguishes between the symphonic employment of themes derived from "folk jazz" and folk music, on the one hand, and concert works based on the idiomatic language of contemporary nonfolk commercial jazz, on the other. *Yamekraw*, for instance, represents the latter tradition. It was the former, so-called romantic musical tradition that received the greatest attention from the spokespersons of the Harlem Renaissance.

I agree with Floyd's implication that there are important similarities between cultural mediation projects like *Yamekraw* and Still's rightfully celebrated incorporation of blues materials in the *Afro-American Symphony* of 1930.[27] Unlike Nathaniel Dett, Florence Price, and William Dawson, who wrote conservative symphonic and choral works, William Grant Still is difficult to firmly place within Locke's account of musical castes in Harlem. Like Langston Hughes, Still is a Harlem Renaissance figure who regularly crossed social and intellectual boundaries. However, in light of Locke's distinction between the symphonic employment of themes derived from "folk jazz" and folk music, on the one hand, and concert works built on the idiomatic language of contemporary nonfolk commercial jazz, on the other, it should be clear that there are important class-based distinctions between projects like *Yamekraw* and the *Afro-American Symphony*. This separation is apparent in the large-scale design of each work, in the local handling of motivic development and harmonic and textural materials, and in the intellectual and cultural background of each project.

Like Floyd, I suggest that there was a broad spectrum of distinct musical activities in 1920s Harlem. These activities ranged from the high-culture ambitions of the New Negro ideals of concert music, on the one hand, to the cultural products of Harlem's popular music, cabaret floor shows, and all-black Broadway musical revues, on the other. Locke's categorical breakdown of black musical activities in the 1920s and 1930s illustrates the importance of the multilevel distinctions between these musical worlds. This said, there are obvious similarities between these social circles. One connecting thread was the lingering impulse from Dvořák's call in the 1890s for the use of

"Negro [folk] melodies of America" as a foundation for "a great and noble school of music."[28] *Yamekraw's* celebration of 1920s race record blues and contemporary Harlem jazz is unique, however, among African American concert works of this era. Johnson's interest in "elevating" the music of Harlem entertainment came in part from his friendship with Will Marion Cook, a former student of Dvořák's. As Maurice Peress has noted, however, the "European models" that the Czech composer "imposed upon his students were not where Cook was heading as a composer."[29]

⅓ CONCEIVING *YAMEKRAW*

The Savannah enclave of Yamecraw (as it was more commonly spelled) was widely seen as a hub of the rich Gullah and Geechee cultures of coastal Georgia and South Carolina. It is likely, therefore, that many 1920s Harlemites interpreted the program of *Yamekraw* as a sign of its intent to express both racial and folk authenticity. Like most of this southern region, the shantytown of Yamecraw was renowned for having retained African traditions and dialects. The larger cultural awareness of Gullah and Geechee cultures in the 1920s was due in large part to the popularity of DuBose Heyward's depiction of the Gullah culture of the Georgia Sea Islands in his 1925 novel *Porgy* and its 1927 dramatization in a highly successful production in New York.

The earliest literary evocation of the Yamecraw community's "religious fervor" likely appeared in James Weldon Johnson's breakthrough poem "Go Down, Death!: A Funeral Sermon." It was first published in April 1927 in the *American Mercury*, but also appeared later that month in Johnson's seminal poetry collection, *God's Trombones: Seven Negro Sermons in Verse*.[30] This poem dramatizes the merciful motives behind God's order for Death to ride down from heaven to release an elderly parishioner from her lifetime of hardship and pain in Yamecraw. In *God's Trombones*, Johnson pointedly discarded stereotyped Negro verse dialect. Johnson recognized that rural southern black preachers did not use black dialect per se but a mix between African American figurative language and another elevated form of language. In the words of Johnson, this hybrid language was "a fusion of Negro idioms with Bible English" (i.e., King James English).[31] Like New Negro art and literature in general, "Go Down, Death!" expresses cultural nationalism through evocations, adaptations, and appropriations of folk art. It is doubtful that James P. Johnson was acquainted with the poem prior to composing *Yamekraw*, although both Johnsons knew of each other's work. James P. was more likely aware that the protagonist of James Weldon Johnson's *An Autobiography of an Ex-Colored Man* had sought to raise ragtime, cakewalks, and other music of southern rural blacks to the level of art music.[32]

Outside of these potential inspirations, James P. Johnson was personally familiar with both Yamecraw and Geechee and Gullah cultures long before their artistic popularity in the late 1920s. His initial contact with these subcultures dated to his teenage years, when he worked as a cabaret and dance hall pianist in the rough black neighborhood of Hell's Kitchen, which was frequented by Geechee and Gullah longshoremen and stevedores from coastal Georgia and South Carolina.

The genesis of Johnson's *Yamekraw* can only be sketchily inferred through an unreliable body of autobiographical commentary by Johnson's associates. These sources are found in the materials assembled for the 1962 Folkways LP, a release that includes liner notes by Perry Bradford and Noble Sissle, and a series of so-called documentary recordings provided by Bradford for side B; supplemental information can also be gleaned from W. C. Handy's 1941 autobiography.

According to Noble Sissle, Vodery and Cook guided the composition of *Yamekraw* by suggesting that Johnson borrow materials from publisher Perry Bradford's compositions to create a more "authentic" American rhapsody:

> When James P. Johnson got . . . the idea of composing a Rhapsody . . . he dropped into Perry Bradford's office and asked a group of fellow musicians to listen to his efforts. Among the listeners was [*sic*] Will Vodery and Will Marion Cook both of whom . . . knew [the] construction of the classics . . .
>
> . . . Cook and Vodery suggested . . . that . . . [Johnson] get one of Perry's Spiritual[s] and Blues and use them as themes . . . [b]ecause . . . an American Rhapsody would have to include these elements.[33]

Whether Cook and Vodery were referring to folk or racial authenticity in the work's borrowings is unclear, especially in light of the commercial nature of Bradford's compositions and his social standing as a Harlem entrepreneur, entertainer, and raconteur. Johnson did follow this advice, as Bradford's commentary on these "borrowings" reveals. This commentary contains details that are frankly wrong or misleading, however. Bradford's synopsis of these supposed borrowings reads as follows:

> The first movement consists mostly of the theme which is *Every Time I Feel the Spirit Moving in My Heart* and *Sam Jones Done Snagged His Britches.* In the second movement you will hear such melodies as *Brothers and Sisters,* whom [*sic*] George Gershwin once said "the *Brothers* song is the most original and tear-jerking tune in a long time." . . . The third and fourth movements—boy, how James P. Johnson spreads and peels his onions with *You Can Read My Letters, but You Can't Read My Mind, Mississippi Roustabouts,* [and] closing with *We Are Leaving for Yamekraw.* . . .
> This jive was put together by . . . Perry Bradford.[34]

Bradford's characterization of these notes as "jive" is an apt description of their historical reliability. Nonetheless, there are certain elements of truth in this text.

To complicate matters, the Folkways LP also includes a series of four recordings that were misleadingly labeled as "THE DOCUMENTATION: Recordings from the Collection of Perry Bradford."[35] These tracks are listed as follows without further discographical information or comment:

Band 1: Sam Jones Done Snagged His Britches (Bradford-Williams)

Band 2: Georgia's Always on My Mind (Bradford-Johnson)

Band 3: That Thing Called Love (Perry Bradford)

Band 4: Shim-me King's Blues (Porter Grainger)

While these songs are certainly "documentation" of Bradford's career, bands 3 and 4 are red herrings for the subject of *Yamekraw,* as they bear no melodic relation whatsoever to the thematic content of the work. However, the first two tracks do relate to *Yamekraw*. In short, Bradford's liner notes and recorded "documentation" imply that Johnson's rhapsody involves at least nine borrowings, but three of these citations bear no relation to the work, two cannot be verified, and the rest involve inaccuracies.

Despite Cook and Vodery's purported advice on the "construction of the classics," *Yamekraw* is built on a loosely formed, episodic structure. This design is an expansion of the type of formal arranging routines employed in Johnson's stride piano compositions. Table 2.1a illustrates the form of the work.

The various episodic sections of *Yamekraw* are closely based on popular music forms—most specifically, blues choruses, popular song form, and sixteen-bar stride strains. The larger whole is built from the combination of these sectional forms, which are based on eight central themes (marked strains A through H in table 2.1a). These building blocks are further combined with an introduction, coda, cadenzas, and interludes, variation choruses, and blues choruses. These strain and chorus statements and their variations are frequently subjected to truncation and augmentation, often in combination with sequential or modulatory extensions or transitional interludes. These transitional passages function as popular culture tropes on classical symphonic development. The composition's structural design is thus appropriately "rhapsodic" in that it is built on both exaggerated, contrasting moods and supposed "folk" themes. Johnson embraces not just quasi-folk jazz and blues themes but also the very idiomatic structures and performance styles of popular music. By the same token, the "classicisms" that one finds in *Yamekraw* are of the sort that Johnson once characterized as the "concert-style" effects of the Harlem "piano ticklers."

In the mid-1950s, Johnson described his early instrumental goal of "building a serious orchestral piano" style. According to Johnson, this style included adaptations of the "orchestral effects" that he had learned from observing the European concert pianists who performed around New York in the second decade of the century. For example, Johnson remembered that "when playing a heavy stomp" as a pianist in the Jungles, he would "soften it right down" then "make an abrupt change like [he had] heard Beethoven do in a sonata." He recalled performing "rag variations on [the] *William Tell Overture*, Grieg's *Peer Gynt Suite* and . . . Rachmaninoff's *Prelude in C-sharp Minor*" in this

TABLE 2.1a. Form of the 1927 piano solo score to *Yamekraw*

M.	Episodic Section	Key	Form/Function	Borrowing
1	Intro.	A♭	Intro.	
17	Strain A	A♭	12-bar blues interrupted at m. 10	*Sam Jones* as a spiritual
27	Var. 1 on Strain A	A♭		*Sam Jones*
41	Strain B ($a^1a^2ba^3$)	A♭	16-bar stride strain	var. on *Soliloquy*
57			Interlude, extension, and transition	
75	Var. on Strain A	A♭	10-bar blues + transition	*Sam Jones*
93	Strain C	G	2 mm. vamp + 12-bar blues with 4 mm. insert	(a) mm. 95–100 = *Brothers* (b) mm. 101–4 = *Letters*
113	Blues chorus 1	Gm	Blues chorus developing Strain C	var. on *Letters*
125	Blues chorus 2	G	Blues chorus developing Strain C	
139			False strain and transition	*Letters* in bass
177	False strain	Gm	Song interrupted (spiritual)	*Brothers*
191	Blues chorus 3	G	12-bar blues interrupted at m. 10	var. on *Letters*
201	False return chorus 1	G	Mm. 201–2 = 113–14 in major	*Letters*
211	Cadenza		Cadenza (m. 212 = m. 133ff.)	
216	Strain D (a)	F♯	12-bar blues with 2 mm. insert	
230	Strain D (b)	F♯m	8 mm. blues + 4 extension	
242	Strain D (a^1)	F♯	14-bar var. Strain D (a) + extension	Mm. 262–9 = *Caprice Rag*
270	Var. on D (a)	D	12-bar blues	
282	Quasi-blues episode	D	Quasi-blues episode	*Stop It, Joe*
296	Strain D^2	E♭	Development of Strain D into 32-bar song (aabc)	
328	Strain E (aa)	B♭	8 + 8	*Georgia*
344	Strain E (b^1b^2)	Gm and B♭m	8 + seq. up to B♭ min (8mm)	
360	Strain E (a^1)	B♭	8 + abrupt modulation	*Georgia*
370	Strain F ($a^1a^2a^3a^1$)	E♭	8 + 8 + 8 + 4	
398	Strain G	Cm	8 + 8 (seq.) + 4 transition	*Charleston Rag*
418	Strain H	Cm	16 + repeated extension	
450	Quote Strain D (a)		Modulatory sequences	
465	Var. quote Strain B	F♯	Only 11 mm. of orig.	*Soliloquy*
476	Var. of Strain D (a)	F♯	2 mm. + 2 seq. + 2 seq. + extension	
486	Strain A	A♭	2 mm. + variations and extensions	*Sam Jones*
498	Strain D ref.		Strain D ref. + brief cadenza	
516	Theme A	A♭	4 mm. vamp + last Theme A	*Sam Jones*

TABLE 2.1b. Alterations to the *Yamekraw* score

	Asch Record	1928 Still Arrangement	1930 Vitaphone
M.	Deviations	Orchestration [(#) = reh. nos.]	Score Deviations
1	**Recording I**	orch vs. pno solo; **(1)**	
19		**(2)** tutti (mel. in reeds) ⇒ oboe solo	
27		**(3)** pno solo	Cut mm. 27–40 (reh. nos. 3–4)
41		**(4)** trbn solo + muted brass vs. reeds (jazz) ⇒ **(5)** tutti vs. pno solo ⇒ tutti	
75	Cut mm. 89–92	**(6)** pno solo ⇒ **(7)** pno + str/wwnds	Cut mm. 75–88
93	**Recording II**	**(8)** orch + trpt solo ⇒ tutti ⇒ **(9)** trbn solo + tutti (emphasis on New Orleans sound)	
113		**(10)** clar/oboe solo + str/wwnds ⇒ tutti ⇒ clar/sax solo + rhythm/str	Cut mm. 113–76 (reh. nos. 13–15)
125		**(11)** pno solo ⇒ sax solo + alternating str/wwnds and brass	Cut
139	Ignores repeat	**(12)** tutti ⇒ **(13)** pno solo + tutti ⇒ **(14)** pno solo	Cut
177		**(15)** clar solo (New Orleans)	
183		pno solo ⇒ tutti ⇒ trpt solo + orch	
191		**(16)** pno solo ⇒ **(17)** sax solo ⇒ tutti	Cut mm. 191–200 (reh. nos. 16–17)
211	Improv. cadenza	pno	New "classical" cadenza m. 211
212		**(18)** sax solo + reeds/pno (jazz texture)	
216	**Recording III**	**(19)** trpt solo + jazz orch texture	
230		**(20)** tutti ⇒ saxes ⇒ sax/trpt/sax solos in alternating jazz orch + symphonic textures	
242		**(21)** pno solo	Cut mm. 242–59
256		**(22)** brass + rhythm ⇒ pno solo ⇒ **(23)** tutti vs. trpt solo with reeds	
270		**(24)** sax/clar solo + reeds and pno (later strings)	31 secs. new "train" music between m. 269 and m. 270
282	Cut mm. 282–93	**(25)** pno solo	Added honky-tonk riffs
296		**(26)** tutti ⇒ **(27)** reeds/rhythm ⇒ tutti	
328	**Recording IV**	**(28)** trpt solo + jazz orch texture	Cut mm. 328–59 (reh. nos. 28–31)
344		**(29)** tutti ⇒ **(30)** pno solo	Cut
360		**(31)** trpt solo + jazz texture ⇒ wwnds/gong	
370		**(32)** horn with pno solos + jazz orch	Cut mm. 370–433 (reh. nos. 32–35)
398	Cut mm. 412–13	**(33)** tutti ⇒ pno solo	Cut
418		**(34)** reeds + rhythm ⇒ **(35)** tutti	Cut (to m. 433)
450		**(36)** trpt solo + tutti ⇒ sax/clar solo ⇒ **(37)** brass + cymb ⇒ sax/clar solo	
476		**(38)** sax/clar solo + reeds ⇒ tutti (repeat)	Cut mm. 482–83
486		**(39)** wah-wah brass + pno ⇒ open brass choir + reeds/pno ⇒ **(40)** tutti ⇒ trpt solo ⇒ pno solo ⇒	(a) mm. 486–99 rearranged (b) Cut mm. 500 ff. (reh. nos. 41)
529		**(41)** tutti with trpt vs. trbn call-and-response solos	

era.[36] Johnson's comments illustrate that it was regular practice among Harlem pianists to signify upon the idiomatic gestures of classical music.[37] Johnson observed that such cross-genre references were "considered very sophisticated in those days as we liked people to know that we could play the classics, too." He explained that he "used to rip off . . . ringing concert-style opening[s] . . . that [were] full of fireworks in the classical manner and then abruptly slide into a solid . . . stomp to wake up the audience and get a laugh."[38] Like the contemporary "ragging" and later "jazzing the classics" vogues, such stylistic mixing was perpetuated in the spirit of what the period called novelty music, a category characterized by signification, wit, and mildly deviant playfulness. In the stride pianists' "jazzing of the classics," this deviance was conducted at the expense of "high" musical masterworks (regardless of the actual canonic status of light classics such as Rachmaninoff's Prelude in C-sharp Minor or Rossini's *William Tell Overture*).

On several occasions, Johnson described his mature "orchestral" piano style in terms of the classical ideals of musical contrast and thematic "development." In practice, these ideals were not directly derived from classical music but were gesturally inspired, as Johnson noted, by what he heard "Beethoven do in a sonata." This aural stylistic model was filtered through an African American cultural perspective and applied to the game rivalry that defined the stride cutting-contest milieu. These "classical" stylizations were applied as secondary, superficial characteristics to the music of the stride pianists. These gestures were meant to sound "artistic" or "classical" because of their melodramatic quality, their pastiche-like quality, or their relative degree of musical complexity.

It is easy to recognize that *Yamekraw* is classically *inspired*. In other words, it aspires to the cultural rituals and performance spheres embodied in the tradition of classical music. These aspirations are readily apparent in the work's extended form; its melodramatic introduction, coda, and modulatory interludes; its cadenzas; its concerns for thematic development and thematic recapitulation; and its artful deviations from the popular music forms that comprise its episodic sections. These elements are not meant to be read as part of the popular music traditions with which Johnson's career was associated. Such high-culture evocations are offset by the supposedly lower artistic nature of the work's episodic structure, its intermusical associations, and its stylistic tropes. In order to build a contextual understanding of the unusual design of *Yamekraw*, it is necessary to consider its formal precedents, particularly *Rhapsody in Blue*.

𝄢 RHAPSODY IN BLUE AND EPISODIC FORM IN SYMPHONIC JAZZ

Yamekraw was published as a piano solo in 1927, a year that witnessed a transition in the formal models of symphonic jazz. In late 1927, Paul Whiteman Publications was founded as a means to publish the orchestral arrangements of this famous band leader. This vanity label was distributed by Robbins Music, which by 1928 took over the Whiteman series and narrowed its focus to popular concert-style works. The Whiteman-Robbins "Modern American Music" score series codified an important three-strain form in symphonic jazz of the late 1920s and 1930s.[39] This form was an extension of a 1920s novelty piano form established in Zez Confrey's *Kitten on the Keys* of 1921. Prior to 1927, most arrangers in the symphonic jazz mold were writing novelty-piano and "orchestral novelty" arrangements, as well as "concert"-style, chorus-variation, and jazzed-classics arrangements. *Yamekraw* does not resemble this emerging three-strain, symphonic jazz formal model, however. Similarly, despite his social proximity to Johnson, Still's *From the Land of Dreams* and *Darker America* (both from 1924) were not models for *Yamekraw*, owing to their greater formal complexity and their sophisticated use of dissonance. As Bradford suggested, the main inspiration for the genesis of Johnson's *Yamekraw* was likely Gershwin's rhapsody. This suggestion is reinforced by evidence of Johnson's connections to early 1920s symphonic jazz.

Yamekraw may not have been Johnson's first attempt at composing an extended, concert-style work based on Harlem's popular music. An undated manuscript entitled *Symphonic Dance: Carolina Shout* shows a concerto-like, orchestral jazz arrangement of Johnson's most famous stride piano composition. Evidence in this manuscript suggests that the work may be related to Johnson's 1923 orchestration of *Carolina Shout* that was used as the overture to the *Plantation Days* revue.[40] The importance of *Symphonic Dance: Carolina Shout* is that this manuscript further underscores that Johnson's initial attempts at extended composition were tied to his artistic milieu during the second and third decades of the century—that is, the worlds of the Harlem piano tick-lers (Harlem's rent parties and cabarets) and black musical theater. The compositional nature of *Carolina Shout* reflects the first tradition, and its likely appropriation as a musical theater overture suggests a fluidity between these cultures that is pertinent to *Yamekraw*.

It is significant that Johnson does not list *Symphonic Dance: Car-olina Shout* in any of his extant, privately assembled symphonic works lists. The earliest composition in these lists is generally *Yamekraw*, but even this title is not always included. Johnson may have considered these early concert works as somehow formally different from his 1932 *Harlem Symphony* and other later compositions.

Johnson's early interest in symphonic jazz is confirmed in com-ments made by both Johnson himself and Sidney Bechet. Johnson re-called that "in 1920 . . . I met George Gershwin . . . He . . . was inter-ested in . . . blues. Like myself, he wanted to write them on a higher level. We had lots of talks about our ambitions to do great music on American themes." Johnson also claimed that in this period of 1916–17, he "was rehearsing 3, 5, 7, and 14 piece combos and trying to introduce small chamber orchestras in symphonic style." He stated that he "wanted to . . . work out ideas and experiments and . . . [to try] out what were known as . . . 'head arrangements.'" He further claimed that these arrangements were "full of counterpoint and contrasting melodies."[41] As was seen in chapter 1, Sidney Bechet's autobiography additionally underscores Johnson's interests in "Orchestrational Jazz, Concert Jazz, and Fancy-Arrangement Jazz" in 1924.[42] This charac-terization better reflects the manuscript evidence of Johnson's *Sym-phonic Dance: Carolina Shout* than the earlier "head arrangements" quo-tation by Johnson, which likely referred to the type of arranging heard in Johnson's band recording of *Carolina Shout* in 1921.[43]

By 1926 or 1927, the published scores of Gershwin's rhapsody and Grofé's *Mississippi Suite* would have been the most obvious "jazz rhap-sody" models for Johnson. However, there is little similarity between the designs of Grofé's suite (which involves the aforementioned three-strain form) and Johnson's rhapsody. Prior to 1927, Gershwin had also composed his one-act opera *Blue Monday Blues* and the Con-certo in F, but the designs of these works also differ greatly from *Yamekraw*. This said, there are significant similarities between *Yamekraw* and the design of *Rhapsody in Blue*. The idea of creating a

Harlem-style jazz rhapsody may have even come from appropriations of this latter work in Harlem entertainment.

In big band jazz, musical theater, and film music, the tasks of composition, orchestration, and arranging each demand a collaborative creative process. This approach is central to both *Yamekraw* and *Rhapsody in Blue*. These popular music traditions saw "works" as dynamic, mutable texts. Beyond the division of compositional and arranging duties, creative collaboration could further include score contributions by band members, contributions of improvised and paraphrased solos that elaborate on written score passages, and band-specific employment of unique instrumental voices. With commercial stock arrangements, scores gained an added mutability by being regularly adapted to widely varying ensembles. This convention was achieved both through cross-scoring (instrument-doubling conventions that allowed a score to be used by multiple instrumental forces) and through the practice of "doctoring stocks," in which stock arrangements were modified for individual needs to create band-specific arrangements. This problem of mutable "form" has been central to the critical reception of *Rhapsody in Blue*.

Concert-style dance-band arrangements, extended symphonic jazz compositions, and certain production number scoring traditions of the 1920s were all closely linked by similar approaches to episodic arranging routines. Even in an idiosyncratic symphonic jazz concert work such as Gershwin's *Rhapsody in Blue*, there are key formal devices that are intimately related to this tradition. This work's relation to popular music has been a long-standing problem in its critical reception. Since its inception, the rhapsody's proponents have put forth a variety of arguments for reading it as a variation on classical form. By contrast, its critical detractors have vociferously claimed that the work involved either a clumsy use of form or had no form at all. These latter arguments claimed that it was laid out as a haphazard (or "rhapsodic") string of episodic thematic statements. This critical tradition was summarized by Leonard Bernstein: "*Rhapsody in Blue* is not a real composition." In his explanation of this remark, Bernstein rightly observed that "you can cut out" any of the "stuck-together sections" in the rhapsody "and the piece still goes on bravely." He suggested that "you can even interchange these sections . . . You can make cuts within a section, or add new cadenzas, or play it with any combination of instruments . . . [I]t can be a five-minute piece or . . . a twelve-minute piece."[44] In his 1928 essay "Jazz Is Music," George Antheil similarly characterized the formal conventions of this era's symphonic jazz concert works as "parade-form," a term that implied "a series of melodies which follow one another without meaning."[45] This derisive description was aimed squarely at Gershwin's rhapsody.

Table 2.2 shows the design of *Rhapsody in Blue* as it was presented in Grofé's 1925 stock arrangement. Roughly three-fifths of the composition (mm. 38-380) is built on a sequence of song-based strains and short connecting and modulatory interludes. In his 1997 study of the rhapsody, the composer-theorist David Schiff presented an innovative analytical overview of the work's foundation on a principle of turning "tunes into themes."[46] Schiff considers both the hypothetical "trunk" or song forms of these tunes and their "theme" forms in the rhapsody. While he does offer a brief interpretation of the overall form of the work, Schiff does not provide a detailed overview of how these tune/strain statements are actually arranged over the course of the work. The concept of "tunes into themes" implies that these tunes transcend their nascent song forms to become classically developed themes. In practice, the tunes are most often cast as near-complete statements that are subjected to strain augmentations, truncations, and so forth. Despite these alterations, the consistent songlike design of these "themes" is readily apparent. The result looks like an elaborate expansion on the multistrain formal models of contemporary novelty ragtime or musical theater production numbers.

The rhapsody is rich in inventive thematic treatments, and these traits are most apparent in the opening seventy-two bars. This passage is best interpreted as an introduction to the main body of the work that begins in earnest at either m. 38 (if the first cut is not taken) or Rehearsal No. 6. Thus, despite its complex design, this passage is only a preface to the greater episodic arranging routine of the rhapsody.

The rhapsody's underlying episodic form does not necessarily imply poor structural design. In fact, like *Yamekraw*, this is an artful expansion of American popular music-arranging conventions. In both works, episodic form is inventively elastic, in that strain boundaries are routinely truncated or extended (through cadential delays, sequential motivic treatments, and related devices). While the broadly conceived form of Gershwin's rhapsody was idiosyncratic, its

TABLE 2.2. Formal outline of George Gershwin's
Rhapsody in Blue, based on the 1925 Grofé stock
orchestration for Harms, Inc.

Reh. Nos./Cuts	M.	Motives
	1	Ritornello
R.1	11	Theme 2
R.2	16	Ritornello
	19	Tag
R.3	21	Ritornello
R.4	24	Tag
A	*30*	
	38	*Ritornello (a¹a²ba³)*
B	65	
R.6–R.8	72	Ritornello (a¹a²ba³)
R.9–R.11	91	Theme 3 (a¹a²ba³)
R.12–R.13	115	Theme 2 (a¹a²ba³)
R.14	138	Theme 4 (a¹a²)
R.15–R.17	146	Theme 4 (b¹b²a³)
R.18	172	Mod. interlude
R.19 + C	*181*	*Theme 2 (a¹a²ba³)*
R.20	*200*	*Theme 2 (a¹a²ba³)*
R.21	*215*	
R.22	*217*	*Ritornello (a¹a²)*
R.23–R.24	*235*	*Ritornello (ba³)*
D	255	
R.25	259	Theme 4 (a¹a²b¹b²)
R.26 + E	*275*	*Theme 4 (a³) + ext.*
R.27	*296*	*Piano cadenza*
F	297	
R.28–R.29	301	Andantino (a¹a²b¹)
R.30–R.31	323	Andantino (a¹a²b²)
R.32	345	
	355	Andantino (a¹a²b¹)
R.33	381	
G	*385*	*Tag*
H	417	
R.34	423	Andantino
R.35	431	Andantino (a¹a²)
R.36	447	Andantino
R.37	459	Tag-based
R.39	485	Theme 2 (a¹a²ba³)
	503	Ritornello + Tag

This arrangement suggests the following cuts for the score: A
to B; C to D; E to F; and G-H. These four cuts are indicated in the
outline above through dashed lines and italicization. Theme
names are based on David Schiff's overview of the work. (See
David Schiff, *Gershwin, Rhapsoday in Blue* [New York: Cambridge
University Press, 1997].) "Ritornello" refers to Theme 1, Schiff's -
"Ritornello" theme. Schiff's Theme 5 is listed here as the "Andan-
tino" theme.

approach to expanding the compositional traditions of novelty rag-time through elastic episodic form and developmental, motive-based interludes was influential, particularly with Grofé. Overall, the pool of "Gershwinesque" symphonic jazz arranging and scoring resources that Gershwin and Grofé created for the rhapsody were an inspiration for much of the Whiteman-Robbins concert work tradition of the late 1920s and 1930s.

Johnson's mid-1920s knowledge of Gershwin's concert work ambitions is sporadically documented. According to the pianist Willie "The Lion" Smith, Johnson, Fats Waller, and Smith were invited to a party "to celebrate . . . Gershwin's new composition *Rhapsody in Blue.*" Smith noted that "we all knew Gershwin," and "he was the one who got us invited." In his recollection of this event, Smith claimed he was worried that Gershwin "was going to stay seated at the piano all night," because Johnson, Waller, and Smith were each "anxious . . . to get at those keys." According to Smith, he finally told Gershwin, "Get up off that piano stool and let the real players take over, you tomato." The three Harlem pianists then took over the party's entertainment.[47] While likely exaggerated, this anecdote demonstrates that the stride circle's cocky game rivalries also extended to interactions with Gershwin. In addition to other evidence from Johnson's estate, there is ample documentation of regular, mutually appreciated interactions between the stride pianists and the white novelty pianists of the Whiteman circle, including Gershwin. Johnson's composition of *Yamekraw* likely began through the same playful one-upmanship that Smith conveyed in his story. This work might be Johnson's way of saying, "Get up off that piano stool and let the real players take over."

♭♭ THE DESIGN OF *YAMEKRAW*

Perry Bradford's liner notes and so-called documentary recordings for the 1962 Folkways LP suggest that *Yamekraw* involves at least nine thematic borrowings. Bradford claims that the opening consists of thematic borrowings from both the well-known spiritual "Every Time I Feel the Spirit Moving in My Heart" and a song Bradford calls "Sam Jones Done Snagged His Britches." While there is no relation between the opening themes of *Yamekraw* and "Every Time I

(a) "Sam Jones" Motive

Sam Jones he done snagged his britch-es. Now he's walkin' 'round here in stitch-es.

(b)

(c)

Example 2.1.   *Yamekraw*'s relation to *Sam Jones Done Snagged His Britches* (Bradford/Williams)

(a) Lead sheet transcribed from the recording by Louis Jordan and His Tympani Five (Decca 7623; recorded March 29, 1939). Melody based on the instrumental head.

(b) Strain A ("Sam Jones" theme) from the *Yamekraw* piano solo, mm. 17–21. James P. Johnson, *Yamekraw: A Negro Rhapsody* (New York: Perry Bradford Music, 1927). © James P. Johnson Foundation. Used by permission.

(c) The common rhythm shared between the *Yamekraw* "Sam Jones" theme and its model

Feel the Spirit," example 2.1a shows a likely thematic relation between *Yamekraw* and Bradford's "documentary recording" of "Sam Jones Done Snagged His Britches," recorded in 1939 by Louis Jordan and His Tympani Five.

The question of this potential intermusical relation is complicated by the fact that the primary melody of the recording only moderately resembles the first theme (strain A) of *Yamekraw* as shown in example 2.1b. Both melodies are based on a standard blues form, albeit in the latter instance the theme is performed with a spiritual-like character. Each melody is built from a two-measure melodic riff. Beyond their similar melodic contours, these blues use the same rhythmic pattern for their riff motives, as shown in example 2.1c. If strain A relates to the "Sam Jones" theme, which I sense it does, then it is constructed as a variant—or very likely based on an earlier undocumented variant—of this song.

While the 1939 Louis Jordan recording had no influence on Johnson's composition, it remains unclear how early Bradford may have "composed" this blues. The melody was apparently in public circulation in the early 1920s, as evidenced in Mark Tucker's interviews with the Harlem musician Garvin Bushell. Bushell refers to the melody in his recollections concerning a September 1921 recording of "Old Time Blues" that he made with the singer Edith Wilson. Bushell comments on two melodic fragments in this recording. The second melody is a brief statement of the riff motive that was used in the 1939 "Sam Jones" recording. Bushell noted, "They used to sing 'Somebody done snagged their britches'" to this tune. This evidence suggests that Bradford's later song was adapted from a bawdy anonymous blues that was in circulation in the early 1920s. The reappearance of this melodic fragment in a two-bar trombone and tuba break in a Bradford-organized, February 1921 recording of "Old Time Blues" by Mamie Smith and Her Jazz Hounds reveals that the passage was a prearranged part of the song.[48] This second recording confirms the melody's direct familiarity in the Bradford and Johnson circle of the early 1920s.

In his Folkways notes, Bradford suggested that *Yamekraw* borrows from a James P. Johnson composition called "Brothers and Sisters" (or the "Brothers Song"). The Johnson estate retains two extant pages from the published score to Johnson and Henry Creamer's "Brothers: A Negro Exhortation." This song was published in 1928, *after* the composition of *Yamekraw*. As shown in examples 2.2a and 2.2b, "Brothers" is adapted from the passage beginning at m. 177 in *Yamekraw*.

Outside a transposition from the original key of B-flat minor to G minor, the refrain of this song is taken virtually note for note from this passage in *Yamekraw*. Beyond the evidence of its copyright date, the first documented appearance of this song is its use as a late 1928 addition to Johnson's revue *Keep Shufflin'*. While "Brothers" almost certainly postdates *Yamekraw*, its title and text suggest a pre-*Yamekraw* association: Will Marion Cook's famous 1912 song "Exhortation: A Negro Sermon." Both works are secondary entertainment derivations of spirituals, and each is a trope on rural southern black preachers and their elevated language.

Bradford suggested that *Yamekraw* further references three songs,

Example 2.2.   Relation of *Brothers: A Negro Exhortation* to *Yamekraw*

(a) Excerpt from *Brothers: A Negro Exhortation* (1928). *Brothers: A Negro Exhortation*, music by James P. Johnson, lyric by Henry Creamer (New York: Perry Bradford Music, 1928). © James P. Johnson Foundation. Used by permission.

(b) Measures 177–88 from the *Yamekraw* piano solo ("Brothers" theme). James P. Johnson, *Yamekraw: A Negro Rhapsody* (New York: Perry Bradford Music, 1927). © James P. Johnson Foundation. Used by permission.

"You Can Read My Letters—But Can't Read My Mind," "Mississippi Roustabouts," and "We Are Leaving for Yamekraw." I have been unable to locate any extant recorded or score materials related to either of the last two songs. By contrast, "You Can Read My Letters" is a reference to a line in the lyrics of Bradford's song "Crazy Blues." In Mamie Smith's historic recording of it, this passage is sung, "Now I can read his letters, I just can't read his mind." Examples 2.3a and 2.3b show that the melodic line underscoring this text parallels the theme that Johnson uses at m. 201 in *Yamekraw*. While this connection to "Crazy Blues" is important because of this song's historical significance, the same melody also freely appears in other Bradford-organized blues recordings of this era. These recordings include two versions of "Liza Johnson's Got Better Bread Than Sally Lee," "New Crazy Blues," and "The Road Is Rocky." Similarly, the common-stock nature of this phrase can also be seen in its appearance as the

(a) Transcribed "Letters" passage from the 1920 Mamie Smith recording (melody in unison with trombone), transposed to B♭

Measures 20–24 of the published version of the song

(b) ⑰ Lento

Example 2.3.   *Yamekraw*'s borrowing of "You Can Read My Letters"

(a) Transcribed passage from the recording by Mamie Smith and Her Jazz Hounds (Okeh 7529-C-OK 4169; recorded August 10, 1920) and mm. 20–24 from the published score to Perry Bradford's *Crazy Blues* (New York: Perry Bradford Music, 1920). Perry Bradford, *Crazy Blues* (New York: Perry Bradford Music, 1920).

(b) Measures 201–3 from the *Yamekraw* piano solo ("Letters" theme). James P. Johnson, *Yamekraw: A Negro Rhapsody* (New York: Perry Bradford Music, 1927). © James P. Johnson Foundation. Used by permission.

main phrase of King Oliver's "(Hello Central Get Me) Doctor Jazz," from 1927.[49] Thus, like the "Sam Jones" theme, this melodic fragment was in popular circulation among Harlem's musical circles of the early 1920s.

Bradford's other useful "documentary" recording is "Georgia's Always On My Mind." This track is a 1928 session by the Gulf Coast Seven, a group that included Johnson, Garvin Bushell, and Bradford. The melody of this song is directly related to the theme used in strain E (m. 328ff.) of *Yamekraw*, but this recording again postdates the composition of Johnson's rhapsody. As shown in example 2.4, despite their different keys and some minimal melodic variations, the song chorus and the "Georgia" theme are clearly related, and each involves the same underlying bass line (outside of the occasional offbeat chordal interjections in the striding left hand of the *Yamekraw* passage). These

Example 2.4.   Relation of *Georgia's Always on My Mind* to *Yamekraw*

(a) Transcription of the first four measures to the chorus of *Georgia's Always on My Mind* (Perry Bradford/James P. Johnson) from the recording by The Gulf Coast Seven (Columbia 14373-D; recorded October 19, 1928). James P. Johnson and Perry Bradford, *Georgia's Always on My Mind* (1928).

(b) First four measures of Strain E (mm. 328–31) from the *Yamekraw* piano solo ("Georgia" theme). James P. Johnson, *Yamekraw: A Negro Rhapsody* (New York: Perry Bradford Music, 1927). © James P. Johnson Foundation. Used by permission.

resemblances do not necessarily imply which work came first. What is important in this intermusical connection is that the melodic materials of "Georgia" are tied to the same black musical theater and race record cultural milieu that defines the "Sam Jones" and "Letters" themes.

There are at least seven intermusical connections that Bradford does not mention. First, strain B of *Yamekraw* seems to involve a paraphrase of the primary theme from Rube Bloom's popular 1926 piano novelty *Soliloquy*. The resemblance between these two themes arises in the idiosyncratic syncopated figurations of the first measures shown in examples 2.5a and 2.5b. Each excerpt involves reiterations of parallel harmonies that move in brief, undulating, neighbor-tone relations before their final chromatic phrase resolutions up to a held harmony (with an accompanying stepwise harmonic motion). This resemblance to *Soliloquy* is the most tenuous of the melodic connections mentioned here. The likely connection between these melodies,

Example 2.5. Resemblance of *Yamekraw* motive to a theme from Rube Bloom's *Soliloquy*

(a) Measures 7–12 of Rube Bloom's *Soliloquy: A Musical Thought* (1926). Rube Bloom, *Soliloquy: A Musical Thought* (New York: Triangle Music, 1926).

(b) Measures 465–72 from the *Yamekraw* piano solo ("Soliloquy" theme). James P. Johnson, *Yamekraw: A Negro Rhapsody* (New York: Perry Bradford Music, 1927). © James P. Johnson Foundation. Used by permission.

however, is reinforced by the fact that at the time of the composition of *Yamekraw*, *Soliloquy* was a well-known work that had been recorded by Bloom, Paul Whiteman's Orchestra, and Duke Ellington's Washingtonians, among others. It is impossible to determine whether the resemblance of strain B to the *Soliloquy* theme was meant to be heard as a borrowing or merely occurred as an unconscious accident.

Second, in mm. 262–69 of *Yamekraw*, Johnson recycles—almost note for note—a modulatory interlude from his *Caprice Rag*, a fast, shout-style number that is important for having been his first solo piano roll recording in 1917.[50] As shown in example 2.6, mm. 262–63 and 266–67 in *Yamekraw* are nearly identical to mm. 55–56 and 59–60 in the 1917 *Caprice Rag* piano roll.[51] The two-bar response phrases to these passages (mm. 264–65 and 268–69 in example 2.6a, and mm. 57–58 and 61–62 in example 2.6b) each involve related melodic and

(a)

(b)

Example 2.6.   Relation of *Yamekraw* mm. 262–69 to an interlude from *Caprice Rag*

(a) Measures 262–69 from *Yamekraw* piano solo. James P. Johnson, *Yamekraw: A Negro Rhapsody* (New York: Perry Bradford Music, 1927). © James P. Johnson Foundation. Used by permission.

(b) Transcription of interlude from Johnson's 1917 piano roll performance of *Caprice Rag* (Metro Art 203176; recorded May 1917). James P. Johnson, *Caprice Rag* (1917). Adapted from the piano roll transcription by Robert Pinsker (unpublished, James P. Johnson Foundation, 1999). Courtesy of the James P. Johnson Foundation.

harmonic material that resolves to similar voicings of the same harmonies. This borrowing likely held some significance to Johnson because *Caprice Rag* was one of a handful of early compositions that remained in Johnson's repertory into the 1950s.

Third, the extant manuscripts to Johnson's 1931 show *Sugar Hill* reveal that he recycled roughly twenty measures from *Yamekraw*'s introduction and strain A in the opening bars to this production's overture. This borrowing underscores the close relation between the musical content of *Yamekraw* and Johnson's work in Harlem musical theater.

Fourth, example 2.7 shows that in mm. 398–413 of *Yamekraw*, Johnson paraphrases Eubie Blake's early composition *The Charleston Rag*, reputed to be his first.[52] In near parallel to Johnson's May 1917 recording debut with *Caprice Rag*, the session that produced the 1917 piano roll of *The Charleston Rag* likewise marked Blake's first foray into this commercial medium. In a retrospective concert in the late 1960s, Blake prefaced his performance of *The Charleston Rag* by noting, "I wrote this . . . in eighteen and ninety-nine. . . . Now the bass

(a)

(b)

Example 2.7.   Relation of *Yamekraw,* mm. 398–411, to Eubie Blake's *The Charleston Rag*

(a) Transcription of mm. 9–17 from Eubie Blake's *The Charleston Rag.* Eubie Blake, *The Charleston Rag* (New York: M. Witmark and Sons, 1917). Transcribed by Terry Waldo, *Sincerely, Eubie Blake* (Eubie Blake Music, 1975).

(b) Measures 398–413 from the *Yamekraw* piano solo ("Charleston Rag" theme). James P. Johnson, *Yamekraw: A Negro Rhapsody* (New York: Perry Bradford Music, 1927). © James P. Johnson Foundation. Used by permission.

you hear, these people [later] called it boogie woogie, [but] we called it the walking bass."[53] The distinctive chromatic walking bass line that Blake mentions is closely paraphrased in Johnson's strain. (See example 2.7.)

The purported composition date for *The Charleston Rag,* 1899, is the year that Scott Joplin's world-famous *Maple Leaf Rag* was published. The correlation is likely not coincidental. Blake's comment possibly reflects a revisionist intent evident in his concern for pointing out that eastern ragtime had employed boogie-woogie bass lines well before the popularity of that stylistic genre in the 1930s and

1940s. While a compositional date of 1899 is possible, it is difficult to believe that Blake wrote the sophisticated *Charleston Rag* at the age of sixteen. The virtuosity and compositional detail in this piece—at least as it was recorded from 1917 forward—significantly surpass the instrumental demands of Joplin's *Maple Leaf Rag*. Regardless, Johnson's paraphrase of this Blake material is homage to his peer and friend, and this thematic connection would have been immediately recognizable to his Harlem entertainment peers.

Fifth, Johnson recomposed yet another 1917 work beyond both *The Charleston Rag* and *Caprice Rag*. Measures 282–95 in *Yamekraw* are built from the first strain of Johnson's 1917 piano roll performance of *Stop It*.[54] Example 2.8 shows that this instrumental recording is related to a Johnson song of the same name (aka "Stop It, Joe") that was published the same year with lyrics by William H. Farrell. It is unknown whether the song or the three-strain rag came first. Johnson's first two published compositions were notably his "Mamma's and Pappa's Blues" and "Stop It." Despite their notable differences (especially in harmonic progressions and phrase lengths), the most direct relation between these three materials—the *Yamekraw* episode, and the piano roll and song of "Stop It"—occurs between the riff of mm. 282–95 in *Yamekraw* and the riff that forms the primary theme to the piano roll strain.[55]

The relation of the piano roll to the song is more complex. Farrell's comic lyrics concern a woman, Miss Mandy, who implores her partner, Lovie Joe, to "stop that wigglin'" on the dance floor (i.e., stop trying to impress her) if he wants to dance "till the band gets thru." The chorus of the song is based on the second strain of the piano rag. The third strain of the piano roll was abandoned entirely. As shown in example 2.8c, the underlying two-bar riff of the vocal (and accompaniment) to the song verse is a loose paraphrase or variation on the riff behind the primary strain of the piano roll.

Last, there are at least two additional publications by Alfred Music that were reportedly derived from that firm's Johnson-Still score of *Yamekraw*. *Yamekraw* reportedly involves a borrowing related to a 1930 dance band arrangement entitled *Hot Curves (Fox Trot)*. In 1931, Alfred Music also published a stock arrangement of a song entitled "Yamekraw Blues." Both of these numbers were attributed to Johnson and arranged by Ken Macomber.[56]

(a) 5

(b) 282

(c)

Miss Man‑ dy John‑son   and   sweet Lov‑ie   Joe,

7

p

Example 2.8.   Relation of *Yamekraw*, mm. 282–93, to the 1917 William Farrell and James P. Johnson song *Stop It* (aka *Stop It, Joe*)

(a) Transcription of mm. 5–6 from James P. Johnson's 1917 piano roll performance of *Stop It* (Universal 203205; recorded August 1917). William Farrell and James P. Johnson, *Stop It* (New York: F. B. Haviland, 1917).Transcribed by Robert Pinsker from the piano roll (unpublished, James P. Johnson Foundation, 1999). © James P. Johnson Foundation. Courtesy of the James P. Johnson Foundation.

(b) Measures 282–83 from the *Yamekraw* piano solo. James P. Johnson, *Yamekraw: A Negro Rhapsody* (New York: Perry Bradford Music, 1927). © James P. Johnson Foundation. Used by permission.

(c) Measures 7–8 from the published sheet music to *Stop It*. William Farrell and James P. Johnson, *Stop It* (New York: F. B. Haviland, 1917).

The above Harlem-entertainment reading of the intermusical content of *Yamekraw* is central to creating an understanding of this work's rich web of cultural meanings. *Yamekraw*'s thematic materials were by no means Dvořák-prescribed melodic borrowings from the "primitive" folk music of Gullah and Geechee communities. Nor were these materials employed within a high-art context governed by New Negro ideologies concerning the mastery of classical form and technique. Johnson presents something quite different. His expression of "the religious fervor and happy moods of the natives of Yamekraw" is filtered through the same sophisticated relation that existed between 1920s black musical theater and the Harlem stride idiom, on the one hand, and the source materials of these traditions, on the other, in ragtime and nineteenth-century brass band, dance, folk, and black religious music.

Both stride and Harlem musical theater in this era relied upon these earlier rural and southern black musical idioms as stylistic tropes that could be developed. This relation is similar to W. C. Handy's method of arranging and combining collected and new materials for his famous blues, or refining such "collected" materials. For example, *Yamekraw*'s evocations of the idiomatic language of spirituals in strain A (m. 19ff.) and the "Brothers" theme (m. 177ff.) emerge from musical theater and entertainment distillations of the spiritual idiom.

As noted, the formal structures of both *Yamekraw* and *Symphonic Dance: Carolina Shout* are closely related to the stride piano tradition. The exact relations of composition, arrangement, and improvisation in the stride idiom in the 1920s are complex. While improvisation per se commonly appears in performances of the blues and popular songs, many stride pianists were also known for their virtuosic arrangements of popular tunes as well as their personal cutting-contest compositions. In this tradition, as I have similarly noted with reference to *Rhapsody in Blue*, a "composition" is a mutable entity subject to variation through either improvisation or further arrangement over time. Thus, the notion of composition principally refers to a set or body of semifixed relationships of both phrases, strains, or sections, and preludes, interludes, and codas, as well as developmental materials, textures, and a basic harmonic template.[57]

The mid-1940s recording of *Yamekraw* for Moses Asch suggests that this stride performance aesthetic was central to Johnson's conception of this work. Example 2.9 compares the original score's mm. 115–20 to a transcription of Johnson's performance of these measures in the Asch recording. While the original notated melodic material remains primary to Johnson's performed realization of this passage, all

(a)

(b)

Example 2.9.   Improvisational elaboration in James P. Johnson's performance of
Yamekraw for Moses Asch

(a) Measures 115–20 from the *Yamekraw* piano solo. James P. Johnson, *Yamekraw: A
Negro Rhapsody* (New York: Perry Bradford Music, 1927). © James P. Johnson Foundation. Used by permission.

(b) Measures 115–20 as performed on the Asch/Folkways recording. James P. Johnson,
Yamekraw: A Negro Rhapsody (New York: Perry Bradford Music, 1927). © James P.
Johnson Foundation. Used by permission.

other elements, including the bass line, internal harmonies, ornamentation, and the presence or absence of contrapuntal lines, were freely subjected to improvisational elaboration. Such minor performance deviations occur throughout the Folkways recording, albeit on a smaller scale than this passage. The fact that Johnson allowed himself such improvisational liberties while reading from the score[58] illustrates his relation to the written text of *Yamekraw* and to the governing tradition for its performance. The arranged and improvisational deviations of the 1930 Vitaphone film score further reflect the continued relation of the work to the performance practices of contemporary jazz and dance orchestras, and Broadway and Harlem musical theater.

In a 1919 study, the celebrated author-columnist H. L. Mencken examined both the American tendency to indiscriminately mix elevated and vernacular languages as well as the national propensity for creating colorful new slang through juxtaposition, modification, and playful contextual manipulation.[59] His source materials for such "novel Americanisms" were culled from popular culture. Mencken notably calls for the artistic rehabilitation of such American vernacular idioms. This viewpoint is appropriate in a consideration of the period in both white and black contexts—culturally and artistically. Mencken's renowned battles against the stultifying strongholds of the "Genteel Tradition" presented an influential and combustible mix of vernacular wit, cultural irreverence, vulgarity, and sophistication. His fascination with such colorful attributes of American mongrelization became a central theme in many cultural products of the era. These attributes also lay at the heart of the symphonic jazz idiom.

The "symphonic slang" of *Yamekraw* is an urban distillation of the folk idioms upon which it signifies. However, while *Yamekraw* and the sermons of *God's Trombones* may each mix black vernacular and elevated gestures, the style and relation of *Yamekraw* to Harlem *popular culture* place it much closer to Mencken's urban vernacular aesthetics than to James Weldon Johnson's folk preachers. While the latter Johnson eschewed dialect, *Yamekraw* celebrates the musical equivalents of dialect, including contemporary hot jazz, blues, the spiritual tropes of popular entertainment, and so forth—popular music that was outside the musical and cultural agenda of most New Negro spokesmen. Last, unlike stereotyped black dialect in literature, which held negative associations for older New Negro writers, Johnson and his peers in Harlem entertainment regarded jazz-based concert works as a means of moving beyond the racial and social constraints of popular music and jazz. This perspective explains Handy's interest in *Yamekraw* for his 1928 Carnegie Hall concert.

3 PERFORMANCE CONTEXT: "JAZZ" EVOLUTION, THE CONCERT IDEAL, AND VARIETY ENTERTAINMENT

The program design of W. C. Handy's Carnegie Hall concert shares important similarities with both the contemporary variety revue and its adaptation in the design of Paul Whiteman's "Experiment" concerts. There have been many accounts of Whiteman's 1924 Aeolian Hall concert, but little attention has been paid to contemporary models for the structure of this unusual program. The program notes to this "Experiment" describe the "purely educational" intent of the concert. Part of this "education" was an attempt to define the term *jazz*. The concert program notes proclaimed that "Mr. Whiteman intends to point out . . . the tremendous strides which have been made in popular music from the day of discordant Jazz . . . to the really melodious music of today, which—for no good reason—is still called Jazz."[60] At one level, this concert sought to demonstrate the "evolutionary" progression of jazz—or rather *white* "jazz"—following its "primitive" beginnings in 1917 with the Original Dixieland Jazz Band. From a more objective distance, it is apparent that this "educational" program was built on the contemporary variety entertainment model.

Like a typical stage revue or vaudeville show, the Whiteman program is divided into two halves and multiple "acts." As outlined in figure 2.1, Whiteman presented eleven "acts." As with variety shows, each "act" is ten to fifteen minutes in length. The program design of variety entertainment in both vaudeville and musical revues was discussed in a 1916 interview with George Gottlieb, the head booker for New York's famous Palace Theatre. In this article, Gottlieb explains that the first act on a bill is usually a "dumb" (nonvocal) act that "will not be spoiled by . . . late arrivals taking their seats."[61] For Whiteman, this "dumb" first act of the 1924 concert was a raucous "jazz" opening that was meant to poke fun at the vaudeville hokum of the Original Dixieland Jazz Band.

1. The True Form of Jazz
    (a) Livery Stable Blues (LaRocca)
    (b) Mamma Loves Papa (Baer)
2. Comedy Selections
    (a) Yes, We Have No Bananas (Silver)
    (b) So This Is Venice (Thomas, adapted from "The Carnival of Venice")
3. Contrast: Legitimate Scoring vs. Jazzing
    (a) "Whispering" (Schoenberger)
    (b) "Whispering" jazzed
4. Recent Compositions with Modern Score
    (a) Lime House Blues (Braham)
    (b) I Love You (Archer)
    (c) Raggedy Ann (Kern)
5. Zez Confrey
    (a) Medley of Popular Airs
    (b) Kitten on the Keys (Confrey)
    (c) Ice Cream and Art
    (d) Nickel in the Slot (Confrey) [with the orchestra]
6. Flavoring a Selection with Borrowed Themes
    (a) Russian Rose (based on "The Volga Boat Song")
7. Semi-Symphonic Arrangement of Popular Melodies
    (a) Medley based on Irving Berlin's "Alexander's Ragtime Band," "A Pretty Girl Is Like a Melody," and "Orange Blossums in California."
8. *A Suite of Serenades* (Victor Herbert)
    (a) Spanish
    (b) Chinese
    (c) Cuban
    (d) Oriental
9. Adaptation of Standard Selections to Dance Rhythm
    (a) Pale Moon (Logan)
    (b) To a Wild Rose (McDowell)
    (c) Chansonette (Friml)
10. George Gershwin (Piano)
    A Rhapsody in Blue (Gershwin, arr. Grofé)
11. In the Field of [the] Classics
    Pomp and Circumstance (Elgar)

Fig. 2.1. Program, Paul Whiteman and His Palais Royal Orchestra, "Experiment in Modern Music," Aeolian Hall, New York City, February 12, 1924

Gottlieb describes the second act on a vaudeville program as "a typical 'vaudeville act.' It . . . should be more entertaining than the first act . . . [so] often . . . a good . . . singing act is placed here. This position on the bill is to 'settle' the audience . . . for the show."[62] For his second "act," Whiteman appropriately presented two "comedy" selections, each of which were well-known Tin Pan Alley novelty songs.

Gottlieb suggests that the third offering should be "a comedy dramatic sketch—a playlet that wakens the interest and holds the audience . . . [until the] laughter-climax at the 'curtain.'"[63] Whiteman's third "act" involved two song groupings. The "comedy dramatic sketch" ideal is evident in the first grouping, which juxtaposes two arrangements of Whiteman's first hit recording, the sentimental *Whispering*. The program describes the serious "pure form" of the original 1920 arrangement as the "forerunner" of Whiteman's "modern" music of 1924. The second, more comedic arrangement was meant to show "how any beautiful selection may be ruined . . . with a Jazz treatment."[64] The second grouping featured "legitimate" arrangements of song hits from recent Broadway shows.

The fourth offering, according to Gottlieb, must "rouse the audience" and "might be the first big punch of the show."[65] For this "first big punch," Whiteman showcased the famous novelty pianist Zez Confrey. Confrey performed solo versions of his *Kitten on the Keys*, along with two other virtuoso specialty numbers. To close the "act," the orchestra joined Confrey in a manic arrangement of his hit, *Nickel in the Slot*. The orchestra then performed another "jazzed classic" arrangement, *Russian Rose*.

For Gottlieb, the fifth act must include a "'big act,' containing a big name." This number "is next to intermission, and . . . must have something really worthwhile to . . . crown the first half of the bill."[66] In a revue like the Ziegfeld *Follies*, the first half of a program would close with a grand production number. Whiteman appropriately presented a grand, "semi-symphonic" medley of songs by Florenz Ziegfeld's favorite tunesmith, Irving Berlin. The medley even features the theme song of the *Follies*, "A Pretty Girl Is Like a Melody." This medley and its "semi-symphonic" arrangement are functionally related to the grand girl-parade showcases that Ziegfeld reserved for this act in a revue.

The first act after intermission, Gottlieb explains, must be "a strong vaudeville specialty, with comedy well to the fore." The purpose of this act is to get "the audience back in their seats without too many interruptions."[67] The second act after intermission is "usually a full-stage act and again must be another big name. . . . It may be a comedy playlet or even a serious dramatic playlet if the star is a fine actor."[68] Following intermission, Whiteman avoided the typical "strong vaudevillian specialty" act and instead featured a suite of Ziegfeld-style exotic "serenades" by the theater impresario's frequent musical collaborator, Victor Herbert.

Gottlieb states that the penultimate act of an evening's entertainment should feature the "hit of the show." This is the top-bill act "for which the audience has been waiting."[69] In musical revues, this second-to-last act was always the biggest production number of the show. For Ziegfeld, this meant an over-the-top display of Ziegfeld Girl pageantry, dancing chorus girls and/or ballerinas, extravagant, revealing costumes, and a grand tableau staging. For Whiteman, this spectacular "act" was Gershwin's *Rhapsody in Blue*. Gershwin himself was the celebrity performer.

Because "some of the audience will be going out" the door during the last number, Gottlieb notes that most vaudeville bookers usually present "a 'showy' act" that "does not depend . . . on being heard perfectly" (he mentions the possibilities of using animal acts, trapeze artists, and a Japanese theater troupe).[70] Whiteman's "showy" closing act was a dance band arrangement of Elgar's *Pomp and Circumstance*.

The programs of the other "Experiment in Modern Music" concerts that Whiteman presented from 1924 to 1938 further support this variety entertainment interpretation. A variety connection is spelled out, for example, in Olin Downes's *New York Times* review of Whiteman's "Third Experiment" concert in 1928.[71] He argues that the enthusiastic praise of the 1924 Aeolian Hall concert had "been instrumental in an ominous decline in the quality of jazz." For Downes, Whitemanesque "jazz" had "begun to put on outrageous airs," and he ultimately compares the evening's potpourri programming—which featured Ferde Grofé's *Metropolis* and Gershwin's Concerto in F—as "musical vaudeville."[72] For Whiteman's proponents, this latter characterization was not likely received as an entirely negative criticism since the Whiteman orchestra was one of the highest paid acts in contemporary variety entertainment, including vaudeville.

In the "Experiment" concert series, works like *Rhapsody in Blue* and *Metropolis* had an entertainment function that was roughly equivalent to the role of extended production numbers in sophisticated variety revues like the Ziegfeld *Follies*. In a manner akin to Whiteman's project to glorify American popular music through concert-style arrangements, the grand production numbers of the *Follies* formed the heart of Ziegfeld's renowned efforts to "Glorify the American Girl." Similarly, like the *Rhapsody in Blue* at Aeolian Hall, the celebrated Ziegfeld girl parades and elaborate tableau presentations were the glamorous raison d'être for an evening of entertainment that ranged from comic vaudeville acts to "spectacular" production numbers.

Whiteman's 1924 "Experiment" sparked a number of attempts to "out-Whiteman" Whiteman among his dance band peers. Several of these subsequent concerts pointedly included references to African American jazz. One of the most prominent efforts to combine symphonic jazz with Harlem jazz and blues can be found in the November 1924 Metropolitan Opera House concert of Whiteman's rival, Vincent Lopez. Lopez noted that "to match Paul Whiteman's coup in signing Gershwin," he "bought original jazz compositions from the leading jazz composers." What Lopez does not mention is that most of this compositional talent was black. The symphonic jazz composition that was positioned to "out-jazz" Gershwin's *Rhapsody in Blue* was a concert work by W. C. Handy. With the help of the arranger Joseph Nussbaum, Handy contributed his "symphonietta in 'jazz' style," *The Evolution of the Blues*. This work was described as "a free-form fantasy [on] the evolution of that specifically American negro emotional quality known as 'the blues.'"[73] The program also involved other African American contributions, such as Fletcher Henderson's *The Meanest Blues* (in an "orchestral development" by Lopez and the arranger Louis Katzman), and Will Vodery's arrangement of Henry Souvaine's *A Study in Syncopation*.[74] Similarly, at the December 1925 Aeolian Hall concert of Harry Yerkes and His Syncopating Symphonists, an elaborate arrangement of Handy's blues was again used as a trump card to "out-jazz" Whiteman. This composition was Albert Chiafarelli's symphony, *Blue Destiny*, which was based on Handy's "St. Louis Blues" and "Beale Street Blues," and also borrowed from Philip Braham's "Limehouse Blues."[75] The programs of the Lopez and Yerkes concerts imply that either Harlem's top entertainment talent (Handy, Henderson, and Vodery) or works based on compositions by Harlem musicians (particularly Handy's blues) could infuse white concert "jazz" events with an element of "authentic" black jazz. The implication was that this latter element was conspicuously absent in the "jazz" of both Whiteman's 1924 Aeolian Hall concert and Gershwin's *Rhapsody in Blue*.

Both the title of Handy's concert work, *The Evolution of the Blues*, and the title of the "Blues Get Glorified" chapter on symphonic jazz in his 1941 autobiography suggest that Handy himself located the project of "glorifying" Harlem music directly in the cultural politics of the concert hall and concert-style works. For Handy, this ideal formed the central premise of his own 1928 Carnegie Hall concert. This concert was promoted as a celebration of the twenty-fifth anniversary of the publication of his famous *Memphis Blues*. His idea was to "give a concert at Carnegie Hall . . . showing the evolution of Negro music."[76] This "educational" intent to illustrate musical "evolution" was clearly yet another attempt to trump Whiteman. Handy's equally revue-like program, shown in figure 2.2, included solo and choral treatments of Handy's blues, work song and spiritual arrangements, several examples of black minstrelsy, spiritual arrangements by J. Rosamond Johnson, piano solos, hit songs from black vaudeville and musical theater, various selections by Will Marion Cook, and a handful of art songs.

This event concluded with a grand "jazz" production number finale that showcased orchestral arrangements of popular tunes by Clarence Williams, Spencer Williams, and Maceo Pinkard. The climax of this "act" was an elaborate orchestra and chorus arrangement of *St. Louis Blues* with Fats Waller as organ soloist. In the position of the second "act" after intermission (a position usually reserved for a "serious dramatic playlet" featuring a big-name star), Handy presented Waller as the piano soloist in Still's arrangement of *Yamekraw*.

Handy's autobiography reveals his pride in the symphonic jazz borrowings of his music by such white orchestra leaders as Paul Whiteman, Don Voorhees, Ben Bernie, Louis Katzman, and Hugo Mariani. However, in his account of his role in the concert jazz of this period, Handy does not discuss his involvement in the white "ultra-modern" composer George Antheil's infamous 1927 Carnegie Hall concert. For this event, Handy was engaged to organize and conduct an all-black concert orchestra for the premiere of Antheil's *Jazz Symphony*. In their self-proclaimed attempt to "out-Gershwin" Gershwin, the organizers engaged Handy after Whiteman was unavailable. Because of the complexity of Antheil's *Jazz Symphony*, Handy's ensemble was put through an unprecedented twenty-five rehearsals, and Handy was ultimately relieved of his conducting duties. As a crowning embarrassment, the

CARNEGIE HALL
Friday Evening, April 27th, 1928.

W. C. Handy's Orchestra
and Jubilee Singers

PROGRAM
PROLOGUE

a. "The Birth of Jazz"   Handy-Smith-Troy
b. "The Memphis Blues"   Handy

SPIRITUALS—ARR. HANDY

1. a. "Steal Away To Jesus"
   b. "Wheel In A Wheel"
   c. "I've Heard of a City Called Heaven"
                        Orchestra and Chorus

BLUES

2. a. "Yellow Dog Blues"   Handy
   b. "St. Louis Blues"   Handy
      Solo-Mezzo Soprano Katherine Handy
   c. "Beale Street Blues"   Handy

PLANTATION SONGS

3. a. "Golden Slippers"   James A. Bland
   b. "Carry Me Back To Old Virginny"   James A. Bland
      Tenor Solo—George E. Jackson
   c. "My Old Virginia Home"   Rucker & Lofton
      Tenor Solo—Russell Smith

SPIRITUALS—ARR. HANDY

4. a. "I'm Drinking From A Fountain"
   b. "Give Me Jesus"
      Orchestra and Chorus

WORK SONGS—ARR. HANDY

5. a. "Goin' To See My Sarah"
   b. "Joe Jacobs"
      Orchestra and Male Voices

PIANO SOLO

6. a. "Bamboula"   Coleridge-Taylor
   b. "Juba Dance"   Nathaniel Dett
      Sidney Brown

SPIRITUALS Arr. J. Rosamond Johnson

7. a. "Didn't My Lord Deliver Daniel"
   b. "O Wasn't Dat A Wide River"
   c. "Witness For My Lord"
      J. Rosamond Johnson and Taylor Gordon

CHARACTER SONGS

8. a. "The Unbeliever"   Bert Williams-Smith-Bryan
   b. "Wouldn't That Be A Dream"   Hogan-Jordan
      Tom Fletcher
      Accompanist, Bernardin Brown

INTERMISSION

PART TWO

9. Cake Walk   Featuring Mme. Robinson
    a. "Dark Town Is Out Tonight"   Will Marion Cook
    b. "Exhortation"   Will Marion Cook
       Male Voices

NEGRO RHAPSODY

10. a. "Yamekraw"   James P. Johnson
       Orchestra
       Piano—Thomas (Fats) Waller

SOPRANO SOLO

11. a. "Spring Had Come" (Hiawatha)   Coleridge-Taylor
    b. "Hear The Lamb A-Cryin'"   H. T. Burleigh
    c. "Joshua Fit De Battle of Jericho"
                                        Arr. Lawrence Brown
       Minnie Brown
       Accompanist—Andrades Lindsey

XYLOPHONE SOLO

12. "Maple Leaf Rag"   Scott Joplin
       W. C. Handy, Jr.

SOPRANO SOLO

13. "Africa"   Ford Dabney
       Josephine Hall

J. ROSAMOND JOHNSON

14. a. "African Drum Dance" No. 1   J. Rosamond Johnson
       Piano Solo
    b. "Under The Bamboo Tree"   J. Rosamond Johnson
       Baritone Solo

JAZZ FINALE

15. a. "Shimmy Like My Sister Kate"   Clarence Williams
       Clarence Williams
    b. "I Ain't Got Nobody"   Spencer Williams
       Male Voices
    c. "I'm Feelin' Devilish"   Maceo Pinkard
       Orchestra
    d. "St. Louis Blues"   Handy
       Organ Solo—Thomas (Fats) Waller
       Orchestra and Chorus

STEINWAY PIANO USED

Management: Robert Clairmont

Fig. 2.2.   Program, W. C. Handy's Orchestra and Jubilee Singers, Carnegie Hall, New York City, April 27, 1928. (Courtesy of the James P. Johnson Foundation.)

Handy orchestra performed beneath "a backdrop of a gigantic Negro couple dancing the Charleston, the girl holding the American flag . . . while the man clasped her ecstatically around the buttocks."[77] Handy's 1928 concert was clearly a personal response to the aforementioned white concerts in which Handy had participated, including the Antheil concert. This latter event, as well as the race-based "evolution" design of the 1928 program, further imply that Handy's Carnegie program was a *racial* challenge to these earlier white symphonic jazz concerts. Johnson's *Yamekraw* represented his African American *Rhapsody in Blue.*

In his autobiography, Handy recalls that Johnson once privately performed *Yamekraw* for Handy and Gershwin's biographer Isaac Goldberg. In this account, Handy describes the work as a simulation of "an ante-bellum Negro preacher." He further relates that Goldberg had compared the work's representation of black "old-time religion" to the experience of listening to "an old-fashioned Jewish cantor."[78] This recollection illustrates that Handy read *Yamekraw* in terms of its mixed evocations of "old time religion" and "spirituals," the mannerisms of the "ante-bellum Negro preachers," and what he calls "the 'pep' and the abandon of popular music." Still's arrangement appropriately builds on these evocations of Harlem's music—from the serious to the syncopated, from the sentimental idioms of Broadway and Tin Pan Alley, to hot nightclub blues. The rich cultural threads that converged in Still's orchestration of *Yamekraw* can be vibrantly illustrated through an examination of the adaptation of this score for the soundtrack to the 1930 Vitaphone film short, *Yamekraw.*

13 FILM ADAPTATION: VITAPHONE, VIRTUAL BROADWAY, AND THE ROAD TO *YAMEKRAW*

In February 1930, Johnson, Bradford, and the Vitaphone Corporation entered into a legal agreement to lease *Yamekraw* for adaptation into a film short.[79] In spite of this agreement, Vitaphone/Warner Bros. had legal difficulties with this film over the next several years. One legal problem arose out of the fact that the company had neglected to clear the rights to adapt Still's arrangement of the work. Meanwhile, Bradford's representatives accused the company of plagiarizing lyrics from Bradford's blues "The Road Is Rocky but I Am Gonna Find My Way." A third legal action brought against Vitaphone claimed that Warners had infringed on an author's 1928 copyrighted scenario and lyrics entitled "The Road to Yamekraw."[80]

Vitaphone's *Yamekraw* short was premiered on August 1, 1930, at New York's Strand Theatre. Like Bradford and Handy, Warner Bros. promoted *Yamekraw* as an African American jazz rhapsody by a famous black popular music composer, but this time with a significantly different cultural spin. A late 1920s Vitaphone Release Index for exhibitors described the *Yamekraw* film short in the following manner:

> "Yamekraw" is a rhapsody of the black man's blues by the noted negro composer, James P. Johnson. It represents the emotional mood of the negro. . . . Murray Roth directed this most unusual and artistic of musical Vitaphone Varieties. It has swiftly changing camera angles, unique lighting effects and . . . futuristic architecture. The picture . . . will delight all lovers of negro music and will reflect credit upon any theatre showing it. The cast includes Louise Cook, colored dancer of "Hot Chocolate[s]," Margaret Sims, Jimmy Mordecai and many others. . . . Johnson composed "Charleston," . . . the score for Miller and Lyles' *Keep Shufflin'* and many popular songs.[81]

In its earlier history, *Yamekraw* was presented by African Americans as a symbol of Harlem's artistic achievements and racial pride. By contrast, the Vitaphone short was designed to appeal to the voyeuristic white upper-middle-class patrons of Harlem's Cotton Club or the *Blackbirds* revues of the white Broadway entrepreneur Lew Leslie. Contrary to the hardships of the real Yamecraw, the Vitaphone short stereotypically depicts this rural community in terms of happy, rhythmic black sharecroppers of the Deep South (Locke's "transposed plantation formula"). The contemporary trade reviews focused on the film's "changing camera angles, unique lighting effects and . . . futuristic architecture."[82] Such traits can be seen, for instance, in the deliberately artificial ("expressionistic"), two-dimensional painted sets and their self-conscious distortions of perspective. This visual sensibility was derived from such influential Weimar-era films as Fritz Lang's *Metropolis* (Universal Film, 1927). In particular, *Metropolis* established a link in the American popular imagination between visual stylization and the adjective *futuristic*. This style is borrowed in *Yamekraw* both for its novelty and its arty cultural currency. The "futuristic" elements starkly contrast with the film's depersonalized black caricatures that are direct outgrowths of the generic entertainment representations of African Americans as "toms, coons, mulattoes, mammies, and bucks" (to borrow from the title of Donald Bogle's book).[83]

The short's primary set is overtly theatrical and centers on a ramshackle cabin populated by a grinning Mammy and Pappy and a yard full of watermelon-eating caricatures of black children as pickaninnies. The film's loose narrative concerns the troubles that arise when a young man leaves his fiancée in rural Yamekraw for the excitement of Harlem. This narrative construct is built upon a paradigmatic tension between city and country, and between domestic fidelity and the fast life of jazz and urban nightclubs. The moral crisis of this parable is played out through the film's third central character, a Jazz Age Jezebel who seduces the young man in a Harlem nightclub.

The initial sequence of the short depicts the carefree pastoral world of Yamekraw and family life around the cabin. The establishing shots of this sequence are underscored first by a wordless choral arrangement of strain A, and then the voices of Pappy (a baritone soloist) and the community/choir. The scene opens with the Yamekraw townsfolk joyfully returning from picking cotton. The young couple soon enters. At the close of this opening sequence, they walk up to the top of a small hill for wooing. A choir emerges around the base of the hill, waving their hands as if they were at an ecstatic camp meeting revival. The choir sings the pseudo-spiritual "For the Road Is Rocky, but It Won't Be Rocky Long." In this second sequence, dramatic lighting is employed to cast oversized, chiaroscuro-like shadows of the fervent church folk on the blank stage scrim set directly behind the choir. The couple return to the cabin and proclaim their love in a passionate moment (set to a newly composed, classical-style piano cadenza). Following this romantic juncture, the woman sings a pseudo-operatic aria concerning the comforts and safety of their rural home. The aria climaxes with the clichéd lines "I'se tryin', cryin', dyin' just to get there some day—to Dixieland, it is so grand, you understand." The man is then handed his suitcase and soon trudges over the hill.

The relationship of this opening sequence to Still's *Yamekraw* arrangement demonstrates the close proximity of this score to well-established entertainment caricatures of black culture and music. The film score was adapted from Still's arrangement by the white radio conductor Hugo Mariani. In the expositional cabin scene that corresponds to mm. 15–56 of the score, Mariani cut mm. 27–40. He also replaced Still's original sax solo (on the "Sam Jones" theme) with choral "oohs" and "ahs." He further recast Still's muted brass solo in this score excerpt as the film's opening baritone solo (the voice of Pappy). Both passages musically and visually underscore this strain's signification on the spiritual idiom. The subsequent "Road Is Rocky" passage (mm. 94–179; see cuts marked in table 2.1a) reveals the validity of Bradford's claim that the film plagiarizes—however briefly—from the 1920 Mamie Smith recording of Bradford's song "The Road Is Rocky."[84] Like Mariani's choral transformation of the "Sam Jones" strain, this latter borrowing illustrates the film's unwitting transformation of another race record blues into Hollywood pseudo-spiritual cliché. Example 2.10 presents a reduction of Mariani's setting of the "Road Is Rocky" passage. This section's arrangement retains the New Orleans jazz-based texture of Still's orchestration. Mariani cut sixty-three measures (mm. 113–76) to segue directly to a clarinet solo in the same New Orleans style. This New Orleans texture is transformed in the film into an urban entertainment signification on the spiritual idiom. This cultural signification simultaneously occurs on textual, musical, and visual levels and is accomplished in a number of ways, each of which directly relate to the popular song genre that I call "entertainment spirituals."

The film's producers meticulously illustrated Johnson's original program concerning "the religious fervor and happy moods of the natives of Yamekraw." This depiction directly draws from the restrictive staging and narrative conventions of the all-black musical-theater and floor shows of the 1920s. Thus, rather than presenting *Yamekraw* as a serious and sincere folk-themed symphony, the film interprets this original program by employing the same Harlem entertainment trappings with which Bradford described the work. In the Vitaphone case, this reading was created from the perspective of Harlem entertainment's white producers rather than from a perspective that might represent the creative and racial uplift concerns of black artists like Johnson who were involved in Harlem's theater and nightclub entertainments.

The importance of reading both Johnson's rhapsody and Vitaphone's *Yamekraw* in terms of the contemporaneous vogue for entertainment spirituals cannot be overestimated. Johnson and the Harlem entertainment circle were actively involved in this trend, and symphonic jazz stylizations were regularly employed in such commoditized spirituals (see chapter 3). Numerous passages in both Johnson's

Example 2.10.   A reconstruction of Mariani's arrangement for the "Road Is Rocky" scene in Vitaphone's *Yamekraw* (measures reference the Still arrangement). Adapted from James P. Johnson, *Yamekraw*, arranged by William Grant Still (New York: Alfred and Co., 1928). © James P. Johnson Foundation. Used by permission.

and Still's versions of *Yamekraw* are indebted to this tradition. The combination of these quasi-spiritual elements, *Yamekraw*'s basis in hot jazz, and the pseudo-folk program of this work suggested a ready-made film narrative to Vitaphone's producers.

Mariani's retention of the score's jazz stylizations throughout the aforementioned plantation sequence is relevant to the larger topic of entertainment spirituals. *Yamekraw*'s eclectic stylistic mix of "old time religion," "antebellum Negro preachers," and "spirituals" with "the 'pep' and . . . abandon of popular music" signifies upon both the contemporary spirituals-as-art and spirituals-as-folk-music camps. This establishing scene is built upon the idea of the call-and-response of a gathered African American community and an interlocutor–folk preacher. The soundtrack's lyrics are defined by a spiritual-like fusion of black figurative language and a stilted, pseudo-biblical text. One key sign that the audience should read this scene in terms of Negro spirituals is both seen and heard at the phrase "Praise Hallelujah Lord!" In this passage, Mariani departs from his normal practice of doubling Still's instrumental parts. In mm. 109–11 (see example 2.10), Mariani set "Praise Hallelujah Lord!" to a newly composed, expansive part-writing. This choral writing creates a type of melodramatic climax that more directly evokes religious choral arranging conventions than Broadway popular song in this context. The choir physically evokes "old-time religion" through camp meeting–style hand waving, rhythmic swaying, and other bodily motions, as well as the fervent black religious vocal stylizations of the performance. These details combine to ensure a reading in terms of black religious expression rather than jazz per se.

A third facet of Mariani's alterations to Still's score is seen in the soprano's aria of the opening plantation sequence (mm. 229–41). Example 2.11 presents Mariani's arrangement of this passage. Here Still's original lyrical alto sax and trumpet solos are sung by the soprano in a quasi-operatic vocal style. Mariani removed the sax section of this passage to underscore a decidedly "classical" texture of strings, oboe, two clarinets, and horns. Like the earlier "classical" cadenza of the film (m. 211 of the score), this aria contributes to an unusual filmic pastiche. Despite the similarity of this passage to a stylistic trope on a Puccini aria (in melodic, harmonic, textural, and performance terms, even despite the presence of blue notes), this music is set in counterpoint to trite stereotyped lyrics and visual shots saturated with inferential racial codes (the sharecroppers cabin, Mammy and Pappy, watermelon, ragtag pickaninnies, etc.). This pastiche of visual Expressionism, a plantation Puccini-style aria, lavish Broadway spectacle, and commercialized black folkloric codes demands to be

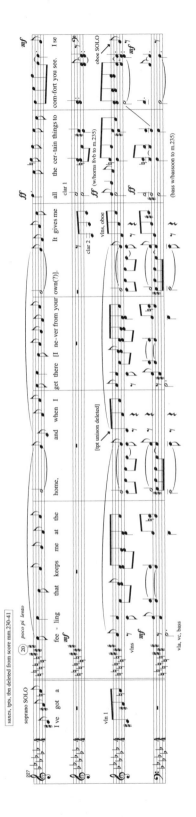

Example 2.11.   A reconstruction of Mariani's arrangement for the fiancé's "Dixieland" aria in Vitaphone's *Yamekraw* (mm. 227–39 of the score). Adapted from James P. Johnson, *Yamekraw*, arranged by William Grant Still (New York: Alfred and Co., 1928). © James P. Johnson Foundation. Used by permission.

read in terms of Hollywood artificiality and excess rather than the assumption that the producer's sought to create "serious" art from African American experience.

The middle sequence of the short concerns the protagonist's trip to Harlem. The sequence begins with a montage of shots depicting train travel. This scene is constructed in an overtly arty manner with oblique angle shots, dramatic lighting, and grainy and soft-focus images. The montage emphasizes shots of the coal-black train, its belching smokestack, and images of the world rushing by. For this montage, Mariani augmented the Still arrangement through an interpolated "noise symphony." In a commercial nod to modernist percussion-based concert works by figures like Still's onetime compositional mentor, Edgard Varèse, Mariani underscores this visual montage with an ensemble that seems to include a bass drum, a pitched bell, a calliope, and wire brushes performed on either a snare drum or a metal sheet. Each of these instruments depicts some aspect of the locomotive experience.

At the conclusion of the train montage, a "motion music" ostinato pattern smoothly segues back into a hot jazz segment of the Still arrangement that now underscores a nighttime street scene outside a Harlem speakeasy. In its skewed proportions, and its flat, artificial sets, the scene outside the nightclub is again derived from the stylized visual worlds of Weimar cinema. While roustabouts play craps on the street curb, the city's workers trudge along the sidewalk—which is set at a thirty-degree angle. In the windows above the nightclub entrance, one can see the shadows of a jazz clarinetist and a couple shuffling in a lascivious embrace. We next see the protagonist admiring his smart new city clothes in what appears to be a convex funhouse mirror.

In this middle sequence, Mariani heightens the "hot" jazz elements of the score to emphasize this transition to Harlem. The music here is built on two consecutive blues-related episodes. The original clarinet solo is given greater hot jazz emphasis in the soundtrack performance through both added melodic ornamentation and scooping inflections on key notes. In the second quasi-blues episode (mm. 282–95, based on the "Stop It, Joe" theme), Mariani's pianist opens up the solo with a short, improvised passage of honky-tonk riffs. At the end of the solo, the protagonist enters the dizzy world of the nightclub.

The club's intoxicating atmosphere is visually depicted through more oblique-angle shots, flashing lights, and a spinning mirrored ball. The club's patrons sing about leaving "that old plantation home" for the excitement of Harlem, all to the same melodic materials as the fiancée's aria. The man is given a front-row seat, the lights dim, and the spotlight hits a female dancer performing a Cotton Club–style, sexually charged, jazz shimmy. A close-up of the dancer's ecstatic face is juxtaposed against a close-up of the protagonist's leering face. As the trumpeter on the soundtrack is given a brief, improvised, hot growl-and-plunger solo (at the repeat of mm. 434–41), the protagonist enters into a lustful dance with the woman. The protagonist's increasingly drunken stupor is conveyed through lightly rocking camera work and a distorted, kaleidoscopic visual effect. The scene then cuts to a private room. The protagonist enters, first smiling, and then quickly changing his facial reaction to shock. This reaction is followed by a reverse shot of the woman in the arms of another man. The two glance at the protagonist, and then return to their lovemaking. The protagonist closes the door and is next seen trudging up the sidewalk as part of the jaded city masses.

The final sequence of the short cuts back to the Yamekraw cabin. It is nighttime, but the cabin light is still on and there is a fire in the fireplace. The figure of the country fiancée is seen in the window. In this sequence, the fiancée assumes a comforting mammy role as the soprano solo sings, "Here I am you child don't cry, come to my arms and lie, Po' Momma's Pappy done died," just as the prodigal son returns from the big city. The protagonist stops to admire his fiancée in the window. She sees him and rushes out. They run toward each other and embrace as the music climaxes—ironically, to the "Sam Jones" theme. They kiss and walk into the cabin. Domestic bliss is achieved, and the choir closes the short by singing a clichéd "Oh, my Lord!"

In terms of contemporary Hollywood product, the *Yamekraw* short was exceptional but was still connected to several cultural trends of the era. First, in 1929 and 1930 there was an unprecedented increase in the numbers of African Americans in commercial films. Such films included all-black features like King Vidor's well-intentioned, spirituals-drenched depiction of the rural South in *Hallelujah!* (MGM, 1929), as well as the cliché-ridden melodrama *Hearts in Dixie* (Fox Film, 1929), each of which was built on demeaning stereotypes and promises of thrilling black entertainment for white audiences. Even in this context, the Vitaphone *Yamekraw* short was unique in its potpourri of Broadway, hot jazz, folk opera, Expressionist-derived sets, and modernist stylizations.

As Vitaphone's promotional description reveals, the short was advertised as a cultural and racial prestige film. This promotional angle relates to the company's earlier campaigns that touted the capacity of sound film to bring New York's sophisticated drama and opera to "every hamlet in the country." By 1930, Vitaphone sought to appeal more to mass than to class aesthetics. *Yamekraw* thus offered an experimental middlebrow compromise with their earlier opera shorts, films that already embodied an agenda of middlebrow artistic democratization. The *Yamekraw* short's second encroachment into middlebrow aesthetics is found in its modernist distillations. These stylizations evoke what Dwight Macdonald later characterized as "*Bauhaus* modernism . . . [seeping] down, in vulgarized form, in the design of [contemporary] vacuum cleaners, pop-up toasters, supermarkets and cafeterias"[85]—a trend that exemplified the middlebrow's special threat to midcentury cultural critics in its recycling of avant-garde inventions as commercially palatable product. Though Johnson's score does not participate in such trends, both the film's visual Expressionism and the interpolated train sequence do. This is not to say that symphonic jazz was not associated with this trend—it very much was. One can observe such modernist "vulgarizations," for instance, in Grofé's *Metropolis* score in 1928 or the visual and musical elements to the "New York Rhapsody" sequence in David Butler's *Delicious* (Fox Film, 1931).

The 1929 *Yamekraw* film short was positioned squarely in the middle of the transition from the silent film era to fully integrated sound cinema (the period from roughly 1924 to 1931). As film scholar Donald Crafton has noted, these early sound shorts were marketed through references to "cinema's capability to suggest a *virtual* presence, an imagined being-there." In both the content and the style of early sound shorts, the sense was that "Broadway, the 'Street of Streets,' was coming soon to the local theater." Crafton has dubbed this phenomenon "virtual Broadway."[86] By 1929–30, the initial form of virtual Broadway (the static recording of discrete performances) gave way to new ideals adapted from Broadway musical revues. In 1929, as Crafton notes, Hollywood's ravenous appetite for New York product had bred a new virtual Broadway aesthetic of "superabundance" that overwhelmed the viewer with dense spectacles that exceeded the physical limitations of productions on the Great White Way. An extravagant production number like the overproduced *Rhapsody in Blue* sequence in Whiteman's 1930 film *King of Jazz*—with its elaborate Art Deco set, hordes of high-stepping chorus girls, and the Whiteman band set atop an enormous piano with multiple pianists—provides an ideal illustration of this aesthetic. While the connection between symphonic jazz arranging and musical theater traditions was certainly made explicit in *King of Jazz*, this association was not merely a concoction of Hollywood producers. The revue setting of *King of Jazz* was presaged by Whiteman's 1928 stage collaborations with the film's later director, John Murray Anderson. Together, Whiteman and Anderson coproduced a series of elaborate film prologue variety shows and touring units for the Paramount Publix theater chain. These specific shows routinely referenced Gershwin's rhapsody, and their production numbers may have rivaled the extravagance of this later film number. This Broadway-to-virtual-Broadway transition clearly parallels the Harlem-to-virtual-Harlem transition seen in the black musical theater borrowings of Vitaphone's *Yamekraw*.

Early sound short entertainments, particularly those by Vitaphone, were commonly modeled after the most popular contemporary entertainment forms of this era. These models included Broadway revues, vaudeville, live musical accompaniment for silent films, lectures, and radio. Like the era's feature-length film musicals, the Vitaphone sound shorts were designed to appeal to "a pre-formed audience . . . [of] sophisticated middle-class urbanites accustomed to high-priced live entertainment at night clubs, roof gardens, and movie palaces."[87] The topical subject matter of both film formats frequently reflected a national curiosity in this period for glimpses of the metropolitan milieu, particularly of New York and Hollywood. Harlem entertainment was an important part of New York's cultural exports to Hollywood. In the Vitaphone Variety of *Yamekraw*, the selling point was the film's capacity to bring first-class Harlem entertainment to the screen and to raise it to a level of artistic spectacle well beyond the original production and geographic limitations of Harlem theater and cabaret.

In conclusion, the history of James P. Johnson's *Yamekraw* reveals a rich web of intertwined trends in American popular culture of the late

1920s and 1930s. First and foremost, the history of Johnson's *Yamekraw* reveals the social tensions between 1920s Harlem entertainment and New Negro aesthetic ideology, on the one hand, and demonstrates the larger racial tensions between white and black "jazz" aesthetics in the 1920s symphonic jazz vogue, on the other. This latter subject also fed into an emerging critical view that defined black jazz aesthetics as art and Whiteman-style symphonic jazz as commercial kitsch. In light of the cultural ambitions of Johnson's professional circle, *Yamekraw* also demonstrates important perspectives on the strategies for racial uplift in Harlem entertainment. By extension, because of the conflicting dual nature of many products of 1920s Harlem entertainment, this tradition—including *Yamekraw*—involved regular efforts to celebrate both black "folk" culture and broader American vernacular idioms. Last, the history of *Yamekraw* illuminates the complex contemporary interactions between class politics, artful entertainment traditions, middlebrow efforts at cultural democratization, and the cross-cultural impact of the variety entertainment model.

three   𝄡   "THE BLUES GET GLORIFIED"

Harlem Entertainment,
Negro Nuances, and
Black Symphonic Jazz

*O*n September 13, 1935, Paramount Studios released *Symphony in Black: A Rhapsody of Negro Life,* a nine-and-a-half-minute film short that featured Duke Ellington and His Orchestra. Despite its commercial origins, this film score has been regularly cited by Ellington's biographers and jazz historians as a key early effort among his extended, concert-style compositions. As argued earlier, the 1930s and 1940s concert works of Ellington and Johnson are steadfastly tied to Harlem's 1920s boom in jazz-derived musical theater, nightclub, and dance-band entertainments. This connection is particularly apparent in an extended score like *Symphony in Black.* In its narrative content and musical arrangement this film represents an ideal microcosm of the hybrid cultural aesthetics that informed a special category of prewar, production-number-derived concert works by Harlem-based popular music composers, including Ellington and Johnson.

The pantomime narrative of *Symphony in Black* concerns a celebrated African American "symphonic" composer—Duke Ellington—

and the "world premiere" of his racially motivated symphony-rhap-sody. The subtitle of this film, like many other "rhapsody"-themed stage numbers and jazz-styled concert works of the day, purposefully alludes to George Gershwin's 1924 *Rhapsody in Blue*. The mixed cul-tural aesthetics and formal design of a work like *Symphony in Black* owe very little to the performance traditions, formal expectations, and generic conventions of Euro-American classical music. *Symphony in Black* actually represents an upward-leaning—or rather "glorified"—extension of a family of production number arranging conventions that were widely shared across dance bands, big band jazz, and the or-chestral idioms of Hollywood and Broadway musicals, interwar radio, and the deluxe movie palace prologues of the day. Such concert-style popular music was central to the theater and stage repertories (as op-posed to dance music repertories) of these orchestral traditions, and the spectacular, jazz-oriented production number arrangements of many period stage and film musicals were among the most visible ex-tensions of these practices. While sections of these stylistically hybrid arrangements may seem to outwardly resemble classical- or concert-style musical textures in their lush orchestrations, expressive devices and gestures, and overall "serious" tone, these idiomatic references are largely stylistic caricatures that hold little substantive connection to the formal expectations and conventions of classical music.

The purpose of this chapter is first to interrogate the strategies of racial uplift that were embedded within African American symphonic jazz, and how and why Ellington, Johnson, and their Harlem enter-tainment peers created these stylistically hybrid musical arrange-ments. Then, by examining three production-number-related con-cert works (including *Symphony in Black*), I hope to reveal the ways in which Ellington's and Johnson's concert jazz compositions of the 1930s and 1940s blurred and manipulated racial, class, and cultural markers, and how these works ultimately embodied a unique, urban-entertainment vision for racial uplift. The key distinction of this agenda lies in this circle's promotion of the elegance, cultural dignity, and high-art possibilities of Harlem's contemporary popular music and popular entertainment forms. This great faith in the art of popu-lar culture directly contrasted with assimilation-based New Negro musical ideologies that promoted black folk music idioms, particu-larly the spiritual, as the proper vessels for racial uplift through the recontextualization, transformation, and synthesis of such materials with Euro-American classical form and style. As these vernacular symphonic jazz concert works draw from music-arranging traditions that have had little critical discussion to date, this argument will be built through additional close studies of a select number of representative musical theater projects, as well as several production numbers from film, stage, and nightclub entertainments. These additional studies will help to articulate the formal, programmatic, and aesthetic sources for Ellington's and Johnson's concert works. The inclusion of Johnson's lesser-known concert works helps to broaden the critical understanding of Duke Ellington's jazz-oriented extended compositions, thereby providing highly valuable community and historical perspectives that have largely been overlooked in critical considerations of Ellington's more widely known extended works.[1]

13 ON "GLORIFIED" ENTERTAINMENT, CULTURAL HIERARCHIES, AND RACIAL UPLIFT IN THE INTERWAR ERA

Despite the absence of chorus girls and even vocals, and despite the score's self-conscious concert-work title, *Symphony in Black* is in essence an extended production number built from an establishing scene and four musical episodes. Each of these episodes readily reveals the film's connections to the all-black Broadway musical and Harlem nightclub revues of the 1920s and early 1930s. Barry Ulanov, Ellington's first biographer, wrote in 1946 that "the short employed most of the clichés usually associated with the dramatic presentation of Negroes. Right out of Oscar Hammerstein's lyric for *Ol' Man River*, big, black colored men sweated and strained, loading heavy bales into storehouses . . . [and stoking] blast furnaces. And then, for surefire audience appeal, there was a brief little story, the eternal triangle, the theme of jealousy [*sic*] underlined heavily . . . [with] blues figurations."[2] By contrast, other critics have conveniently ignored the entertainment overtones of the film. For example, in his monumental 1989 book, *The Swing Era*, the jazz historian Gunther Schuller found *Symphony in Black* to be a "major [compositional] effort," and "not only an early extended work of Ellington's but also a direct forerunner of *Black, Brown and Beige*" both "programmatically and in overall concept."[3]

The juxtaposed historical and critical views of Ulanov and Schuller suggest that this rhapsodic film score and its pantomimed narrative mix a range of class-status signs for both art and entertainment. These juxtaposed views underscore long-standing themes in the reception of the film and its score, particularly the opinion that the image and narrative can dually represent a perpetuation of racist entertainment clichés and Ellington's abilities to elevate such clichés to a serious artistic expression of African American experience. What has been routinely overlooked is that the hybrid musical territory of the score parallels white symphonic jazz as well as the concert-style popular song arrangements of contemporary stage and radio orchestras. Bandleaders and popular music arrangers who promoted the hybrid symphonic jazz idiom sought to position this idiom not so much as high art, but as smart and sophisticated popular music. This "glorified" entertainment aesthetic directly grew out of the theatrical and musical spectacles of contemporary variety entertainment. Similar glorified jazz leanings also lie at the heart of *Symphony in Black*, although in this specific case the glorified music is authentic Harlem jazz. This aesthetic was certainly not foreign to Harlem's popular culture, and, as shall be demonstrated below, a similar intent lies at the core of both Ellington's and James P. Johnson's shared aspirations for concert jazz.

Few music scholars have given much thought to the pervasive variety entertainment aesthetic that governed American popular culture in the 1920s and 1930s. While there has been a recent boom of research in American musical theater, most of this work has studied piano-vocal song scores that more directly reflect the specific contributions of the composer of a show rather than how that music was *actually realized* through the original arrangements and period performance practices. This composer-centric—and notation-centric—critical focus has been complemented by a high-culture interest in identifying strategies of narrative and musical coherence and unification. More specifically, this new musical theater research has largely focused on the rise of the plot- and character-driven book musical that rose to prominence after the great success of Jerome Kern's *Show Boat* in 1927. This genre, with its emphases on quasi-realism (regardless of the fact that characters routinely break into song) and the integration of script, musical themes, and musical style, became the predominant production model only after Rodgers and Hammerstein's *Oklahoma!* in 1943. Up to this point, and even somewhat beyond, musical theater was guided by the entertainment-for-entertainment's-sake, variety-oriented aesthetic of the musical revue, a stage institution that emphasized celebrity singers, actors, dancers, and comics, the art of the songwriter and arranger, massed displays of the female body, and—above all—spectacular production values. Naturally there were some middle-ground genres of the musical, like the frivolous, lighthearted musical comedies of the 1920s (such as the Gershwin brothers' *Lady Be Good!* in 1924) and the popular backstage film musicals of the 1930s (such as *42nd Street* in 1933), that comfortably combined loose plots and lavish displays of spectacle in song, dance, and staging. While the post-1940 book musical ultimately found ways to integrate some of these time-tested entertainment strategies into the more lofty ideals of that genre, rarely do these accommodations approach the revue tradition's penchant for eye-popping extravagance for its own sake in rich costumes, striking dance choreography, lush sets, grand girl parades, and the sort of extended musical arrangements that turned two- and three-strain popular songs—or multiepisode medleys of such songs—into elaborate production numbers that could last upwards of fifteen minutes. Such glorified musical arrangements prominently featured regular shifts in instrumentation, style, tempi, and key, as well as a rich palette of expressive devices. While there is significant overlap between the arranging conventions (and arrangers) of the book musical and the musical revue, it is in the latter context—including revue-oriented musical comedies—that extravagant production numbers most fully realized this glorified entertainment aesthetic.

Revue-based productions of the 1920s and 1930s existed in a variety of related entertainment traditions. Broadway and Hollywood stage and film musicals stood at the top tier of this world. These productions generally had significant budgets and nearly unlimited access to top talent, a bevy of chorus girls, full theater orchestras, and so on. Below this, there was a second tier that included the top nightclubs, the first-class vaudeville circuits, and the deluxe movie palace variety prologues that aspired to a similar extravagance, though they often made-do with smaller budgets, casts, and orchestras and fewer sets. Nevertheless, these second-tier productions often featured original music or arrangements, as well as top celebrity talent. Below this was another teeming world of less-spectacular revues in smaller night-clubs, cabarets, restaurants, and second-class vaudeville and movie houses. Here, less elaborate Tin Pan Alley stock arrangements (which could still be somewhat sophisticated in the higher-priced "special," "concert," or "symphonic" arrangement categories), lesser-known local talent, and small bands (or a single pianist) dominated, and acts generally did without significant sets or chorus girls. It is in the top two tiers, then, that glorified entertainment thrived. This connection is wholly apparent even with a venue like the Cotton Club, where Duke Ellington rose to fame, and which ultimately billed its offerings as "The Ziegfeld Follies of the Colored Race." Again, despite the great cultural breadth of these glorified entertainments, few scholars have actually examined how revue entertainments were structured, the varieties of music that were performed in them, and how this music was arranged and functioned within each part of an evening's enter-tainment. Despite obvious connections to nineteenth-century Ameri-can and European theatrical genres, these interwar revue traditions are nevertheless generically and historically distinct in and of them-selves. Their prevalence in American interwar entertainments de-mands critical consideration. My concern here is specifically the raison d'être of this musico-theatrical spectacle: the production number. This extended arrangement model formed the central cue for the Harlem entertainment concert jazz tradition. While the concert works discussed later directly derive from earlier revue production numbers, these formal and programmatic inspirations nevertheless informed many other concert works by Ellington and Johnson that have less ob-vious connections to commercial entertainment.

The formulaic narrative and musical designs of Johnson's and Ellington's concert works pose a significant problem for critical as-sessment if they are evaluated solely through the lens of traditional Euro-American art and classical music ideologies. The root of this problem is the long-held binary opposition of art and entertainment. The class-based cultural ideology behind this opposition deems any merging of these realms as suspiciously middlebrow, and hence a marginal artistic effort. A great degree of this marginalization has to do with the complex relationship between the critical ideologies that have shaped the accepted historical narratives of jazz and Euro-Amer-ican concert music, as well as the long-derided cultural position of middlebrowism. From the early 1920s, popular symphonic jazz was manifest as an entertaining and artistically democratic hybrid idiom that rested along the fault line between jazz and the culture of concert music in America. After the symphonic jazz idiom gained a significant presence in popular culture of the late 1920s, this hybrid music provided an exemplary target in the critical war against culturally "homogenizing" middlebrow commercialism. For example, in 1938, the jazz critic Winthrop Sargeant attacked what he variously termed "commercial sweet jazz," "lush . . . movie-house spotlight . . . jazz," and "the big variety-show type of jazz band." For Sargeant, all of these musical entertainment forms were synonymous with the 1920s vogue for "symphonic jazz," an idiom characterized by its "fusion of the pretentious and commonplace," its "slick and striking," "gilded, exotic, orchestral effects," and its excessive use of "instrumental, melodic and harmonic variations, and . . . modulations."[4] While this criticism is largely leveled at white symphonic jazz, the cultural history and compositional intent behind Johnson's and Ellington's production-style concert works clearly open them to similar criticism, particularly if a critic were to insist on the cultural priority of the traditional ideologies of classical, or "Art," music.

Because of their direct entertainment lineage, the concert work efforts of Ellington and Johnson are quite distinct from many other contemporary African American strategies of racial uplift through music. The ideals of racial uplift emerged around the turn of the century and centered on the belief that African Americans could attain social mobility through self-conscious cultural assimilation. As the historian Kevin Gaines has articulated, this agenda promoted the visible adoption of contemporary white middle-class values, including "self-help, racial solidarity, temperance, thrift, chastity, social purity, patriarchal authority, and the accumulation of wealth."[5] Even in the latter decades of the nineteenth century, music was an important cultural front for efforts at black uplift. Thus, as the musicologists Ray Allen and George P. Cunningham have noted, "The turn-of-the-century emergence of conservatory-trained black instrumentalists, singers, and composers embodied the ideal of racial uplift." Harlem composer-conductor Will Marion Cook's aspirations for a concert career ideally represent this movement, both in his training as a concert violinist and composer and in his close connections to his supporter and family friend, Frederick Douglass, a major proponent of this early vision for racial uplift.[6]

As Allen and Cunningham observe, however, early interpretations of this uplift ideology were recalibrated under a new ideal of cultural transformation, which, by the time of the Harlem Renaissance in the 1920s, involved both "cultural uplift through the synthesis of African American musical materials with European style and form, and the transformation of those materials into new [race-based] expressions rather than a *de facto* accommodation to European American artistic norms."[7] Thus, across the peak years of the Harlem Renaissance (just following the war and up through the early 1930s), uplift ideology had expanded to include the self-agency and racial-identity politics of the New Negro movement, which argued that universal standards of beauty and aesthetics were not intrinsically based on white culture. The new belief was that racism and pervasive negative stereotypes could be combated through the promotion of racial pride, cultural demonstrations of intellect and education, and the production of African American–themed art, literature, and music that demonstrated a mastery of high-art traditions while foregrounding black aesthetics, cultural perspectives, and traditions. As Allen and Cunningham note, in this environment, conservative black intelligentsia promoted spirituals as "the privileged genre of African American folk expression for cultural transformation and elevation." Such transformation and elevation was to be accomplished through "careful [musical] arrangement . . . according to principles of Western harmony, tonality, and form," and with an eye toward the dignified, high-culture performance practice traditions of the concert hall.[8] While the symphonic jazz efforts of the Harlem entertainment circle certainly share the belief in concert music as a marker of racial and cultural progress, and while their intent was to lift a lower-class African American musical tradition to this purported higher cultural stage, their approach to musical transformation notably did not involve self-conscious displays of the mastery of classical form and technique, but rather an expansion on the compositional practices, stylistic idioms, and programmatic topics of Harlem entertainment.

The greatest cultural divergence between New Negro ideology and Harlem symphonic jazz lay in the latter's elevation of urban popular entertainment rather than "folk" music idioms. It was not just the depictions of black culture that these cultural leaders were uneasy with, but the new jazz-derived music as well. That modern "jazz" culture lay far from the middle-class mores of most concert spiritual proponents can be readily seen in the body of white and black criticism, journalism, editorials, and letters to editors in the 1920s, heatedly denouncing the (presumably) corrupting cultural influence of these (supposedly) decadent new musical and entertainment trends, many of them indebted to lower-class and southern black musical traditions. This is not to say that the commercial success and racial uplift strategies of certain black jazz artists were not acknowledged in New Negro circles. Especially important was the promotion of a dignified professional appearance and demeanor among Harlem's top jazz orchestras. While their music, lyrics, and cabaret and dance hall performances may not have befitted the New Negro cultural agenda, as Jeffrey Magee has noted, the high professional standards and polished appearance of these organizations (which featured tuxedo-clad performers, expert reading musicians, shined shoes and instruments, impeccable grooming, and an orchestral-type stage presentation) proved to be an effective strategy for promoting an elevated white reception for this music.[9] Ellington was widely considered the apogee of sophisticated Harlem orchestral jazz in the late 1920s and 1930s. As the cultural historian Lewis Erenberg has noted, by "extending the possibilities of black [popular] music—especially its tonal range and harmonic complexity—Ellington demonstrated its equality with classical traditions" to an ever-growing number of music and cultural critics, musicians, and fans from the late 1920s forward.[10] For Ellington and his peers, the next logical step in uplift via Harlem entertainment was to gain acceptance for their music in American concert halls. This agenda was nothing new, however, as Johnson's and Ellington's quests for the high-culture aura of Carnegie Hall had been foreshadowed at least a decade earlier in efforts by Harlem's elder musicians.

13 "AMERICAN MUSIC FOR AMERICANS" AND *NEGRO NUANCES*

Across the 1920s, the older generation among Harlem's celebrated literary and art circles was aligned with the mores of middle-class America, where Jazz Age popular culture was largely stigmatized. By contrast, several younger members of the New Negro circle found vibrant sources of racial inspiration in this commercial world. This generational shift was pointedly articulated by the poet Langston Hughes in 1926 when he proclaimed, "Let the blare of Negro jazz bands" and "the bellowing voice of Bessie Smith singing the Blues penetrate the closed ears of the colored near intellectuals until they listen and perhaps understand."[11] While James Weldon Johnson (born 1871) pointedly discarded stereotyped black dialect in his famous poetry collection of 1927, *God's Trombones*, Hughes (born 1902) and such peers as the poet Sterling Brown (born 1901) and the illustrator-artist Aaron Douglas (born 1899) found a vital racial essence in the "dialects" of black vernacular, urban culture. Similarly, the concert works of Johnson and Ellington wholeheartedly embraced contemporary black popular culture. Their artistic visions owed a great deal to the musical aesthetics espoused by James Weldon Johnson's contemporary, the composer-conductor Will Marion Cook.

As implied in the nickname he received from the younger generation, "Dad" Cook was a mentor for many Harlem musicians who began their careers in the 1920s. The theater, nightclub, society, dance, and concert orchestras led by Cook, James Reese Europe, Ford Dabney, Luckey Roberts, and other Harlem bandleaders in the World War I era formed a key backdrop for the strategies of racial-cultural uplift of African American dance bands and nightclub or theater orchestras of the 1920s. With the onset of the war, the arrival in New York of the influential Original Dixieland Jazz Band in 1917, the untimely death of James Reese Europe in 1919, and the arrivals in New York of the sweet-style orchestras of Art Hickman and Paul Whiteman in 1919 and 1920, respectively, black Manhattan lost its once-dominant hold on the New York dance orchestra market. Nevertheless, many elder statesmen of Harlem entertainment remained quite active professionally from the end of World War I into the 1920s through their work in all-black musical ensembles for Broadway and cabaret or nightclub productions as well as by leading several of New York's most important society orchestras. These ensembles were also early sources of pickup work for Ellington, Johnson, and other musicians of their generation. It is in these social contexts that Ellington and Johnson interacted with Cook. This contact seems to have fostered both Johnson's and Ellington's concert work ambitions.

A greater understanding of Cook's pre-1920s professional career is thus essential background for understanding this relation.

Cook's success with *Clorindy, or the Origin of the Cakewalk* in 1899 established him as a central figure in subsequent black productions on Broadway up through the war years. Throughout this period, Cook harbored an interest in establishing a distinctly African American concert music tradition, and this goal is reflected in his persistent efforts to found all-black concert orchestras throughout the era of World War I and the 1920s. In 1918–19, Cook led a highly successful series of twenty-six- to fifty-piece syncopated concert orchestras. Though most commonly known as the New York Syncopated Orchestra, Cook's ensemble was also variously called the Southern Syncopated Orchestra, the Will Marion Cook Syncopated Orchestra, and the American Syncopated Orchestra. This latter organization's European tour in 1919 awakened many Europeans to African American jazz.[12]

In contrast to the string- and percussion-heavy Clef Club orchestras, the instrumental makeup of Cook's concert ensembles more closely reflected his own roots in musical theater. According to one reliable report, in their 1919 European tour, the Southern Syncopated Orchestra included "two violins, a cello, a saxophone, two basses, two clarinets, a horn, three trumpets, three trombones, drums, two pianos, and a banjo section."[13] In this hybrid instrumentation, Cook's syncopated ensembles foreshadowed the mid-1920s Paul Whiteman symphonic jazz concert orchestras. Cook's anticipating the Whiteman orchestra and its variety-based, concert-style entertainment model is further evidenced in the American Syncopated Orchestra's concert program in Chicago in 1919 (reproduced in the section of photographs in this book). This program provides a rare window onto the exact repertory and reception of this ensemble, which has been quite underresearched in the growing literature on Cook.[14] Though described through a minstrelsy-derived, racist frame of reference that is typical of African American entertainment designed for white audiences of this era, this program's emphasis on the characteristically "American" nature of Cook's orchestra and its variety-styled repertory clearly suggest important precedents for Paul Whiteman's mid-1920s concert-centered tours.[15]

While in performance the Cook orchestra was apparently quite free with number interpolations, this printed program gives a good representation of the ensemble's typical concert repertory. It includes both straight and ragged versions of light classical works (each performed in a decidedly nonclassical instrumentation), traditional concert spirituals and "entertainment spirituals," orchestral arrangements of black Tin Pan Alley tunes, jazz- or blues-oriented numbers (likely with improvised solos), and concert works in a characteristically African American idiom. As African American musicians coming of age just before 1920, both Ellington and Johnson were very much aware of both the cultural significance of the syncopated orchestras of Cook and James Reese Europe, and they each likely witnessed—or heard about—performances by these ensembles prior to meeting Cook in the 1920s. Johnson's connections to Cook's cultural ambitions in the early 1920s illustrate Cook's likely influence on these younger composers.

In the mid-1920s, Cook tried to use the contemporary interest in black musical theater to build an audience for a new concert-style syncopated orchestra that would double as the pit band for an all-black stage revue. In 1924 this venture produced Cook's *Negro Nuances*, a musical revue that included musical contributions by Johnson and the saxophonist-clarinetist Sidney Bechet. The extant evidence concerning this project provides information on both the relation of Cook to younger Harlem entertainers, and the unusual concert music aspirations of this circle in general.

On June 1, 1923, Cook's associate, a Mr. C. A. Parker, wrote a letter on Cook's behalf describing Cook's intentions to develop a new all-black revue. The key passage is Parker's note that "this [project] will be the beginning of some large activities in the entertaining line." Parker claims that "there is a chance for [building] a colored Symphony and the men backing Cook are eager to help make it international in scope."[16] As there is no mention of classical symphonic literature, this "symphony" idea seems to have been a Jazz Age update on Cook's earlier syncopated orchestras. Parker's brief mention of the talent that would be involved in this revue-with-orchestra venture demonstrates Cook's intention to build a high-class variety revue that could appeal to all the "brows"—high, middle, and low. *Negro Nuances* was promoted through advertisements like the two shown in figures 3.1a and 3.1b. According to these documents, the show's talent roster was based on the high-class vaudeville model that was implied in

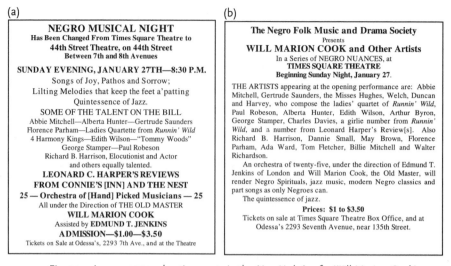

(a)

NEGRO MUSICAL NIGHT
Has Been Changed From Times Square Theatre to
44th Street Theatre, on 44th Street
Between 7th and 8th Avenues

SUNDAY EVENING, JANUARY 27TH—8:30 P.M.

Songs of Joy, Pathos and Sorrow;
Lilting Melodies that keep the feet a'patting
Quintessence of Jazz.
SOME OF THE TALENT ON THE BILL
Abbie Mitchell—Alberta Hunter—Gertrude Saunders
Florence Parham—Ladies Quartette from *Runnin' Wild*
4 Harmony Kings—Edith Wilson—"Tommy Woods"
George Stamper—Paul Robeson
Richard B. Harrison, Elocutionist and Actor
and others equally talented.
LEONARD C. HARPER'S REVIEWS
FROM CONNIE'S [INN] AND THE NEST
25 — Orchestra of [Hand] Picked Musicians — 25
All under the Direction of THE OLD MASTER
WILL MARION COOK
Assisted by **EDMUND T. JENKINS**
ADMISSION—$1.00—$3.50
Tickets on Sale at Odessa's, 2293 7th Ave., and at the Theatre

(b)

The Negro Folk Music and Drama Society
Presents
WILL MARION COOK and Other Artists
In a Series of NEGRO NUANCES, at
TIMES SQUARE THEATRE
Beginning Sunday Night, January 27.

THE ARTISTS appearing at the opening performance are: Abbie
Mitchell, Gertrude Saunders, the Misses Hughes, Welch, Duncan
and Harvey, who compose the ladies' quartet of *Runnin' Wild*,
Paul Robeson, Alberta Hunter, Edith Wilson, Arthur Byron,
George Stamper, Charles Davies, a girlie number from *Runnin'
Wild*, and a number from Leonard Harper's Review[s]. Also
Richard B. Harrison, Dannie Small, May Brown, Florence
Parham, Ada Ward, Tom Fletcher, Billie Mitchell and Walter
Richardson.
An orchestra of twenty-five, under the direction of Edmund T.
Jenkins of London and Will Marion Cook, the Old Master, will
render Negro Spirituals, jazz music, modern Negro classics and
part songs as only Negroes can.
The quintessence of jazz.
Prices: $1 to $3.50
Tickets on sale at Times Square Theatre Box Office, and at
Odessa's 2293 Seventh Avenue, near 135th Street.

Fig. 3.1. January 1924 advertisements in the *New York Age* for Will Marion Cook's *Negro Nuances* revue: (a) from the *New York Age*, January 19, 1924, p. 6; (b) from the *New York Age*, January 26, 1924, p. 6.

Parker's 1923 letter. Actor-singers like Paul Robeson and Abbie Mitchell contributed to the more "serious" numbers of the show. Harlem's contemporary blues divas are emphasized, in that the show included Alberta Hunter, Gertrude Saunders, and Edith Wilson. One advertisement's added reference to "a girlie number from [James P. Johnson's musical comedy] *Runnin' Wild*" underscores a nod to low-brow, voyeuristic revues. Of greater significance is the information that these documents provide on the musical elements of the revue. Each advertisement emphasizes the size of the show's orchestra, twenty-five players—roughly the same size and instrumental makeup that Paul Whiteman employed a year later in his historic Aeolian Hall concert. These advertisements also seem to imply that the show was performed in a semiconcert setting, an approach that probably involved a modest staging but not the elaborate, fully-staged productions associated with Harlem or Broadway theater. The program's tag line, "the quintessence of jazz," was likely meant to tap into several ideas that were associated with the term *jazz* in the 1920s. In terms of musical style, this tag line could equally refer to either Harlem jazz and blues or even contemporary Whiteman-style dance bands (which was emulated by several black orchestras in this period). (The minimal materials extant do not reveal much about the show's actual orchestral arrangements or performances.)[17]

Negro Nuances was largely a pastiche of recycled materials, most of which were by Cook. As seen in figure 3.2, an outline to *Negro Nuances* illustrates the program's basic structure, which was based on a common Africa-to-Dixie-to-Harlem narrative model employed in many of the all-black shows of the 1920s. (Though this show's "Fourth Nuance" is set in New Orleans, this staged locale is trumped by an overriding emphasis on modern Harlem through the episode's big finale borrowing from James P. Johnson's *Runnin' Wild.*) The basis of this musico-geographic structure is its progression from "primitive/jungle" themes, to "country" topics and black folk music of the old South, to a "city" theme that celebrated the contemporary cultural riches of Harlem. (Readers should note that this basic migrational progression—of Africa, to the Deep South, to the urban North—forms the basis of the traditional narratives of jazz history.) In this historical focus, the revue revised the black historical pageants that Mark Tucker has discussed with regard to the program design of Ellington's *Black, Brown and Beige*.[18] As Tucker's research centered on both the artistic-cultural influences in Ellington's Washington, D.C., youth and the intellectual history of *Black, Brown and Beige*, his overview of this recurrent "evolution of Negro music" narrative trope is quite cursory, and he understandably provides only a brief list of Harlem shows and production numbers that employed variations on this idea. Considering the significant importance of this narrative model and these program topics to Harlem entertainment across the 1920s and 1930s, there is a great critical need to explore in detail several non-Ellington applications of this program model. This subject and its relation to Harlem adaptations of the variety entertainment aesthetic is central to interpreting nearly all of the musical studies that follow in this book. In 1920s and 1930s all-black entertainments, these historical/musico-geographic program topics allowed a producer to incorporate a broad spectrum of African American popular music, including popular "savage"-style dance numbers, slave-era work songs, plantation songs, cakewalks, spirituals, blues, Tin Pan Alley ballads and novelties, love songs, minstrel songs, hot jazz numbers, nods to Creole culture, and so forth. This same dual-purpose historical/variety-entertainment focus was transposed to Harlem entertainment's concert aspirations, as

Negro Nuances: Episodes in the Musical Life of the Negro (The Soul of a Race Told in Music, Drama, and Dance), in two acts, by Abbie Mitchell, Will Marion Cook, with additional music by James P. Johnson and Sidney Bechet.

FIRST NUANCE

Scene 1: 10-12.5 minutes. African jungle, mud house, trees, palms, fire flies, insects. Soft fanciful lighting effects and weird noises. Set in the African night. Scene opens with a hymn of praise to the God that this particular tribe worships. An idol is prominently displayed. Nine men are dressed in the skins of wild animals. One woman is true to type—beautiful, but with African beauty. Includes: (1) "Hymn of Praise"; (2a) "Song of War"; (2b) "Barbaric Dance"; (3a) "African Love Song" (9.5-10.5 minutes; includes characteristic African dance and a burlesque on the "Love Song"); (3b) "Marriage," natural and with comedy effects; and (4) "Dance of Death," wild, passionate, and fearful.

INTERLUDE

Scene 2: "The Ghost Ship" (3 minutes). This number will be sung by full chorus, during which pictures will illustrate the story. The story is that of a slave ship that sailed from Africa hundreds of years ago with a thousand slaves. During the mutiny of the slaves, every soul on board perished. Tradition has it that any ship meeting with the specter of this slave ship is doomed to destruction.

SECOND NUANCE

Scene 3: A five-minute (dramatic?) scene growing out of songs written by Jean Toomer. Set in the cotton fields of Georgia. Costumes: bandanas, overalls, calicos. In this scene, there must only be sorrow songs. Exhortation in songs, all without orchestral accompaniment. Ensembles, quartet singing, and finishing up with a prayer, in which all humbly, and fervently, sing and pray; song dying away like a last sob of a broken heart. (Perhaps "I'll Be Ready" to lighten the tension.)

INTERLUDE

Scene 4: Abraham Lincoln, Frederick Douglas, and colored soldiers during the Civil War. Numbers: (1) "Orchestral Overture"; and (2) "On Emancipation Day" tableau (10 minutes). A man dressed in old-fashioned minstrel clothes who can play banjo, sing, and dance. Small boys and girls as well. Ensembles are based on the type of music that immediately precedes and follows 1860.

THIRD NUANCE

Scene 5: "Clorindy, or The Origin of the Cake Walk" (30 minutes). Scene just outside New Orleans. Numbers: (1) "Opening Chorus"; (2) "Hottest Coon in Dixie"; (3) "Lover's Lane"; (4) "Who Dat Say Chicken in Dis Crowd"; (5) "Creole Dance"; (6) "Cake Walk"; (7) "Darktown Is Out Tonight"; and (8) "Finale."

INTERLUDE

Scene 6: "Garden of Flowers" (6 minutes), very tropical. Song. [*ED. NOTE: The remaining text is lost here.*]

FOURTH NUANCE

Scene 7: New Orleans or the Land of Jazz. Dance garden. Costumes elaborate as [?]. [*ED. NOTE: The remaining text is lost here. One discernible text fragment is "classics."*] Numbers: (1) "Opening Chorus"; (2) "Memphis Gouge"; (3) "Darky Love Song"; (4) "Sunshine Sammy"; (5) "Schottische"; and (6) "Charleston Dance."

Fig. 3.2. An abridged and edited version of the working outline to Will Marion Cook's *Negro Nuances* (1924). From the Will Mercer Cook Papers of the Moorland-Springarn Research Center, Howard University. (Courtesy of the Moorland-Springarn Research Center, Howard University.)

can be seen in *Negro Nuances*. In the summer before W. C. Handy's Carnegie Hall concert of April 1928 (which similarly sought to show "the evolution of Negro music"), as noted in the introduction to this book, the columnist H. L. Mencken had provocatively asked: "Why did Negro composers wait for Gershwin to do his *Rhapsody in Blue*? Why did they wait for Paul Whiteman to make jazz a serious matter?" As the production of *Negro Nuances* in 1924 suggests, the answer is that they did not wait, but their efforts before 1927 had little impact in the larger commercial world that Whitemanesque symphonic jazz had so thoroughly conquered.

13 THE VAUDEVILLE AESTHETIC, PRODUCTION ARRANGEMENTS, AND MUSICAL TOPICS

The nightclub floor show and stage revues that Ellington and Johnson built their early careers in were defined by the era's predominant interest in variety entertainment forms. Film scholar Henry Jenkins's concept of a "vaudeville aesthetic" provides a model description of the precepts governing musical revues of the late 1920s and 1930s. Jenkins has observed that the "logic of the variety show rested on the assumption that heterogeneous entertainment was essential to attract and satisfy a mass audience.... [I]ndividual acts ... [were] juxtaposed together with an eye toward the ... highest possible degree of novelty and variety ... [W]hat vaudeville communicated was the pleasure of infinite diversity in infinite combinations."[19] As George Gottlieb's account of vaudeville programming in 1916 shows, both acts and shows were structured to build toward well-placed climaxes. In musical revues, the two key climactic, spectacular acts were typically extended song-and-dance production numbers. In the 1920s and 1930s, such extended popular-song arrangements were likewise governed by a formal interest in building internal diversity through contrasting themes, textures, tempi, keys, and variations. This variety-based production number ideal was closely related to conventions of symphonic jazz arranging.

Leonard Reed was one of the celebrated Cotton Club choreographers and producers who worked with Ellington, Cab Calloway, and other famous Harlem acts in the 1930s.[20] In a 1997 interview, Reed noted that "variety was the essence" of his productions.[21] Reed explained that these floor shows were only seventy-five minutes in length (with two shows an evening). Even individual act "didn't do eight minutes of . . . the same thing. [They] had to have that variety, and that's what made them so great."[22] Dan Healy, the producer of the Cotton Club shows, similarly observed that in both act and show, "the chief ingredient was pace, pace, pace!"[23] This overriding interest in variety and pace translated into shows that, according to Reed, were "generally built around [act] types"[24] (as Gottlieb had similarly noted), with widely contrasting combinations of talent, and acts ranging from solo, duet, and small-group singing, dancing, novelty, and comedy acts, to large ensemble song-and-dance numbers, all of which could cover a broad range of musical styles and genres.

Reed explained that the big opening number of a show "would break down in three or four different segments." Following a spectacular full-ensemble introduction with a "line of girls, twelve to sixteen girls, which would open the show dancing," a "boy and girl [would] come in and sing a song, with the girls," after which the music "would go back to the . . . original [up] tempo for an ending." To provide contrast, the next act after this multipartite opening would be "a single tap dancer or a ballroom dancer."[25] After describing possible middle acts, Reed observed that he would typically place a "spectacular" dance act—"one that's really sensational"—as the penultimate number of an evening. When an act like the phenomenal tap-dance duo of "the Berry Brothers finished, in the midst of the great applause, the [grand ensemble] finale went on." For the production numbers of his Cotton Club shows of the 1930s, Reed was influenced by the elaborate film musical choreography of Busby Berkeley and MGM's musicals.[26]

Both the program design that Reed outlines and the extended song-and-dance production numbers of this revue tradition greatly informed Johnson's and Ellington's concert jazz works of the 1930s and 1940s. The connections between these two musical worlds can be seen in four key areas: (1) the aforementioned Africa-Dixie-Harlem program topics; (2) symphonic jazz intermixtures of "elevated" and "black" musical topics; (3) the design of "production"-style arrangements; and (4) jazz "rhapsody"-themed production numbers in the era's all-black revues.

In the various arranging traditions related to symphonic jazz,

James P. Johnson outside his Harlem home in the late 1920s. (Courtesy of the Institute of Jazz Studies, Rutgers University Libraries, Rutgers University.)

A 1940s publicity photo of James P. Johnson. (Courtesy of the Institute of Jazz Studies, Rutgers University Libraries, Rutgers University.)

A 1933 publicity photo of Ellington made before his orchestra's tour of England. This is one of the best-known images of Ellington, and it reflects the Cotton Club famous tag line, "The Aristocrat of Harlem." (Courtesy of the Institute of Jazz Studies, Rutgers University Libraries, Rutgers University.)

A composerly publicity photo of Duke Ellington from the 1930s. (Courtesy of the Institute of Jazz Studies, Rutgers University Libraries, Rutgers University.)

Duke Ellington and His Orchestra, 1930. (Courtesy of the Institute of Jazz Studies, Rutgers University Libraries, Rutgers University.)

A 1919 concert program for Will Marion Cook's American Syncopated Orchestra. (Courtesy of Cambria Master Recordings and Archives.)

AMERICAN SYNCOPATED ORCHESTRA

——— and Singers ———

WILL MARION COOK
Conductor

GEORGE EDMUND DULF
Conductor

"THE HIT OF THE SEASON"

TRINITY AUDITORIUM

Thur. Eve. Nov. 13 $\overline{8:15}$
Friday Mat. Nov. 14 $\overline{2:15}$
Sat. Eve. Nov. 15 $\overline{8:15}$

Prices 50c - 75c - $1.00 - $1.50 - $2.00
ON SALE NOW at TRINITY BOX OFFICE

Exclusive Management
JAMES R. SAVILLE
3623 PINE GROVE AVENUE, CHICAGO

Specimen Program

American Syncopated Orchestra
and Singers

WILL MARION COOK
Conductor

≡ ≡ ≡

American Music for Americans

≡ ≡ ≡

PART I.

ORCHESTRA—"Swing Along"	Cook
ORCHESTRA—"Moaning Trombone" (Characteristic)	
QUARTETTE—(Spirituals)	
ORCHESTRA—"Call of the Woods"	Tyers
FOLK SONG—"I Got a Robe"	
ORCHESTRA—(a) Plantation Melody	Lamen
(b) Hungarian Dance No. 5	Brahms
"LISTEN TO THE LAMBS"	Dett
Soloist and Orchestra.	
ORCHESTRA—"Arabian Knights"	David
ORCHESTRA—"Exhortation"	Cook
ORCHESTRA—"Suwannee Ripples"	
SOLO—"Mammy o' Mine"	Pinkord

PART II.

DRUM SOLO	
MASSED CHORUS—In Modern Part Songs	
ORCHESTRA—(a) "Humoresque"	Dvorak
(b) "Admiration"	Tyers
TENOR SOLO—"Mammy"	Cook
ORCHESTRA—"Russian Rag"	
TROMBONE SOLO—"Ad Lib"	
ORCHESTRA—"Mid the Pyramids"	Jones
ORCHESTRA—"Dixieland in France"	Henry Saparo
ORCHESTRA—"Ramshackles"	
ORCHESTRA—"Rain Song"	Cook

What Is A Syncopated Orchestra?

The AMERICAN Syncopated Orchestra and Singers

is an organization of thirty negro musicians, under the direction of Will Marion Cook, who give to the public the negro music, both vocal and instrumental, including not only the present day music, but the original plantation melodies.

It is not only an orchestra of strings, banjos, wind, wood and brass, but each member is a singer as well as an instrumentalist.

Will Marion Cook, the conductor, is acknowledged as one of the greatest musicians in the negro race. To him has fallen the duty of the gathering together of this orchestra, which has proven the wide musicianship with which he has been credited.

"This organization has had the sense to yield to the call of the blood and do the things they can, and which they can do as no other men can approach. With their bland and childlike smile they can sing their 'spirituals' running from the depths of religious emotion to a little light and airy persiflage, with things sacred, yet with such spontaneous expression of the negro point of view, that it is not the slightest sense of irreverence. It is the same with their ragtime. What in the white man's hands becomes coarse and vulgar suggestion, as they do it, it is simply infectious in its gaiety," as said by one of the foremost critics of the country.

Taken altogether, it is the most wonderful organization of its kind in existence. It is what the people want, what they demand, and what they are going to insist upon having. AMERICAN MUSIC FOR AMERICANS.

READ WHAT THE CHICAGO CRITICS SAY:

HERMAN DEVRIES IN CHICAGO AMERICAN.

They are the rage of the hour. It is not difficult to understand the crowds or their vivid appreciation. If the orchestra is a popular idol, the conductor as popular as you would be able to get.

Will Marion Cook is a genius in his particular way.

The orchestra is a band of excellently schooled musicians, and whatever they offer has some peculiar, unique personality that seems a part of no other like band I have heard.

Nothing is untouched by their keen native intelligence, and the musicianship is thoroughly refined. Even in its most humorous aspects, it never becomes coarse.

They are the musical aristocrats of their race.

FREDERICK DONAGHEY IN CHICAGO DAILY TRIBUNE.

Sly and salubrious showmen, these Negroes, with diversions and didoes that, as Mr. Stock said, have been worked out with brains.

The orchestra's are distinctly unmitted by these minstrels, and both worship and fun were, in the naive text and tune of "Tis Me, O Lord."

Nothing else in hearing is at all like this band, with its flare for raffish rubato and its special technique for the high pulse of melody. Lawrence Gilman, twenty-five per cent of yesterday's audience, Mr. Vogesil maliciously explained, was of Chicago Symphony subscribers.

HENRIETTE WEBER IN HERALD EXAMINER.

The orchestra, players, singers, everything, went through a heterogeneous program to which they gave not only to an uncertainty as guide, so many were the additions and the seemingly spontaneous amplifications.

From orchestra numbers to plantation melodies, from moaning trombone to humorous part songs, and back again to orchestra music, ranging from Brahms to sublime minstrel ragtime, kept the musical ball rolling, with everyone keyed up to the highest pitch.

In fact, the audience that occupied not the seats but the front edge of every seat in Orchestra Hall was as much of a show as the artistic minstrels on the platform. Every countenance was wreathed in a happy smile, and only here and there was the deprecatory highbrow who really could not see it, or rather hear it at all. And of the professional musicians encountered, a few were sniffy, while others patted themselves for their bigness in being able to like this sort of thing, but for the rest, it was simply a vast throng of regular human beings who were having the frank enjoyment of the thing they liked.

It was a great show, a wonderful entertainment and beautiful music. And cheers and applause met the movement of the orchestra at the intermission that the orchestra would come again.

KARLETON HACKETT IN CHICAGO EVENING POST.

It was a terrible evening for the highbrows in Orchestra Hall, for you could hear the tough

cordage of their musical self-respect rending strand by strand until it fairly hung in tatters about them and was not even fit to serve as camouflage for the time being. They were there in shoals and droves, so that, while the audience was somewhat spotted, like the leopard, large portions of the highbrowed forehead were people arrayed as for the opera. To be perfectly fair, most of them threw up their hands at once in token of absolute surrender, but I saw one fair Brahmin with features set like a graven image of the Great Stone Face up in the New Hampshire mountains while Will Cook and his men were showing how how Brahms really ought to be played.

The charm of what these people do is infectious. It is very skillful, but there is something vastly more appealing in it than the most startling exhibition of technical skill could produce, and this comes from the sheer beauty of the best of it and the spontaneous joy these people get from the mere doing.

In the midst of the most crazy "jazz" they will suddenly settle into a tone of the most exquisite beauty, for, after all, they are music-makers. They gave the highbrows a jolt even before they started, since at the head of the program was printed—"American Music for Americans"—which, I guess, means you something to think about. Also it would be quite a task to deny the essential fact, since if generations on American soil makes an American the forebears of these colored folk have been here pretty nearly as long as anybody and as for their music—well, the one brand of music which carries the name "America" on it and is known the world over the moment it is heard, is rag. Denounce it, view with alarm its pernicious influence over the young, curse it in good set terms and do anything else to it which your musical morals demand of you—but don't go to hear these people give some examples of the real thing unless you are prepared to fall from grace. They won't touch your nerves nor call up uncertain names for you when they have said; they don't have to. But bit by bit, with bland and childlike wiles, they will insinuate some of these strains within your ears, and even tho you be as one with the wax of Puritan prejudgment, sealing them tight they will find some chink thru which to worm their way. The only thing for such a one to do is to stay at home, safe out of sound, and then rave to his heart's content.

MAURICE ROSENFIELD IN CHICAGO DAILY NEWS.

Mr. Cook's syncopated band is far removed in character from the more sedate and formal symphonic orchestra, but it is unique and has a distinct place in the musical activities, especially of America.

Its instrumental combination is anything but orthodox. Its numbers are vastly different from the so called classic music which is heard at the concerts of our leading orchestras. But these differences and their own particular kind of music, have an instant appeal to those who consider music purely as a diversion than an uplift.

Mr. Cook, who had trained his personnel carefully, painstakingly and musically, often lets his people cavort and amuse themselves in the course of the program, but always within the bounds of good taste and always with a regard for that might be termed musical propriety. The singers often "rag" their tunes but it is all done with spontaneous, negro humor, and one bobs and wiggles along with them while they do their stunts.

It is a very exhilarating performance while these musicians present, and well worth going to hear and see.

EDWARD C. MOORE IN CHICAGO DAILY JOURNAL.

Once again those highly agreeable syncopationists that perform under the direction of Will Marion Cook came to Orchestra Hall last night, and once again they tested the capacity of the house. The organization itself needed the stage, so there was no chance to accommodate the late comers, but if there had been more seats in the house there would have been a larger audience. It was the only way that it could have been larger.

As the program of eight days before had been so much of a hit, it was repeated in all of its essentials on this occasion consequently the printed announcement was of less service than the former one had been. But what matter? It made very little difference what these gifted minstrels did; they apparently have a wide repertoire, and it is all attractive.

So the players performed their Hungarian dance, their waltz, and the other specimens of supposedly concert music, interspersing it with "blues" and "jazz". One of the matters that show brains in the construction of this entertainment is that it is what the photographers call contrasty. There is never too much of anything. A hair-raising and shoulder-joint loosening "jazz" is immediately followed by a piece of music played with as fine a tone and as delicate a nuance as you would be able to get out of a symphony orchestra of similar proportions, perhaps better, for when orchestra players develop to the point of being able to get a good tone, they have usually developed out of a taste for such music as this syncopated organization plays. And should there be any possibility of your having too much of even this style of playing, there is the singing singers entering, sometimes with a song, that has come straight from the south, sometimes with something that has been put into notes for just such a performance, sometimes, fortunately not too often, with the product of tin-pan alley.

It was a good show, the best of its kind that has ever come to Orchestra Hall. There was no danger of any of the numbers being wide-spread in performance, the frank enjoyment of the participants in their own performance took care of that. They liked their own music so well that they did it well. Consequently the audience liked it as well as they did. It was the best lesson in the world on the state of mind that any performing artist ought to be in before he ventures to appear on the stage.

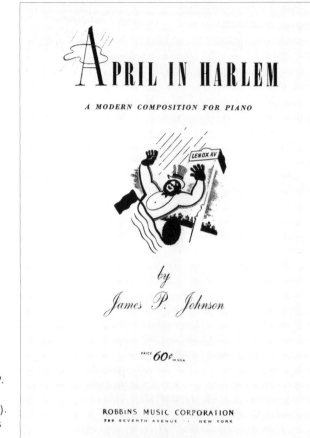

The folio cover to James P. Johnson, *April in Harlem* (New York: Robbins, 1944). (Courtesy of EMI/Robbins Music Corporation.)

From the concert program to the "First Concert of Symphonic Works by James P. Johnson," Heckscher Theatre, New York City, March 8, 1942. (Courtesy of the James P. Johnson Foundation.)

A 1935 Brunswick Records advertisement for the release of Duke Ellington's *Reminiscing in Tempo*. (Courtesy of the Institute of Jazz Studies, Rutgers University Libraries, Rutgers University.)

After the 1955 performance of Duke Ellington's *New World A-Comin'* with the Symphony of the Air. *Left to right:* Donald Shirley, Jinx Faulkenberg, Duke Ellington, Lena Horne, and Lenny Hayton. (Courtesy of Dr. Donald Shirley.)

Duke Ellington conducting pianist Donald Shirley with the Symphony of the Air in a 1955 Carnegie Hall performance of Ellington's *New World A-Comin'*. (Courtesy of Dr. Donald Shirley.)

there was a great emphasis on building variety in arranging routines through juxtapositions of different styles of popular music and other "characteristic scoring effects" (textures) that referenced familiar ethnic and nationalistic musical styles and their distinct instrumental combinations, rhythmic components, and melodic and harmonic traits. These "characteristic effects" directly relate to the idea of referential musical topics, as articulated by Leonard Ratner, Robert Hatten, and other scholars.[27] Quite notably, Jeffrey Magee has recently applied topical analysis to the study of 1920s musical theater traditions. In this context, Magee quotes Hatten's equally useful definition of topics as "patches of music that trigger clear associations with [musical] styles, genres, and expressive meanings."[28] It is in this specific sense that "characteristic scoring effects" tap into the broad, musico-cultural coding systems of Jenkins's "vaudeville aesthetic."

The term *routine* specifically denotes a given arrangement's ordering of popular song strains (i.e., the verse, patter, and chorus), the repetitions and variations of these elements, their combination with instrumental textures and effects, and the use of an introduction, interludes, and coda. On this larger structural scale, as the 1920s symphonic-jazz arranger Arthur Lange advised, "An arrangement . . . must be full of contrast," and since "a change in tempo is contrary to . . . dance music, the only way to eliminate monotony is by means of modulation" or changes in "instrumental color."[29] In a 1926 overview of symphonic jazz arranging, Lange remarks that the use of a patter strain—or another type of third strain—in an arrangement is another common means for creating musical variety, particularly within extended arrangements. This three-strain episodic form notably approaches the greater thematic complexity of many Whiteman-style concert works as well as the era's grand production numbers. With these contexts in mind, beyond the subject of the dance band market, Lange discusses arranging for "concert situations"—that is, arranging for concert jazz, theater, or movie palace orchestras, contexts that purportedly allowed "greater rhythmic complexity, tempo variation, and the use of non–dance oriented" scoring effects.[30] Similarly, in his 1946 essay "Arranging for Radio," the radio arranger Tom Bennett discusses the "type of orchestra which . . . play[s] popular music in a concert manner rather than in a dance tempo. . . . a style that [was] created to make the sometimes banal and trite music of the day interesting to listen to rather than interesting to dance to."[31] Of particular interest is Bennett's overview of "the big, spectacular arrangements." These numbers correspond directly to Lange's concert-style arrangements. Bennett notes that such numbers "are usually of some length, running four or five minutes," and "they usually present a tune, or several tunes, in a startling variety of treatments."[32] In radio, Broadway musicals, and in sound-era Hollywood films, such spectacular production numbers were often constructed in a manner that resembles both symphonic jazz dance-band arranging and Whiteman-style, popular idiom concert works.

One key interconnection between Harlem entertainment, symphonic jazz arranging, and production number routines can be found in symphonic jazz–styled admixtures of "elevated" and African American–themed effects. This type of scoring texture can be ideally seen in the era's "entertainment spiritual" vogue. From the age of minstrelsy to the 1940s, the spiritual idiom was manifest in a broad range of cultural activities. What seems to have been forgotten in the critical literature on spirituals is that the idiom was also a significant part of popular entertainment. As "entertainment spirituals" were generally jazz-inflected, mildly irreverent parodies of religious spirituals, and as they were routinely performed in an exaggerated fashion that emphasized physical and vocal stereotypes of rural, southern African American religious expression, these sorts of performances were regularly denounced by black and white proponents of racial uplift through concert spiritual arrangements.[33]

A model entertainment spiritual can be seen in Spencer Williams's "Moan, You Moaners! (Fox Trot Spirituelle)," which was published in the 1930 *Joe Davis Folio of Paul Whiteman's Favorite Modern Rhythmic Spirituals*.[34] "Moan, You Moaners!" was recorded by a variety of artists, including a 1930 rendition by the famous blues singer Bessie Smith and her favorite pianist, James P. Johnson.[35] Though lacking in symphonic jazz affectations, the Smith-Johnson recording is fascinating because it marks an intersection of stride piano, 1920s Harlem blues, an emerging black pop-jazz vocal quartet tradition (which leads to groups like the Ink Spots), *and* the entertainment spiritual idiom. The thirty-two-bar Tin Pan Alley chorus contains a small number of tropes on the spiritual idiom, including melodic passages that recall such popular spirituals as "Deep River," alternating major and minor melodic thirds, and stereotyped chordal motion of close parallel fourth and fifth harmonies. All of the "modern rhythmic spirituals" in this folio are marked by intertextual parodies of spiritual lyrics and their performance practice ("let the good Lord hear you shout," "hear them sisters groanin', . . . repentin' and atonin'," etc.). Such markers indicate that some aspect of the entertainment spiritual idiom is in effect. On stage and film, as well as in recordings, these tropes were augmented in performance by exaggerated, often campy, aural and physical enactments of African American worship, as can be readily heard throughout the Smith-Johnson performance of "Moan, You Moaners!"

The type of symphonic jazz stylizations that were typically found in the arrangements of entertainment spirituals can be seen in example 3.1, which presents an excerpt from the score to a spiritual-based number from Johnson's 1931 show *Sugar Hill* (the text has unfortunately been lost).[36] This number's dramatic introduction abounds in details that were intended to impart a sense of serious austerity, including dramatic diminished harmonies, a "movie music" employment of frequent sequential repetitions, a tremolo bass in the low strings and piano, and so forth. This number likewise underscores its spiritual-derived melody with a potpourri of stylistic topics that merge the spiritual idiom with popular and "serious" or "elevated" musical scoring. These elements include a faux-primitivist bass drone, a jazz texture (the muted trumpets) set against an "austere" string choir, a slow rate of harmonic change over minor and diminished chords, and a homophonic accompanimental texture. These are common hallmarks of intersections between the entertainment spiritual and symphonic jazz idioms.

A related jazz-spiritual choral tradition of Harlem, Broadway, and Hollywood can be briefly illustrated through RKO's 1929 film short *St. Louis Blues* with Bessie Smith. It featured an orchestra led by Johnson (with members of the Fletcher Henderson Orchestra), the Hall Johnson Choir, and musical direction by J. Rosamond Johnson. Example 3.2 presents a short passage from W. C. Handy's published version of the Rosamond Johnson choral arrangement that was used in this RKO film and that may have been reemployed in one of Lew Leslie's *Blackbirds* revue editions or his 1931 *Rhapsody in Black* revue.[37] While the film's soundtrack makes overt reference to symphonic jazz

Introduction to *Spiritual*

Example 3.1.   Measures 1–25 from the "Spiritual" number in James P. Johnson's score to *Sugar Hill* (1931). © James P. Johnson Foundation. Used by permission.

Example 3.2. Measures 41–48 from J. Rosamond Johnson's arrangement of "St. Louis Blues" in the film short *St. Louis Blues* (RKO, 1929). Sheet music of "St. Louis Blues" written by William C. Handy, courtesy of Handy Brothers Music Co., Inc. (International copyright secured.)

when Johnson's band briefly quotes from Gershwin's *Rhapsody in Blue*, the point of this example is the frequent intersections of the entertainment spiritual choral style with symphonic jazz affectations. In the film short, the interactions between Bessie Smith and the choir of nightclub patrons again signify upon the relation between a testifier and a congregation. Handy's secular blues is edged into the idiom of entertainment spirituals through the choir's frequent cries of "Lawd" and "Moan, sister." A heightened, pseudo-classicism is seen in the decidedly nonjazz, "elevated" choral writing of such lines and the non-spiritual-like, triplet chromatic runs in example 3.2 (these details derive from Handy's original score). The collective effect openly approaches the mongrel jazz-classical stylistic boundaries of symphonic jazz. Most of the extant production numbers of Johnson's stage scores and Ellington's performances in the Cotton Club floor shows reveal similar designs and formal traits.

A good example of the connections between these all-black stage traditions, symphonic jazz scoring affectations, and "production"-style arranging routines can be seen in the eight-plus-minute musical arrangement featured in the *St. Louis Blues* short. A formal outline of the film's production arrangement can be seen in table 3.1. While the arrangement may not display as broad a range of texture, key, and tempo changes as some contemporary Broadway and Hollywood production numbers, the overall routine for *St. Louis Blues* reveals a similar means of extending a popular song, and a similar sensitivity to ever-shifting textures, stylistic topics, tempi, and keys—all of which are key outgrowths of the variety aesthetic and symphonic jazz-style arranging conventions.

Beyond such limited evidence as the arrangement heard in this widely circulated 1929 film short, the study of production numbers in 1920s and 1930s Harlem entertainments is seriously hampered by a dearth of extant score and recording materials that accurately document these practices. For example, despite the wealth of score materials available in the archives devoted to Johnson and Ellington, only a very small number of extant theater and floor show arrangements from the 1920s and 1930s can be identified with any certainty, and most of those materials are either incomplete representations of the actual arrangements and performances or they originate from less-important (or failed) productions.[38]

Among Johnson's extant scores, I have been able to identify only one reasonably complete manuscript that reflects an actual production number arrangement from one of Johnson's staged theater works. This number is the "Moving Day" finale to Johnson's aforementioned 1931 show, *Sugar Hill,* which closed after eleven performances in January 1932. No script has been found for the show, and most (though not all) of the lyrics are also lost. The design of the finale is shown in table 3.2. This outline is based on an incomplete set of orchestral parts. It is unclear who the arranger of this number may have been, though it was likely either Johnson himself or William Grant Still (who is credited on two other arrangements in the show). A typescript program outline that charts out the form of the number also exists.

TABLE 3.1. Formal outline of J. Rosamond Johnson's arrangement of "St. Louis Blues" in the film short *St. Louis Blues* (RKO, 1929)

Time	M.	Section	Key	Texture
6:52	1	Intro. (chorus a^2b twice)	C	Slow. Bessie Smith solo. "My man's got a heart like a rock . . ."
7:42	13	Piano intro.	F	Medium-slow lope. Harlem stride (pno solo).
7:55	17	Vocal verse A^1	F	Medium-slow with stilted rag-like swing. Entertainment spiritual. Smith with choir-band backing. "I hate to see . . ."
8:31	29	Vocal verse A^2	F	"Feelin' tomorrow . . ." Smith with choir-band backing . . .
9:04	41	Vocal verse B^1	Fmin	"St. Louis woman . . ." Smith with choir-band backing . . .
9:47	57	Vocal chorus^1	F	Medium-slow. Smith with choir-band backing. "Got de St. Louis Blues . . ." Rubato final phrase.
10:24	69	Trumpet break	F	Solo trumpet break (no band)
10:28	71	Vocal verse A^3	F	Male choir in call and response with Smith. "Let me be your big dog . . ."
10:59	83	Dual trumpet break	mod.	Picking up tempo Dual trpt. break (no band).
11:03	87	Inst. chorus var.^{1}	G	Up-tempo, hot Harlem big band. Trpts. with clar. trio riff background.
11:14	99	Inst. chorus var.^{2}	G	Continues
11:26	111	Inst. chorus var.^{3}	G	Big band. Solo clar. with sustained brass/reed background.
11:37	123	Inst. chorus var.^{4}	G	Continues
11:48	135	Inst. chorus var.^{5}	G	Big band. Riff-based clar. solo with brass response. Mordecai enters.
11:59	147	Inst. chorus var.^{6} (shout)	G	Big band. Riff-based ensemble, shout-chorus type texture.
12:09	159	Inst. chorus var.^{7}	G	Big band. New Orleans–style texture. Mordecai dance showcase.
12:20	171	Inst. chorus var.^{8}	G	Big band. Hard cadence stop.
12:30		*Narrative break*		*Confrontation of Smith and male lead*
12:52	183	Inst. chorus^2	G	Slow bump-and-grind. New Orleans lowdown with trpt. lead.
13:22	195	Inst. chorus^3	G	Mordecai steals Smith's money and casts her to the floor.
13:50	207	Choral break	G	Rubato choral break (no band)
14:00	209	*Rhapsody in Blue*	G → mod.	*Rhapsody in Blue* paraphrase with trpt. lead. Mordecai leaves.
14:18	215	Vocal verse B^2	Fmin	Moderate tempo. Climactic arr. for Smith/chorus.
14:57	231	Vocal chorus^4	F	"Got de St. Louis Blues . . ."

This document describes the finale's form as follows: "Act III, 4. Moving Day: Intro 1, 4, Last ending 4/4. Hanging round door 1 ch Eb, 1 ch. of Honey Bb, 1 ch. Happen to me D stop. Intro, Boston 1 chs. Break stop."[39] Johnson's notes on "Hanging round door," "Honey," "Happen to me," and "Boston" are references to earlier *Sugar Hill* songs that are reprised in this finale. In each case, rather than performing a newly arranged version of that music for the finale, the musicians needed to turn to a previous chart to perform that music. Thus, as should be apparent from this outline, the finale was arranged largely in the manner of a medley overture, though this ensemble finale also included vocal and choral elements that are now missing. These added vocal textures can clearly enhance the "spectacular" and "elevated" qualities of this sort of extended arrangement. Though it seems far more mundane than the formal structure of *St. Louis Blues*, this sort of multitune, medley arrangement conforms to many of the production ideals that were noted by Lange and Bennett, including regularly shifting contrasts in musical textures, stylistic treatments, mood, and key. This extended number also likely involved vocal solos, duets, choral ensembles, and a range of musical episodes from tender ballads to up-tempo, big-band-styled orchestrations.

TABLE 3.2.　Formal outline of the "Moving Day" finale to James P. Johnson's *Sugar Hill* (1931)

M.	Section	Length	Key
1	Intro./Vamp	2	D♭
3	"Moving Day" (Verse) (aab^{1}b^2)	16	
19	"Moving Day" (Chorus^1) (a^{1}a^{2}ba^3)	32	
51	"Moving Day" (Chorus^2)	32	
83	"Moving Day" (Chorus^3)	32	
115	"Moving Day" (Ensemble chorus^4)	32	E♭
147	"Moving Day" (Ensemble chorus^5)	32	
179	"Moving Day" (Ensemble chorus^6)	32	
206	"Moving Day" (Instrumental chorus^7)	32	
238	"Hanging Around Your Door" Reprise (chorus^1) (a^{1}a^{2}ba^3)	32	E♭
270	"Hanging Around Your Door" Reprise (chorus^2)	32	
302	"Hanging Around Your Door" Reprise (chorus^3)	32	
334	"Yes, I Love You, Honey" Reprise (chorus^1) (a^{1}ba^{2}c)	32	B♭
366	"Yes, I Love You, Honey" Reprise (chorus^2)	32	
398	"Something's Going to Happen to Me and You" Reprise (chorus^1) (a^{1}a^{2}ba^3)	32	
430	"Something's Going to Happen to Me and You" Reprise (chorus^2) *break?*	32	
462	Intro. "Boston"	4	F
466	"Boston" Reprise (chorus) (a^{1}a^{2}ba^3)	32	
498	"Break stop"/Coda?	10	

The production numbers of the Cotton Club floor shows pose somewhat different problems for study than Johnson's stage scores. The Ellington orchestra's exact contributions and the actual music the band performed in the Cotton Club revues are subjects that have been oddly overlooked in the critical commentary on the bandleader's pivotal years at this establishment. While Ellington recorded commercial versions of many individual numbers from Cotton Club revues, the great majority have no pretense of replicating exact arrangements and performances from the shows. Very few of the vocal recordings include the singer from the revue the number originated in, and none involve the choral arrangements that were used in special numbers like grand finales. Moreover, these commercial 78 rpm recordings include at most only four and a half minutes of music, less than a bare minimum for a closing production number. Thus, while certain specialty dance numbers in these revues could have been performed with the commercially recorded arrangements as their backing music, the extended opening and closing arrangements of the type that Reed discussed are not accurately represented in Ellington's commercially recorded output. Similarly, the band's extant recorded broadcasts do not document actual floor show performances but rather band features.[40] It is clear that these broadcasts present the latter part of an evening's entertainment, when the Cotton Club bands provided music for dancing rather than broadcasting live floor show performances.

The extant manuscripts for the "Swanee River Rhapsody" finale to *The Blackberries of 1930* revue represent the frustrating problems of determining the formal principles employed in the Cotton Club production numbers. Ellington wrote both the songs and arrangements for this show. For this number, there exists published piano-vocal sheet music of the basic song and a four-page sketch (short score) manuscript. The manuscript contains only very limited details of the arrangement. It is written in three-stave stave groupings that outline ideas for a sixteen-bar verse, a thirty-two-bar vocal chorus (to be repeated), and ideas for two instrumental choruses. There is a key change from C major to F major in the second instrumental chorus. Each section indicates unadorned melody and bass lines that deviate little from the sheet music. Both documents also include the novelty juxtaposition of Ellington's chorus melody and Stephen Foster's

"Swanee River." The content of the compositional sketch ranges widely from two to five voices. The only instrumentation specifics are in the reed section indications of the instrumental choruses, which shift Foster's melody to the forefront. If performed as written in the manuscript, the arrangement would run under three minutes. Such materials clearly do not reflect the "rhapsodic" character of the number, the "mélange of melody" described by the show's program, or even the likely minimum length of a grand finale to a fast-paced, ten-act, seventy-five-minute revue. This number would have to have been at least seven to eight minutes in length if all acts were of equal length. Such a balance between acts would have been quite unusual, however, so a finale would likely have been several minutes longer than most of the acts. In sum, the show's performance of "Swanee River Rhapsody" was likely eight to twelve minutes in length. These sketch materials show no indication of how Ellington chose to do this. Although we lack evidence of its "rhapsodic" arrangement, "Swanee River Rhapsody" was clearly part of a significant trend in "jazz rhapsody" production numbers in Harlem stage and floor show entertainments of the 1920s and early 1930s. Ellington's and Johnson's stage and nightclub work involved numerous examples of this trend.[41]

𝄢 THE PRODUCTION-STYLE CONCERT WORKS OF ELLINGTON AND JOHNSON

For both Ellington and James P. Johnson, the formal, cultural, aesthetic leaps from production number models to concert jazz compositions were surprisingly small. A prime illustration of this latter mode of compositional thinking can be seen in Johnson's manuscripts for his *Mississippi Moan: Symphonic Poem*, a cantata-like concert work that Johnson likely composed in the late 1930s. It exists in two manuscripts. The first is a collage-like, sixteen-page score that involves clipped-and-pasted excerpts from commercially published piano-vocal sheet music mixed with new musical material and pasted-on music paper staves that place newly edited (or additional) music over the borrowed sheet music. The second manuscript is an incomplete, fifty-six-page, 338-bar orchestration of the work. This score expands the collage manuscript through repetitions of certain passages and through limited insertions of new music. This full score is written for a large theater-type ensemble consisting of piccolo, flutes, oboes, English horn, clarinets (three), bass clarinet, bassoons, a saxophone section (alto, alto, tenor, baritone), French horns (four), trumpets (three), trombones (two tenors and a bass), tuba, a drum set, timpani, guitar, harp, a choir (SATB), a standard string section, bass, and piano.

Figure 3.3 shows two typical pages from the collage manuscript. The source of the original score is a 1928 folio, *Dixieland Echoes: A Collection of Five Descriptive Negro Songs*, "composed and edited by Perry Bradford and James P. Johnson," and published by Perry Bradford Inc. *Mississippi Moan* adapts the songs "Echoes of Ole Dixieland" (as the tone poem's "Prologue") and "Mississippi River Flood" from this folio. The foreword to the folio provides descriptive copy about each of the songs. For "Echoes," Bradford and Johnson note: "We picture a log cabin scene in Alabama, with fathers, Mothers, Sons and daughters after their evening meal at sundown." The authors describe "Mississippi" as "A Negro Musical Poem, of the [1927] Mississippi River Flood, with style descriptive." The subsequent title of the concert work is reflected in two popular songs that were contemporary with this folio. The first is a 1926–27 song, "Muddy Water: A Mississippi Moan," with music by the white composers Peter De Rose and Harry Richman, and lyrics by Jo Trent (an African American who was an early songwriting partner to Ellington).[42] The second precedent or parallel is Ellington's own instrumental, "Mississippi Moan" (Irving Mills also receives writing credit), recorded in April 1929.[43] This said, Johnson and Bradford included a "Mississippi Moan" segment in the first act grand finale to their 1929 stage revue, *Messin' Around*. The same show even featured Johnson performing his *Yamekraw (Piano Symphony)*, as it was billed, as a piano solo in the extended final number of the show, "Harlem's Midnight Frolic." According to the show's program, the three-part, first-act finale, titled "Mississippi," began with a "Roustabouts (Song)" segment for four soloists, choir, and chorus girls and boys (dancers and singers). The second episode, "Mississippi Moan," was staged for a male soloist and the "entire company," as was the last segment, "Mississippi (Song)."[44] (Bradford claimed elsewhere that this "Roustabouts" song was related to a theme in Johnson's *Yamekraw: A Negro Rhapsody*.)[45]

The "Mississippi River Flood" in the song folio has an extended

Fig. 3.3. Pages 8–9 from James P. Johnson's collage-like short score to *Mississippi Moan* (ca. 1930s). (Courtesy of the James P. Johnson Foundation.)

dramatic narrative built into its song lyrics. The song also displays lengthy programmatic instrumental passages that depict the storm and its approach, and there are numerous shifts in musical tempo and texture—and even spoken passages—in the score. This "descriptive," eight-page piano-vocal score was ready-made for the staged production number that gave the symphonic poem its name. The connection between the song and the production number is circumstantially affirmed in one reviewer's observation that "the lyrics [of the show] have a way of rhyming 'Mississippi' with 'have pity,'" a couplet that occurs in the middle of "Mississippi River Flood."[46] Most of the reviewers panned the show for its formulaic content and lack of decent comedic material. As one reviewer noted, the show "messes around with all the stock ingredients of negro musical revues and produces fair entertainment" through its "almost continuous clogging, black-bottoming, Charlestoning, blues-sobbing and spiritual singing."[47] Most reviewers commented favorably, however, on what one critic called the show's "Broadwayized spirituals" and "broadly burlesqued camp meeting song[s]."[48] By contrast, it appears that the "Mississippi" production number prompted only lukewarm interest. One critic noted that "a pretentious number called 'Mississippi' failed to hit its mark."[49] Another noted that "the 'Mississippi Moan,' with the familiar hands over head, bending forward and backward gestures, shows that the big 'Porgy' funeral scene should not go on forever." This latter comment is a reference to the many black entertainment recyclings from the hit 1927–28 production of DuBose Heyward's play, *Porgy*, which also tapped into the period's spiritual vogue in its aforementioned scene.[50] In both his *Mississippi Moan: Symphonic Poem* and the "Mississippi" stage number, Johnson created extended dramatic and programmatic collages of contemporary musical and programmatic narrative topics—or rather "stock ingredients"—from contemporary all-black stage productions.

Another concert work with a similar stage/entertainment pedigree is Johnson's 1942 orchestral *Drums: Symphonic Poem*, premiered at a special event billed as the "First Concert of Symphonic Works by James P. Johnson."[51] The program notes that this work was based on a "poem by Andy Razaf," a detail that cryptically points to the obscured origins of this composition. There are several extant scores that reveal much about the history of the work prior to its 1942 premiere. One of these items is an undated, three-page song manuscript titled "Can't You Hear Those Drums?" Though the score notes "music by James P. Johnson" and "lyric by Langston Hughes," no lyrics are included. Nevertheless, the two-stave music clearly marks off a piano accompaniment and melody to a song with a sixteen-bar verse, a thirty-two-bar chorus, and a thirty-two-bar patter strain marked "Chant." (See example 3.3a–c.) A separate lyrics sheet for this Hughes-Johnson song also exists, but it bears the title "Those Jungle Drums." The chorus begins, "In my heart beats the jungle drums. To their rhythm the jungle hums. By moonlight in the sweet night, [c]an't you hear the drums?"[52]

The next step in the transformation of the song into a concert work seems to have been a thirty-one-page short score on three-stave systems. This short score is dated "11/16/42" in Johnson's hand, and titled *Jungle Drums: Can't You Hear Those Drums*. This manuscript turns the original Hughes-Johnson song into a 485-measure instrumental composition. The form of the work is outlined in table 3.3. While the vocals and lyrics have been excised from the composition, the score reveals a design that seems a cross between the compositional approach of *Mississippi Moan* and production number arranging. Johnson builds his composition through artfully paced instrumental variations of the three song strains, with occasional strain extensions, and motivically related bridging interludes. He expands these basic materials by adding a driving, percussion-based introduction, and by devising a fourth strain (from a variation on the chorus) that he actually introduces as the first theme of the work (labeled "Pre-chorus"; example 3.3d and table 3.3). Like *Mississippi Moan*, *Drums* adapts an earlier Harlem floor show–type song, and his full score is also notably marked with such stage-related annotations such as "Dance," "Dance A," "Verse," "Chorus," and so on (all marked in bold on table 3.3).

Other extant archival materials[53] reveal that Johnson wrote the original song for the 1932–33 Connie's Inn show, *Harlem Hotcha*, which featured songs by Johnson and Razaf, music performed by Don Redman and His Connie's Inn Orchestra, and a cast that notably starred Earl "Snakehips" Tucker and Bessie Dudley, both of whom starred two years later in *Symphony in Black*. Like *Messin' Around*, this nightclub revue, *Harlem Hotcha*, featured its own fair share of "stock ingredients of negro musical revues." Unfortunately, there are no extant manuscript score materials from this show. One reviewer noted,

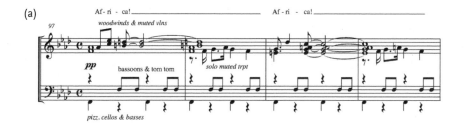

Example 3.3.   Themes from James P. Johnson's *Drums: A Symphonic Poem* (1942).
(Used by permission of the James P. Johnson Foundation.)

(a) Verse Strain theme

(b) Chorus Strain theme

(c) Chant Strain (Patter) theme

(d) Pre-chorus Strain orchestral theme

TABLE 3.3.   Formal outline of James P. Johnson's *Drums: A Symphonic Poem* (1942); timings from the Concordia Orchestra performance (1994)

Time	M.	Section	Length	Key	Texture
0:00	1	**"Dance"**/Intro. (a) + (b)	16 + 16	Fmin	Timpani intro. m. 16ff. new patterns with occasional brass stingers
0:44	33	**"Dance A"**/Pre-chorus $(a^1a^1b^1a^1b^2b^2a^2a^3)$	32	Fmin	Based on Chorus 1 (a) phrase but transformed into a stride-style strain
1:19	65	Prechorus^{var} $(a^4a^5ca^6)$	32	Fmin	Prechorus (a) is doubly augmented. (c) replaces (b).
1:52	97	**"Song"** Verse (abac)	16	Fmin	
2:15	113	**Chorus** (aaba)	32	Fmin	(b) phrase emphasizes Charleston rhythm.
2:51	145	**"Brass Coda"** $(a^{6var1} + a^{6var2})$	16	Fmin	Based on harmonies of (a^6) in Pre-chorus^{var}. Percussion recalls mm. 1–8 and 17–24.
3:13	161	**"Tom Tom Solo"**	16	Fmin	New percussion material
3:33	177	**"Dance D"**/Chant $(a^1a^2ba^3)$	32	Fmin	Patter strain. "Chant" (a) phrase involves a variation on the Chorus (a) phrase.
4:05	209	Interlude 1a	8	Fmin	Mm. 209–16 based on mm. 81–88 = Pre-chorus^{var} (c).
4:11	217	Interlude 1b	8	Fmin	Mm. 217–24 involve a 4-bar Verse motive and sequence.
4:22	225	Interlude 1c	8	Fmin	Mm. 225–32 involve a Chorus (b) phrase var. and a varied repeat.
4:33	233	Chant 2 $(a^1a^2ba^3 + a^{3var})$	32 + 4	Fmin	Mm. 265–68 involve a strain extension through a varied repeat of mm. 261–64.
5:07	269	Chant^{var} interlude	32	Fmin	Flute and tom tom interlude built as a variation on Chant materials
5:42	301	Chant 3 (a^1a^2)	16	Fmin	Incomplete statement
5:57	317	Interlude 2a	8	mod.	Mm. 317–24 built on mm. 209–16 and 81–88 = Pre-chorus^{var} (c).
6:04	325	Interlude 2b	16	mod.	Mm. 325–40 = vars. on Verse. Modulates B♭min to Fmin to Cmin.
6:26	333	Pre-chorus^{var} $(a^7a^8ca^9)$	16	Cmin	
6:43	357	Interlude 3	8	mod.	Modulating interlude based on Chant materials
6:51	365	Chorus 2 (aa)	16	Gmin	Half of Chorus strain
7:09	381	Interlude 4	8 + 6	mod.	Mm. 381–88 built on Prechorus^{var} (c). Mm. 389–404 based on 4-bar sequences.
7:37	405	Chant 4 $(a^1a^2$ + extension)	16 + 4	Gmin	Mm. 421–24 extend Chant through two held chords.
7:56	425	Interlude 5 (Intro Recap)	16	Fmin	2/2, recalls mm. 1–8 and 17–24. Sense of recapitulation.
8:16	441	Pre-chorus Recap (aaba)	16	Fmin	Includes a lengthy extension built on motivic sequences
8:52	473	Coda	8	Fmin	Recalls Intro. and includes a ref. to Pre-chorus phrase (a)

however, that "Louise Cook [offered] in 'Drums!' a barbaric African conception." She was said to be "very tom-tom, with Willie Jackson doing the 'Black Captive' stuff." (By "tom-tom," the critic is referring to the aforementioned African and "jungle" program tropes in Harlem entertainment.) This reviewer also explains that Cook was "the tossing torso who's been a panic at Connie's for several seasons now with her torrid" dancing.[54] From this evidence, it seems that this number featured up-tempo frenetic dancing and a narrative conceit borrowed directly from the Cotton Club's famous "dark Africa" routines that were backed by Ellington's "jungle music."[55]

Though the jazz historian Marshall Stearns was likely right that "the citizens of Harlem neither knew nor cared about any jungle," and that "they didn't identify themselves with Africa,"[56] Johnson, Ellington, and their peers regularly reemployed this sort of Harlemized African/jungle program in artistic projects that celebrated the sophistication and racial heritage of modern African Americans, and particularly Harlemites. A similar scenario forms the basis for the first scene of Cook's *Negro Nuances*, for example. Likewise, the extant scripts and poems for Ellington's opera *Boola*—which became the basis of the program for *Black, Brown and Beige*—include an extended opening section set in Africa with obligatory references to "jungle drums." Though the later concert work dropped the African roots of this story, this programmatic connection to musical theater cannot be overemphasized.[57] There is also a small possibility that the germinal idea for the opera *Boola* may have come directly from Harlem musical revues, as can be seen in the program to a minor, early to middle 1930s cabaret show called the *Plantation Revue*—a production that notably included an African-themed number (with "native maidens") based on Donald Heywood's tune "Boola."[58] Regardless, all of these connections between the variety-derived, formulaic programmatic and musical topics from Harlem entertainment's concert works underscore the importance of these conceptual building blocks to the compositional thinking and cultural concerns of Johnson, Ellington, and their peers.

The fundamental purpose of the aforementioned Africa-Dixie-Harlem program model of interwar entertainment was to glorify or celebrate modern Harlem as the glamorous apotheosis of the rich diversity of black musical culture. In many realizations of this theatrical narrative, the roles of the Africa and Dixie musico-geographic topics were entirely secondary to the Harlem theme. In practice, one or both of these topics could be deleted altogether to provide greater focus on the diverse genres of black music that were manifest in contemporary Harlem alone. The theater historian Allen Woll has similarly commented on the predominant modern show-business perspective that was applied to the historical/musico-geographic program topics of Africa and Dixie. For example, in his discussion of Lew Leslie's all-black productions, Woll notes that in these revues "'Broadway' often dominated 'Dixie.'"[59] Woll also suggests that as the all-black Broadway productions evolved over the 1920s, they began to present "a modern New Negro, the new vision of the Harlem Renaissance."[60] I suggest that this "new vision" specifically represents the quintessentially modern, urban vernacular aesthetics of the Harlem entertainment renaissance. This reading reinforces the composer-pianist Eubie Blake's firm assertion that "music and entertainment" *was* the Harlem Renaissance.[61] This latter personal perspective underscores the fundamental meanings behind the Africa-Dixie-Harlem tropes in this community's creative efforts in musical theater, nightclub revues, and concert jazz. This said, because of the Great Migration, contemporary urban Harlem represented *all* the varied cultural tributaries for African American heritage, and thus this community was positioned as the figurative melting pot of black America. Such sophisticated, musico-theatrical celebrations of Harlem's near-mythical role as the cultural apex of modern African American life were thereby employed as a key strategy among black entertainment efforts at racial uplift. This dual celebration of black America's musical heritage and the glamour of modern (1920s) Harlem entertainment were Will Marion Cook's central legacy in the concert works of his most celebrated protégés, Ellington and Johnson.

While it may never have been performed as a concert work in the manner of *Black, Brown and Beige*, Ellington's score to *Symphony in Black* has been received nonetheless by critics as a de facto concert work akin to that later effort. In fact, this "extended composition" is best viewed as a bridge between, on one hand, the aesthetic and cultural interests of 1920s Harlem revues, and, on the other, Ellington's concert works of the 1940s, many of which took similar multimovement, suite-based designs, and nearly all of which programmatically celebrated the rich spectrum of "Negro nuances" in modern black culture. This intersection of entertainment and art fully defines the intent of *Symphony in Black*.

The film's general concept was most likely the work of the film's director and producer, Fred Waller, and its "continuity" writers, Milton Hocky and Fred Rath. Beyond the film's narrative design, one unusual conceit of this production is its avoidance of spoken dialogue in favor of pantomime acting and dancing. While Ellington receives only a compositional credit in the film's main titles, at least one interview of the day suggests that he did provide some input on the film's narrative. The implication is that while Ellington contributed to the development of this scenario, this production—like most all films—was a collaborative and commercial project for mass entertainment.

Like Johnson's *Drums*, Ellington's score for *Symphony in Black* closely adheres to the production number model, as can be seen in table 3.4. The film opens with a two-part establishing scene that juxtaposes Ellington composing in his "music studio" and shots of Ellington and his orchestra presenting the work's premiere performance. These paired events function as bridging devices that connect the disparate "movements" of the filmic "symphony." The short's visual narrative is subsequently built from intermingled sequences that consecutively present Ellington composing in his attic atelier, the work's premiere performance, various intertitle cards—presented as Ellington's music manuscript pages—that signal episode titles, and evocatively staged depictions of the programmatic themes that supposedly inspired each musical episode. After the introduction, the film presents the four-part "Rhapsody of Negro Life."

The main titles and introductory scene are suitably underscored with self-consciously "rhapsodic" concert-style musical gestures built from fanfare-like rising solo trumpet figures, homophonic brass and reed responsorial phrases, and "symphonic" timpani rolls. (See example 3.4.) Later in the film, this music returns in the "Jealousy" segment of "Part Two." The establishing shot pans in on the door to the "Duke Ellington Studio," where a letter is dropped into the mail slot. A new introductory musical passage is synchronized to dramatically underscore a close-up zoom on the text of the letter: "Just a reminder that the world premiere of your new symphony of Negro Moods takes place two weeks from today."

The first episode begins in earnest with Ellington performing the

TABLE 3.4. Formal outline of Duke Ellington's score to *Symphony in Black* (Paramount, 1935)

Time	M.	Section	Key	Texture	Image Narrative
0:00	1	**Intro.** ("Jealousy") ($a^1a^2a^2b^1$) + repeat	mod.	Fast. "Straight" fanfare trpt. + brass, reeds, tymp.	Main titles
0:30	34	*Transition*	mod.	4/4. "Swing" show band style.	Intertitles about symphony
0:55	49	*Piano prelude*	C/Amin	Rubato solo piano	Ellington composing
1:12	57	**(1) The Laborers** ($a^1ba^2a^3$)	Amin	Slow. Work-song. Alto + trbn. solos.	Concert to laborers
2:34	89	**(2) A Triangle.** Piano vamp.	A♭	Medium swing. Solo piano vamp.	
2:40	93	"Dance" ($a^1a^2ba^3$ + tag)	A♭	(a^1) solo trbn.; (a^2) plunger trpt. solo; (b) reed soli; (a^3) sax soli.	Ellington concert to couple dancing to radio in Harlem
3:33	127	"Jealousy" ($a^1a^2a^2b^1$)	mod.	= mm. 17–39. Fast cut-time.	Couple encounters Holiday
3:57	152	*Piano cadenza*	mod.		Ellington composing
4:11	156	"Blues" (*clar. cadenza*)	B♭	Clar. *Rhapsody in Blue* cadenza.	Orchestra in concert
4:33	162	Chant	B♭	Fast to medium. Brass feature.	Holiday cast in the street
4:47	168	Blues chorus 1	B♭	Medium tempo. Trbn. solo.	Orchestra in concert
5:20	180	Blues chorus 2	B♭	Vocal with reeds	The "lost-my-man blues"
5:53	192	Chant (no vocal)	B♭	As at m. 162ff.	Orchestra in concert
6:19	202	*Solo piano introduction*	mod.	Solo piano	Ellington composing
6:26	204	**(3) A Hymn of Sorrow** ($a^1a^2a^1b^1b^2a^1b^3$)	F	Slow 2/2. Sec. a = preacher (muted trpt. solo). Sec. b = choir (reeds).	Orchestra concert to black congregation mourning
8:00	232	*Solo piano transition + intro.*	mod.	4/4, up-tempo, stride piano intro.	Ellington composing
8:10	240	**(4) Harlem Rhythm** Blues chorus 1	D♭	Swinging trpt. solo with sustained reeds	Concert to Harlem montage
8:22	252	Blues chorus 2	D♭	Reed ensemble with brass responses	
8:36	262	Blues chorus 3	D♭	Trbn. ensemble with rhythm	
8:49	272	Blues chorus 4	D♭	Shout chorus call and response (trps./reeds)	
9:02	284	Extension and tag	D♭	Tutti	Orchestra concert + credits

introductory solo piano part underneath an iris shot of the title of the manuscript he is supposedly working on: "Symphony in Black, Part One, The Laborers." The Ellington band then begins an original theme inspired by African American work songs. The number fea-

Example 3.4.   Introduction/"Jealousy" theme from Duke Ellington's score to *Symphony in Black* (Paramount, 1935)

tures a call-and-response texture between the wailing alto saxophone of Johnny Hodges and the "laboring" responses of the trombones and timpani. The sequence presents a greatly expanded Ellington "concert" orchestra set on semicircular risers with the pianist-composer conducting from a grand piano. The band is in full formal dress and has been augmented from a fourteen-member dance band to the more "symphonic" proportions of a twenty-four-man orchestra, even though only the smaller orchestra is heard on the soundtrack.[62] As the soundtrack presents a contrasting bridge theme for solo trombone and reed backing, there is a dissolve to artful, shadowed images of muscled African American men shoveling coal into a furnace. After a quick cut back to the orchestra, there is yet another "labor" scene of black workers bearing heavy loads in a factory.

"Part Two, A Triangle," presents a new, tripartite episode. The first segment, "Dance," features an up-tempo reworking of Ellington's 1932 "Ducky Wucky," which is used here to underscore a joyful, private dance between a couple in a Harlem apartment. The couple is played by Bessie Dudley and Earl "Snakehips" Tucker, a dance team that had been Cotton Club performers and was also part of Ellington's 1935 stage revues.[63] Shots of the couple are interleaved with shots of the spurned woman—played by a young Billie Holiday—down in the street below the elevated train. Holiday looks up at the dancing shadows in the window of the apartment. As the couple leaves the apartment, the score returns to the introduction's fanfare theme, now introduced (by intertitle card) as "Jealousy." There is a street confrontation, and the spurned lover is cast brutally to the ground. After a cut to Ellington playing prelude-type piano figurations in his music studio, an intertitle card introduces the next segment, entitled "Blues." This card is followed by a "concert" shot of the Ellington orchestra and Barney Bigard, who provides a solo clarinet introduction replete with a *Rhapsody in Blue*–style glissando. The subsequent "Blues" number is a reworking of Ellington's "The Saddest Tale" of 1934, recast here as a vocal feature for Holiday, who moans, "I've got those lost-my-man, can't-get-him-back-again blues."

In a December 1935 article, Ellington discussed his vision for the "Part Three, Hymn of Sorrow" episode. The movement was said to depict "the death of a baby." In the film, there are images of a sorrowful congregation and a white-haired African American minister with a small, child-sized coffin at his feet. Ellington saw this scene and the accompanying "dirge" (which is not quite a spiritual, but close) as "true to and of the life of the people it depicted." Ellington also remarked that this episode was meant to be "the high [point of the film] and should have come last, but that would not have been commercial, as the managers say."[64] True to form, for this "commercial" grand finale ("Part Four"), the film features an up-tempo, dance-oriented "Harlem Rhythm" episode that revels in exotic nightclub imagery associated with Ellington's Cotton Club performances. This hot jazz grand finale features superimposed shots of Tucker's famous sexually charged, "snakehips" dance routine, a line of Cotton Club–style chorus girls, and shots of black nightclub patrons. Despite such "commercial" considerations, when Ellington described part 3 of the *Symphony* as "true to the people it depicted," he could have been referring to the larger collection of Harlem vignettes that he sought to incorporate in this score, as many of these clichéd Harlem entertainment topics are presented in a newly respectful and "serious" light by the film's director. In a similar manner, the film score presents common production number arranging conventions in a newly respectful, serious light, as it self-consciously evokes various textures, musical qualities, and gestures from both Harlem entertainment and traditional concert music.

𝄢 BLACK SYMPHONIC JAZZ AND AFROLOGICAL VERNACULAR MODERNISM

Johnson's and Ellington's concert works of the 1930s and 1940s were closely aligned with Cook's vision for a new black concert music built from the music of Jazz Age Harlem. The cultural ambitions of Cook were based on the transformation of the musical and programmatic matter of Harlem entertainment into something that could express racial pride. In the interwar era, this musico-cultural elevation had to occur under the veneer of symphonic culture—a project that in the 1920s was intimately tied to the idea of symphonic jazz. Johnson's and Ellington's concert works were largely constructed as extensions of Harlem entertainment musical idioms. Though transposed to the medium of instrumental music, these concert works reclaimed a racially positive reading of their underlying programmatic sources in Harlem's theatrical entertainments.

In a recent article, the jazz scholar Jeffrey Magee articulates how Miles Davis's lifelong interest in the blues was part of a larger field of "Afrological" and "vernacular modernist" trends in mid-twentieth-century African American creative traditions. While these two specific terms are derived from the writings of George Lewis and Miriam Hansen, respectively, Magee's interpretation of Davis's "Afrological vernacular modernism" is primarily built on Guthrie P. Ramsey's conception of "Afro-modernism," an artistic aesthetic that was manifest "in efforts to blend or juxtapose the earthy and the urbane, the down-home and the cosmopolitan, the simple and the sophisticated."[65] Ramsey identifies the spiritual heart of Afro-modernism in "North-South cultural dialogues" within African American communities, a phenomenon that was specifically manifest through "the flow of black migrants to urban commercial centers." This trend "supplied northern cultural spaces with 'southernisms' that constantly interacted with urban modernity and with European and American cultural practices."[66] Building on earlier work by Samuel Floyd, Houston Baker, and others, Ramsey largely situates the Afro-modernist moment in the postwar 1940s, but he underscores significant connections between this later cultural moment and the creative boom of 1920s Harlem, which he describes as an important "symbol of black urbanity, [and] black modernity."[67] This is the very perspective that defined the racial uplift strategies of both Harlem entertainment and Ellington's and Johnson's concert jazz. Both Ramsey and Magee find the "chief musical conduit of Afro-modernism" to be the influence of the blues.[68] More specifically, Ramsey finds an aesthetic centrality in the practice of "bluesing," a concept that he builds from Samuel Floyd's description of the broader historical continuum of adaptations of blues conventions—

melodically, harmonically, and lyrically—in African American popular music from its roots in Africa to modern "genres like country blues, urban blues, gospel, jazz, R&B, and even the classical music of black composers."[69] Again, for the Harlem entertainment circle, the practice of "blues-ing" represented not a universal folk idiom promoted by New Negro conservatives, but rather a quintessential musical "symbol of black urbanity and black modernity" due to the relation of this fundamental African American musical aesthetic to contemporary jazz.

Johnson's and Ellington's compositional interests in concert works based on black, urban vernacular music markedly increased during the 1930s and into the early 1940s. In 1942–43, both artists were featured in breakthrough performances of these works in symbolically important venues such as Carnegie Hall and Town Hall in New York. Though quite different from the Afro-modernist agenda of the postwar 1940s bebop community that Ramsey has examined, the production-style concert jazz compositions discussed in this chapter offer quintessential examples of the cross-cultural syncretism that defined midcentury Afro-modernist musical aesthetics. The impulse to "blend or juxtapose the earthy and the urbane, the down-home and the cosmopolitan" can be found at every level of the intellectual processes that created these works. Moreover, these compositions were inherently built to bridge—and revel in the juxtaposition of—"the simple and the sophisticated," whether at the level of down-home blues in glorified concert dress, or the act of taking Harlem nightclub entertainment into a venerated concert hall. In their recurrent Africa-Dixie-Harlem programs and mixed musical topics, the compositions mentioned here and other works in this same vein by Johnson and Ellington fully embody North-South African American cultural dialogues, and richly embed such matters within larger American discourses of class status (high, middle, low) and race (spanning black, brown, beige, and white). The Afrological vernacular modernism of these works demands that interpreters locate artistic meaning and value in these rich, cross-cultural exchanges and in their Afro-modernist blues-ing of music for the concert hall.

four 𝄢 ELLINGTONIAN EXTENDED COMPOSITION
AND THE SYMPHONIC JAZZ MODEL

*A*cross the late 1920s to early 1940s, despite Paul Whiteman's continued popularity as a bandleader, there was a new critical desire to redefine the concert work tradition of symphonic jazz through the aesthetics of African American–style hot jazz. The origins of this shift are found in the development of the unique public image of Duke Ellington, the "serious jazz composer." This image was linked to both the agenda of Ellington's own publicity machine and his more sophisticated compositions of the late 1920s and 1930s. This development culminated in the publicity and criticism for Ellington's landmark of 1943, *Black, Brown and Beige*, a "Tone Parallel to the History of the Negro in America."

In his 1993 essay "The Genesis of *Black, Brown and Beige*," Mark Tucker explored the models and antecedents that Ellington drew upon to conceptualize and compose his "Tone Parallel."[1] Tucker concluded by proposing several avenues of further research. First and foremost, he suggested the need to examine Ellington's composition against the backdrop of earlier "large-scale jazz works designed for the concert hall," especially the concert-style works promoted by Paul Whiteman. I contend that the design of *Black, Brown and Beige* (or *BB&B*) does in fact represent the apotheosis of Ellington's unique adaptations of—and expansions on—the model of Whitemanesque symphonic jazz.

The relationship between Whitemanesque and Ellingtonian symphonic jazz is tied to questions of both cultural reception and structural design. This relationship is evidenced in Ellington's concert-style works of the 1930s and early 1940s, up to and including *BB&B*. Ellington developed his compositional models for *BB&B* in the 1930s, a period when such efforts were received as part of a greater sphere of Whiteman-style symphonic jazz activities. The form of *BB&B* rises above the "elaborate recipes for giving a jazz tune extended form" that 1930s jazz critics like Winthrop Sargeant had contemptuously identified with Whitemanesque symphonic jazz.[2] *BB&B* also reveals Ellington's emerging interest in extended, multimovement suites. His expansions on the symphonic jazz idiom are found at multiple structural levels in *BB&B*—in the large-scale arranging routines of its various episodic segments, in the construction and function of its various "developmental" interludes, in the unusual structures of its themes, in its rich network of motivic cross-references, and so forth. It is important to identify the ways in which this work expands upon the characteristic "recipes" of symphonic jazz form. These relations are revealed through comparisons between the compositional design of *BB&B* and the concert jazz models that came before it, both by Ellington and his peers. This chapter examines the relationship between Ellingtonian "extended" composition and the symphonic jazz model through a study of the compositional devices and forms employed in Ellington's concert-style works up to and including *BB&B*.

𝄵 JAZZ POLITICS AND THE WHITEMAN-ELLINGTON CONNECTION

The jazz world still harbors deep concerns about the public's understanding of Whiteman's music. Nowadays, this reaction is less likely to result from a negative aesthetic assessment of Whiteman's music than from a protective reaction deeply rooted in concerns about policing the boundaries of the jazz canon. The divisive argument about whether or not Whiteman's music can rightfully be called jazz has a long history that is bound up in the ideological politics of jazz criticism, musical style, and race, and dates back to the 1925 essay "Jazz

Contra Whiteman" by the American critic Roger Pryor Dodge.[3] While Whiteman's legacy has undergone a small degree of reassessment over the last several years, the bandleader remains almost a taboo subject among jazz proponents. This said, even some modern-day critics are less concerned with proper assessments of Whiteman's legacy than with demarcating a firm division between canonic jazz figures and popular music.[4] This bifurcated view of American culture as consisting of either "art" (i.e., the bona fide jazz tradition) or "entertainment" does not take into consideration the hybrid nuances that can exist between high and low cultures. These concerns over policing the canonic boundaries of jazz are shaped by essentialist views of the jazz tradition and its relation to race and artistic creativity. Such perspectives do not often acknowledge the many pluralistic gray areas in American culture, identity politics, and racial interchange. Whiteman's career is an exemplary model of the hybrid middlebrow culture that overlapped with the first half century of the jazz tradition. The social and aesthetic complexities of this pluralistic commercial middle ground are far more interesting than the dated question of whether Whiteman is or is not part of the jazz tradition.

In any consideration of the broad range of popular music discussed in 1920s "jazz" criticism, one must bear in mind that the primary attributes that post-1930 jazz critics considered essential to "true" or "hot" jazz (improvisation, the blues, swing, race, etc.) were not nearly as commonplace or prominently featured in syncopated popular music until the later 1920s. Even at that point, despite the sweet-versus-hot distinction having come into circulation, "authentic" jazz was lumped together critically and popularly with the music of sweet dance bands, hotel bands, and symphonic jazz. The divisions between these stylistic idioms were clean-cut only in theory and in individual recordings. In practice, popular music of this era encouraged stylistic confluences. Moreover, many bona fide jazz musicians— white and black—pursued diverse careers as professional musicians for hire, regardless of the stylistic demands and performance context of a given job. This broad, variety entertainment–based musical culture of the 1920s was a major concern for post-1930 jazz critics who believed that the journalism of the 1920s was far too inclusive and confused about what constituted jazz and which elements in this novel music contributed to its infectious vitality.

In their quest to define a stylistically pure tradition, post-1930 jazz critics sought to divorce authentic jazz from the messy family of overlapping musical traditions that were called jazz in the 1920s. The musicologist Charles Hamm has rightly noted that the terminological confusion with the idea of jazz in the 1920s originated in part from the "questionable theoretical assumption . . . that 'jazz' was a product of white American culture in the 1920s and that it grew out of the New York–based Tin Pan Alley style of songwriting."[5] The white critics in the 1930s who sought a more exclusive definition of jazz were promoting stylistic and ethnic traits that they personally valued in improvisation-based, hot-style black jazz. This post-1930 need to construct a historical narrative of jazz authenticity required a firm delineation of stylistic boundaries. To achieve aesthetic priority, these critics—including Roger Pryor Dodge, Hughes Panassié, Frederic Ramsey Jr., and Charles Edward Smith—also sought to redefine authentic jazz as an art, with the music of Duke Ellington being central to this agenda. The critical project to reposition the public's perception of jazz from lowly commercial popular culture to an intellectual high art underscores the power of the myth of class mobility in American culture. The driving impetus behind this project was the belief that authentic jazz—and jazz musicians—should be afforded the same rarefied aura of high-culture prestige, status, and artistic entitlement that was tied to the classical music tradition. This class-based elevation of the style and performance aesthetics of black jazz (whether improvised or precomposed) was entwined with a simultaneous critical devaluation of the symphonic-style, arranged "jazz" of Whitemanesque entertainment. This development is the root of the critical fall of Whiteman from the jazz canon, as well as the dialectical opposition between Ellington and Whiteman as the respective signifiers for jazz and non-jazz stylistic poles.

In constructing the boundaries and narrative framework of an "authentic" jazz tradition, these critics were successful in demoting the privileged cultural authority of other syncopated popular music styles of the 1920s, especially symphonic jazz. A central ideological tool employed by this new critical school was the powerful dialectic that devalued "commercial" interests in favor of disinterested, creative "art" or "folk art" expressions (a romanticized notion of folk culture lay at the heart of much of this new criticism). This critical tool constructed a virtuous aura of artistic purity around black improvised instrumental jazz and simultaneously damned Whiteman and symphonic jazz. While this shift in the definition of jazz forged modern jazz historiography and ultimately elevated the improvised black jazz tradition to the privileged position of an art, it greatly narrowed our present-day understanding of the larger cultural context of the bona fide jazz tradition in the first half of the twentieth century.[6]

There is a great value in this narrower, present-day definition of the jazz tradition—one that I am not willing to jettison. However, this definition requires more nuance concerning the tradition's overlaps with popular culture, since throughout its history authentic jazz has by no means existed in an isolated cultural ghetto. To this end, Scott DeVeaux has made a useful distinction between the "core and boundaries" of the jazz tradition.[7] For many post-1930 jazz critics, Ellington was a key figure for defining the core jazz tradition, while Whiteman came to represent the "confused" (and thus dangerous) "boundaries" represented by the aforementioned popular culture "jazz" (jazz in quotes) that John Szwed has identified.

This chapter examines the compositional roots of Ellington's early extended works. Evidence suggests that part of Ellington's compositional development involved the adaptation, expansion, and ultimate transcendence of a formal model that was popular among his white arranger peers. The wholly American tensions of race, class, and cultural identity that unduly attach themselves to this observation create an unfortunate potential for misunderstanding. Not all the possible paths of influence in Ellington's compositional process can be adequately debated, supported, or refuted here. As Mark Tucker and others have revealed, Ellington drew upon a wealth of intellectual inspirations for creating the narrative program of *BB&B*.[8] In writing the *music* for *BB&B* and other concert-length works, he likely drew inspiration from an equally diverse number of sources. At the most concrete level, the compositional act can involve transparent adaptations of generic or individual formal models; but it can also be far more abstract, in which case there may be no real evidence of formal connections between a work and its inspiration. Beyond the formal evidence that Ellington might have adapted a generic formal model from the forgotten concert works of the Whiteman camp, there is also significant biographical evidence of Ellington-Whiteman connections. This evidence does not mean that Ellington did not draw more abstract compositional inspiration from African American peers—and friends—like James P. Johnson and William Grant Still. He very likely did to some level, but I have found few obvious signs of formal modeling, or even biographical evidence linking Ellington's extended jazz works to the concert works of these two individuals.

To say that Ellington's concert works have compositionally based connections to popular culture, or to white popular music, does not in any way diminish his cultural accomplishments or his authenticity as a jazz musician or black artist. In the early to middle twentieth century, the very idea of a "jazz" concert work already implied a mixture of art and entertainment (i.e., high and low culture) and black and white music. It should not come as a surprise, then, that a musician of Ellington's great talent might occasionally adapt formal models from contemporary arrangements and compositions—composers have always done this, regardless of their training (or lack thereof) or their professional or stylistic orientation.

As Ellington openly acknowledged, he and Whiteman had a long personal association. In his autobiography, Ellington stated:

> Paul Whiteman was known as the King of Jazz, and no one as yet has come near carrying that title with more certainty and dignity. . . .
>
> We knew him 'way back when we were at the Kentucky Club [1924–25] . . . Whiteman . . . very loudly proclaimed our musical merit. . . .
>
> In 1939 [sic; the concert occurred on December 25, 1938], Paul Whiteman organized . . . his most successful [Carnegie Hall] concert. He . . . chose several people . . . to write original compositions connected thematically . . . with bells. I was honored to be among them, and my work was *The Blue Belles of Harlem*.[9]

Another typical expression of Ellington's respect for Whiteman can be found in an interview that was published just after the Carnegie Hall concert of December 1938:

> Mr. Whiteman deserves credit for discovering and recognizing ability or genius in composers whose works would not normally be accepted in dance bands. Whiteman makes it possible to commer-

cialize these works. . . . [H]e has maintained a "higher level" for many years, and . . . there is no doubt but that he has carried jazz to the highest position it ever has enjoyed. He put it in the ears of the serious audience and they liked it. He is still Mr. Whiteman.[10]

Mark Tucker suggests that this latter interview displays Ellington's "familiar smiling mask of diplomacy" and that it was rare for Ellington to "air . . . negative opinions publicly."[11] Noting the context of this quotation (a *Down Beat* article concerning Ellington's views on contemporary bandleaders), Tucker contends that Ellington's concluding sentence ("He is still Mr. Whiteman") was just such an act of tactful, "ambiguous" diplomacy. This issue is more complex than Tucker suggests, in that Ellington's autobiography and various interviews (over many years' time) reveal a long-held respect and admiration for Whiteman's promotion of jazz-derived concert works. While there probably is some note of ambiguity in this quotation, there is also an element of genuine (if guarded) appreciation for Whiteman. Ellington seems to have viewed Whiteman as a unique bandleader set apart from his peers by the ambitious concert jazz projects that he was singularly associated with.

Ellington seemed quite appreciative of Whiteman's aforementioned efforts to encourage and promote the young composer's talents, as evidenced by essays under Ellington's name, his extant publicity materials, and numerous contemporary interviews. For many years, Ellington's promotional-management agencies were proud to advertise that Whiteman's orchestra had performed *Creole Rhapsody* at the presentation of Ellington's award for best American composition of 1932 (by the New York Schools of Music). Ellington's publicists likewise made good use of the fact that Whiteman conducted Ellington's *Mood Indigo* in a 1933 New York Philharmonic Symphony concert at the Lewisohn Stadium of the City College of New York. (The number was arranged by Whiteman's staff arranger, Carroll Huxley, with the Philharmonic augmented by Whiteman's musicians.)[12] In addition, as noted, Whiteman commissioned Ellington to write his *Blue Belles of Harlem* for the former bandleader's 1938 Carnegie concert. Lastly, in 1944–45, Ellington was invited to contribute a composition to Whiteman's new *Contemporary Composers Concert* radio series on the Blue Network (later the American Broadcasting Corporation).[13] This commission resulted in Ellington's *Blutopia*, a four-and-a-half-minute, concert-style work that was premiered by Whiteman's radio orchestra on November 21, 1944. This last project strongly suggests both Whiteman's continued commitment to Ellington's concert work efforts, and his favorable opinion of the extended compositions from Ellington's first two Carnegie Hall concerts.[14] (Ellington premiered a big band orchestration of this work at his December 19, 1944, Carnegie Hall concert.)

During this period, a number of other conductors in the Whiteman mold also invited Ellington to contribute concert works to various programs and projects. In 1941, for instance, the conductor and composer Meredith Willson commissioned "Music for Americans," a ten-part score series that included Ellington's *American Lullaby*. Willson premiered the composition series on his radio show, performed it as a suite with the Los Angeles Philharmonic at the Hollywood Bowl, and recorded the scores with his Whiteman-modeled, thirty-piece concert orchestra. These works were additionally issued as piano solos in the Whiteman-originated Modern American Music score series published by Robbins Music.[15] In 1950, NBC and Arturo Toscanini announced a suite of popular-style score commissions, similar in aesthetic scope to the *Music Out of the Blue* and Willson projects, to be called *Portrait of New York*.[16] This commission resulted in one of Ellington's most important concert works, *Harlem*, which he premiered with his own orchestra in 1951 (see chapter 6).[17] These events and commissions are little discussed in Ellington literature, but evidence suggests they were not peripheral to his ambitions as a composer.

A final connection between Ellington and Whitemanesque concert jazz can be found in Ellington's long association with Jack Robbins. Robbins was a close friend and business associate of Whiteman. Most importantly, several key compositions that connect Ellington to the symphonic jazz formal model were published in Robbins Music's aforementioned Modern American Music score series.

𝄢 WHITEMANESQUE SYMPHONIC JAZZ

The formal procedures of *Black, Brown and Beige* represent Ellington's most thorough exploration to that date of the techniques of "extended jazz composition" that he had experimented with since his earliest concert-style work, his *Rhapsody Jr.*, copyrighted in 1926. The etymological roots of these ideas—"jazz composition" and "extended jazz" form—are uniquely tied to Ellington's development as a composer in the 1930s. In contemporary critical efforts that sought to culturally elevate the blues, African American aesthetics, and the music of Harlem entertainment, the idea of jazz composition was held to be distinct from both jazz arrangement and Whitemanesque symphonic jazz. For this reason, it is important to understand this latter tradition before exploring Ellingtonian symphonic jazz.

The symphonic jazz arranging idiom was a product of the early 1920s. In Ferde Grofé's influential arranging work for Whiteman, this tradition is built on several related topics, including (1) "characteristic" scoring effects; (2) the concept of an arranging routine and its use in creating extended episodic form; (3) the Tin Pan Alley "modern" idiom and its use of extended harmony, modulation, and sequence; and (4) the relation of this arranging tradition to contemporary novelty ragtime. The governing aesthetic of this dance-band idiom is based on stylistic variety, entertainment value, and novelty.

In his most complex scoring routines, Grofé's arrangements involved three separate thematic strains, a diverse palette of instrumental effects, regular modulation, and some combination of introduction, interludes, and coda. These concert-style song arrangements were a foundation for the Whitemanesque concert work tradition, and they in turn owed a great deal to both novelty ragtime and the scoring routines of the grand production numbers of contemporary variety entertainments.

The novelty piano tradition, a 1920s, virtuosic, white extension of ragtime, served as a structural model for the Whitemanesque concert work tradition. A typical three-strain novelty rag form is outlined in example 4.1. This three-strain form is derived from the strain form models of classic ragtime and nineteenth-century marches. This model became the central formal template for the novelty rag tradition following the 1921 publication of Zez Confrey's immensely successful *Kitten on the Keys*.[18] In this tradition, strains are generally sixteen or thirty-two bars in length. Modulation commonly occurs between the first and second strains, usually by third relation. Following the B strain, there is a return to the initial key and the A strain,

Intro. → ‖: A :‖ → ‖: B :‖ → Interlude → A → ‖ Intro. → ‖: Trio: C :‖ → A

Example 4.1.   The typical form of 1920s "novelty piano" compositions

often by way of a modulating interlude. The so-called trio C strain is set in the key of the subdominant. Introductions and interludes are frequently four to eight measures in length. As contrasting modulatory passages, these episodes are generally colored with "modernistic" Tin Pan Alley chromaticism or whole-tone-based or extended harmonies. All these traits are important to the symphonic jazz concert work tradition.

Symphonic jazz most fully flowered as a concert work idiom in the period from 1926 to 1930. This era is also significant in that commercial "concert edition" dance band orchestrations and piano solos in the symphonic jazz style had become big business for Tin Pan Alley publishers. This trend is particularly evident in the Whiteman-Robbins Modern American Music score series. The relation of novelty piano to Whitemanesque Modern American Music can be articulated by examining one of the latter idiom's most popular and prototypical concert-style works: Louis Alter's 1928 *Manhattan Serenade*.[19] Table 4.1 shows a formal outline of this composition. Novelty form is apparent in the work's structure of three sixteen-bar strains, two four-bar modulatory interludes and a four-bar introduction, modulations that occur between each strain, and a third strain in the trio key of the subdominant. There are several significant departures from the novelty tradition. The most immediate difference lies at the level of basic musical character. While novelty compositions were based on an unvarying dance pulse, *Manhattan Serenade* displays rather melodramatic, widely varying tempi, performance expressions, and dynamic shadings, and liberal smatterings of ritards and rubato cadenzas. Formally, there are expansions on the novelty idiom both in the way the music is organized and in a more elastic approach to episodic form. In particular, strains B^1 and C^2 reveal this new sense of episodic elasticity. For instance, B^1 is extended by cadential delay and the four-bar, varied restatement of its (b) phrase. In C^2, the episode departs from its original strain form in its eighth measure, and thereafter repeats two measures and segues to interlude 2.

The Modern American Music idiom further differs from the novelty tradition in its use of both classically styled cadenzas and the expansion of interludes to include development-type material. Music critics have historically used the ideological rhetoric of classical development as a central tool for either discrediting or defending the compositional achievements of many concert jazz works. These types of critical responses permeate the reception histories of both George Gershwin's *Rhapsody in Blue* and Ellington's early extended compositions. In this sort of critical reception, the ideal of thematic development is understood to mean the rigorous intellectual standards of post-Beethovenian "organic development" in the classical repertory. In this tradition, musical form must be largely through-composed and logically unfold—or rather, "organically" unfold—through the perpetual structural transformations of thematic materials. The classical tradition and Western music in general exhibit many means of thematic development that are far simpler than the organic development model of Beethoven's Fifth Symphony. In fact, various 1920s and 1930s texts and articles on popular music arranging—most of which were produced by symphonic dance band arrangers—casually speak of employing thematic "development" techniques in the interludes of dance band arranging routines. This tradition can be seen in the 1926 book *Arranging for the Modern Dance Orchestra* by Arthur Lange, who was the mid-1920s arranger for Whiteman's rival, Roger Wolfe Kahn. In this text, Lange discusses the desirability of "developing" verse and chorus themes in the interludes and third "arranger's chorus" of typical arranging routines of the day. He even refers to these passages simply as the "development" sections of a routine, as if alluding to sonata-allegro

TABLE 4.1. Formal outline of Louis Alter's *Manhattan Serenade* (1928)

M.	Section	Key
1	Introduction = 4 mm.	Cmin
5	Strain A = 16 mm. ($a^1b^1a^2b^2$)	Cmin
21	Strain B^1 = 16 + 4 extension ($a^1a^2b^1a^3 + b^2$)	A♭
40	Strain B^2 = 16 mm. ($a^1a^2b^1a^4$)	A♭
56	Interlude 1 = 4 mm.	chrom.
60	Cadenza	—
61	Strain C^1 = 16 mm. (a^1a^2bc)	F
77	Strain C^2 = 10 mm. of orig. ($a^1a^2b^2 \rightarrow$ interruption)	F
89	Interlude 2 = 4 mm.	mod.
93	Strain A^3 ("recap") = 16 mm. + 2 mm. extension	Cmin

form.[20] The idea of using thematic "development" textures in popular music arranging has a long history that extends well beyond symphonic jazz. In jazz-derived concert works, the "development idea" began as an expansion of these simple developmental conventions in 1920s dance band arranging. In the context of the concert work tradition of symphonic jazz, these gestures of motivic manipulation were meant to be signs of musical sophistication. Most of the Modern American Music scores exhibit fairly simple approaches to the "development idea." In this repertory, there is clearly a shared body of development conventions that has passed between various composers and arrangers. Most of this idiom's thematic transformations are employed as a means for strain extension, and these transformations are based on only slight melodic elaborations and changes in orchestration. The idiom thus employs both the "development idea" and the melodramatic, rhapsodic style of "serious" concert music in much the same way that a 1920s symphonic jazz arranger like Ferde Grofé had employed "characteristic" scoring effects within dance music.

The relation of Whitemanesque concert works to the "development idea" can be illustrated by a brief consideration of Ferde Grofé's *Metropolis*, from 1928.[21] This twenty-minute work represents a new level of sophistication in its expansion on the symphonic jazz formal model and its developmental motivic and strain manipulation techniques. An outline of this composition's form is shown in table 4.2. This work expands the novelty compositional model to its limits. *Metropolis* is constructed from four strains, three of which are sixteen-bar forms. What is evident in table 4.2 is the extent to which introductions and interludes have expanded and taken on new developmental functions. *Metropolis* displays an even greater elasticity in strain forms than *Manhattan Serenade*. It has an underlying tongue-in-cheek playfulness, a sense that for every instance of highbrow posturing, there is some element of entertainment to counter such seriousness. This is seen in a brief contrast of the work's popular, classical, and hybrid stylistic references. Its first twenty measures, for instance, establish a stereotypical "classical" texture in the aptly described "pomposo" introduction, *marcato* brass fanfares, rolled timpani, and a quasi-Lisztian piano cadenza. The sincerity of such rhapsodic, "pomposo" scoring effects is seriously undermined in the comic vocal trio of strain C, which is scored for a dance band rhythm section and the jazz-pop vocal harmonies of the Rhythm Boys (a group that included Bing Crosby). Lastly, a merging of the jazz voice with a classical characteristic effect is heard in strain B³, which presents a four-voice "Fugato" section scored in New Orleans–style jazz polyphony.

The "pomposo" introduction to *Metropolis* ideally illustrates this work's expansion upon the novelty-derived interludes of a composition like *Manhattan Serenade*. Like most novelty ragtime interludes,

TABLE 4.2. Formal outline of Ferde Grofé's *Metropolis* (1928)

M.	Section	Comments
1	Intro.	Based on Strain A ("Skyline"*) motive
63	Strain A¹	"Skyline" 16 mm. (a¹a²bc)
79	Strain A²	8 mm. → interrupted (10 mm. extension)
97	Strain A³	10 mm. → interrupted (10 mm. varied end)
New	Piano Cadenza	Recording inserts piano cadenza (rel. to m. 134ff.)
114	Strain B	16 mm. + 4 mm. insert (a¹ba²a³). Phrase a³ includes 4 mm. insert between 1st and 2nd mm.
134	Interlude 1	At m. 146, false Strain B (4 mm. only). At m. 161, there is a transposed variation of m. 134ff.
193	Vamp	vamp (4 mm.)
197	Strain B(b)¹	8 mm. original → 10 mm. rhythmic extension of an A minor chord
215		vamp (4 mm.)
217	Strain B(b)² + extension	8 mm. original in minor key → 10 mm. rhythmic extension of an A♭ chord (and its neighbor chord)
262	Interlude 2	Piano cadenza at m. 262. Foreshadows Strain C.
321	Strain C	"Fox Trot" 16 mm. (aabc)
337	Strain B(b)³	"Fugato" 16 mm. (two 8 mm. themes)
New	"Fugato" cont.	Two additional entries (8 + 8)
369	Interlude 3	
438	Intro. to Strain D	
444	Strain D¹	"Fox Trot" 12 mm. → 2 mm. extension
458	Strain D²	12 mm. → 2 mm. extension
472	Strain D³	4 mm. → interruption
476	Interlude 4	
488	Strain D⁴ (problematized)	12 mm. + extension (mm. 499–507 = rhythmic palindrome)
508	Interlude 5	Extended sequence–based passage from m. 522: (a) 4×; (b) 12×; (c) 5× repetition of final m. of (b)
544	Strain A	"Recap" 10 mm. → 7 mm. extension
560	Coda	Mm. 569–72 = 9 mm. rhythmic palindrome

Outline derived from both Whiteman's 1928 Victor recording of *Metropolis* (Victor 35933, 35934; recorded March 13–17, 1928) and the Paul Whiteman "Condensed Score" from the Paul Whiteman Archives of Williams College. This "Condensed Score" (written on its cover) is an annotated copy of the Robbins 1928 piano solo. This publication was adapted as a conductor's score for Whiteman at some later date. This score includes an insert for the "Fugato" section that is included in the 1928 recording, as well as extensive cuts that are not observed in this recording.

*In 1945, Robbins Music published a short piano solo entitled *Skyline* that was derived from Strain A of *Metropolis*.

Example 4.2.   Measures 63–93 from Ferde Grofé's *Metropolis*

the structure of the entire introduction to *Metropolis* is derived through the combination, recombination, sequence, and modest variation of two- to four-measure building blocks. In this "development" passage, these materials are almost entirely derived from the first phrase of strain A. The first full statement of strain A is shown at the beginning of example 4.2 in mm. 63–78. The extended form of the introduction involves eight major passages, each of which is built on the sequence and repetition of these two- to four-bar motives derived from strain A. The use of these two techniques amounts to roughly 90 percent of the introduction. Variation may be introduced by either technique. The most common means of variation are simple melodic variation, and rhythmic diminution or augmentation. One of the more complex applications of such variation techniques is seen in the ending to strain A² (mm. 87–92), shown at the end of example 4.2. In this passage, variation techniques extend the strain's fourth phrase, first by diminution and sequence of a submotive, and then by the addition of a six-beat chromatic variation on the opening of the strain A motive. This larger two-bar phrase is sequenced up a whole tone in mm. 89–90. In m. 90, a new four-note chromatic motive is then itself subjected to variation and a series of sequences, each rising by whole tone. This whole-tone-based passage again modulates to the dramatic m. 93 statement of a chromatic variation on the strain A theme. In total, these simple techniques of sequence and repetition expand a sixteen-bar strain to twenty-one measures. Another common variation tool is the introduction of harmonically or contrapuntally complex elements in subsequent restatements of melodic material. Again, this is a process in which subsequent strain variations are built through the addition of ever-more-complex elements. Such devices include ornamental chromatic or whole-tone harmonies and counterpoint, elements that are generally superficial and do not significantly change the original melodic materials.

4.3 ELLINGTON AND "MODERN AMERICAN MUSIC"

In the post-1930 criticism that damned Paul Whiteman as the antithesis of true "jazz," two key themes were an intent to elevate Ellington's music to the level of high art and an effort to define "jazz composition" as a concert idiom based on African American–style hot jazz. In the late 1920s and early 1930s, this criticism was largely written for an audience of classical music devotees. As such, Ellington's music was routinely discussed in terms of classical ideology and placed in the heady company of Stravinsky, Delius, and other classical composers.[22] Writers like R. D. Darrell and Constant Lambert based this criticism on a dialectic that set Ellington's masterpieces of the "ten-inch record form" (Lambert's term)[23] in opposition to White-manesque concert jazz. This criticism was recycled by Ellington's publicity managers over the 1930s, first at Mills Music, and then at the William Morris Agency. Contrary to the aesthetic opposition of Whiteman and Ellington that was central to the critical arguments of early jazz critics like Darrell and Lambert, both Ellington and his publicists regularly situated his early extended jazz efforts directly within the sphere of Whitemanesque symphonic jazz.

The importance of public relations to Ellington's image can be sensed in a William Morris Agency *Manual for Advertising* that was prepared for Ellington in 1938. This document illustrates the role management played in building the image of Ellington as a "serious jazz composer." In a passage titled "Exploitation," for instance, the agency provides the following advice on how to introduce the artist:

> Ellington's genius as a composer, arranger and musician has won him the respect and admiration of such authorities as Percy Grainger, head of the department of music at the New York University; Leopold Stokowski, famed conductor . . . ; Paul Whiteman, whose name is synonymous with jazz; and many others. Sell Ellington as a musical genius whose unique style and individual theories of harmony have created a new music. He has been accepted seriously by many of the greatest minds in the world of music, who have regarded it a privilege to study his art and to discuss his theories with him.[24]

A related passage titled "Ellington's Ability as Composer Given Serious Approval" states that

> the jazz blues era [has] produced few musicians whose accomplishments as composers and conductors have received serious critical approbation. The men who have achieved something more than popular and evanescent acclaim can still be numbered on the strings of one violin—George Gershwin, Paul Whiteman, Ferde Grofé and Duke Ellington.[25]

As these excerpts illustrate, William Morris's spin on "Ellington, the serious composer" places him distinctly within the realm of Whiteman-related symphonic jazz.

Ellington's interviews and essays of the 1930s suggest that he had long aspired to compose concert-style works. This goal was progressively realized through such works as *Rhapsody Jr.* (copyrighted 1926; published 1935), *Creole Rhapsody* (1932), *Reminiscing in Tempo* (1935), the score to the film short *Symphony in Black* (1935), *Diminuendo and Crescendo in Blue* (1937), and several lesser-known 1930s Modern American Music scores for Robbins Music and Paul Whiteman.

In his symphonic jazz-based activities of the 1930s, it is hard to separate Ellington's artistic self-conception from the image promoted by his publicity machine. These blurred boundaries between publicity, manager, and client are even apparent in the origins of Ellington's earliest concert-style works. According to Ellington's son, Mercer, for instance, the motivating factor behind the composition of Ellington's *Creole Rhapsody* was Irving Mills's managerial scheme to broaden Ellington's audiences by encroaching on Whiteman's signature cultural territory.[26] In fact, Mills's fundamental tools in steering Ellington's career up a complicated ladder of symbolic cultural achievements were his promotions of Ellington as the bon vivant maestro and "serious composer" in the manner of Whiteman and Gershwin, respectively.

Prior to discussing Ellington's landmark extended concert works of the 1930s and 1940s, we need a brief overview of Ellington's Whiteman-Robbins commissions and piano solos. Ellington's professional ties to Robbins began in 1923, after Ellington and his early songwriting partner Joe Trent wrote a musical show, *Chocolate Kiddies*. As Ellington recalled in his autobiography, "We played and demonstrated [*Chocolate Kiddies*] for Jack Robbins, who liked it and said he would take it. . . . Jack . . . published several of my piano solos around that time, such as *Rhapsody Junior* and *Bird of Paradise*."[27] *Rhapsody Jr.* was not copyrighted until October 21, 1926, by the Robbins-Engel company.[28] The discrepancy between this copyright date and Ellington's recollection of a connection between these piano solos and his initial association with Jack Robbins suggests a three-year window for the compositional dates of these piano solos. The histories of both *Rhapsody Jr.* and *Bird of Paradise* are further complicated by the fact that the company waited nine years (until 1935) before publishing these compositions as Modern American Music piano solos. (Contrary to Ellington's recollection, there is no evidence that these piano solos were published in the mid-1920s.) Lastly, in late 1938, after he broke with his longtime manager, Irving Mills, Ellington signed with both the William Morris Agency and Robbins Music. As part of this latter association, Robbins published Ellington's other Whiteman-related piano solos, *American Lullaby* and *Blue Belles of Harlem*, in 1942 and 1943, respectively.

The formal design and certain stylistic elements of *Rhapsody Jr.* and *Bird of Paradise* strongly suggest they were composed closer to 1926, after the premiere of Gershwin's *Rhapsody in Blue* in 1924 (though Ellington's piano pieces bear no direct formal relation to this work). This hypothesis is largely based on the extant information for the history of *Rhapsody Jr.*, though certain compositional details in *Bird of Paradise* equally support this belief, as will be discussed later. The assumption that *Rhapsody Jr.* was composed much closer to its copyright date than to the period of *Chocolate Kiddies* (1923) is partly based on Jack Robbins's early promotions of *Rhapsody Jr.*, which appeared in 1926–27. Mark Tucker has observed that a January 1927 article on Ellington's Washingtonians lists *Rhapsody Jr.* as Ellington's "latest composition" for Robbins-Engels. There was also a 1926 trade announcement of this work as a Robbins "exclusive." Despite these connections to Robbins, no evidence has yet surfaced to confirm an actual 1926–27 publication of this score.[29] One further clue to the genesis of *Rhapsody Jr.* can be found in an extant lead sheet from this era, which unfortunately is undated.[30] In light of the October 1926 copyright by Robbins-Engels, it is further possible that Irving Mills encouraged Ellington to compose this work years before *Creole Rhapsody*. (Mills likely began his professional association with Ellington in the summer of 1926.) Ellington never recorded *Rhapsody Jr.*, and it was another decade before Jimmie Lunceford's band recorded a significantly altered arrangement of it in 1935.[31] In the same year, Robbins Music published both a stock orchestration of *Rhapsody Jr.* (arranged by Lyle "Spud" Murphy) and a piano solo (presumably arranged by Ellington, since no arranger-editor is cited), which was included in the company's Modern American Music score series.

Both the 1926 and 1935 versions of *Rhapsody Jr.* are based on an episodic combination of thirty-two- and sixteen-bar strains. The few writers even to mention this little-known work have generally been dismissive. For instance, in *Ellington: The Early Years*, Mark Tucker remarked that "with its ninth and augmented chords, its whole-tone melodies and parallel triads, *Rhapsody Jr.* shows Ellington displaying some of the hallmarks of mid-twenties jazz modernism," or more accurately, Whitemanesque Modern American Music. These characteristic traits of "mid-1920s jazz modernism" are tied to the work's thirty-two-bar A strain. Though these elements are somewhat heightened in the arrangements of the 1935 Robbins scores (the stock orchestration and the piano solo), they are equally evident in the undated, mid-1920s lead sheet.

Tucker's assessment of the parallels between *Rhapsody Jr.* and the symphonic jazz idiom are undeniably accurate. *Rhapsody Jr.*'s rough compositional date of 1923–26 places it in a somewhat curious chronological position with regard to the emergence of the Modern American Music idiom. Paul Whiteman Publications did not begin operation until 1927. Before 1926–27, with the exception of Grofé's symphonic-length compositions of 1924–27 (including *Broadway at Night*, *Mississippi Suite*, and *Three Shades of Blue*), most of the composers who were later associated with Whitemanesque, multithematic extended compositions were still composing in the novelty piano tradition or producing Grofé-style chorus-variation and jazzed-classics arrangements. In addition, before 1927, the only true Whiteman-Robbins-type concert work to be formally published was Grofé's *Mississippi Suite* (for Leo Feist) in 1926. Related formal models from this period are found in the mid-1920s vogue for novelty piano and orchestral novelty compositions. Because of the early 1920s Whiteman-Ellington association, it is likely that Ellington was keenly aware of Whiteman's various concert work activities, even during Ellington's early years at the Kentucky Club. The readily available published scores to Gershwin's *Rhapsody* and Grofé's *Mississippi Suite* were the most obvious "jazz rhapsody" models for the young Ellington to emulate in 1925–26. However, Grofé's suite was the only pre-1927 published score to display the emerging multithematic, novelty-based formal design that came to define the Modern American Music concert work tradition. Before 1926, of course, Gershwin had also composed his one-act opera *Blue Monday Blues* (aka *135th Street*) and the Concerto in F, but the Gershwin concert works as a whole are much more formally complex than either mid-1920s orchestral novelty compositions or the standard structure of a late-1920s, novelty-influenced, Whitemanesque work such as *Manhattan Serenade*. It is the latter tradition that *Rhapsody Jr.* most closely resembles.

With regard to the formal design of *Rhapsody Jr.*, it seems less probable that Ellington drew directly from jazz-based concert work models in Harlem's musical circles of the mid-1920s. (James P. Johnson's *Yamekraw* did not appear until 1927.) One likely influence may have been multistrain, stride piano cutting contest works. Despite the close stylistic kinship between 1920s Harlem stride and the white novelty piano tradition, none of the Harlem stride pianists in 1926 were yet known for the type of mid-1920s novelty piano modernism found in *Rhapsody Jr.* It does seem possible, however, that a Harlem symphonic jazz ensemble like Leroy Smith's orchestra could have been performing an abbreviated "jazz" arrangement of Gershwin's *Rhapsody* in 1926. (Smith recorded his three-minute, novelty-style, fox-trot arrangement of the *Rhapsody in Blue* in 1928. His popular Whiteman-style orchestra began a high-profile extended engagement at the famous Harlem nightclub, Connie's Inn, in 1926.)[32] In the end, the most plausible formal inspirations for the "jazz modernism" of *Rhapsody Jr.* were mid-1920s Whitemanesque dance band arrangements, as well as novelty compositions like the popular Zez Confrey examples. These stylistic connections are revealed in an examination of the extant scores to this work.

Tables 4.3a and 4.3b present formal outlines to the 1926 and 1935 scores of *Rhapsody Jr.* In its initial 1926 form, *Rhapsody Jr.* was based on four strains. Strain A displays the work's stylistic borrowings from mid-1920s "jazz modernism" in both its melodic and harmonic construction. This strain is built in a simple a^1ba^2c form. Though it is

TABLE 4.3a.   Formal outline of *Rhapsody Jr.*, 1926 copyrights lead sheet

Section	Form/Function	Length	Key
Strain A	Whole-tone based	32	C
Strain B	Jazzed "Spring Song" (Mendelssohn)	16	D♭maj
Strain C	Ragtime/stride styled	16	D♭maj
Strain A		32	C
Interlude		8	Fmin
Strain D		32	Cmin

TABLE 4.3b. Formal outline of *Rhapsody Jr.* (1935)

M.	Section	Length	Key	Form/Function
1	Introduction	4	—	Whole-tone based + sequential
5	Strain A¹	32	C	Whole-tone based
37	Strain B	16	D♭	Obscures 1926 borrowing
53	Strain A²	36	C	Var. + extension (= aba [c+])
89	Strain D	32	Cmin	
121	Strain A³	31	C	

TABLE 4.3c. Formal outline of *Bird of Paradise* (1935)

M.	Section	Length	Key/Form
1	Introduction	4	Sequential and chromatic
5	Strain A¹	16 + 4	E♭. a¹ba² (c) with (c) extended
24	Strain B	16	
40	Strain A²	20	Repeat
60	Interlude	4	Mod.
64	Trio Strain	16 (+14)	Fmin→A♭. Expands 20-bar strain.
94	Strain A³	20	E♭

TABLE 4.3d. Formal outline of *American Lullaby* (1942)

M.	Section	Length	Key	Form/Function
1	Introduction	12	Fmaj → mod	a¹a²b. Elides with Interlude¹.
13	Interlude¹	5	Cmaj → mod	Acts as intro. to Theme
19	Theme¹	(16)	(Cmaj)	
33	Interlude 2	5	(Cmaj)	Interlude repeated
39	Theme²	(16)	(Cmaj)	Rescored Theme
53	Coda	4	Cmaj	Transposes mm. 1–4 (A¹)

TABLE 4.3e. Formal outline of *Blue Belles of Harlem* (1938)

M.	Section	Length	Key	Form/Function
1	Introduction	14	A♭	Orch
15	Strain A¹	38 (= 32*)	A♭	Pno solo (* = with 12 mm. in 2/4, hence an underlying standard 32-bar form)
53	Extension	4	mod.	
57	Strain B	12	B♭ → E♭	Pno solo with orch
69	Strain B	13	mod.	Pno solo
82	Strain C¹	32	E♭	Orch → pno solo → orch
114	Strain C²	8 (+1)	A♭ → mod	Incomplete
123	Strain A²	(12) = 8†	F	Pno solo → orch († = with 4 mm. in 2/4, hence an underlying standard 8-bar phrase)

based on whole-tone and extended harmonies, and includes small passages of chromatic voice-leading, the strain is firmly rooted in C major.

The sixteen-bar B strain undergoes a telling shift in the 1935 score. In its mid-1920s form, the melody of this strain is a jazzed version of Mendelssohn's *Spring Song*, a perennial chestnut of the jazzed- and ragged-classics repertories.[33] The 1935 score alters the main melodic notes of the strain's first two measures, thereby obscuring its original melodic borrowing and its roots in mid-1920s, Confrey-style novelty ragtime.

The idiomatic origins of strain C, which appears only in the un- dated, mid-1920s lead sheet, lie squarely in the compositional models of Harlem stride piano. Though the lead sheet's melody provides the only surviving score materials for this strain, it seems significantly in- debted to James P. Johnson's rags of the years up to the early 1920s. This resemblance is seen both in strain C's construction through riff manipulation rather than a melodic conception, and in its use of a three-over-four rhythmic tension, a contemporary cliché in both novelty and stride piano.

In melodic terms, *Rhapsody Jr.*'s D strain is virtually the same in each score. This theme is set in a standard thirty-two-bar song form (aaba), and is meant to be performed "with decided rhythm" (marked out by a standard-issue, novelty/stride oom-pah bass). This strain's minor-key setting and various stylized figurations (particularly a fre- quent neighbor-note, triplet figure) lend a somewhat classicized air to its overall character. In the 1935 score, this touch of "classicism" is complemented with a newly composed, "modernistic" (and dra- matic), whole-tone-based introduction.

While both the 1926 and 1935 scores invoke various novelty sty- listic traits, neither displays a straightforward basis in contemporary, three-strain novelty form. In the harmonic schemes of each version, *Rhapsody Jr.* modulates only between C major/minor and D-flat major. Thus both arrangements are rather distant from the novelty tradition's template for key relations between strains. (Unlike most novelty works, for instance, *Rhapsody Jr.* has no clear trio strain set in the key of the subdominant.) The episodic forms of the stride idiom were much less orthodox with regard to their large-scale harmonic organization and the number of episodes (and their variations) in any given composition (or its performance). For example, a classic stride composition like James P. Johnson's *Carolina Shout* has four strains, a number of variation episodes, and some combination of introduction, interludes, and coda. The precise number and ordering of many of these elements (particularly strain variations and transitional interludes) could vary between performances. With this model in mind, it seems that the four-strain, 1926 score of *Rhapsody Jr.* was constructed in a hybrid episodic form that equally adapts contemporary novelty and stride piano idioms.[34]

By contrast, the formal revisions of the 1935 score bring this composition in alignment with the then-established norms of the Modern American Music tradition. The arrangement's new sequence-based, harmonically drifting, whole-tone introduction assists this goal. The reduction to three strains and the removal of the uncharacteristic ragtime strain (the original strain C) equally reposition *Rhapsody Jr.* within the Whiteman-Robbins idiom, as does the melodic alteration and harmonic complication of the B strain. The 1935 score also displays a certain Whitemanesque episodic elasticity in its recomposition of strain A^2, with a newly varied strain ending that involves an expansion phrase built from both sequential repetition and a new motive based on dramatic, chromatically shifting, diminished chords.

Table 4.3c presents a formal outline of *Bird of Paradise*, a composition that closely accords with the symphonic jazz formal model. Ellington once suggested that this work was composed in the mid-1920s, about the same time as *Rhapsody Jr.*[35] This early date seems unlikely in that the style of the 1935 Robbins-published score is entirely out of character with the mid-1920s novelty and stride strain models that had been the basis of the mid-1920s version of *Rhapsody Jr. Bird of Paradise* displays a far more sophisticated use of integrated strain expansions and phrase extensions (both within and at the end of strains) and it also reveals a much more refined compositional approach to the symphonic jazz formal model than any composer-arranger besides Grofé had demonstrated by this time.

American Lullaby presents a unique adaptation of the standard Whitemanesque model, departing from, or more accurately, *dissipating* the multistrain format of this idiom. This work, Ellington's contribution to Meredith Willson's 1938 radio project, is simple in its formal outlay, as shown in table 4.3d. *American Lullaby* differs from the

Whiteman-Robbins structural model by including only one real strain or theme, though other episodic materials do assume certain quasi-strain-like formal functions. The main theme is sixteen bars in length and built through four-bar phrasing (a^1ba^2c). This theme presents a fluid use of cadential phrase elisions that is rarely found in Whiteman-Robbins concert works. The twelve-bar introduction, with its four-bar coda reprise, does somewhat resemble strain form in both its opening (a^1a^2b) structure and in the placement of its restatements in the work's overall layout. This passage is never stated as a full musical period, though. In the work's introduction, for instance, there is a missing fourth four-bar phrase (which would create a sixteen-bar strain), and the (b) phrase—the strain's bridge phrase—melodically drifts away from strain-style construction as the episode segues to a cadenza-like passage in mm. 11–12. The work's harmonically static interlude also avoids clear periodic phrasing through its cadential elisions. This interlude functions somewhat like a secondary introduction that leads into the main theme, as opposed to the more autonomous episodic interludes associated with the symphonic jazz formal model. Despite these various formal deviations, this structural design still betrays its origins as an extension of the Modern American Music–based formulas that defined the 1935 *Rhapsody Jr.* score and *Bird of Paradise*.

Of Ellington's four Modern American Music compositions, the sole score that he wrote expressly for Whiteman, *The Blue Belles of Harlem*, displays the most thorough merging of Whitemanesque form and the "Ellington Effect," to borrow Billy Strayhorn's famous phrase. In this expression, Strayhorn meant to capture both Ellington's habit of composing and orchestrating specifically for the individual musical talents and unique instrumental voices of his band members, and the distinctive greater whole that was produced when these individual instrumental voices sounded together in the performance of Ellington's compositions.[36] My assessment of *The Blue Belles of Harlem* is based on Billy Strayhorn's significantly reworked, six-minute quasi concerto arrangement for piano solo and jazz band that was performed at Ellington's Carnegie Hall concert of January 1943.[37] In many ways, this later arrangement looks forward to the rich merging of Ellingtonian and Whitemanesque ideals in Ellington's 1943 composition *New World A-Comin'* (discussed in chapter 6). As shown in table 4.3e, *Blue Belles* is built from an elastic, three-theme episodic form based on modifications of thirty-two- and twelve-bar strains. In a manner akin to Grofé's late-1920s concert works, the 1943 *Blue Belles* arrangement involves sophisticated compositional devices for manipulating episodic boundaries to create larger structural forms. Ellington had initially explored most of these resources in his first "extended" composition, the 1931 *Creole Rhapsody*.

13 EARLY ELLINGTONIAN EXPERIMENTS IN "EXTENDED" FORM

The January and June 1931 recordings of *Creole Rhapsody* are positioned in the Ellington literature as landmark events in Ellington's aspirations to compose in "extended" forms.[38] (These two-part recordings took up both sides of ten- and twelve-inch 78 rpm records, respectively.) According to Ellington's autobiography, this work was composed after Irving Mills suggested that the bandleader write "a new long work—a rhapsody." In response, Ellington "went out and wrote *Creole Rhapsody*" overnight. He claimed that he had written "so much music for [this work] that we had to cut it up and do two versions."[39] This latter claim is somewhat misleading—the second version of *Creole Rhapsody* was clearly a revision of the first arrangement. Ellington characterized this composition as "the seed from which all kinds of extended works . . . later grew."

In his review of the 1959 LP recording of *Black, Brown and Beige*, the critic Robert Crowley asserted that in 1943 *BB&B* was "acclaimed [only] in the popular music trade papers," and that "the more astute the critic, the more adverse the criticism of the only really relevant aspect of the piece, its form or structure." From this perspective, Crowley argued,

> What Ellington produced in [*BB&B*] is distinguished . . . by the delightful originality of its details. It is a series of loosely related or unrelated smaller pieces, interrupted rather than integrated by arbitrary "classical" transitions. Since reiteration is almost the only means of extension used, the music . . . seems excessively repetitious. The program . . . is absolutely essential to one's accepting it as a single work.[40]

While Crowley's description of its formal construction is not entirely accurate, his description of this work as a "series of loosely related smaller pieces, interrupted rather than integrated by arbitrary 'classical' transitions" echoes the 1930s classically biased criticism of Constant Lambert, R. D. Darrell, Roger Pryor Dodge, and others. In each case, the rhetoric of form is employed as a tool of critical empowerment. Neither Crowley nor these 1930s critics made any real effort to identify the assumed models of classical composition that they thought were relevant to their idea of jazz composition, nor did they provide any substantial discussions of what Ellington actually wrote. This critical scenario changed in the late 1960s, when authors such as Gunther Schuller and A. J. Bishop reemployed the rhetoric of classical form to again promote the idea of Ellington as a "serious" composer. Both Schuller and Bishop built their respective canonization projects on revisionist analyses of Ellington's "seeds" of extended composition, his *Creole Rhapsody* and the 1935 recording of *Reminiscing in Tempo*. In each instance, but particularly with *Reminiscing*, these authors de-emphasized—or missed entirely—the episodic, strain-based foundations of each composition. For example, Schuller first discussed these two works in a 1957 essay entitled "The Future of Form in Jazz." Eleven years later, Schuller returned to the basic themes of this earlier essay in the Ellington chapter of his landmark 1968 book *Early Jazz*.[41] Over the last decade or so, this pioneering text in jazz scholarship has been frequently attacked for its notational (or score-oriented) bias, and its critical foundation on formal ideals that derive from the classical tradition. Schuller's discussion of *Creole Rhapsody* is a case in point. The roots of these problems originate in the 1957 essay, one of Schuller's lesser-known, late-1950s manifestos on the ideals of "third stream jazz" (a term that he himself had coined the previous year). While his assessment of *Creole Rhapsody* is important in and of itself, he notably identified both this work and *Reminiscing* as key forebears to his own third-stream ideals for "extended jazz composition."

In this essay, Schuller argued that jazz was evolving into "a music to be *listened* to." This "evolution" demanded that jazz must "reach out for more complex ideas, harmonies and techniques," and develop "more complex musical forms." He characterized this quest to create "tonal materials on a larger scale" as a dangerous project for jazz composers who were merely "satisfied . . . [to] complacently reach . . . over into the classical field" and borrow "forms upon which to *graft* [their] music."[42] Schuller claimed that in his vision of extended jazz composition, form needed to evolve "out of the material itself" and from "within . . . [the] domain forms [that were] much more indigenous to its own essential nature."[43] This statement articulates key concepts for the accepted definition of Ellington's "extended" compositions. However, Schuller's emphasis on advanced harmony, unusual phrase lengths, and complex form in his analyses of these two works was more indigenous to the rhetoric of classical form than to jazz of the 1920s and 1930s.

Though he expressed his earnest appreciation of Whiteman in both essay and act,[44] Schuller's comments about borrowed classical forms being grafted onto jazz read as an effort to distinguish his so-called third-stream aesthetics from the poor reputation of the heterogeneous designs employed in Whitemanesque symphonic jazz. However, the Whiteman-Robbins concert work tradition had more to do with glorifying the idioms of American popular music than grafting popular music themes onto actual classical forms. In short, Schuller does not observe any connection between the Whitemanesque and Ellingtonian uses of strain-based episodic form in their respective concert-style works. Similarly, in his important 1963 essay on *Creole Rhapsody*, the critic A. J. Bishop does not consider the possibility of Whiteman-Robbins forebears to the work's structural designs. Instead, Bishop described the January 1931 version of *Creole Rhapsody* as a "broad" (ababcba) compositional structure that he likened to classical sonata rondo form.[45]

Tables 4.4a and 4.4b present the formal structures of the two recorded versions of *Creole Rhapsody*. The January 1931 version is built on three strains of thirty-two-, sixteen-, and twelve-bar lengths. As shown in table 4.4a, despite important differences, the three-strain design clearly resembles an elaboration on the three-strain Whiteman concert work model. As shown in table 4.4b, Ellington completely recomposed the latter half of *Creole Rhapsody* for its second recording in June 1931. The importance of this recomposition is its introduction of a new level of structural complexity. From m. 89, this later version is built from four variations of a new thirty-two-bar strain C. In the interlude of mm. 203–26, Ellington displays his first

TABLE 4.4a. Formal outline of first version of *Creole Rhapsody* (Brunswick, 1931)

M.	Section	Length	Key
1	**Part I. Theme A^1** (a^1)	8	A♭/E♭m[a]
9	(a^2)	8	A♭/E♭m
17	(b) Bridge	4 + 4	G → (B♭)
25	(a^3)	8	A♭/E♭m
33	**Theme B**, Part 1	12	B♭maj
45	Theme B, Part 2	12	E♭maj
57	**Theme A^2** (a^1) + (a^2)	16	A♭/E♭m
73	(b) Bridge	8	G → (B♭)
81	(a^3)	8	A♭/E♭m
89	**Part II. Intro.** (Thm. A var.)	8	A♭maj
97	**Theme B, Part 2**	12	E♭maj
109	**Interlude**	4	E♭maj
113	**Theme C**	16	E♭maj
129	**Theme B, Part 1**	12	A♭maj
141	**Theme A^3**	35	A♭/E♭m
176	**Coda**	6	E♭min

Note: Theme A involves a certain degree of tonal ambiguity in that it cadences in E♭ minor though Ellington wrote the passage in A♭ major. In addition, in the phrase turnaround, E♭min changes to E♭maj^9.

TABLE 4.4b. Formal outline of second version of *Creole Rhapsody* (Victor, 1931)

M.	Section		Length	Key
1	**Part I. Theme A^1** (a^1)	♩ = 144	8	A♭/E♭m
9	(a^2)		8	A♭/E♭m
17	(b) Bridge, Part 1		4	G
22	Bridge, Part 2 (var.)		4	mod.
25	**Theme B**, Part 1	♩ = 120	12	B♭maj
37	Theme B, Part 2		12	E♭maj
49	**Theme A^2** (a^{1}a^{2}ba^3)	♩ = 144	32	A♭/E♭m
81	**Interlude 1**		8	
89	**Theme C^1** (a^{1}ba^{2}c) (new)	♩ = 92	32	A♭maj
121	**Part II. Intro. to Part II** (Theme A var.)		4	mod.
125	**Theme C^2**	♩ = 112	32	B♭maj
157	**Interlude 2**		34	mod.
191	**Theme C^3** (incomplete)	♩ = 108	12	Fmaj
203	**Interlude 3**.a (Theme A var.)	♩ = 116	8	mod.
211	Interlude 3.b, based on Theme A(b), Part 1	♩ = 108	4	Gmaj
215	Interlude 3.c, based on Bridge, Part 2		4	mod.
219	Interlude 3.d, based on Theme A (var.)		7	mod.
226	**Theme C^4**		16	Cmaj
242	**Interlude 4**		4	mod.
246	**Coda** (= Theme C)		5	A♭maj

real experiments with the "development idea." In this interlude, variously sized, smaller phrases are constructed into a larger modulatory episode. Each of these smaller segments is constructed through a truncated and varied statement of theme A materials. Ellington's approach is different from Grofé's motivic manipulation techniques, but the compositional intent was likely motivated by the same principles. The "development idea" was manifested by Grofé through the combination, sequence, and modest variation of small motivic building blocks derived from a work's thematic episodes. With Grofé, the "development idea" was a means of linking up themes and expanding episodic frames through phrase extension and the construction of independent interludes.

While *Creole Rhapsody* was certainly a "seed" for Ellington's later extended works, the four-part *Reminiscing in Tempo* represents Ellington's first transformation of symphonic jazz episodic form. Again, however, this framework has been overlooked in the work's critical reception. Schuller, for example, in his ten-page *Reminiscing* analysis in his 1989 book *The Swing Era*, still holds roughly the same classical critical bias and musico-political agenda displayed thirty years earlier. Schuller takes the 1935 recording as a definitive text, and provides a confusing chart of thematic permutations to demonstrate the work's "organic" development. From this chart alone, one is left with the impression that each part of the work is essential to the composition's "structural unity."[46] Or is it? In his 1936 response to the negative reviews that followed the work's release, the critic Enzo Archetti observed that "on one point only do all reviewers . . . agree: that only the last side of *Reminiscing* is somewhat understandable."[47] While I do not necessarily agree with this assessment, its contemplation opens up new vistas on this work.

In recent years, a number of documents have emerged that provide insight into the form of *Reminiscing*. First, the Smithsonian Institution possesses Ellington's sketches and band parts for the 1935 recording. Second, several mid-1940s concert recordings have been commercially released.[48] These include an ABC July 21, 1945, radio broadcast from the Fieldston Ballroom in Marshfield, Massachusetts; Ellington's November 13, 1948, Carnegie Hall concert; and a December 10, 1948, concert at Cornell University. The most striking information from these three sources is that Ellington performs *Reminiscing* as a continuous work, and this form consists *only* of Parts I through III. Contemporary critics routinely interpreted Part IV as a typical, Ellingtonian "ten-inch record masterpiece" in and of itself, but they were baffled by the form of Parts I–III. The sketch materials are revealing on this matter. First, though "Rem. I" is written on the opening page, this title is in darker ink than the rest of the manuscript. In addition, the score materials are bipartite, with a through-composed score for Parts I–III forming one division, and Part IV forming the other. In the band parts, Part IV is written on a separate page. In the sketches, Part IV is on different paper. This evidence suggests that the divisions between parts were imposed by recording technology, and Part IV of the recording was created to fill out the fourth side of the two discs.

Table 4.5b presents an outline of Part IV, which is based on two thirty-two-bar chorus statements. The arrangement further includes a middle, cadenza-like piano solo, and a recycled vamp introduction. Is Part IV complete in and of itself? Yes, and its structure provides insights into the form of Parts I–III. Table 4.5a outlines Parts I–III, which I will refer to as "the work." *Reminiscing* is built from a small collection of motives, each subjected to slight variation, truncation, and/or extension. In addition to its two eight-measure themes, the work also includes a number of two- to eight-bar interludes, and one sixteen-bar development-type interlude.

Reminiscing is undeniably rich in motivic references, manifest both in Grofé-style developmental passages and a new technique that is best termed "motivic saturation." With this term, I refer to the score's perpetual references to a small number of motives. The sophistication of Ellington's manipulation of these motives can be sensed both in the permutational relations that exist between several motives, and in his dense employment of these cells. This technique is seen in the passage that extends from theme A^2's six-bar phrase extension and the subsequent mm. 33–36 transition to theme A^3. This passage is shown at the end of example 4.3, where the motives are labeled A through E. The extension to theme A^2 begins in m. 27 and initially involves two statements of motive C. From m. 29 forward, the passage is saturated with a string of motive references to create a larger developmental impression. On the larger level, the work's two-theme structure seems unrelated to the Whitemanesque model. For instance, despite

TABLE 4.5a. Formal outline of *Reminiscing in Tempo* (1935)

M.	Section	Part	Length	Key
1	Vamp/Intro.	**I**	2	F
3	Intro. (pretheme)		10	
13	Theme A^1		8	
21	Theme A^2		7 + 5 ext.	D♭
33	Transition		4	B♭
37	Theme A^3		6 + 4 ext.	
47	Transition		2	
49	Theme A^4		8	
57	Interlude (= development)		16	
73	Vamp (var.)		4	
77	Vamp	**II**	4	F
81	Theme A^5		6 + 4 ext.	
91	Theme A^6		6 + 4 ext.	
101	Theme B^1 (= bridge)		8	
109	Interlude		8	
117	Vamp + extension		6	
123	Interlude		8	
131	Theme A^7		8	
139	Theme A^8		8	
148	Transition (Theme B ref.)	**III**	4 (incompl.)	
152	(Theme B ref.)		3 (incompl.)	
155	(Theme A ref.)		5	
160	Extension		8	D
168	(Strain A ref.) (development)		4	
172	Extension		8	D → A
180	Transition to Vamp		4	
184	Vamp		4	
188	Theme A^9		6	
194	Extension		12	
206	Vamp		4	
210	Theme A^{10} (coda)		14+	

TABLE 4.5b. Formal outline of *Reminiscing in Tempo* (1935), Part IV

M.	Section	Length	Key
1	Vamp	4	F
5	**Song A^1**/Theme A (32-bar song form)	8	
13	Theme A	8	
21	Theme B	8	
29	Theme A	8	
37	Cadenza	6	
43	**Song A^2**/Theme A	8	B♭
51	Theme A	8	
59	Theme B (var.)	8	
67	Theme A	9	

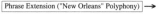

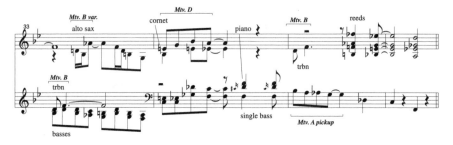

Example 4.3.   Measures 21–36 from Part I of Duke Ellington's *Reminiscing in Tempo* (1935). *Reminiscing in Tempo*. Words and music by Duke Ellington. Copyright © 1935 (Renewed 1962) by Famous Music LLC in the U.S.A. This arrangement copyright © 2008 by Famous Music LLC in the U.S.A. Rights for the world outside the U.S.A. controlled by EMI Mills Music Inc. and Warner Bros. Publications U.S. Inc. International copyright secured. All rights reserved.

Example 4.4. Measures 5–36 from Part IV of Duke Ellington's *Reminiscing in Tempo* (1935). *Reminiscing in Tempo*. Words and music by Duke Ellington. Copyright © 1935 (Renewed 1962) by Famous Music LLC in the U.S.A. This arrangement copyright © 2008 by Famous Music LLC in the U.S.A. Rights for the world outside the U.S.A. controlled by EMI Mills Music Inc. and Warner Bros. Publications U.S. Inc. International copyright secured. All rights reserved.

the work's length, theme B is only presented once in its entirety, and its second reference is in an unusual development passage that begins Part III. Theme B is also unusual in that it gives the impression of being an out-of-context, eight-bar song bridge. This impression can be explained through a further examination of Part IV.

Example 4.4 presents mm. 5–36 of Part IV, where themes A and B are set in a perfect thirty-two-bar song form. Theme B is the song bridge, and all of the cell motives are key parts of this chorus. Without the cadenza, Part IV resembles a standard jazz arranging routine for a thirty-two-bar chorus. What is one to make of this relation? It appears that the thirty-two-bar chorus of Part IV was the first music written, and this strain represents the template that was deconstructed to build Parts I–III. This evidence suggests that Parts I–III were conceived through an episodic, glorified popular song arranging aesthetic that grew out of Whiteman-style symphonic jazz. This hypothesis is further supported by the evidence of Ellington's ties to this idiom in his *Creole Rhapsody* and Modern American Music piano solos.

𝄢 BEYOND SYMPHONIC JAZZ: "JAZZ COMPOSITION" AND THE DESIGN OF *BLACK, BROWN AND BEIGE*

The meaning of "extended jazz composition" requires some explanation. Across the first two-thirds of the twentieth century, the term *composition* carried significant class hierarchy overtones that emerged from the period ideologies of "good" music. As the scholar Paul Lopes notes, from the late nineteenth to mid–twentieth centuries in the United States, "'good' music referred to the European [classical and concert] music repertoire and legitimate techniques of professional bands and orchestras" that played and promoted this repertory.[49] As Lawrence Levine has demonstrated, across the late nineteenth and early twentieth centuries, the American advocates of "good" music and high culture were highly successful in promoting a range of divisive cultural ideologies.[50] H. Wiley Hitchcock has rightly characterized this development as a schism between the American "cultivated" and "vernacular" musical traditions. As Hitchcock notes, the former tradition was "based on continental European models, looked to rather self consciously," and promoted by "pretenders to gentility." The vernacular tradition was "a 'popular' music in the largest sense," governed not by the "abstract aesthetic standards" of good music but by the lower commercial standards "of the market-place."[51] One result of this art-versus-entertainment schism was that music educators, aesthetes, and professional musicians typically encouraged a restriction of the term *composition* to mean music that reflected the lofty ideals of high culture. Naturally, this term was still used somewhat more loosely in mass culture, but this practice was generally adhered to across the classes. For instance, musicians who wrote songs were almost uniformly characterized as "tunesmiths" and "songwriters" rather than as "composers." Similarly, in period critical descriptions of music creation practices in big-band and dance-band work, the term *composition* is used quite sparingly despite the great amount of creativity and originality that went into building the repertories of most bands. Instead, this creative work is most commonly called by the lower-class term *arranging*, even when the work in question is based on entirely new material.

Granted, the class-based restrictions on the use of the term *composition* are generalized here. Indeed, the belief in this high-culture restriction was highly subjective and could vary from person to person, even among close friends. Such an ideological schism can be seen in the long friendship of Ellington and Donald Shirley, the pianist who performed the 1955 Carnegie Hall premiere of the symphony-plus-big-band orchestration of Ellington's *New World A-Comin'* (with Ellington conducting Shirley and the NBC orchestra, aka the Symphony of the Air; see chapter 6). During the 1950s and 1960s, Shirley was part of a close circle of friends that included Ellington, Billy Strayhorn, the arranger Luther Henderson, and Ellington's doctor, Arthur Logan. In a 2007 interview, Shirley forcefully insisted that Ellington could not be called a "composer," nor could a work like *New World* rightfully be called a "composition." Shirley is the first to admit that this close-knit Ellington circle liked to chide him for being a high-minded intellectual and an advocate of high culture (Shirley speaks eight languages and holds doctoral degrees in psychology, music, and the liturgical arts).[52] Shirley's comments were made in the context of his recollections of working with Ellington, Strayhorn, and Henderson on *New World*. Shirley conveyed a story of Ellington, Strayhorn, and Henderson manically searching through all of the orchestral parts, hunting for one wrong note that was heard in a rehearsal. Shirley told them exactly where the problem was, but he was astounded to learn that Ellington's team had no full score for the orchestration and that they were still busily trying to correct, polish, and even write areas of the orchestration during rehearsals with the orchestra (even after having performed this symphonic arrangement in 1949 and 1951, neither performance of which Shirley was aware of). While this sort of collaborative, last-minute work was *de rigueur* for the Ellington organization, as well as most big bands and musical theater productions of the day, from Shirley's perspective as a classical musician—a musician who was rigorously trained at the Leningrad Conservatory of Music and elsewhere—this approach to music and even the music itself (i.e., the formal and stylistic content of *New World*) lay far from the ideals of high culture. Though he viewed Ellington, Strayhorn, and Henderson as his musical brothers and close friends, Shirley's cultural position was emphatically clear when he remarked that "it's an insult to Johann Sebastian Bach if you're going to call [my friend Duke Ellington] a composer."[53] (He maintains this opinion even despite his great appreciation for traditional popular music before the era of rock and roll.) Most readers of this book will likely take great offense to Shirley's view that Ellington cannot be called a proper "composer," but one should bear in mind that the highly restrictive use of this term has a long history in the American schism between cultivated and vernacular music traditions. In fact, this profound schism—and the resultant imbalance of cultural privilege—is one of the primary factors that motivated many popular musicians to attempt to write concert-style works in an effort to gain greater cultural respect for America's vernacular music traditions. As noted previously, however, most of these midcentury efforts, both black and white, were typically derided as middlebrow, populist art.

Beginning with the 1930s writings of R. D. Darrell, Roger Pryor Dodge, and Constant Lambert, Ellington's music came to be positioned as the very definition of "jazz composition." The meaning of this newly coined term was still tied to the class ideologies of this era. This perspective is seen in Alain Locke's aforementioned account of black musical hierarchies. His second-tier "worthwhile jazz"/"jazz classics" musical grouping included the subcategory of "jazz composition," with Ellington as Locke's exemplar. In this category, however,

Locke also included African American arrangers like Don Redman and Benny Carter, who were working in a "typically racial or 'pure' [black] style."[54] In this period understanding then, "jazz composition" was defined specifically through sophisticated big band arrangements that balanced written scores and detailed orchestrations with room for improvisational contributions; which relied upon a performing collective of individual musical voices; and which embraced African American musical aesthetics. This 1936 understanding of a "jazz composition" tradition took hold in the jazz community across the Swing Era. As noted, however, Locke additionally described Ellington as the most promising "classical jazz" composer. This latter term formed yet another higher tier of jazz composition. Locke's conception of "classical jazz composition" is an important ideological root for the elevated cultural implications of the later term, *extended jazz composition*. For Locke, this tier "transpose[d] the elements of . . . jazz idioms . . . [to] more sophisticated . . . musical forms" that aspired to the ideals of "good" music.[55]

Though Ellington's distinctive musicians and the balance between composition, orchestration, and improvisation are typically the central issues for critical considerations of Ellington's status as a composer (or as a "jazz composer"), the primary critical concern with regard to his longer concert works has almost consistently been Ellington's use of "extended form." As with the ideals of "composition" in the classical music tradition, the period uses of this latter term naturally reference issues of formal construction and thematic development. Extended form also strongly implies that these concert works "extend" the indigenous jazz arranging principles that Ellington employed in his "ten-inch record form" arrangements (to paraphrase Lambert). Thus, in large part, this term implies "extended *jazz* form."

Various synonyms for "extended jazz form" began to appear in the popular journalism on Ellington just after the release of his *Creole Rhapsody* of 1932. This formal idea became particularly important to the era's classically biased Ellington criticism. In a 1934 essay by Warren W. Scholl, for instance, the critic noted that with the two twelve-inch records of *Creole Rhapsody* Ellington had "expand[ed] to larger forms."[56] Ellington himself had used the term *extended work* in an interview that followed his 1943 Carnegie Hall concert. In this article, the term arises in the context of both his praise for Paul Whiteman's symphonic jazz accomplishments and Ellington's attempt to articulate the contrasting African American foundations of his own music. As he noted, Whiteman "gave composers a chance to write new, *extended works*," but the Ellington orchestra "came in with a new style," and "we put Negro feeling and spirit in our music."[57] In this article, the interviewer also comments that Ellington preferred to characterize his orchestra's performance style as "Negro music" rather than jazz per se. This latter point reflects Ellington's lifelong aversion to stylistic categorization, particularly when he was confronted by journalists and critics who sought to label him a "jazz composer." This position is evidenced in a 1935 Ellington interview that presaged the composition of *Black, Brown and Beige*. Ellington said that he planned to "compose an immortal symphony to commemorate the history of his race." The interviewer added that "Ellington [didn't] intend to abide by the recognized rules of 'conservatory' music. He intends to apply his own thoughts to interpret characteristics of his race."[58] Racial expression was thus a key conceptual ingredient behind Ellington's "extended jazz" compositions of the 1930s and 1940s.

In a 1933 *Metronome* article, the critic Doron Antrim asked the question, "After Jazz—What?: Is American Music Stymied or Are We Going Somewhere?"[59] Though it is not entirely explicit in its title, Antrim's essay deals with Whitemanesque concert jazz, not the bona fide, improvisation-based jazz tradition.[60] Despite this Whitemanesque focus, Antrim observes that "jazz as was and is, probably has its truest exponent today in Duke Ellington." When asked "the question before the house," Ellington responded:

> It is my honest belief that . . . jazz will never bow out . . . I do feel . . . that its accepted forms are due for radical changes but that there will remain in the background the jazz element, based on primitive jungle rhythms.
>
> I have always believed in musical experimentation. . . . Just as a scientist in his laboratory mixes and remixes his chemical elements again and again to reach a new discovery, so must the musical experimenter mix and re-mix his musical elements, trying different harmonies, melodic strains, tempos, rhythms . . .
>
> My belief is that the new form will be "sophisticated jazz"—a more subtle, a more startling form than ever before. . . .

I have just completed a Victor recording of my latest composition called *Rude Interlude*. In it are contained new departures in musical tempo and arrangement—some pretty daring departures—but I offer it as my first contribution to what I sincerely believe is due to be the new form of "sophisticated jazz."[61]

By implication of the larger context of this article as a whole, this desired "expansion" implies a goal to develop "seven or eight minute numbers" in a contemporary "American idiom" that reflected the "music of the people"—in other words, the idioms of contemporary popular music. (However, Ellington's own example of "sophisticated jazz," the fascinating *Rude Interlude*, is better described as a prime model of Ellington's mastery of the "ten-inch record" form.) In this article, Ellington's "sophisticated jazz" is positioned as a clear extension to Whitemanesque symphonic jazz, though Antrim read his efforts in this direction as being a "truer" expression of "jazz as was and is," a comment that likely was meant to reflect Ellington's interest in racially characteristic musical expression.

Through the course of his career, Ellington mainly explored two formal models in his pursuit of "extended jazz" composition. His initial efforts at extended composition were based on adaptations of the multithematic, novelty/stride and symphonic jazz episodic models. Ellington's second formal model was the extended suite, first represented by his 1935 score to the film short *Symphony in Black*. The suite model—meaning an ordered collection of largely unrelated instrumental movements—ultimately overshadowed the importance of the symphonic jazz formal model in Ellington's postwar extended compositions. The larger ambitions behind Ellington's pre-1940 extended compositions were revealed only after the premiere of the hour-long *Black, Brown and Beige*, at his January 23, 1943, Carnegie Hall debut. This work represents the most comprehensive synthesis of Ellington's models of symphonic jazz and the jazz suite. The formal procedures employed in it also represent Ellington's richest exploration to that date of the accumulated techniques of jazz composition he had experimented with since *Rhapsody Jr.*

While the cultural identity politics of *Black, Brown and Beige*'s rich program—the work's "parallel to the history of the American Negro"—require a separate essay, a degree of contextual background is useful here. At its 1943 premiere, the conceptual program behind the work was conveyed in both the concert program and in Ellington's own spoken introductions to the work's three movements. This narrative is most succinctly stated in a prefatory section of the concert program:

> In this "tone parallel to the history of the American Negro," three main periods of Negro evolution are projected against a background of the nation's history. "Black" depicts the period from 1620 to the Revolutionary War, when the Negro was brought from his homelands, and sold into slavery. Here he developed the "work" songs, to assuage his spirit while he toiled; and then the "spirituals" to foster his belief that there was a reward after death, if not in life. "Brown" covers the period from the Revolution to the first World War, and shows the emergence of the Negro heroes who rose to the needs of these critical phases of our national history. "Beige" brings us to the contemporary scene, and comments on the common misconception of the Negro which has left a confused impression of his true character and abilities. The climax reminds us that even though the Negro is "Black, Brown and Beige" he is also "Red, White and Blue"—asserting the same loyalty that characterized him in the days when he fought for those who enslaved him.[62]

Though it omits much of the greater detail that Ellington conveyed in the performance introductions and the concert program, this brief statement captures the broad intellectual scope and cultural work that Ellington ascribed to this composition. It was intended as a powerful racial and cultural statement on the African American experience. This serious social intent and its detailed program greatly distance this work from the white symphonic jazz of the 1920s and 1930s.[63] For the concerns of this chapter, it is useful to consider how the *Black, Brown and Beige* program adapts and diverges from earlier popular culture programmatic models in symphonic jazz and Harlem entertainment.

The programmatic imagery associated with symphonic jazz centered on both the mythic—or glorified—aspects of the modern American metropolis and the modern metropolitan lifestyle so richly portrayed in the popular media of the interwar period. The web of cultural associations manifest in this new American metropolitan mythology are primarily represented in the cultures of both white and black Manhattan. Programmatically, symphonic jazz was associated with a small pool of perpetually recycled themes that can be divided into six primary categories:

1. The suave urbanity of the Park Avenue or the smart-set metropolitan lifestyle (i.e., evocations of penthouses, ritzy nightclubs, furs, champagne, caviar, limousines, etc.)
2. The idea of the metropolitan environment as "city symphony," a subgroup of themes that included the mythological aspects of the skyscraper and the glorification of the machine, as well as the omnipresent noise and hectic ambiance of the urban milieu
3. The idea of the city as theater, with the gaudy and gilded nature of Broadway and jazz nightclub life being central topics
4. The modern metropolis as a rich cultural and ethnic melting pot
5. The mythology of Harlem as "Black Manhattan" (as James Weldon Johnson observed, Harlem represented the "miracle" of a "black metropolis" that contained "more Negroes to the square mile than any other spot on earth" and existed as a parallel universe "in the heart of the great Western white metropolis")[64]
6. Evocations of the stylized themes of Harlem entertainment

Black, Brown and Beige's program intersects this thematic pool in categories 3, 4, 5, and 6. The most relevant intersections involve the celebration of Black Manhattan and themes from Harlem entertainment.

Harlem entertainment's curious mixture of racial pride and negative racial stereotypes was intimately tied to African American signification practices.[65] The restrictive programmatic formulas and clichéd character types of this theatrical tradition were central to most manifestations of black musical theater throughout the war years and the 1920s. Only in the 1930s were minor changes introduced within these narrow conventions.

Mark Tucker has noted the conceptual relation between *Black, Brown and Beige* and previous depictions of African American history both in the black historical pageants that were presented in Washington during Ellington's youth, and in interwar theatrical conventions. These conventions sought to portray black heritage in a highly stylized manner, particularly the Africa-Dixie-Harlem topical model that shaped Harlem musical theater productions and floor show revues of the 1920s and 1930s.[66] The serious cultural intent of *Black, Brown and Beige*'s program rises above these entertainment roots of the Africa-Dixie-Harlem program topics, but this transcendence involves the reclaiming and retooling of this tradition rather than its abandonment. Ellington had already attempted a similar refashioning of stereotypes in 1941, when he, Billy Strayhorn, and fifteen writers produced the Hollywood musical revue *Jump for Joy*. Following the twelve-week run of this revue, Ellington told a newspaper interviewer that his intent was "to give an American audience entertainment without compromising the dignity of the American people. . . . [E]very Negro artist . . . runs afoul of offensive stereotypes, instilled in the American mind by whole centuries of ridicule and derogation. The American audience has been taught to expect a Negro on the stage to clown and 'Uncle Tom.'" According to this interview, the problem Ellington attempted to solve in this revue was "how to present the Negro as he is, without sacrificing entertainment features."[67] (Though this statement is not presented as a direct quote from the bandleader, it is presumed to represent Ellington's personal opinion.) This project reclaimed and refashioned negative generic conventions for a new, positive social intent. Such confrontational numbers as "Uncle Tom's Cabin Is a Drive-In Now" openly signified on previously negative entertainment practices, but these numbers were meant to be *entertaining* and not didactic. As the show's primary composers, Ellington and Strayhorn similarly employed musical arrangements and stage revue conventions that came directly out of interwar Harlem musical theater traditions. In the same interview, Ellington directly links the social project of *Jump for Joy* with his ongoing work on an opera that intended to depict "the story of the Negro people." This latter work was *Boola*, the aborted project that gave birth to *Black, Brown and Beige*, which, like *Jump for Joy*, refashions Ellington's musical roots in Harlem entertainment traditions and big band jazz for a new type of artistic statement. Through the recontextualization of this music in a concert work form, he sought to convey a serious cultural message that was wholly foreign to the earlier symphonic jazz concert work traditions that the composition most closely resembled.

Black, Brown and Beige has been subjected to a number of analyses over the last thirty years, the most significant of which are a 1974–75 essay (published in three parts) by Brian Priestley and Alan Cohen, and Gunther Schuller's discussion of this work in his 1989 book, *The Swing Era*.[68] While each of these studies has provided rich insights, they were conducted largely in a critical vacuum with little reference to the extended compositional forms and constructive devices that Ellington had employed in previous extended works. Neither analysis considers non-Ellington formal models.

After the disappointing critical reception to the premiere at Ellington's first Carnegie Hall concert, it was nearly thirty years before this work was performed again in its entirety.[69] It is intriguing that a work that remained little heard during Ellington's lifetime has recently become a popular topic in cultural, historical, and musical criticism on Ellington. While this belated attention stems partly from the Ellington centennial of 1999, it also has to do with the work's status as Ellington's most "symphonic" composition in length and conception, and its rich racial program.[70]

In 1928, as I have noted, the composer George Antheil derisively characterized the formal conventions of symphonic jazz concert works as "a series of melodies which follow one another without meaning."[71] This classically biased, negative characterization of the multithematic, episodic forms employed in interwar symphonic jazz concert works was later reflected in Robert Crowley's description of *Black, Brown, and Beige*. Within the Whitemanesque tradition, the term *syncretization* can indicate the same sort of string of episodic juxtapositions, although it equally refers to juxtapositions of disparate strains and characteristic "rhapsodic" or "classical" scoring effects. Both implications of this term are relevant to the complicated design of *Black, Brown and Beige*.

On the larger scale, each of the work's three movements is divided into multiple episodes.[72] For example, the *Brown* movement comprises three episodes: "West Indian Dance," "Emancipation Celebration," and "The Blues." These large-scale episodes within each movement are self-contained, even though certain episodes are dovetailed together (as in the *attacca* segue between the "West Indian Dance" and "Emancipation Celebration" episodes of *Brown*). As shown in tables 4.6 and 4.7, the internal episodes of each movement further break down into smaller arranging routines based on combinations of song chorus and multistrain forms, along with interludes, introductions, and codas. (By "song chorus form" or "popular song form," I refer to big band arranging routines built from reiterations of a single popular song refrain, rather than arrangements built on two or three strains from the verse, patter, and refrain sections of a popular song.) The formal designs of these episodes are not without precedent in Ellington's compositional work, both small and large scale. Many of the internal episodes are closely related to big band arranging routines or some variation on Ellingtonian "ten-inch record form." The large-scale design of *Black, Brown and Beige* is thus built on nested episodic layers that only loosely relate to each other through both the progression of the work's program and a rich network of motivic cross references. Among symphonic jazz concert works of the late 1920s to early 1940s, this extensive motivic web is unique, but it is also an extension of Ellington's previous experiments with "motivic saturation" and the "development idea."

There are complications in choosing a hierarchical terminology for the work's nested relationships between movements and internal sections and subsections. For example, in his spoken introductions to each of the three movements at the 1943 premiere, Ellington referred to the larger divisions of the work as "movements" and the internal movement subsections as "themes." Ellington's use of the term *theme* implies a more organic, through-composed movement form than is warranted in the nested episodic design of *Black, Brown and Beige*. Schuller fairly accurately refers to it as a "work in three movements and innumerable subsections," but he most frequently calls these subsections "episodes."[73] Priestley and Cohen describe the larger work as a triptych, its three larger sections as "parts," and the internal subsections of each part as "movements."[74] While this latter approach seems the most logical because of the self-contained design of the episodes, Schuller's terminology seems the most appropriate in light of Ellington's description of the work.

The longest and most complex of the three movements is the first, *Black*, which comprises three episodes: "Work Song," "Come Sunday," and "Light." In this movement of over twenty minutes, these three episodes are joined together through transitional bridges, each of which is indebted to the hyperbolic, quasi-rhapsodic interludes of the symphonic jazz tradition. Specifically, Ellington's interludes display prominent textural shifts (often involving a move from a big band texture to solo instruments); dramatic changes in tempo with added rubato phrasing; cadenza-like passages over whole-tone, diminished, or extended harmonies; and fanfare-like introductory bridges and other related "rhapsodic" musical effects. These exaggerated symphonic jazz devices—like symphonic jazz form—gradually lose their prominence in Ellington's subsequent concert works from the mid-1940s onward.

On an intellectual and artistic level, the work's program introduces a wealth of cultural and racial concerns that Ellington continued to revisit for the rest of his life in his large-scale compositions. With regard to the more limited concerns of the compositional models discussed in this chapter, *Black, Brown and Beige* is unique among Ellington's large-scale compositions. It exhibits a multilevel merging of both his future interest in extended, multimovement suites, and his continued exploration of the developmental and quasi-rhapsodic devices that derive from the symphonic jazz model. "Work Song" is Ellington's most complex transformation of this latter model.

Table 4.6 presents a formal outline of "Work Song." This eight-minute episode is without a doubt the most complex unit in the work. The design of "Work Song" bears a noticeable structural resemblance to the multithematic models of both Whiteman-Robbins novelty-based form and the more freely designed multistrain form of stride piano cutting contest works. More precisely, "Work Song" is based on a form of three themes that are connected and introduced by a recurrent "Tom-Tom" vamp figure and various developmental interludes. "Work Song" displays a wealth of novelty-type sequential and chromatic structures, with typical symphonic jazz concerns for frequent modulation (in its latter half) and quasi-rhapsodic properties, such as a varied and elastic tempo; flexible, expressive dynamics; and varied performance character.

Where "Work Song" departs from the complex novelty-based, multithematic formal model of a work like Grofé's *Metropolis* can be seen most directly in the construction of Ellington's three primary themes and in the unique structures of his developmental interludes. For instance, as shown in example 4.5, theme A bears no relation to strain form. The thematic section A^1 (m. 3ff.) consists merely of three statements of a one-and-a-half measure motive (motive A). After these

statements, Ellington introduces a developmental transitional interlude that combines variation and sequential treatments of the theme A
motive. In theme A^2 (m. 27 ff.), these three motive A statements occur
in more rapid succession because of the deletion of the original half-
measure rests that separated each statement in theme A^1. The third
motive A statement in A^2 is furthermore elided with a phrase extension.

TABLE 4.6.   Formal outline of "Work Song" (*Black, Brown and Beige,* 1943)

M.	Section	Length	Form/Function
1	Vamp	2	*E♭ major.* ♩ = 108. Tom-tom figure.
3	Theme A^1	6	Tutti. Motive A (mm. 3–4) stated 3× (call and response between reeds and trpts).
9	Transition	18	Slight accel., ♩ = 120. Transitional interlude. Saxes, trbns, rhythm. Mm. 25–26 = trpt fanfare elided into Theme A^2.
27	Theme A^2	10	Three-plus Motive A statements passed between trbns, saxes, and trpts. Mm. 31–36 of trbns are a phrase extension that foreshadows Theme B.
37	Theme B, "Work Song"	18	Saxes and rhythm. In a call-and-response type of structure.
55	Vamp Var.	8	♩ = 108. Vamp and dramatic interlude.
65	Theme A^3		Tutti. Followed by baritone sax phrase extension that functions as a 4-bar break.
75	Interlude (= development)	40	♩ = 110–20. Bari sax solo continues.
115	Theme A^4	6	♩ = 104. Tutti.
121	Interlude, Part A	12	Gradually slowing. Trpt cadenza and solo.
133	Interlude, Part B	10	♩ = 116. Reeds and rhythm.
143	Solo, Part A	10	Extended plunger-muted trmb solo. Allusions to Themes A, B, and C.
153	(brass sec.)	4	*D major.* Call and response between trbns and trpts. Foreshadows Theme C (with reeds referencing Motive A).
157	(trpts soli)	8	*C major.* Trpts unaccomp. soli. Quasi-variation on trpt solo of m. 121ff.
165	Trbn solo cont.	15	♩ = 75. Trbn solo continues.
180	Trbn solo, Part B = Theme C	8 (A^1)	Trbn solo continues. Set in an (A^{1}A^{2}BA^3) form that includes several modulations.
	(32-bar song)	8 (A^2)	*D♭major.* Brass on melody (reeds initially reference Motive A). Trbn solo returns in m. 191. Foreshadows *Religioso* transition of m. 211ff.
		8 (B)	F major. Trbn solo continues.
		7 (A^3)	*D♭major.* ♩ = 108. Call and response between trbn solo and trpts/reeds.
211	Coda + Transition	6	*Religioso.* ♩ = 76. Alto sax solo leads into "Come Sunday."

Note: Performance markings are based on the *Black, Brown and Beige* score reconstruction by Maurice Peress (1999).

The most straightforward theme in "Work Song" is the thirty-two-bar ($a^1a^2ba^3$) song chorus form of theme C, but this simple design is complicated by two elements: an internal chromatic modulation (at m. 188), and the situating of this chorus-style theme as the latter half of an extended, plunger-muted trombone solo by "Tricky" Sam Nanton. The internal half-step modulation from C major to D-flat major in m. 188 (from [a^1] to [a^2] in the song form) is related to the type of clichéd final chorus modulation "for brilliancy" that the 1920s symphonic jazz arranger Arthur Lange advocated in his 1926 book *Arranging for the Modern Dance Orchestra*.[75] (The third relation modulation of D-flat to F for the theme's bridge is also a typical Tin Pan Alley convention.) The more vexing issue with theme C is how it nonchalantly emerges out of the first part of the trombone solo. Part (a) of this solo is a thirty-seven-bar episode that formally falls somewhere between a theme and a developmental interlude. Although this passage melodically sounds like a lyrical thematic statement (as opposed to a sequence-based interlude), it is largely constructed through a perpetual series of varied allusions to previous and forthcoming motives related to themes A, B, and C. This unique passage is furthermore constructed as a means of modulation, first from E-flat major to D major, and then from D to C major. In short, this first half of the trombone solo carries many of the same formal functions as a typical symphonic jazz interlude.

Although the eighteen-bar length and opening measures of theme B (the "Work Song" theme) suggest a more traditional strain form, this episode's actual structure is significantly more complicated. As seen in mm. 37–54 of example 4.6, the first eight measures begin as a 4 + 4 bar, strain-style phrase. From m. 44, this phrase is briefly extended through varied riffing on the melodic material of mm. 43–44. Measures 47–48 begin as a variation on motive B (mm. 37–38). This "call" is then sequenced down an octave in mm. 48–49 as a "response," and subsequently truncated to a new, one-bar "call" phrase in m. 51. This truncated motive is in turn repeated an octave higher (the second "response"). Finally, there is a concluding two-bar statement of this varied motive in mm. 53–54. While theme B outwardly resembles a sixteen-bar strain form, it is complicated by an internal two-bar phrase extension and developmental antecedent phrase built on call-and-response variations of motive B.

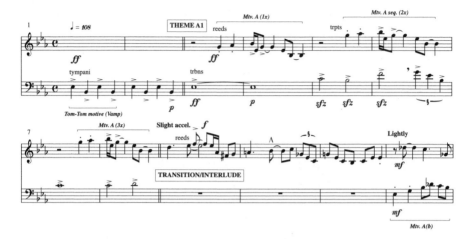

Example 4.5.   Measures 1–12 from "Work Song" (*Black, Brown and Beige*, 1943).
Worksong Theme. By Duke Ellington. © 1946 (renewed) by G. Schirmer, Inc. (ASCAP).
International copyright secured. All rights reserved. Reprinted by permission.

There is an abstract relation between the opening figures of
themes A and B (see mm. 3–4 and 37–38 in examples 4.5 and 4.6).
Both themes begin with a two-beat ascending rhythmic figure. Each
theme follows this figure with a three-beat, descending triadic arpeg-
giation.[76] This similarity is not accidental. The two-beat rhythmic
cell, for instance, is one of several motivic details that are referenced
repeatedly throughout the work's rich thematic and motivic fabric. In
fact, all three of the "Work Song" themes seem like permutations of
one another. As in the design of *Reminiscing*, these close thematic relations suggest a sensitivity to thematic and rhythmic transformation
that is largely absent in the concert works of the Whiteman tradition.

Within *Black, Brown and Beige* as a whole, Ellington's concern for
thematic transformation and cross-reference is most pronounced in
the developmental interludes of "Work Song." The interlude of mm.
75–114, shown in example 4.7 is arguably the most complicated of
these connective interludes. This passage is elided to the end of
theme A³ (mm. 69–74) by means of the underlying baritone sax solo.
Soon thereafter, the baritone sax becomes the central voice of the interlude. Unlike the single-motive, developmental passages of a composition like Grofé's *Metropolis*, mm. 143–179 of "Work Song" con-
tain a dense fabric of semivaried statements and references to motives

Example 4.6. Measures 37–54 from "Work Song" (*Black, Brown and Beige*, 1943). *Worksong Theme.* By Duke Ellington. © 1946 (renewed) by G. Schirmer, Inc. (ASCAP). International copyright secured. All rights reserved. Reprinted by permission.

A and B, and a third submotive. This passage represents a further step in the development of Ellington's "motivic saturation" technique. Like the typical symphonic jazz interlude, these motivic materials are subjected to various repetition- and sequence-based serial statements. These motives are also subjected to a greater degree of varied melodic and contrapuntal combinations than one typically finds in either Whiteman-Robbins concert works or Ellington's extended compositions of the 1930s. In short, while multistrain form seems to have been the underlying template for "Work Song," Ellington's compositional design uniquely avoids the "elaborate recipes for giving a jazz tune extended form" for which Winthrop Sargeant had rightly chastised Whitemanesque symphonic jazz.[77]

Ellington transcends the symphonic jazz formal model at multiple levels in *Black, Brown and Beige*. First and foremost, he returned to the suite-based multimovement design that he had first explored in *Symphony in Black*. In *Black, Brown and Beige*, the suite concept is further

Example 4.7.   Measures 69–96 from "Work Song" (*Black, Brown and Beige*, 1943).
Worksong Theme. By Duke Ellington. © 1946 (renewed) by G. Schirmer, Inc. (ASCAP).
International copyright secured. All rights reserved. Reprinted by permission.

enriched through nested episodic layering processes. This design is completely unlike the greater production number medley/suite model that *Symphony in Black* was built on. At the episode level of each movement in *Black, Brown and Beige*, Ellington relies upon slightly more complex and/or lengthy versions of Ellingtonian "ten-inch record form." This act has come to form the very definition of Ellingtonian "extended jazz," as Ellington's post-*BB&B* concert works are most commonly composed as suites built from "extended" chorus-based arranging routines. This new vision of extended jazz is uniquely entwined with the rhapsodic and developmental gestures of symphonic jazz. However, for perhaps the first time, the symphonic jazz aesthetic is richly interwoven with the core musical and arranging traditions of African American big band jazz from the Swing Era. Gone are the Whitemanesque strings and other orchestral instruments; the mixed ensemble of classical, theater, dance band, and jazz musicians; and the secondary "jazz" stylizations and novelty elements of the symphonic jazz dance bands.

Over the course of Ellington's Carnegie Hall concerts of the 1940s, the residual rhapsodic bridging elements that saturate every level of *Black, Brown and Beige* are far less frequently employed. (There are notable exceptions, however, in such works as the 1943 *New World A-Comin'* and the 1950 *Harlem*, both of which are discussed in chapter 6.) As Ellington moved away from the symphonic jazz model, his postwar concert works focused more exclusively on extensions of compositional and arranging practices from the big band jazz tradition that Ellington's orchestra embodied. These elements include a primacy of the blues idiom and African American musical aesthetics (slurs, blue notes, melismas, call-and-response patterns, riff-based textures, swing, etc.), greater elements of improvisation, and chorus-based forms. Like many of his "ten-inch record" masterpieces and *Black, Brown and Beige*, Ellington's postwar concert works also begin to routinely reference a wealth of prejazz, African American musical traditions that form the bedrock of both Ellington's own musical language and American popular music in general. This deep well of African American musical inspiration includes ragtime, nineteenth-century brass band music, southern dance tunes, stomps, drags and set dances, jubilee, gospel and spiritual traditions, and rural and urban blues. (These same idioms greatly influenced the

Harlem stride piano tradition that was the cornerstone of Ellington's early musical education.) These idioms are often employed as stylistic topics—or "tone parallels"—for the programmatic content of Ellington's concert works. Like *Black, Brown and Beige*, many of Ellington's postwar suites involve programmatic statements about larger social, cultural, and political concerns of their day, with special emphasis on African American experience.

From a strictly musical perspective, Ellington's postwar concert works achieve a greater naturalness and uniformity of idiomatic expression than interwar symphonic jazz, with its self-consciously hybrid stylizations. By the time of Ellington and Strayhorn's *Far East Suite* in 1966, Ellington's concert works were almost entirely based on suite-style collections of disparate movements. Some movements, such as the nearly twelve-minute "Ad Lib on Nippon" from this suite, still involve lengthy chorus-based arranging routines, rhapsodic solo piano bridges, and instrumental cadenzas. However, these elements are far less frequently employed, and they less self-consciously reference a classical sound. Such passages are also far more likely than similar passages in *Black, Brown and Beige* to involve improvisational input from band members. (Jimmy Hamilton's frequent clarinet cadenzas in *The Far East Suite* are a case in point.)

A good example of this new type of suite-based, Ellingtonian "extended jazz" in *Black, Brown and Beige* is "Come Sunday," the second episode from *Black*. The sophistication of this episode is on par with many Ellingtonian "10-inch record" masterpieces. As seen in table 4.7, the "extended" song-based arranging routine of "Come Sunday" is built on a thirty-two-bar (a¹a²ba³) song chorus (which did not yet have lyrics in the 1943 performance). As shown in table 4.7, the rich, spiritual-based theme of "Come Sunday" is nearly as prominent as the theme of "Work Song" in the larger work's intricate web of motivic references. Where the "Come Sunday" episode departs from the typical arrangements of Swing Era big bands, however, is in the great liberties it takes with the chorus-variation routines of this tradition. Another key difference is this episode's employment of introductory and interlude passages saturated in motive-based, intramusical and intermusical references.[78] A clear, thirty-two-bar statement of the "Come Sunday" theme does not arrive until m. 68, two-thirds of the way through this episode, with Johnny Hodges's sensuous alto sax lead evoking the moaning, wailing, and gesticulating intonations of rural, African American deacons and ministers. With a multitude of slurs, blue notes, and melismas, Hodges engages in a fervent and emotional call-and-response with a church-like brass background (which also includes occasional tenor and baritone sax countermelodies). This texture is meant to invoke the musical "tone parallel" of a testifying deacon-minister and his congregation. (These associations were made explicit in the 1958 rerecording of this number with lyrics added for the gospel singer Mahalia Jackson.) The motivic material for this theme is referenced several times leading up to the full theme statement that starts on m. 68. There is a certain kinship between this episode's design and the relationship between Parts I–III and Part IV of *Reminiscing in Tempo*, although the chorus-derived arrangement of "Come Sunday" is far less abstract.

Even before its formal beginning, the "Come Sunday" episode is foreshadowed in the closing textures of "Work Song." The deacon-like phrasing of "Tricky" Sam Nanton's final "Work Song" solo segues directly into a bridge with a "religioso" reed backing and a gospel-tinged Hodges alto sax solo. The *attacca* segue between these episodes leads to an eleven-bar introduction with preluding gestures built from fragmented, out-of-order statements of motives in the "Come Sunday" theme. Before the start of the full, thirty-two-bar statement of this theme (in m. 68), Ellington presents multiple variation statements of phrase A from this chorus, written for the trombone of Juan Tizol. The series of prechorus phrases that begin the "Come Sunday" arrangement somewhat recall the more involved reiterations of the eight-bar phrase A in *Reminiscing in Tempo*. In the three prechorus passages of "Come Sunday," there is one initial major-key statement of phrase A (at m. 12) and two minor-key statements that are somewhat obscured by a busy obbligato violin solo. Beyond the stylistic significations on African American religious music, "Come Sunday" also includes intermusical allusions to "Swing Low, Sweet Chariot" (at m. 22), the dark background reed scoring and harmonies of Ellington's famous 1926 composition "East St. Louis Toodle–Oo" (beginning at the violin solo strain at m. 35), and a typically Ellingtonian, big band train effect for the second interlude (from m. 59). "Come Sunday" ends as it began, with a reed-based, "religioso" bridging interlude that segues directly into the next episode of the movement.

While the delayed-theme design of "Come Sunday" is atypical of Ellington's big band arrangements, it is far more indebted to earlier Ellington compositions than to the symphonic jazz model. The six-minute "Come Sunday" episode is clearly constructed as an extended, chorus-based arranging routine. Such big band arranging extensions also typically involve the prominent use of motivically related interludes, introductions, and codas. These interlude elements were favored in symphonic jazz dance band arranging of the 1920s, but they played a greatly diminished role in the arranging routines of the Swing Era. The arranging routine of "Come Sunday" has a clear dramatic or rhetorical structure, in that a listener hears progressively more complete statements of a protean song theme—the phrase A "idea" of the movement—as the arrangement unfolds. This pregnant "idea" is briefly explored in multiple guises until its full potential is passionately revealed at the end of the episode. By extending the parameters of standard arranging conventions through such innovative means, Ellington introduces a new approach to articulating the "development idea" from within the jazz tradition. This said, *Black, Brown and Beige*'s intricate web of references to "Work Song" and "Come Sunday" motives—many involving rhythmic and melodic transformations—still clearly owes a great deal to the symphonic jazz-derived "motivic saturation" technique that he developed in the 1930s.

As seen in tables 4.7, 4.8, and 4.9, the remaining episodes of *Black, Brown and Beige* beyond "Work Song" and "Come Sunday" involve multiple levels of negotiation between chorus-based "extended jazz" arranging and the multistrain symphonic jazz formal model. Likewise, there are regular interchanges between Ellingtonian big band jazz and symphonic jazz rhapsodic textures. For example, "Light" is largely built through a *Reminiscing*-style "parade" sequence of eight-bar subsection episodes, but it includes a full song-form strain, and a sizable developmental display of motivic references. By contrast, the suite-within-a-suite design of the *Brown* movement involves rather straightforward, chorus-based arrangements for both "West Indian Dance" and "The Blues," although the latter episode notably merges the blues idiom with various rhapsodic textures and gestures.

Beyond *Black, Brown and Beige*, the Ellington Carnegie Hall concerts of the 1940s inspired the composer to write an important series of large-scale concert works. Like Paul Whiteman's series of "Experiment in Modern Music" concerts from 1924 to 1938,[79] each Ellington Carnegie Hall appearance during the 1940s featured several concert-style works within a larger variety entertainment program format. Each Ellington Carnegie Hall concert, like the Whiteman concerts, featured the premiere of at least one major extended composition written expressly for that event. At his Carnegie Hall concert of December 11, 1943, for instance, Ellington premiered his quasi-piano concerto, *New World A-Comin'*, a work that represents his most thorough synthesis of Whitemanesque and Ellingtonian symphonic jazz aesthetics.[80] Both these Carnegie appearances and their resultant concert

TABLE 4.7. Formal outline of "Come Sunday" and "Light" from *Black* (*Black, Brown and Beige*, 1943)

"Come Sunday"

M.	Section	Length	Key
1	Intro. (uses motives from Chorus)	11	B♭ → mod.
12	Pre-chorus 1 (var. phrase from Chorus)	12	F
24	Interlude 1	11	F/Dmin
35	Vln Solo Strain	8	Dmin
43	Pre-chorus 2A → 2B	8 + 8	Dmin
59	Interlude 2 (Train)	8	mod.
67	Cadenza (piano) ("church"-style)	1	mod.
68	Chorus (32-bar [aa¹ba²], with alto sax as gospel "vocalist")	24	D♭
92	Coda/Bridge (*attacca* segue to "Light")	10	D♭

"Light"

M.	Section	Length	Key
—	Intro. Part A → Cadenza (trpt)	11	D♭ → mod.
1	Intro. Part B	16	B♭
17	Strain A (aa¹ba², with 16-bar [b])	39	B♭
56	Interlude (WS motives)	21	B♭ → E♭ → C
77	Subsection 1 (aa¹ba²)	13	B♭
90	Subsection 2 (WS motives)	8	B♭
94	Subsection 3	8	B♭
102	Subsection 4 (WS var.)	8	Gm
110	Subsection 5 (CS var.)	8 + 6	B♭
126	Subsection 6 (CS statement)	7 + 4	B♭
136	Subsection 7 (CS var. + WS motives)	8 + 6	B♭
150	Interlude (CS motives)	16	mod.
166	Coda, Part A (shout chorus style, with dense WS + CS motives)	42	A♭
208	Coda, Part B (flag-waving coda)	14	A♭

Note: WS = "Work Song" references. CS = "Come Sunday" references.

works fueled heated critical debates about the merits of jazz versus "serious" music, the place of jazz in the concert hall, and Ellington's ability (or lack thereof) to compose extended works. After 1944, Ellington devoted his large-scale compositional efforts almost entirely to suite-based extended forms, though many of these works continued to display applications and developments of the motivic and episodic techniques that Ellington had first explored in his extended compositions

TABLE 4.8. Formal outline of *Brown* (*Black, Brown and Beige*, 1943)

"West Indian Dance"

M.	Section	Key
1	Intro. Part A (drums, march-style)	—
5	Intro. (orch.), Part B (ref. to "The Girl I Left Behind")	D♭
15	Chorus 1 (a^1ba^2c, where [a] is a var. on "Come Sunday")	F → A♭
47	Interlude (train-style)	A♭
55	Chorus 2 (variation)	A♭
99	Coda	A♭
106	Transition (rhapsodic, with quotes from "Swanee River" and "Yankee Doodle")	mod.

Note: Across mm. 67–99, there are numerous disjunctions between the January 23, 1943, premiere performance of this movement and the brass, reed, and rhythm parts of Maurice Peress's reconstructed score to *BB&B*. This disjunction is corrected in the Peress score through his use of the original manuscript charts. The score and recording align again at m. 99.

"Emancipation Celebration"

M.	Section	Length
1	Emancipation Celebration (a^1ba^2c, with [a^1] phrase 7 mm). In B♭.	31
32	C phrase var.	8
40	B phrase	8
48	B phrase var.	8
58	Bass solo (harmonic progression rel. to Chorus)	8 + 8
67	Interlude	8
75	C phrase	8 + 8
84	A phrase (piano solo with rhythm)	8

"The Blues" (a.k.a. "Mauve")

M.	Section	Key	Length
1	Intro. (grand, fanfare-like)	D♭	6
7	Chorus 1 (vocal)	Cmin	16
23	Chorus 2 (vocal)	Cmin	12
35	Bari Solo Strain (strainlike harmonic progression)	(B♭)	16 + 1
52	"Carnegie Blues" Strain (12-bar blues)	D♭	11
63	Interlude/Intro. (solo tenor sax)	D♭	2
65	Blues Vocal Strain (vocal; = 8 mm blues chorus)	D♭ → Cmin	8
73	Coda (9-bar variation on the setting of Chorus 1)	Cmin	9

of the 1930s. The symphonic jazz imperative for the hyperbolic display of rhapsodic and developmental structural elements played a much-diminished role in Ellington's compositions beyond 1950. In 1950, Ellington composed *Harlem*, a masterly, fourteen-minute work that is the apogee of Ellington's mature, post-symphonic-jazz conception for external form, and Ellington's richest exploration of thematic development.

TABLE 4.9. Formal outline of *Beige* (*Black, Brown and Beige*, 1943)

M.	Section	Key
1	Intro. ("jungle"-style with important 4-note Intro. Motive)	E♭
70	Cadenza (piano)	—
71	"Bitches' Ball" (ragtime solo)	Gmin
91	Interlude 1 (based on Intro. Motive)	Fmin
100	Intro. to Waltz (3/4 time; var. of "Sugar Hill Penthouse")	B♭
108	Sugar Hill Waltz, Chorus 1 (32-bar, a^{1}bca^2)	B♭ → C
140	Interlude 2, Parts A, B, and C	mod.
164	Sugar Hill Waltz, Chorus 2 (with 6 mm. [a^2] statement)	C
195	Interlude 3 (4/4 time, slowed tempo, hard swing)	mod.
199	Sugar Hill Waltz, Chorus 3 (only [a^1] stated before cadence)	E♭
207	Cadenza (baritone sax)	
209	Intro. (baritone sax cadenza continues in 3/4)	
213	Waltz 2	E♭
253	Cadenza (bari. → piano) (refs. to "Work Song" and "Sugar Hill Penthouse")	mod. → F
263	Intro. to Song (4/4)	F
267	Song (Chorus 1) (a^{1}bca^2, 32-bar but [c] and [a^2] extended)	
305	Interlude 4 (false chorus)	F
311	Song Variation (Chorus 2) (a^{1}bca^2, but [a] is 14 mm)	mod.
392	Cadenza (piano)	mod.
399	Anthem (trpts.) → False Coda Bridge (false codalike interlude)	A♭
422	Motivic Recap. Coda (with refs. to "Work Song" and "Come Sunday")	A♭

Note: All the preceding analyses are based on the *Black, Brown and Beige* score reconstruction by Maurice Peress (1999). Both Brian Priestley and Mark Tucker have suggested that "Bitches' Ball" may not have been composed by Ellington. See Brian Priestley and Alan Cohen, "Black, Brown & Beige," in *The Duke Ellington Reader*, ed. Mark Tucker (New York: Oxford University Press, 1993), 200n, and Mark Tucker, *Ellington: The Early Years* (Urbana: University of Illinois Press, 1991), 39–41.

five   𝄽   "HARLEM LOVE SONG"

The Symphonic Aspirations of
James P. Johnson, 1930–1945

*A*fter 1930, James P. Johnson largely retired from popular entertainment and turned his attentions to the composition of racially expressive, jazz-based concert music. Beginning with his 1932
Harlem Symphony, Johnson produced symphonies, orchestral suites,
symphonic poems, piano concertos, hybrid jazz-classical piano character pieces, orchestral expansions on several of his early ragtime
compositions, a ballet, works for chorus, two operas, and a string
quartet, among other extended compositions.[1] Unlike Duke Ellington's big band–based extended works, most of Johnson's concert jazz
compositions are written for more conventional symphonic or theater
orchestra instrumentations. Nearly all of these works are indebted,
however, to Johnson's foundations in Harlem jazz. Similarly, most of
these compositions involve descriptive programs centered on Harlem
culture and other racial topics. Beyond his *Harlem Symphony*, Johnson's racially themed symphonic works include his *Concerto Jazz a
Mine* for piano and orchestra in 1934, his *American Symphonic Suite*
(based on W. C. Handy's "St. Louis Blues"), also from 1934, and his
incomplete, mid-1930s *Symphony in Brown*. Similar African American

topics can be found in the programs of his symphonic works for ballet, which included *Manhattan Street Scene (Romance of a Hurdy Gurdy)* and *Sefronia's Dream: Negro Fantasy*. His celebrations of Harlem culture and entertainment are further evident in his symphonic orchestrations of several earlier compositions, including his *Symphonic Dance: Carolina Shout*, and the orchestration in 1941 of his *Liberty: A March Fantasia*, a work from 1917 that he dedicated to Harlem's celebrated all-black 369th Infantry Regiment (an outfit that included James Reese Europe's "Hellfighters" band).

Many of these compositions include important musical paraphrases and borrowings. For example, both *Yamekraw* and the *Harlem Symphony* include self-borrowings from early popular music and musical theater compositions, as well as references to blues and spirituals that were popular in the 1920s. By extension, Johnson's one-act operas, *De Organizer* (with a libretto by Langston Hughes) and *Dreamy Kid* (based on a play by Eugene O'Neill), center on stories from black Manhattan, and each owes a great deal to black musical theater conventions. In sum, Harlem permeates Johnson's concert works in conception, formal details, and programmatic content.

Unfortunately, Johnson was never able to organize and maintain the type of long-standing, commercially stable ensemble that Duke Ellington had used as an invaluable platform for promoting his own concert work ambitions. Nonetheless, through the dedication of a small group of conductors, entrepreneurs, and patrons, some of Johnson's compositions did ultimately receive modest exposure through piano solo publications, through occasional radio performances and commercial recordings, and through several important concerts of the late 1930s and 1940s.

In both 1937 and 1942, Johnson unsuccessfully applied for Guggenheim Fellowships that he hoped could provide financial support and institutional recognition for his compositional projects.[2] Johnson's extant 1942 application provides a wealth of information about his concert work activities to that date, his extended efforts to further his formal musical education, and his goals, ambitions, and views of himself as a composer. These materials also notably outline the pre-1943 performance histories of Johnson's concert works. Among the concert work performances noted on the 1942 fellowship application, for example, Johnson lists seven performances for his *Yamekraw: A Negro Rhapsody*, though three of these events are radio orchestra performances and two are film short adaptations. Johnson notes six pre-1943 concert performances of his *Harlem Symphony*: Brooklyn Museum, 1939; Carnegie Hall, 1940; Academy of Music, Brooklyn, 1940; Lima, Peru, 1941; Bolivia, 1941; and Brooklyn's Hecksher Theatre, 1942. This symphony was clearly his most performed concert work. In its account of the various pre-1943 performances of Johnson's concert works, this application suggests a burgeoning symphonic career that was unfortunately never fully realized. In fact, after the 1942 Brooklyn concert at the Hecksher Theatre, Johnson only heard one last orchestral performance of his concert works in his lifetime. This final event was a 1945 Carnegie Hall showcase of the full, cross-genre breadth of Johnson's rich legacy as a musician and a composer. Again, *Harlem Symphony* was a featured work.

Johnson's long careers as a popular music performer and composer are amply documented in commercial recordings and smaller number of scores that have circulated well beyond his death in 1955. Without a similar legacy of widespread documentation, after his 1945 Carnegie Hall showcase, Johnson's concert music languished for decades in almost complete obscurity until the early 1990s, when Johnson's family (especially through the efforts of Johnson's grandson, Barry Glover) ultimately made his extant scores available to scholars and performers. Among the wealth of Johnson-related materials preserved in the family estate, *Harlem Symphony* is again the best represented concert work among the extant sketches, full and part scores, private transcription recordings, personal correspondence, and scrapbook clippings that relate to Johnson's efforts as a symphonic composer. For these and other reasons that are explained later, this composition is arguably the best resource for articulating Johnson's mature vision of a new, jazz-derived symphonic tradition.

13 BRIDGING THE CULTURAL DIVIDE

After 1930, Johnson increasingly sought to find artistic legitimization in "serious" composition and self-education in classical compositional methods. As in *Yamekraw*, his later extended works sought to transplant Harlem's popular music into the soil of American symphonic traditions. Part of Johnson's efforts to gain cultural recognition for his work in this latter era also involved attempts to expand his artistic circles and professional contacts. For example, beginning in 1936, Johnson started to write various (former) New Negro authors to inquire about possible opera collaborations and other professional concerns. This correspondence documents an important bridge across the cultural divide between 1920s Harlem entertainment and leading figures from the New Negro movement. This divide is clearly seen in two letters exchanged between James P. Johnson and James Weldon Johnson, the celebrated father figure of the Harlem literary renaissance of the 1920s and early 1930s. At some point in late 1936, James P. Johnson wrote:

Dear Sir:

You will perhaps remember me from my association with Cecil Mack when we wrote [our] *Runnin Wild* show together.

Sometime ago I was speaking with your brother Rosamond & he said he had written you concerning myself.

Dr. Johnson I am desirous of obtaining the Gugenheim [*sic*] Fellowship & I am appealing to you to help me.

My "Yamekraw" Negro Rhapsody was played by the W.P.A. Theatre Orch. as an overture to *Macbeth*. It also has been synchronized very sucessfully [*sic*] by Warner Bros. and Pathe Motion Picture Companies.

I have in manuscript a "Symphonic Suite" on *St. Louis Blues*, 2 symphonies, a piano concerto & other compositions for major symphony orchestra [and] also [solo] piano pieces. My reputation in the popular field is well known here & abroad. Namely

Runnin Wild—Miller & Lyles
Keep Shufflin'—" "
Sugar Hill—" "
Plantation Days—O'Neil & Greenwal[d]
Messin Around—Louis Isquith

Also interpolations for the late [Florenz] Zeigfeld [*sic*], Earl Carroll, George White, Shubert [i.e., the Shubert Brothers] &

others. I need money & would like to continue & complete my musical education & compositions.

> Hoping you will help me.
> I remain sincerely
> James P. Johnson[3]

James Weldon Johnson's response was as follows:

My dear Mr. Johnson:

Of course, I know who you are, and I am familiar with your work.

The first step you need to take in trying for a Guggenheim Fellowship is to write Mr. Henry Allen Moe, Secretary . . . In writing him you may mention my name. When you file your application you may give me as one of your references. I shall be glad to use any influence I may have to help you in securing the award of a fellowship.

> With best wishes, I am
> Sincerely yours,
> James Weldon Johnson[4]

These two letters make clear the social distance between the composer and the author. James P. clearly knew Rosamond Johnson, likely through their mutual work in various 1920s and 1930s musical theater projects. James P. and James Weldon, however, did not personally know each other, but each had become aware of the other through their high-profile cultural activities. James P.'s deferential tone and his assumption that James Weldon's influence could help in an application for a competitive and prestigious Guggenheim Fellowship underscores James P.'s knowledge of the senior author's reputation. In the late 1920s and early 1930s, James Weldon Johnson was perhaps the most visible black American intellectual because of his work as a literary critic and author, his earlier fame in musical theater, and his 1925 and 1926 collections of spirituals, among other projects. James P. Johnson's extensive references to his concert works, their nontraditional performance history, and his significant reputation in popular music suggests a fairly egalitarian view on the cultural distance between these significant accomplishments. Nevertheless, James P. felt it was necessary to mention his hope of "complet[ing]" his "musical education," by which he means a formal education in classical composition and music theory. In other words, despite his significant career, James P. Johnson's desire for "education" is colored by a class-based need for legitimization in the world of classical art music.

Despite his adherence to the compositional models of Harlem entertainment in most of his concert works, from the mid-1920s forward, James P. Johnson regularly worked to improve his compositional craft in writing extended forms. In his considerable efforts to pursue a more formal musical education from the mid-1920s forward, it seems that Johnson was "forever in pursuit of a conservatory equivalency diploma," as Maurice Peress has noted of Gershwin's similar quest for legitimacy in the concert music field.[5] Evidence suggests, though, that Johnson's educational efforts were far more extensive and rigorous than those of his friend, George Gershwin.

In his desire to move from a "lowly" career as a popular music composer to the "high" culture sphere of concert music, James P. Johnson likely saw certain parallels with James Weldon Johnson's earlier transition from musical theater to "serious" literature. James Weldon Johnson long supported such bootstrap cultural ambitions, and he clearly believed James P.'s concert music aspirations were worthy of his support, though he was not likely familiar with Johnson's compositions in this vein.

In his 1942 application package—that is, his second attempt—for a Guggenheim Fellowship, Johnson provides an extended overview of his career that emphasizes his "musical education," the "plan of work" for the proposed grant, and a multipart composition list. Johnson's multiple artistic personalities are ideally summarized at the end of his "Creative Work: Accomplishments" essay:

> Having played the piano and conducted bands in dance halls, cabarets and on the stage from the South to Broadway and in all the principal cities of the United States and abroad, and having trained choruses and choirs for big [Broadway] shows and radio in addition to having acquired . . . classical technique, I feel that I am exceedingly close to my race with an extensive musical life comparable to few others in the field. I have written "blues," big

ensembles, original spirituals, classic songs and seen life from the most primitive to the highest stage in America.[6]

This emphasis on the cultural diversity of his musical background was likely unique among the Guggenheim Fellowship applications of that day. While many forgotten musicians won Guggenheim Fellowships for composition, this honor was bestowed upon some of the most celebrated art music composers of the interwar era. The composition fellows from 1925 to 1942 (i.e., from the award's inception to the time of Johnson's second application) included Aaron Copland, Roger Sessions, Roy Harris, Randall Thompson, Ruth Crawford Seeger, Otto Leuning, William Shuman, and Carlos Chávez, among others.[7] In this era, it is not surprising that a small number of fellows had dabbled in merging traditional concert music and jazz-derived stylistic gestures. For example, Copland was a fellow in 1925, and he wrote his 1926 jazz-oriented Piano Concerto during his time as a Guggenheim fellow. By contrast, when George Antheil became a fellow in 1932–33, he had lost interest in his earlier jazz-derived idioms. There is an important distinction to be made, however, among these 1920s "jazz"-influenced "serious" concert works. In general, composers like Copland and Antheil approached their jazz and popular music borrowings from "above"—or outside—jazz culture. For example, neither Copland or Antheil had any performance experience or training in contemporary jazz or popular music.

With their mutual backgrounds in music for the theater, Marc Blitzstein (a fellow in 1940–41) and Robert Russell Bennett (a fellow in 1928–29) are two recipients who had professional backgrounds somewhat comparable to Johnson's. While Blitzstein's populist-oriented, agitprop stage works of the 1930s and 1940s borrow from accessible, vernacular music traditions, his elite pedigree as a composer influenced the public's reception of his musical theater works as high culture. By contrast, prior to his 1928–29 Guggenheim award, Bennett's training as a composer largely consisted of conventional music studies with the Danish composer-conductor Carl Busch (who led the Kansas City Symphony), as well as an on-the-job education through his arranging work in Broadway productions and for Tin Pan Alley publishers. However, since Bennett was the preeminent Broadway arranger of the 1920s and 1930s, his application likely carried influential references from America's top musical theater composers, and most especially George Gershwin and Jerome Kern. With this specific background, Bennett's 1928–29 fellowship probably offers the most relevant comparison to Johnson's application. Like Johnson, he had an interest in merging popular music and concert music traditions in some—though by no means all—of his concert works. Bennett's award in part funded his compositional studies with Nadia Boulanger in Paris. Johnson obviously hoped to pursue a similar opportunity.

Another important comparison can be made to William Grant Still, who was the only African American composition fellow from 1925 to 1942. Like Bennett and Johnson, Still had a very active career in popular music of the 1920s and 1930s. Like Johnson, Still was an intimate member of the Harlem entertainment circle. Unlike Bennett or Johnson, Still had acquired extensive formal compositional training, most notably from both George Whitefield Chadwick, who directed the New England Conservatory, and the "ultramodernist" composer Edgard Varèse. At the time of his 1934–35 Guggenheim fellowship, Still had just gained a measure of fame as a "serious" composer through the success of his *Afro-American Symphony* of 1930. While there are certainly jazz- and blues-derived elements in this famous work, this composition also displays a host of formal details that set it apart from the concert jazz ideal that Johnson later developed in his extended works of the 1930s and 1940s, as will be discussed later. In light of their long personal and professional friendship, however, it seems likely that Still's award was the impetus for Johnson's interest in pursuing this avenue of support.

With the exception of Bennett, all of the Guggenheim fellows mentioned earlier had significant pedigrees in contemporary "serious" composition. I use the term *serious* as a means to underscore the perceived cultural chasm between "high" concert music culture and "low" popular entertainment. The highbrow/lowbrow paradigm obviously carries powerful, implicit notions about cultural prestige and privilege. The era's inherent prejudice against "low" popular music compositional traditions likely played a great role in Johnson's ambitions to achieve respect as a concert music composer. Johnson seems to have recognized that this goal could only be achieved through recognition from established "serious" composers, from prestigious cultural awards like the Guggenheim Fellowship, and through the prestige afforded by a "proper" compositional pedigree with esteemed teachers. With these criteria in mind, in his 1942 application essay, Johnson humbly notes that he "managed to become a member of the League of Composers," the esteemed New York organization that promoted performances of contemporary music. To underscore the merits of this accomplishment, Johnson cites Igor Stravinsky's, Arnold Schoenberg's, and William Grant Still's memberships in this organization.

Johnson's 1942 application essay also suggests his concerns about the comparative quality of his formal education in that he provides extensive details to document his formal training in classical composition and literature. Johnson mentions his early piano studies with Bruto Giannini, where he "studied Kohler-Bertini's Etudes [i.e., some of Henri-Jerome Bertini's keyboard etudes arranged by Louis Koehler], [Muzio] Clementi's Preludes and Exercises . . . [in] *Gradus ad Parnaseum* [*sic*], Handel's Fughetle's [*sic*] and Bach's little preludes and exercises." He adds that "in addition to other classics," he "also studied over a period of six years several of Chopin's waltz's [*sic*], preludes, nocturnes, [his] Polonaise and Beethoven's 'Moonlight Sonata.'" Despite his emphasis here on a classical pedigree, Johnson further adds that "while studying [the classics] I was working in various cabarets and composing by ear at the same time." After mentioning a series of his early ragtime compositions and popular songs, as well as his vaudeville and musical theater work around the country, Johnson again turns to an additional discussion of his continued balance between furthering his formal music education and his efforts to build a professional career. He mentions studying composition and Percy Goetschius's 1892 *The Theory and Practice of Tone-Relations: An Elementary Course of Harmony with Emphasis upon the Element of Melody* with "E. A. Jackson a private pupil of Dr. Goetchins [*sic*] himself and a graduate of the Institute of Musical Art" (which was later renamed Juilliard). He further adds that at roughly the same time (1917), the Q.R.S. piano roll company "engaged me as a staff pianist and my rolls were a sensation overnight. I went out to Chicago and helped produce a musical revue called 'Plantation Days', with the music by George Gershwin and the Negro parts by myself, which played all the key cities of the United States and . . . in London, England."[8]

After this initial educational overview, Johnson provides an extensive list of his hit songs, musical theater scores, and nightclub revue work. Johnson then claims that in 1930 he "resolved to complete [his] musical education." To do this, he "began to study strict counterpoint with a teacher named Mr. Markham, a Royal Fellow from Royal College, London." Soon thereafter, he "resumed, with Ea. A. Jackson, 'Homophonic Forms,' 'Applied Counterpoint,' 'Larger Forms,' all of Dr. Goethchins [*sic*] works and Prout Instrumentation." (He is referring to Percy Goetschius's 1898 *The Homophonic Forms of Musical Composition*, Goetschius's 1902 *Counterpoint Applied in the Invention, Fugue, Canon and Other Polyphonic Forms*, Goetschius's 1915 *The Larger Forms of Musical Composition*, and Ebenezer Prout's 1877 *Instrumentation*.)[9] After providing a descriptive account of his post-1930 concert works, Johnson returns to yet more evidence of his training in classical music:

> I had studied Richter's *Harmony* [Ernst Friedrich Richter's 1912
> *Manual of Harmony*] and Prout's *Counterpoint* [Ebenezer Prout's
> 1890 *Counterpoint: Strict and Free*] with Mr. Furgieule in the years
> of 1927 and 1928 and 1929 and piano with E. E. Troumann under
> whom I studied Chopin [é]tudes, Mochele's *Finishing Studies*
> [unknown], Beethoven's Sonata *Pathétique* and G Major Concerto
> [i.e., Piano Concerto no. 4 in G Major, op. 58], Schumann's
> *Soaring* [*Aufschwung*, for solo piano], Liszt's *Rigoletto Paraphrase* and
> Second and Twelfth Rhapsodies, [Carl Maria] Von Weber's Rondo
> in E-Flat [i.e., *Rondo brillante* in E-flat Major, for solo piano], and
> Bach two and three part inventions, well-tempered Clavichord
> [*Well-Tempered Clavier*] and Classic Repertoire in general. I had to
> analyze Haydn, Mozart, Beethoven and most of the masters in my
> composition studies. In 1935 I took up instrumentation studies with
> Mr. Boris Levinson, a pupil of Rimsky-Korsakoff, studying the
> aforesaid Masters' Treatise [his book *Principles of Orchestration*].[10]

In a likely effort to offset the dated, nineteenth-century focus of these formal studies, Johnson further claims that he is "busily engaged in the study of the Impressionistic, Atonal and Polyatonal Schools of Composition." Alongside the conservative nature of his private classical education studies, his mistaken use of the word "polyatonal" for "polytonal" suggests that Johnson had a fairly limited formal knowledge of contemporary art music. This hypothesis is further verified throughout his extant personal notes on concert works that Johnson felt he should study (or that he had heard over the radio or in live performances). Almost all of the works cited in these notes are from the nineteenth-century warhorse concert repertory that was promoted by popular radio conductors like Arturo Toscanini and Leopold Stokowski. This conservative, behind-the-times understanding of the classical tradition is further reflected in his description of his "Plan of Work" for his application. In this section, he suggests that the programmatic "symphonic tale" of Beethoven's Symphony no. 3, the *Eroica*, could be adapted for a symphonic account of African American history. He states that in his proposed composition he will "endeavor to depict the Negro's loyalty and gallantry from our Country's beginning up to the present time."[11] The history- and race-based patriotic program he outlines for his proposed symphonic suite, which he titles *The U.S.A.: Remember the Blood, We, Too Have Shed for Thee*, has significant resonances with Ellington's *Black, Brown and Beige*. There may even be some unknown thread of mutual influence between these two works. In both these compositions, and nearly all of Johnson's and Ellington's other concert work efforts, each composer focused almost exclusively on programmatic compositions. The concert jazz tradition that Johnson and Ellington were building is certainly related to nineteenth-century Romantic repertories, specifically small character pieces and symphonic tone poems. However, there was also likely an influence from the more middlebrow descriptive concert music traditions of American theater and movie palace orchestra repertories.

Because of the heated politics of contemporary American cultural hierarchies, it is not likely that the Guggenheim selection committee placed much cultural value on Johnson's significant popular music and commercial accomplishments. The inherent prejudices against popular music in the interwar culture of American classical music likely tainted the Guggenheim committee's reception of Johnson's application. Beyond his commitment to a compositional idiom built on popular music, race may have been a factor to contributing Johnson's two-time failure to win a fellowship. Johnson himself proudly stated that he may have been too "close to [his] race" and have had too "extensive [a] musical life" when compared to "others in the field" of "serious" composition. Regardless, Johnson's richly varied career to 1942 differed drastically from the accomplished group of Guggenheim fellows outlined earlier.

Johnson's failure to win an award of this nature by no means reflects poorly on the high quality of his concert works. It says far more about the class, race, and cultural barriers of the day that impeded his artistic ambitions. Despite the rather conservative nature of Johnson's formal music studies, his actual compositions are in fact quite up-to-date in their wholehearted embrace of modern popular music in formal structure, idiomatic language, and even aspects of orchestration. This vision sought to bridge American race and class divisions, particularly among the worlds of entertainment and art. Johnson's first—and arguably his most successful—realization of these ideals can be found in his *Harlem Symphony*.

13 THE PERFORMANCE HISTORY OF JAMES P. JOHNSON'S *HARLEM SYMPHONY*

The manuscript sketches for Johnson's *Harlem Symphony* state that the work was "conceived [in the] Winter of 1930" and "completed June 27th 1932." The work received its debut at a rather extraordinary event on November 21, 1937. The occasion was the premiere performance of the American Negro Ballet company at the Lafayette Theatre in Harlem. Founded in 1933, this Harlem-based ballet company was the brainchild of the white impresario Eugene Von Grona, a German-born dancer who had emigrated to New York in 1926. Von Grona initially made a name for himself by introducing German expressionist dancing to American mass audiences in movie prologue performances and at other similar venues. With the financing of the movie palace mogul "Roxy" Rothafel, Von Grona placed an open call for dancers in Harlem newspapers in 1933. His objective was to found a modern black dance company that would both reflect contemporary dance and the cultural heritage of its dancers.[12]

The importance of this 1937 event to Harlem music was that the company's premiere also fostered the founding of a Harlem orchestra. Over the several weeks of its tenure at the Lafayette, the ensemble was variously listed in show programs (and the press) as the Harlem Symphony Orchestra, the New York Negro Symphony Orchestra, the

Negro Symphony Orchestra, and even the American Symphony Orchestra.[13] The inspiration for this orchestra may have come from the Negro Theatre Orchestra (aka the Negro Unit Orchestra) that was organized by the WPA Federal Theatre Project in 1936. This latter ensemble was part of the Lafayette Theatre's production of *Macbeth*, directed by Orson Welles. (This all-black interpretation of Shakespeare's masterpiece is commonly known as Welles's "Voodoo Macbeth" because the locale of the play was moved to the contemporary West Indies.) This WPA orchestra performed incidental music for the play, as well as an overture and several other orchestral works. For its entire eight-month run, the chosen overture was Johnson's *Yamekraw*.

The dual premieres of the American Negro Ballet company and the New York Negro Symphony Orchestra received wide press coverage in the national black press, local papers like the *New York Times*, and such magazines as *Down Beat, Time,* and the *New Yorker.* Most of these sources favorably mention the performance of Johnson's symphony. On November 20, 1937, the *New York Amsterdam News* announced that the orchestra was scheduled to perform "for the first time, Jimmy Johnson's *Symphonie Harlem,* [a] brilliant new opus . . . Mr. Johnson will direct as guest conductor for the overture Sunday." The *Amsterdam News* also reported that the event would also include "a short address by James Weldon Johnson."[14] This address spoke of the evening as being an "epochal event in the cultural history of the American Negro."[15] The program describes Johnson's symphony as

a new symphony in four movements by [the] noted young composer James Price Johnson, of which two are presented for the first time at this concert. In the first movement we hear the subway train pulling into Penn Station, the rush and bustle of the crowds jamming into the car before the door closes and then the ride uptown. At 110th Streets, strains of Yiddish songs and dances are heard. At 116th Street, the tempo changes to the rhumba of the Spanish section. Men and women are heard rushing for the doors to change trains at the 125th Street stop and the ride goes on to 135th Street. We are in Harlem. In the next movement, we are in Harlem's crowded tenements. A boy and girl have quarreled and he pours his broken heart out in a blues song. She forgives him and the song becomes a melody of love.

The orchestra's contributions attracted enough attention that at least one of its performances was broadcast locally on the radio station WOR on November 21, 1937.[16]

Much of the nationally circulated press coverage for the ballet-orchestra premiere remarked on the racial novelties in the production, and comparisons were regularly made to other Harlem entertainment traditions. For example, *Time* magazine noted that "in the pit an all-Negro 'symphony' orchestra, sporting a single saxophone as a concession to racial idiom, played lukewarm jazz." They found similar novelty interest in the racial dynamics of Von Grona's project as a whole. In reviewing the evening's performance, *Time* remarked that "the attempted emulsion of ballet technique and [jazz-derived] hot-cha failed to mix. *St. Louis Woman* . . . was straight hot-cha, and might have done better at the Cotton Club."[17] Despite a critical reception colored by expectations of "Harlem hot-cha," the publicity for the event underscored Von Grona's paternal interest in providing "artistic opportunities" to Harlem performers.[18]

These documents (and others) illustrate the rich cultural milieu that introduced Johnson's *Harlem Symphony*. This ballet-orchestra project marked a highly unusual collision of cultural, racial, commercial, and philanthropic interests. The broad spectrum of perspectives represented in these documents reflect a rich cross-section of racial and cultural views that emerged from this meeting of white and black Manhattan's performance communities.

Johnson's symphony was next performed on March 11, 1939, at the Brooklyn Museum as part of the Brooklyn Civic Orchestra's annual "Schubert Festival." The ensemble's conductor, Dr. Paul Kosok, became an important proponent of the work over the next several years. This performance marked the full work's premiere (as we have seen, the American Negro Ballet program notes state that only two movements were used as an overture).

In this 1939 performance, the *Harlem Symphony* appeared just after intermission on a program that included Franz Schubert's Symphony no. 4 ("Tragic"), two Schubert orchestral overtures, two orchestral lieder by Schubert, and an orchestral rhapsody by Emmanuel Chabrier. The concert program provides nearly the full descriptive program as it appears in the symphony's manuscript score:

Symphonie "Harlem" (First Performance) James P. Johnson

1. Maestoso—Allegro moderato—Andante grandioso.

    A subway journey—Pennsylvania station. 110th St., Jewish neighborhood; 116 St., Spanish neighborhood, 125th St., Shopping district . . . (Female shoppers gossiping) 135th St., Negro neighborhood; 7th Ave. promenade.

2. Andante Espressivo—Song of Harlem.

3. Allegro con brio—The Night Club.

4. Largo—allegro; In a Baptist Mission.[19]

This performance apparently attracted very little press coverage. Johnson's scrapbooks only include a single preperformance newspaper announcement of the concert, and a single review clipping from a local paper.[20] The concert was notably broadcast locally, however, over New York's WNYC radio station. Despite this minimal press attention, the extant transcription recordings to this performance reveal a very enthusiastic audience response with nearly two minutes of applause by both the audience and the orchestra while Johnson took several bows to acknowledge their appreciation.[21]

On October 2, 1939, excerpts from the symphony were performed at Carnegie Hall in a concert organized by W. C. Handy and ASCAP. The performance was billed as "Symphonic, Spirituals, Musical Comedy Songs and Compositions Written by [African American] Members of A.S.C.A.P." The concert was a celebration of the diversity of Harlem's music, with special emphasis on the artistry in Harlem popular entertainment. Johnson is said to have conducted "excerpts" from his symphony. William Grant Still, Handy's onetime musical assistant, similarly performed excerpts from his *Afro-American Symphony*. Beyond three short orchestral segments of this sort, and in addition to a handful of choral performances of famous spirituals, the majority of the evening was given over to performances of African American popular music. Johnson's *Harlem Symphony* was given the prominent performance slot following a massive opening choral performance of "Lift Ev'ry Voice and Sing" (the so-called "Negro National Anthem" by James Weldon and James Rosamond Johnson).[22] In sum, with the performance of his symphony and his multiple performance roles as a conductor and pianist (as a soloist on Scott Joplin's *Maple Leaf Rag*, and as a song accompanist for performances of his own "Charleston" and "Old Fashioned Love"), Johnson was positioned as a central symbol of the rich art of Harlem's popular music.

The conductor Paul Kosok gave his second performance of the symphony with the Brooklyn Civic Orchestra on April 31, 1940, at the Brooklyn Academy of Music. One preperformance newspaper announcement of this concert noted that Robbins Music was planning to publish the symphony. Contrary to this report, the Robbins Music association only produced a piano solo arrangement of the second movement from the symphony. As can be seen in the score cover reproduction in the section of photographs in this book, the movement was published under the title "April in Harlem: A Modern Composition for Piano." The subtitle shows that this publication was part of the Robbins Modern American Music publication series discussed previously. With its minstrelsy-derived, blackface caricature of a man in a tuxedo and top hat, this piano folio's cover imagery differs significantly from the cover themes of the rest of the series. Here, the man is set under the street sign of Lenox Avenue, in the heart of Harlem. With his hands in the air and an ecstatic facial expression, the image seems to invoke period stereotypes of African American "old time" religious expression, particularly the physicality of camp meeting–style hand waving, rhythmic swaying, and other bodily motions. Despite this movement's character as a slow, lyrical "Harlem love song," the prominent motion lines and large, black eighth note at the bottom of this image strongly contribute to the image's mixed stereotypes of black "religious fervor" and the jazz-fueled delirium of Hot Harlem nightclubs. These same themes from Harlem entertainment are readily seen in this newspaper article's account of the symphony's program as "the musical story of the reactions of a sightseer in Harlem. The first movement is his subway ride from Pennsylvania station to the Negro metropolis. Next comes his acquaintance with the romantic life of Harlem, the hectic hours in the night club belt and the religious fervor of a Baptist mission meeting."[23]

In late 1940 and 1941, Kosok gave multiple performances of the symphony on his South American tour. His performances in Peru and Bolivia are chronicled in multiple scrapbook clippings that Johnson saved. (These out-of-the-way performances reflect the unusual international profile of Kosok's career rather than any specific agenda in promoting Johnson's orchestral works.) Kosok wrote to Johnson that fifteen thousand people had heard the symphony in an outdoor concert in Lima, Peru, where the work "was received with a tremendous lot of applause, [and] in fact I had to repeat the Nightclub movement."[24] This account of Lima's fifteen-thousand-person audience was notably reported in the *New York Post*, the *Amsterdam News*, and other regional and national newspapers. At the end of his letter, Kosok asks Johnson if he would be interested in helping to organize an all-Johnson concert upon Kosok's return to New York. This suggestion led to the most important performance of the *Harlem Symphony* (and Johnson's symphonic works in general).

In December 1941, an organization calling itself the "Friends of James P. Johnson," circulated an initial announcement of a forthcoming all-Johnson program of "serious" symphonic works in honor of the pianist-composer. The committee had engaged Kosok and the Brooklyn Civic Orchestra to perform at Manhattan's Heckscher Theatre (in the El Barrio neighborhood at Fifth Avenue and 104th Street). The concert was organized and directed by George W. Lattimore, a Harlem impresario who had once managed Will Marion Cook's Southern Syncopated Orchestra. The initial eighteen-person "Friends" committee consisted of some of Harlem's most famous citizens, including singer Paul Robeson, Reverend Adam Clayton Powell Jr., actress and singer Mercedes Gilbert, Walter White (the famous civil rights activist and executive secretary of the NAACP), various relatives of W. C. Handy, and Fats Waller, among others. This announcement touts that the *Harlem Symphony* "will be performed again by popular demand." It was also the hope of the "Friends" that

> The concert will express our America—its culture and democratic
> traditions. Only in our America could Mr. Johnson's music have
> been conceived. Only in a democracy in these troubled times
> [World War II], could one hear these universally appealing sym-
> phonies written by a Negro, conducted by a White and played by a
> mixed group of artists.[25]

The group planned to have a fully sponsored program with free admission, and their announcement asked for both donations and sponsors for the event.

By the time of this "First Concert of Symphonic Works by James P. Johnson," on March 8, 1942, the event was prominently billed as being "Under the Patronage of His Honor Fiorello H. La Guardia, Mayor of the City of New York." La Guardia had become chairman of the "Honorary Committee," a now interracial organization that had expanded to include the conductor Leo Barzon, the jazz critic and promoter John Hammond, the poet Langston Hughes, music historian and critic Sigmund Spaeth, composer and critic Deems Taylor, and other impressive sponsors. The program opened with the *Harlem Symphony*, followed by the premiere performance of two movements from his *American Symphonic Suite on "St. Louis Blues,"* three orchestral songs (two of which were from his 1942 one-act opera, *Dreamy Kid*), the first movement of Johnson's *Jazzamine* piano concerto, and his *Drums*.[26]

This event received a significant amount of national press, and the *Harlem Symphony* was singled out as the highlight of the evening's program. Among Johnson's scrapbook press clippings is a fairly astute review—of Johnson's concert jazz ambitions, and of the inherent musico-cultural politics in the *Harlem Symphony*—by a critic named O. V. Clyde. Clyde claims that Johnson's major contributions to popular music are

> enough to secure his niche in American music. But Mr. Johnson is grappling with a musical problem . . . of extraordinary interest. Johnson has been trying for years to find a solution for the problem of how to embody the genius of jazz and the blues in larger symphonic forms. . . .
>
> In my opinion, the performance of this music constitutes an historic event . . . This is true regardless of the specific success or failures in Mr. Johnson's effort to synthesize the jazz idiom to a full orchestra. It is the effort which was significant.
>
> It was not made by some musician from the politer regions of the academies who spoofingly or ineptly tries to "adapt" some jazz syncopation to a modernistic score with the delusion that he is "utilizing" the rough diamonds of jazz for his own glittering diadems. On Sunday evening, the Negro and white audience heard one of jazz music's true monarchs at work in more traditional forms. . . . Mr. Johnson is . . . tackling what may prove to be one of

the more crucial creative problems of the coming American composer as well as of the present musical generation.

In my opinion, Johnson's courageous efforts do not quite succeed simply because I think that he has permitted himself to be too much awed by the teachings of the traditional schools. He is too much impressed by conservatory harmony books, and the ordinary tricks of the orchestral trade. The result is a curious mixture of original jazz ideas overcast with conventional harmonizations. This was true of the *Harlem Symphony* and of the *St. Louis* suite. . . .

Salute to James P. Johnson and the people who made his concert possible! Let New York have many more. And let Mr. James P. Johnson tell the music teachers where they get off instead of letting them tell him where he gets off. What they've got can be learned. What he's got can't.[27]

Clyde's attention to the differences in creating concert jazz from outside the culture of black jazz and from inside, as Johnson had, is crucial to understanding the intended project of the symphony. In historical retrospect, this concern is not just a compositional issue but also a matter of performance realization, as will be discussed later. Clyde's mixed praise is founded on his sense that Johnson's project was hampered by his deference to the admonitions of the conservative textbooks he had studied to acquire "classical technique." While I do not fully agree with this sentiment, there is something to this hypothesis in that the musical score does reveal evidence for identifying several of Johnson's compositional models.

Four years after this orchestral concert, Lattimore organized yet another major performance showcase for Johnson. The concert was held at Carnegie Hall on May 4, 1945, and it was billed as a "'Jazzfest' and 'Pop' Concert" featuring Johnson. While Johnson's orchestral, vocal, and piano compositions and performances were the backbone of the evening's program, the concert also included other notable performances. A preconcert flyer for the event notes that the evening's conductor, Josef Cherniavsky, would be "assisted" by an orchestra of fifty "star players" and a chorus of fifty singers, as well as other guest artists.[28] The evening featured three orchestral works by Johnson, including the premiere of his tone poem *Reflections,* and a performance of Still's arrangement of *Yamekraw* (with Bruce Wendal at the piano rather than Johnson). The second and fourth movements of Johnson's symphony were central features in the concert, although the work had been renamed *Harlem Suite*, and the second movement was listed under the Robbins title of "April in Harlem." Slight variations also appear in the program's description of the ideas behind these two movements:

> In "April in Harlem" a musician plays a nostalgic lament in blues style. This is followed by a "Love Song Across the Airshaft," [which is] directed to a woman watching from an opposite window. "Baptist Mission" is based on a typical kind of [African American] congregational singing. Eight variations over an ostinato supply the structural contour.[29]

In explaining Johnson's diverse compositional pursuits, the program suggests that his concert works were "products of a difficult 'after hours' schooling" process, but these works are "rooted in the same mode of feeling that underlies all of Johnson's creative activity." While there is no evidence that this concert was broadcast, there are extant radio transcription recordings for the performance of these two movements (thanks to the fact that Carnegie Hall included state-of-the-art recording and broadcast capabilities). Johnson's other contributions to the evening's performance were not recorded, however.

After the post-intermission performance of Cherniavsky's *St. Louis Fantasy* (oddly subtitled "A Russian Tribute to W. C. Handy"), Johnson himself took the stage and dominated the remainder of the concert. First he acted as accompanist for the singer Edith Sewell's renditions of two of his songs. Then Johnson performed five of his own "piano specialties." This segment was followed by the piano-vocal premiere of the composer's *[Ode to] Dorie Miller*, an extended patriotic work by Johnson and lyricist Andy Razaf. The work is dedicated to the African American sailor famous for his heroism during the attack on Pearl Harbor. This number was followed by a "jazz-jamboree" jam session with Johnson and guest artists performing several of his popular compositions. The finale for the concert was an orchestral arrangement of Johnson's *Victory Stride*, originally a ragtime-based piano work from the second decade of the century.

After this 1945 performance, the *Harlem Symphony* was lost for nearly fifty years until the conductor Marin Alsop gained access to the Johnson family's collection of extant manuscripts. Alsop ultimately reintroduced this work with her Concordia Orchestra on February 21, 1992, at Lincoln Center's Avery Fisher Hall in a concert devoted to Johnson's symphonic compositions.

13 JAMES P. JOHNSON'S *HARLEM SYMPHONY* AND THE IDEA OF CONCERT JAZZ

A considerable body of archival materials exists for Johnson's unpublished *Harlem Symphony*. Beyond the transcription recordings of the 1939 and 1945 performances, there are individual working sketches for each movement. These short-score sources hold clues to Johnson's compositional process—they provide early forms of themes, details on his linking together of separate ideas and passages, and a wide variety of rudimentary thoughts on accompaniment and orchestration details. In addition, there are two to three sets of extant instrumental parts for each movement, most of which show evidence of performance use. There is likewise a separate set of parts and a short-score conductor's part from the 1945 performance for "April in Harlem," the second movement of the symphony.

The most important extant full score is a composite, comprising printed full scores to movements 2 through 4, as well as a holograph manuscript for most of the first movement (which oddly includes printed pages for only the introduction). Throughout this document, both manuscript and printed score pages include penciled conducting notes and extensive revisions and refinements to musical content in Johnson's hand. This composite manuscript also includes a printed cover on thick, bright-red paper with the text "Symphony Harlem by James P. Johnson." In addition to this composite score, there are holograph full scores to movements 1 and 2, each of which is marked as "revised." Despite this notation, when compared to the composite score, these so-called "revised" scores are seen to be earlier versions of these movements. Beyond minor variations in musical content, the most significant difference between the composite score and the earlier "revised" scores lies in orchestration. The "revised" manuscripts are written on preprinted music manuscript paper for theater ensembles of the early 1930s. This orchestration includes a single flute, a single oboe, a first clarinet part (the second clarinet line is not used), a bassoon, a four-part sax section, a three-part trumpet section, a two-part trombone section, a drum part, a part for guitar in the second movement (the stave on the printed page is for banjo or guitar), a string section (with four violin parts), a part for "bass or tuba," and a piano part. (The French horn stave is not used.) For half of the first movement, the first three saxophonists double on clarinet (above the remaining baritone sax). In the second movement, the two alto saxophonists double on clarinets, with the tenor sax joining on yet another clarinet halfway through. By contrast, the composite manuscript is written for a more traditional orchestra with two flutes (the piccolo stave is not used), two oboes, three clarinets, two bassoons, four French horns, three trumpets or cornets, two tenor trombones and a bass trombone, tuba, timpani, and a full string section that includes the double bass. (The harp staves are not used.) The notable nonsymphonic instrument is a part for drums (i.e., a drum kit) and auxiliary percussion. Throughout all the movements, the composite score expands on the orchestrations and accompanimental materials seen in the "revised" scores. The composite score is clearly heard in both the transcription recordings of the 1939 and 1945 performances. Thus, in light of the presence of saxophones and the hybrid theater orchestration, the "revised" scores likely represent the original orchestration for the 1937 American Negro Ballet company performances of the symphony (as we have seen, one of the reviewers for these early performances noted the presence of a saxophone).

In his 1942 Guggenheim Fellowship application, Johnson noted his orchestration and instrumentation studies around both 1930 and 1935. The orchestration notes in Johnson's short-score sketches suggest that Johnson conceived the symphony for the type of orchestra in the composite score, since these manuscripts only include references to "woodwinds," "oboes," and "clarinets," and there are no indications for saxophones. Nevertheless, the "revised" score suggests that the American Negro Ballet performances necessitated a hybrid orchestration along the lines of his earlier *Yamekraw*. Johnson's subsequent reworking of this initial full orchestration, then, reveals his first attempts to translate this more hybrid idiom to a self-consciously symphonic instrumentation. There is even evidence in the composite score that he was learning classical-style instrumentation by trial and error, as he subsequently refined his "symphonic" orchestration through a multitude of adjustments after rehearsals and performances.

The third movement of the *Harlem Symphony* is an ideal model for articulating several key aspects of Johnson's mature conception of concert jazz. As Johnson's biographer Scott Brown has suggested, the symphony is constructed as a "programmatic travelogue through Harlem."[30] The third movement, entitled "The Nightclub," purportedly takes the listener into the heart of Harlem entertainment. Table 5.1 shows an outline of the form of the movement, which looks like a variation on a standard three-strain stride composition, including a requisite "trio" strain set in the key of the subdominant. In fact, the movement is a modest recomposition of Johnson's early piano ragtime composition *Innovation*. In October 1917, four months before the first recording of his *Carolina Shout*, Johnson recorded *Innovation* as a piano roll for the Universal Music Company. This roll is Johnson's only recording of the composition. Each of the symphonic movement's strain themes are directly adapted from the melodic materials of this earlier ragtime work, although they are each transposed down a half-step from the 1917 performance. Though recorded in 1917, *Innovation* was probably written several years earlier, when the teenage Johnson was a cabaret and dance hall pianist in the Jungles and just beginning to circulate in the world of Harlem entertainment. Thus, the "nightclub" depicted in this movement is likely tied to an image from a Clef Club engagement, a rough-and-tumble cabaret from Johnson's youth in Hell's Kitchen, or even a prejazz Harlem nightclub from the war years like Barron Wilkins's establishment (which moved to Harlem in 1915).

The composite score for the third movement of the *Harlem Symphony* includes the printed notation that the movement is written in "3 Part Song Form / 2 Trios." This description is misleading. Formally, there are not two trios, but one, which Johnson labels "Trio I." This sixteen-bar strain is subjected to five successive variations, with a third-relation key change from A-flat major to C major for the final three variations. The sketch score for the movement includes a passage marked "Trio II." However, this passage corresponds not to a new thematic strain but to music that was used in mm. 165–78, the final trio variation.

TABLE 5.1.   Formal outline of James P. Johnson's *Harlem Symphony* (1932)

Movement 1 ("Subway Journey")

M.	Section	Length
A-P	Intro., Parts A and B	8 + 8
1	Strain (a^1ba^2) Subway Journey + 110th St. Jewish Neighborhood	8 + 8 + 8
25	Interlude 1	4
29	116th Street Spanish Neighborhood Var. 1 of Strain A (a^1ba^2)	8 + 8 + 8 + 5
58	125th Street Shopping District. Lady Shoppers Gossiping. Interlude 2 with Jazz Clarinet Cadenza A	4 + 6 + 2
70	Var. 2 of Strain A (a^1b)	8 + 8
86	135th Street Negro Neighborhood Interlude 3	6
	Jazz Clarinet Cadenza B	4
96	7th Avenue Promenade Var. 3 of Strain A (a^1)	8 + 2
106	Interlude 4	8
114	Var. 4 of Strain A (a^1)	8 + 2 + 4
129	Coda	8

Movement 2 ("Song of Harlem")

M.	Section	Length	Key
1	Strain A^1 (a^1a^2bc)	15	B♭
16	Interlude 1	8	mod.
24	Strain B^1 (a^1ba^2c) ("Harlem Love Song")	32	F
56	Interlude 2	4	mod.
60	Strain A^2 (a^1a^2bc)	16	B♭
76	Interlude 3	9	
85	Strain B^2 (a^1ba^2c)	32 + 3	

Movement 3 ("The Night Club")

M.	Section	Length	Key
1	Intro.	12	B♭
13	Strain A^1 (a^1ba^2c)	16	
29	Strain A^2 (a^1ba^2c)	16	B♭
45	Strain B (a^1ba^2c)	16	E♭
61	Strain A^3	16	
77	Interlude (var. on Strain B(b))	8	mod.
85	Trio (a^1ba^2c) (= Trio I)	16	A♭
101	Trio var. 1	16	
117	Trio var. 2	16	
133	Trio var. 3 (= Trio II)	16	C
149	Trio var. 4	16	
165	Trio var. 5	14	
179	Cadential extension	8	

Movement 4 ("Baptist Mission")

M.	Section	Length	Key
1	Intro. Initial Theme Statement	14	Gmin
15	Intro. to Var. 1 (basso ostinato)	4	
19	Var. I	16	
35	Var. II	16	
51	Var. III	16	
67	Var. IV	16	
83	Var. V	16	
99	Intro. to Var. 6	14	
113	Var. 6 ("The Prayer")	14	
127	Var. VII	16	
142	Finale, Coda, Parts A, B, and C	14 + 13 + ?	

Johnson's self-conscious reference to a "3 Part Song Form" might initially seem to reference the underlying three-part instrumental stride form. However, this assumption is problematic in that Johnson expands on stride form by subjecting the "Innovation" trio strain to five successive variations. The arrangement also departs from stride-based piano ragtime in other interesting ways. For example, Johnson scored the last variation in a manner that distinctly evokes the hot-style "out chorus" tradition employed in big band arrangements of the late 1920s and 1930s. The scoring even includes quasi-improvisatory clarinet breaks.

Johnson's purposeful characterization of the movement as a "3 Part Song Form / 2 Trios" may in fact be a self-conscious classical reference to his lessons from Goetschius's *The Homophonic Forms of Musical Composition*. If so, Johnson takes certain liberties with Goetschius's original formal prescriptions. Goetschius devotes about one-third of his *Homophonic Forms* text (roughly one hundred pages) to an overview of "Three-Part Song Form," a design that he identifies with the tripartite form of a minuet and trio movement in the classical tradition. According to Goetschius, the "three-part song form" is comprised of a final "trio" appended to a "two-part song form" (a Classical-era double-period form with the first part coming to a complete tonic cadence in the dominant key, and a second part moving from the key of the dominant back to the original tonic key). In articulating his understanding of a "Song-Form with One 'Trio,'" Goetschius states that this design involves "a broader exposition of the 3-Part Song-form, in which each 'Part' has expanded into a complete 'Song-form.'"[31] In this quotation, Goetschius is describing a two-part compound "song form" with a standard double-period "song" (described earlier) and "trio," which is described as a harmonically complete "song form" in a related key. Goetschius describes one possible "enlargement" of this form as a "Song Form with Two 'Trios,'" in which a composer can add a new (second) "trio" instead of repeating the first one. If Johnson's description of the design of this movement was a nod to Goetschius, then he clearly was not slavish in following his textbook. Rather, he likely saw a correlation between ragtime form and both Goetschius's "Three-Part Song Form" and "Song Form with Two 'Trios.'" In shoehorning these textbook models onto ragtime strain form, a myriad of small prescriptive details are ignored. Most importantly, the first two strains are harmonically complete "song forms" that derive from a compositional tradition significantly removed from the minuet traditions of Haydn and Mozart (even if there are remote connections between these forms via eighteenth- and nineteenth-century Euro-American dance music traditions). This said, Goetschius does not discuss the merging of variations and "three-part song form" in either *Homophonic Forms* or *The Larger Forms of Musical Composition*, books that Johnson had studied. This latter idea was likely his own, and it represents a merging of piano ragtime form and multistrain big band and dance band arranging conventions from the 1920s (where arrangements could include verse, chorus, and patter strains).

Johnson's conception of variation technique in this movement also owes more to piano jazz and orchestral jazz, or even orchestral ragtime of the World War I era, than it does to Goetschius's prescriptions for classical variation forms. The theme of the "Innovation" trio strain is scored for oboes and violins. As seen in example 5.1a, the theme has a typical ragtime character with a cut-time syncopated melody that features an initial downbeat rest on many measures, and a simple accented, offbeat, neighbor-note figure as its primary melodic material. These details are complemented by a busy, ragtime-style flute obbligato part, a sustained harmonic accompaniment in the brass and violas, and a rudimentary pizzicato bass line on chord roots and fifths on beats 1 and 3 in each measure.

Like most chorus variation forms in 1920s and early 1930s big band jazz, there are few significant harmonic variations introduced between the successive variations of the sixteen-bar trio strain. Variation is accomplished largely through thematic variation, changes in accompanimental materials, and changes in scoring textures. On the larger scale, the basic idea here is a string of chorus variations that build in intensity. Over its six statements, the scoring of the trio strain progressively thickens, tempo gradually quickens, and the dynamics also gradually increase. Each of these traits helps to build up to the hot "out chorus" (the final variation). The basic musico-narrative model of this idea can be found in many big band and dance band arrangements of the day, as well as the arrangements used in the popular dance production numbers of contemporary musical comedies and nightclub floor shows. In the first variation, the theme is presented by the oboes. A variation on the jazzy obbligato part is given to a clarinet trio (another favorite contemporary big band texture), and the string section introduces a ragtime oom-pah accompanimental texture. The theme then shifts to the trumpets (with violin doubling) in the second variation. Though now scored for flutes and French horns, the obbligato retains its outline from the previous variation. The theme is temporarily dropped in the third variation (now in C major) and replaced by call-and-response glissandi between the woodwinds and brass (trading ones), which also join in unison at phrase turnarounds. The fourth variation expands on both this idea and the previous dynamics, but both the brass and woodwinds take on larger one-bar call-and-response phrases (again trading ones). The fifth variation reintroduces the theme in full orchestral unison (though with a return of the simple bass line). This latter episode is truncated and elides with an eight-bar cadential extension. The extension begins with hot-style clarinet breaks and sparsely stated, full orchestral interjections, thereby suggesting a cadenza texture. The movement then closes with a rousing four-bar orchestral coda.

The "Nightclub" movement as a whole begins with a short introduction, like an orchestral or piano rag. This brief, opening passage involves three varied statements of a sustained, four-bar chord scored for brass and low woodwinds. This gesture is complemented by a responsorial ornamental phrase scored for an orchestral ragtime trio of flute, piccolo, and clarinet.

The tempo picks up at the first strain (see example 5.1b). The orchestral ragtime scoring of strain A involves a dance tune theme played by the first violins, a flute obbligato part, a simple harmonic backing with a quarter-note pulse in the middle strings and clarinets, and a rudimentary bass line in the tuba and cellos. The sketch score describes this episode as an "allegrto [sic] di stomp." The restatement of strain A introduces very little melodic variation, but it modulates to B-flat major from the tonic E-flat major. The theme is scored here as a jazzy trumpet solo (marked "swing") with a New Orleans–jazz-derived clarinet obbligato. The final eight bars of the strain statement (phrases a^2c) are scored with an additional clarinet trio backing (with bassoons). Strain B (see example 5.1c) returns to the key of E-flat. This sixteen-bar strain is constructed as a call-and-response between two different orchestral textures (one dominated by brass and woodwinds,

Example 5.1a.   Theme from the "Innovation" trio strain of the third movement ("The Nightclub") from James P. Johnson's *Harlem Symphony* (1932). © James P. Johnson Foundation. Used by permission.

Example 5.1b.   Strain A from the third movement ("The Nightclub") of James P. Johnson's *Harlem Symphony* (1932). © James P. Johnson Foundation. Used by permission.

Example 5.1c.   Strain B from the third movement ("The Nightclub") of James P. Johnson's *Harlem Symphony* (1932). © James P. Johnson Foundation. Used by permission.

and the other a syncopated response for clarinets and strings) that shift between each four-bar phrase. This single episode is followed by a third statement of the A strain with roughly the same scoring as original statement, but with one interesting change: Johnson adds an eight-bar countermelody phrase in the upper string parts of the four-bar (c) phrase of strain B. This countermelody then carries over into the first phrase of strain A^3 (in mm. 61–64). Lastly, the trio is introduced through an eight-bar modulatory interlude. The interlude involves the sequence of a four-bar, brass-scored phrase that is actually a variation on phrase (b) of strain B.

Some of the compositional thinking behind this movement can be discerned from the extant sketch materials. Of these seven pages, four include early sketches for what became mm. 1–100 and 165–86. Basic orchestration notes are included, and the primary elements of the music are sketched out over groupings of three-stave systems. Among these notes, there is a telling personal note for the passage that relates to the second A strain. Here Johnson writes "Boston effect," "Boston," and "Slap Stick." These notes are likely reminders to score this passage in the manner of William Grant Still's orchestration of Johnson's song "Boston" for the 1931 musical comedy *Sugar Hill*. In this show, "Boston" was a jazz-based, dance production number. This extant show orchestration involves a similar bass drum and slap stick percussion part. This show orchestration also includes backing strings that provide pizzicato accompaniment chords on beats 2 and 4 over every measure. The key orchestration difference between the symphonic movement and the dance number is that the melodic lead for "Boston" is given to a sax trio, while strain A^2 is scored for a swinging trumpet solo with a solo clarinet obbligato part.

While the sketches for the "Nightclub" movement are written on three-stave systems, much of the music could be easily condensed to a two-stave piano score. Thus the overall initial design of the movement looks like a typical piano rag or stride composition. This is particularly true of the movement's formal design of an introduction, a short interlude, and three strains that are repeated one to three times each. While harmonic materials and melodic and rhythmic content all undergo varied degrees of refinement before the final score, and while ornamental filigree and countermelodies are likewise added to the full score, most of this eight-page sketch maps directly onto the final orchestral composition. The main difference lies in the trio materials. Over pages 6–7 of the sketch, the materials that become the first orchestral statement of the trio strain are simply labeled "Trio" and likewise set in A-flat major.

Over pages 7–8 of the sketch, the materials that become mm. 165–86, or rather trio variation 5 and its cadential extension, are labeled "Trio II" and set in C major. The key change is what seems to identify the aforementioned idea of a second trio strain, and this section seems to have been somewhat of a compositional afterthought. In this working sketch though, the use of two trio strain statements is clearly more akin to piano-based stride compositions than to traditional orchestral writing or the structural models of the classical symphonic tradition. The subsequent theme-and-variations design for the trio is likely meant to bridge these various perspectives. The paper of one page differs from the other pages of the sketches. On one side of this page, Johnson wrote "Harlem Symphony / 3rd Movement / James P. Johnson." On the other side as well as an additional page, there are additional sketches with randomly ordered materials and orchestration notes for the variations of the trio. This evidence seems to indicate that these ideas came at a later point in the compositional process.

O. V. Clyde's claim that Johnson was "too much impressed by conservatory harmony books" when writing this symphony simply does not hold up to the evidence presented above. If Johnson's fellowship essay recollections of his classical composition studies are correct, then between 1930 and 1932 his most important "conservatory books" on form were Goetschius's books, *Homophonic Forms* and *The Larger Forms of Musical Composition*. Goetschius's texts are extremely conservative, and the symphonic tradition that they advocate is wholly Germanic, and heavily weighted toward the models of Mozart, Beethoven, and Brahms. Goetschius even warns that since the symphony is "the most serious and dignified form of musical composition, it is not customary to introduce . . . any movements of a less distinguished . . . type than the Sonata-allegro or Rondo forms," with the sole exception of "the conventional Minuet, Scherzo, or allied Song-form with Trio."[32] Despite its label as a "3 Part Song Form / 2 Trios," in both harmony and form, Johnson purposefully advocates a "less dignified" formal model than Goetschius might have approved. For Johnson, big band jazz and Harlem musical theater arranging conventions, as well as orchestral ragtime and stride piano, were all highly worthy subjects of symphonic elevation and appropriate "modern" counterparts to the minuet and scherzo models advocated by Goetschius.

The remaining movements of the symphony display many of the same aesthetic concerns that are present in the "Nightclub" movement, though in less obvious ways. The first movement is a case in point. While the music may not slavishly illustrate all of the colorful, extramusical city scenes that Johnson's first movement program describes, he peppers his orchestration with a variety of conventional instrumental effects borrowed from popular entertainment (film music, musical theater, etc.) to depict certain events. For instance, the second part of the introduction (mm. I–P [in the score, the introduction's measures are labeled with letters rather than numbers]) is labeled "Train."[33] The scoring here involves a number of common "train effect" instrumental devices. A key element in the effect deployed here is the drum part, which starts with alternating double eighth notes between a bass drum and snare to evoke the initial turning of the train's cranks and wheels. This instrumental part is paired with similarly repetitive low/high figures in the trombones, clarinets, and bassoons. At m. M, which is marked "train effect—wire brushes," a solo drum part begins to accelerate the tempo. The scraping of the wire brushes depicts something like releases of steam from a train's boiler (though the New York subway is electric powered). Over mm. O–P, the score introduces a tremolo bass drum under an accelerating clarinet ostinato, all of which depicts the train picking up speed as it starts to pull away from the platform at Penn Station to begin its subway journey. At the beginning of strain A (m. 1), Johnson again writes "train effect" on the score. The drums—now a snare drum with brushes and a bass drum—continue to evoke the straining pistons of the train. The cellos and third clarinet introduce a two-bar, busy eighth-note figure labeled "basso ostinato." The repetitive figure again depicts a "machine" or motion effect to evoke the train pulling away from the station. Lastly, there is also a small note that states "side to side" over the trombone part. This comment seems to indicate that at least at one performance or rehearsal, the trombone section was asked to physically exaggerate the train motion by moving their horns side-to-side, as one might see in various big band stage routines. Similar entertainment scoring effects can be heard later in the "7th Avenue Promenade" section of the movement, where John-son notes that a trombone figure is meant to represent a "bus horn" in one passage (from m. 92), and he furthermore characterizes another drum part as the "roll of [the] bus" (from m. 96).

The first movement is based on a single, twenty-four-bar a^1ba^2 song strain (see example 5.2). Each phrase is eight bars in length. In the sketch score for the movement, Johnson labels this theme "P.T.," which stands for "Principal Theme." On the second page of the sketch score, Johnson labels another episode of music "S.T.," for "Subordi-nate Theme." These terms probably derive from Goetschius's *Larger Forms* and its description of sonata-allegro form, or rather first-movement form in the Classical-era symphonies of Mozart and Beethoven. Despite the self-conscious "classical" characterization of these themes, Johnson does something quite different from sonata-allegro form. The so-called subordinate theme is not a secondary sonata theme, nor is it transposed to a related key, as one would expect in the classical model. Rather, the "S.T." episode corresponds to the first variation of strain A (m. 29 forward). The variation involves both modest thematic embellishments and orchestration changes. This episode is far from a contrasting second sonata-allegro theme. Simi-larly, though Johnson's sketch score includes two personal notes to "develop this phrase" (in both cases set over bare melody lines), his final composition is quite distinct from the exposition-development-recapitulation model of classical sonata-allegro form. Rather than a classical-style sonata-allegro thematic development, Johnson's "devel-opments" at these two points prove to be merely short phrase exten-sions at the end of strain variations. This sort of fluid, quasi-develop-mental approach to expanding episodic boundaries can be found widely in early 1930s Tin Pan Alley, dance band, and Broadway ar-ranging. The latter traditions, not the advice of Goetschius, were the guiding models in this case.

The distance between Johnson's composition and sonata-allegro form was not the result of ignorance. Had Johnson desired, it would have been very straightforward to follow Goetschius's prescriptions for a two-theme, sonata-allegro symphonic movement. Instead, Johnson builds his first-movement tour of Harlem from a statement and four variations of his strain A, along with a two-part introduction, four short connecting interludes, two jazzy clarinet cadenzas, and a

Example 5.2.   Strain A from the first movement ("Subway Journey") of James P. Johnson's *Harlem Symphony* (1932). © James P. Johnson Foundation. Used by permission.

short coda. (See table 5.1.) In most respects, this design suggests an extended song arrangement along the lines of what might be used in a musical theater production number. This said, Johnson takes important artful liberties with truncations and augmentations of the strain variation statements. In sum, to paraphrase O. V. Clyde, Johnson sought to expand a "synthesize the jazz idiom" to the idiomatic instrumental palate of "a full [symphonic] orchestra" rather than impose idiomatic symphonic forms and developmental conventions upon jazz-styled melodic and harmonic thematic materials. This intent can be seen in a comparison of the theme statement and the fourth variation.

Sketches suggest that the two-part introduction was added after the composition of the main body of the movement. Measures A–H highlight a grandiose theme scored for the brass (first trombones and later trumpets) and rolling timpani. The woodwinds provide a busy, decorative background. This material also forms the eight-bar coda to the movement. The grandiose theme of the introduction and coda additionally foreshadows the "basso ostinato" motive of strain A (which starts at m. 1). Measures I–P introduce the train effects discussed earlier. Phrase (a) of the first strain statement (see example 5.2) is labeled "Penn Station" and "Subway Journey," and this passage continues the previous train effect, though it picks up to a steady *allegro moderato tempo*. The train effect underscores the simple primary theme in the violins. This theme is nothing more than a two-note pattern (based on a grace-note figure) that shifts register in each measure. It is more like a ragtime or stride piano theme than it is a lyrical principal theme for a classical symphony. Though labeled "basso ostinato," the countermelody in the cellos is hardly as rigid as the basso ostinato variation technique described by Goetschius in *The Larger Forms*. Beyond its first two statements in mm. 1–4, this motive leaves its initial materials behind to become more of a general perpetual motion figure. The motive is notably an eighth-note diminution of the quarter-note grandiose brass theme in the introduction. The contrasting bridge phrase for the strain (mm. 9–16) presents a lyrical French horn solo backed by strings, muted brass, and clarinet. The bridge is meant to depict the "110th St. Jewish Neighborhood" (though the lyrical horn melody and clarinet counterpoint are not particularly evocative of a "Jewish" musical topic). There are only slight scoring alterations in the return of the (a) phrase at m. 17. At m. 24, there is a repeat sign with the note to "repeat to horn solo," but this instruction is not observed in the 1939 Kosok performance. If followed, the strain would have yielded a standard thirty-two-bar song form.

Following its visit to the "110th St. Jewish Neighborhood," the audience continues its musical tour of north Manhattan. The first variation of the movement strain depicts the "116th St. Spanish Neighborhood" (using 1920s dance band–style clarinet trio underscored with the "Spanish" flavor of wood-block and temple-block percussion parts). At m. 58, the tourist arrives at Harlem's famous "125th St. Shopping District," and one can supposedly hear "Lady Shoppers Gossiping" (where a light string- and woodwinds-based passage gives way to a hot-style jazz clarinet cadenza). After the second variation, a third interlude brings the tourist to the "135th St. Negro Neighborhood" (where a second jazzy clarinet cadenza is introduced; the final bar of the cadenza includes a Gershwinesque or Klezmer-style clarinet glissando, as well as a trombone figure labeled "bus horn"). After arriving at the "Negro neighborhood," the tourist begins a "7th Ave. Promenade" (this passage is set against a dense texture that includes a busy trombone figuration that is likely meant to evoke either walking or the aforementioned bus).

Following the fourth interlude, the movement arrives at a quasi recapitulation as Johnson presents one final strain variation. This passage only involves phrase (a), and Johnson essentially presents an enriched, tutti reorchestration of mm. 1–8, though at a slightly brisker tempo and with double forte dynamics. The main theme stands firmly in the foreground, as the original strings are doubled by the oboes, clarinets, and trumpets. In the 1939 Kosok performance, the passage has the character of a slightly out-of-control orchestral ragtime performance or a jazzy, floor show dance production number. The eighth bar of the phrase (m. 121) is repeated, before a three-bar phrase extension spins out a number of related jazz-like figurations in the strings and woodwinds (the 1939 recording reveals a clarinet trio emphasis here). This extension is then further prolonged by a cadential delay through chromatically rising, "grandioso" chordal statements as the tempo slows to andante. At m. 129, the trombones and cellos reintroduce the "basso ostinato" theme of the introduction. This theme is set against a long, held chord in the woodwinds, horns, trumpets, timpani, and remaining strings. The final measure closes on an emphatic tutti cadence.

In sum, while Johnson's first movement includes a number of small nods to his lessons from Goetschius's texts, he seems to have had little concern for emulating classical sonata-allegro form in the first movement of his jazz-based symphony. Instead, he builds an artful, quasi-symphonic expansion on the compositional and arranging traditions of musical theater production numbers, and possibly even the more elaborate popular song arrangements of 1920s symphonic jazz dance bands. Here, one does not find formulaic principal and subordinate first movement sonata-allegro themes, nor a rudimentary thematic development section. Nevertheless, by avoiding a clear strain theme statement between m. 1 and the return of a strong theme statement at m. 114, there is a sense of semisymphonic recapitulation. This quality is complemented by the bookends of the "basso ostinato" theme in the introduction and coda. Movements 2 and 4 are designed in a similar fashion.

Movement 2, the "Song of Harlem," has a far less descriptive program than the previous section of the work. Nevertheless, the drama of the protagonists in this "Harlem Love Song" is virtually acted out in the movement's performance descriptions: *Andante expressivo* (labeled "Song of Harlem"); *Andante amoroso* ("Harlem Love Song"); *Affettuoso; tranquillo; morendo; Agitato; dolce; largamente passionato; grandioso; alargando; tranquillo;* and *tenderamente sostenuto.* By reading these descriptions, one can easily imagine a stereotypical narrative for a love story in a musical comedy. A couple meets and gazes longingly at each other. There is a slow, amorous first encounter, followed by a moment of tranquility before some problem arises. Resolution comes through a grandiose, passionate proclamation of love. The couple reunites, and lives happily (tenderly) ever after. The work's reviewers interpreted the number this way. Most significantly, this reading is explicitly conveyed in the 1937 Von Grona program ("A boy and girl have quarreled and he pours his broken heart out in a blues song. She forgives him and the song becomes a melody of love"). The 1945 program described the movement in similar terms ("a 'Love Song Across the Airshaft,' directed to a woman watching from an opposite window").

The movement is based on two very expressive song-form strains. (See example 5.3.) While it seems that both themes were newly composed, there are many small details in the second theme that are appropriately reminiscent of the chorus to the song, "Yes, I Love You Honey," from the 1931 Johnson, Miller, and Lyle production, *Sugar Hill.*[34] Though the 1944 Robbins piano solo reduction of this movement involves only two strains, the arrangement of both the piano

Example 5.3a.   Strain A from the second movement ("Song of Harlem") of James P. Johnson's *Harlem Symphony* (1932). © James P. Johnson Foundation. Used by permission.

Example 5.3b.   Strain B from the second movement ("Song of Harlem") of James P. Johnson's *Harlem Symphony* (1932). © James P. Johnson Foundation. Used by permission.

solo and the symphonic movement bears great resemblance to the three-strain, Whiteman-derived formal model of works in this score series. (In the piano solo version of this movement, the editor Domenico Savino inserted a typical symphonic jazz-derived, arpeggiated cadenza that conforms even more closely to the genre conventions of this series.) As can be seen in table 5.1, the overall form of the symphony movement involves two statements of each strain, and three short modulatory interludes. As in the first movement, this episodic form involves truncations and expansions of strain statements. Overall, the movement has the character of either a romantic ballad or a ballad-based ballet dance number in a musical theater production of the day.

The final movement is built in a theme-and-variations design. The central descriptive program of the movement—the depiction of a Harlem "Baptist Mission"—is fundamentally evoked through both the thematic borrowing of the traditional spiritual, "I Want Jesus to Walk with Me," as well as the aural imagery of various orchestral textures. The movement begins directly with an initial theme statement of "I Want Jesus." Johnson's source for his version of this theme is unclear. This spiritual does not appear in the most widely circulated spiritual anthologies of the day, with the sole exception of a collection by the Harlem choral arranger Edward Boatner.[35] Boatner's four-part arrangement was definitely not followed by Johnson (they differ in both rhythmic and melodic details, as well as length). Johnson may have derived his theme from memory, based on either performances in his youth or in contemporary Harlem.

As seen in table 5.1, the overall design of the movement involves a theme statement, seven variations, an extended introduction to the penultimate variation, and an extended, three-part finale. The initial statement is a pious rendering of the theme by strings alone. At m. 15, there is a four-bar introduction built from two statements of a true "basso ostinato" motive in unison low strings. This descending, chromatic lament motive (see the bass line of example 5.4) saturates most of the movement. The first and second variations retain basically the same "classical" textural character. At the third variation (m. 51 forward), a muted trumpet solo takes the lead. A clarinet trio, scored in unison, provides a jazzy countermelody against a background scoring of strings and horn. At the fourth variation (m. 67 forward), the scoring

Example 5.4.   "I Want Jesus to Walk with Me" theme from the fourth movement ("Baptist Mission") of James P. Johnson's *Harlem Symphony* (1932). © James P. Johnson Foundation. Used by permission.

density increases yet again. Dynamics have risen to forte. In a move that likely depicts the characteristic physicality of a passionate hymn rendition at a Harlem Baptist church, the fifth variation increases both the scoring density as well as its contrapuntal contributions and its sense of swing (prominently heard in both the 1939 and 1945 recordings). This episode achieves an important first climax in the narrative of the movement. Unison flutes, oboes, and clarinets take the melody, and a full trumpet section provides a jazzy, hot-style obbligato part.

After this climactic rendition, a pious "classical" composure returns as the congregation calms for "The Prayer" indicated at the extended introduction to variation 6 (m. 83). Here, the ostinato bass temporarily ceases. Dynamics cut back to piano. A series of canonic exchanges begins between woodwinds and brass, while strings drop out. In m. 102, there is a prominent cadential phrase that is notably derived from the famous "Let My People Go" line of the spiritual "Go Down Moses." In the G minor tonic, the phrase emphasizes a ♩♩♪♩. rhythmic pattern and melodic movement between the minor tonic (G), a raised leading tone (F-sharp), and the dominant (D). Both these elements help to reinforce this hymn allusion. This "Let My People Go" reference soon becomes a recurrent motive (in various permutations) from this point through to the end of the movement. At the sixth variation (m. 113 forward), the basso ostinato motive starts again in the low brass. The main theme appears in the horns and clarinets against a background scoring for brass and woodwinds (with strings out). The statement concludes with a prominent "Let My People Go" cadence.

The seventh variation (from m. 127) begins the buildup to another major climax for the movement. The music shifts here to a double-forte, tutti texture. Horns and trombones present the theme over cascading basso ostinato motive statements in most other instruments. The variation segues directly into the first part of the finale, which begins at m. 143. Here, the tempo picks up even more, and the basso ostinato motive drops out. This cadential extension is primarily built on chord interjections that are connected by responsorial string figurations. This passage leads to a big pause at the cadence of m. 156. Thereafter, the first two bars of the "Jesus" theme reenter as a motive for rising sequential statements which build in both dynamics and scoring density, and the music builds to two grandiose held cadential chords at m. 169. The finale closes on a varied tutti statement of the spiritual motive and another cadential variation of the "Let My People Go" motive.

13 INTERWAR CULTURAL POLITICS AND BLUES-ING THE SYMPHONIC TRADITION

The program to Johnson's 1945 Carnegie Hall concert suggests both that his orchestral works were "products of a difficult 'after hours' schooling" process and that, despite his quest for a "conservatory equivalency diploma," these compositions were still rooted in the creative traditions that he had professionally thrived in outside the concert hall. Despite his extended studies of classical compositional techniques, Johnson seems to have felt little obligation in practice to adhere to the generic formal prescriptions of the classical symphony beyond a four-movement form, a standardized symphonic instrumentation, and basic thematic variation principles (which in his case are only loosely related to the motivic development ideals of the classical tradition). His idea of concert jazz more accurately involves an artful expansion on formal compositional techniques and arranging routines borrowed from popular music and jazz. Like his production-number concert works of this same era, the *Harlem Symphony*—as well as Johnson's other original concert works—revels in the cultural dialogics of "Afro-modernism."[36] As with the cross-cultural ideals that defined Johnson's production-number concert works (like *Drums*, for instance), the concert jazz aesthetics of a composition like the *Harlem Symphony* are equally centered on a highly individual "blues-ing" of the symphonic tradition. By this, I mean that while Johnson does dress Harlem entertainment up in glorified symphonic form, this cultural transposition taps directly into the rich historical continuum of African American adaptations and reinventions of idiomatic blues and jazz conventions.

Johnson's late-career symphonic ambitions, his extended educational quest, and his subsequent correspondence with various New Negro literary figures, all underscore his post-1930 interests in mediating Harlem's two cultural universes—that is, the lowly, earthly worlds of "the jook, . . . rent parties, cabarets, and after-hour joints," on the one hand, and the more lofty ideals of high literature, the "concert hall, the art gallery, and the composer's studio," on the other hand.[37] While these endeavors were all transparent signs of his ambitions for upward mobility and racial uplift, and thus a movement toward New Negro cultural ideology, his steadfast faith in the art of Harlem entertainment was clearly distinct from the 1920s New Negro aspirations, social requirements, and high-minded goals for African American concert music. In specific, as suggested by Clyde, Johnson's vision for concert jazz was quite egalitarian, especially in his desire to "find a solution for the problem of how to embody the genius of [authentic] jazz and the blues in larger symphonic forms." This egalitarian perspective, however, was also tied to the social vision embodied in the descriptive programs of Johnson's Harlem-centered concert works. In a sense, the optimistic, multifaceted cultural view of Harlem that Johnson hoped to paint for his audiences shares much with the postwar racial optimism that was later expressed in Roi Ottley's 1943 book, *New World A-Coming: Inside Black America* (see chapter 6).

The egalitarian ideal of elevating lowly popular music to "classical forms" is a recurrent theme in interwar American popular culture. The concert jazz compositions of both Johnson and Ellington are undeniable extensions of these trends, despite the important racial, cultural, and idiomatic differences that distinguish these works from this near-parallel tradition. Regardless of these differences, each of these musical traditions taps into key facets of interwar middlebrowism. Despite a great deal of the cross-fertilization between all strata of American musical life during this period, most historical accounts of American musical culture from World War I to midcentury tend to rely upon a rigid generic delineation between popular music (including jazz) and classical music. Johnson's and Ellington's concert jazz compositions of the 1930s and 1940s inhabit this very same cross-cultural territory. The hypothesis that interwar American musical culture is defined by its culturally democratizing activities is supported by the evidence of such trade magazines as *Metronome* and *Down Beat*. Present-day histories of interwar jazz might give the impression that these periodicals were solely devoted to coverage of jazz and swing. However, in the 1930s and early 1940s, both magazines were committed to addressing a large cross-section of American musical activities. For its first several years of operation in the 1930s, the front-page title banner of *Down Beat*, for instance, proudly proclaimed that its coverage extended to "Ballroom, Cafe, Radio, Studio, Symphony and Theater." Notice that jazz is not even mentioned. As might be surmised from this logo, these magazines regularly reported on the doings of such popular conductors as Stokowski and Toscanini (*the* world of American symphonic music in the 1930s and 1940s, at least in this popular-culture frame). Both magazines were particularly interested in stylistic border crossings and the cultivation of performances of distinctively "American" music, much of which stylistically fell in or near the symphonic jazz idiom.

On one end of this spectrum, academic studies of interwar American art music have confined themselves to a now-canonical pool of figures and themes centered around both the immigration of European modernists to the United States and the generation of American composers who had established themselves as equals on the field of international modernism (Charles Ives, Aaron Copland, Virgil Thomson, Henry Cowell, Charles and Ruth Crawford Seeger, etc.). Outside of a few recent contributions, such as Joseph Horowitz's book *Understanding Toscanini*, little scholarly attention has been given to the contextual relation of these canonical subjects to the much larger musical culture in which they occurred, nor to the complex interactions between radio, mass marketing, and the culture of classical music in this era (both the traditional and contemporary art music varieties).[38]

Along with Horowitz, a number of historians have recently taken up the quest to redraw the imposed boundaries in American society between high art and popular, mass, or vernacular culture. A primary inspiration for such studies has been Lawrence Levine's *Highbrow/Lowbrow: The Emergence of Cultural Hierarchy* from 1988, an engaging account of the sacralization of high culture and the parallel emergence of American cultural hierarchies in the late nineteenth and early twentieth centuries.[39] One important extension of Levine's work can be seen in Joan Shelley Rubin's 1992 book, *The Making of Middlebrow Culture*.[40] This latter study details the further stratification of American culture during the interwar era and explores the later implications of the cultural trends that Levine first articulated. Examining the rise of such institutions and phenomena as the Book-of-the-Month Club, journalistic reviews of new books, and the American middle-class desire for self-education and cultural self-improvement, and considering the ideologies behind the popularity of great book lists and book programs on commercial radio, Rubin uncovers the "unjustly neglected . . . emergence of American middlebrow culture" in the 1920s, 1930s, and 1940s.[41]

As Horowitz and Rubin both rightly note, the jaundiced highbrow critical perspective on mass culture at midcentury, on the American anti-intellectual tradition, and especially on interwar attempts at democratizing high culture for the masses, had significant roots in the theories of the Frankfurt School (particularly the writings of Theodor Adorno) and Leo Lowenthal. By the mid-1940s, this criticism had begun to "filter down from the ivory tower toward mass-circulation newspapers and magazines" by way of the essays of Dwight Macdonald, Clement Greenberg, Russell Lynes, and others.[42] For Macdonald and his peers, the most disconcerting manifestations of this cultural democratization lay in the market-driven proliferation of inexpensive copies of canonical artworks (particularly the midcentury boom in "quality" paperbacks, books of collected art reproductions, and the phenomenal sales success of classical records)[43] and in the era's boom in institutions for the arts. In highbrow critical circles, these phenomena were not the subjects of praise. The primary manifestations of cultural democratization in the world of music, as Joseph Horowitz amply demonstrates, included the Toscanini cult, the music appreciation "racket" (Virgil Thomson's characterization), and a diversity of related broad cultural efforts at popularization of a frozen repertory of "nineteenth-century [European] warhorses [that] were recycled to amass a primer for radio-era listeners."[44] While large audiences faithfully tuned in to these performances for exposure to classical music and cultural enrichment (James P. Johnson was one of these very same listeners), to Macdonald and his counterparts in the inner circles of the classical musical community, these trends lay at the heart of the dreaded middlebrow intrusions into high musical culture.

This interwar middlebrowism bears on Johnson's idea of concert jazz. In raising this subject, I do not mean to disparage the artistic accomplishments of Johnson's concert works. Rather, I mean to understand these efforts in the distinct historical and cultural context of their day. To paraphrase Clyde once again, for Johnson's "musical generation," egalitarian, middlebrow ideology lies at the very heart of "the problem of how to embody the genius of jazz and the blues in larger symphonic forms." Beyond such basic symphonic jazz ideals, the many ways in which interwar middlebrow culture may have shaped Johnson's symphonic ambitions are also partly suggested in his perpetual pursuit of musical self-education (his "conservatory equivalency diploma"), and the relation of this quest to the extensive jottings and reminders in his private notebooks on the nineteenth-century concert-music repertory that was promoted by radio conductors like Toscanini and Stokowski (in fact, many of these private notes refer to radio performances by these conductors). That said, the cultural mediation agenda of Johnson's mature concert jazz aesthetic also bears a significant resemblance to the literature and art of several important younger New Negro authors who found artistic inspiration in Harlem's commercial entertainment.

Despite the incendiary tone of his call for "the blare of Negro jazz bands" to "penetrate the closed ears of the colored near intellectuals until they . . . understand"[45] and appreciate this new music, Langston Hughes—like the poet Sterling Brown and the artist Aaron Douglas—

retained close ties with older figures like James Weldon Johnson. This cross-generational respect can be seen in Johnson's preface to Brown's landmark 1932 poetry collection, *Southern Road*, where Johnson noted that Brown had "infused his poetry with genuine characteristic flavor by adopting as his medium the common, racy, living speech of the Negro in certain phases of *real* life."[46] In spite of James Weldon Johnson's general aversion to post-1920 popular culture, in his response to James P. Johnson's inquiry in 1936 about the Guggenheim Fellowship, it is clear that James Weldon Johnson's long-held interest in cultivating the artistic aspirations of younger talent could easily extend across the art/commercial divide, a breach he himself had crossed in the war years as he left behind the world of musical theater for his loftier ambitions in literature.

As documented in other letters, during the middle and late 1930s, James P. Johnson was actively seeking a librettist for collaboration on an opera. This objective was likely the proposed project for his now-lost 1936 Guggenheim Fellowship application. Beyond William Grant Still's 1934–35 award, Johnson may have also found inspiration in the award of a Guggenheim Fellowship to Langston Hughes in 1935. Indeed, it appears that during December 1936 Johnson both submitted his fellowship application and wrote a letter to Hughes to suggest a collaboration on a "grand opera." As with his letter to James Weldon Johnson, the composer used a formal "Dear Sir" salutation. A January 24, 1937 response from Hughes confirms their previous lack of acquaintance, as the poet responded in kind with "Dear Mr. Johnson." Hughes seems to have been quite pleased with this new contact, though, as he notes, "I have long known and admired your work, and once met you some years ago."[47] In response to Johnson's remark that he was "convinced" that they "ought to do a strong Negro opera" together, Hughes noted that he would "very much like to hear the ideas which you have in mind. I think we could work out something really Negro, modern, and interesting." From March to May 1937, Johnson began similar exchanges of letters with Sterling Brown. Like Hughes, Brown responded enthusiastically to this new contact: "Dear Mr. Johnson: I have heard Dad [Will Marion] Cook mention you frequently, and I have been anxious to meet you."[48] This latter exchange resulted in several months of efforts to turn Brown's play, *Natural Man*, into a "grand opera," a project that was ultimately abandoned. Though it took several years and several aborted projects, the proposed collaboration with Hughes later produced *De Organizer*, a "blues opera" premiered in a 1940 concert performance in New York under the auspices of the International Ladies Garment Workers Union. The vernacular "Negro" and "modern" qualities of the work were derived directly from 1920s and 1930s jazz, swing, and blues idioms, as well as ragtime, Tin Pan Alley popular song, and a wealth of African American idioms that Johnson had regularly mined in his earlier musical theater work.

These 1936–37 exchanges with Hughes and Brown suggest that the vernacular, urban literary aesthetics of these younger authors offer the New Negro counterparts most analogous to Johnson's mature, post-1930 visions for concert jazz compositions. While in the 1930s he aspired to the broad artistic recognition that these literary contemporaries had achieved, Johnson followed a far more commercial career path in the 1920s than either of these authors or even his friend and sometime orchestrator, William Grant Still, a figure whose concert works came to embody the more traditionally symphonic musical aspirations promoted by the senior New Negro leaders (like James Weldon Johnson). Whereas Still saw clear artistic distinctions between his commercial work as an orchestrator and the high-culture ambitions of his concert works, Johnson's artistic vision resolutely sought to merge these worlds and to celebrate both vernacular musical form and style. In both his long career as a commercial musician and composer, and in his 1930s reinvention as a "serious" concert-music composer, Johnson's music wholeheartedly embraced the "common, racy, living . . . *real*" idiomatic language and dialect of Harlem's popular music traditions. This pride in the historic, social, and artistic accomplishments of Harlem as a community, as well as this rich, egalitarian vision for African American concert music, were also notably shared in the mature extended compositions of Johnson's friend and onetime piano protégé, Duke Ellington.

six 𝄢 "CARNEGIE BLUES" AND THE
SYMPHONIC ELLINGTON

HARLEM!
Black metropolis!
Land of mirth!
Your music has flung
The story of "Hot Harlem"
To the four corners
Of the earth!

Listen:
Soft voices laughing,
shuffling heels,
a kaleidoscope of color,
the savage moan of the saxophone,
the primeval beat of the jungle . . .
. . . .
And so, your song has stirred the souls
Of men in strange and distant places.
The picture drawn by many hands
For many eyes of many races.
But did it say to them

Of what you *really* are?

. . . .

And was the picture true of you,
The camera eye in focus
Or was it all a sorry bit
Of ofay hocus-pocus?

—Duke Ellington, *Black, Brown and Beige*[1]

*T*he widely publicized January 23, 1943, Carnegie Hall premiere
of *Black, Brown and Beige* was pivotal in establishing Duke Ellington's lasting reputation as a "serious" composer for the concert hall.
Following this celebrated performance, Ellington instigated an eight-
year-long series of near-annual Carnegie Hall appearances (with one
notable additional performance occurring at the Metropolitan Opera
House). Each of these well-promoted events featured the premieres
of one or more new concert compositions, as well as a number of
newly expanded, concert-style arrangements of popular Ellington instrumentals and song hits. From 1949, Ellington further increased his
reputation as a "serious" composer-performer by expanding his diverse performance schedule to include appearances with symphonic
orchestras.

Each of these occasions emphasizes Ellington's continued development of his unique cross-class professional image. An amalgam of
high and low cultural symbols formed a perpetually refined professional image of, on the one hand, a commercially savvy musician,
maestro, entertainer, and businessman who wrote hip but "serious,"
sophisticated popular music and, on the other hand, an internationally lauded, "serious" concert music composer. My emphatic use of
the malleable, midcentury notion of "serious" artistic expression underscores Ellington's masterful control of contemporary American
class discourses across his career. This skill can be seen in a December
1945 interview, for example, where the composer was asked his opinion on the *New York Times* review of his December 19, 1944, Carnegie
Hall concert. The *Times* reviewer had suggested that "there are those
who seek in Mr. Ellington's music a growing affinity between jazz and
serious music. Actually, . . . his work is based on . . . the jazz idiom
only and employs an instrumental technique utterly different from

that of symphonic music." According to the interviewer, "the Duke listened to the quotation with a smile." He then responded:

> *Serious* is a confusing word. . . . We take our American music seriously. If *serious* means European [concert-classical] music, I'm not interested in that. Some people mix up the words *serious* and *classical.* They're a lot different. . . . There is no such thing as modern classical music. There is great, serious music. That is all.
>
> Critics are a funny bunch of people. They use words to their own advantage. They live in one world and we live in another. . . . All music critics think jazz musicians are trying to get into the symphonic field. Ninety-nine percent of the jazz people aren't interested in symphony techniques at all.[2]

While critics, public relations firms, and artists certainly use "words to their advantage," in this interview Ellington himself works the very same territory of shaping public opinion for self-promotion. In this succinct statement, Ellington's vigilant devotion to the control of his public image is evident. He portrays himself as both a humble man of the people and a patriotic proponent of "serious" American music. Moreover, while the article's regular references to jazz convey Ellington's unspoken commitment to African American idioms, he positions his concert music not as jazz, and not as "classical" music, but as both "serious" and "modern" *American* music. In 1940s and 1950s journalism on Ellington, he routinely describes the "Negro idiom" as a core aesthetic of his "serious American music." In the context of an interview titled "Why Duke Ellington Avoided Music School," these themes underscore Ellington's self-conscious promotion of a decidedly democratic—or even classless—view of American musical culture. Despite his avowed indifference to "symphony techniques," by several means Ellington taps into the archetypal imagery, rhetoric, and social privileges of classical music in midcentury America: in his adoption of the concert performance model, in the very idea of appearing at Carnegie Hall, and especially in his emphasis on the culturally elevated idea of "serious" music. At the same time, his response evokes anti-intellectual stereotypes that distance American vitality, originality, and supposed virility from the often effete reputation (in America) of European classical music and musicians, while his implied attributes of character position him as an exemplary model of the self-made American composer-artist. The cultural populism of this multilayered public image places Ellington's views on the artfulness of African American jazz and popular music at the forefront of his vision for a serious American concert music. This vision is built on a purposeful blurring of the contemporary cultural boundaries that separated art from entertainment and black from white. The larger aesthetic implications of this project are most prominently seen in Ellington's later forays into symphonic territory.

Beyond the Whiteman-style concert orchestra performances of Ellington's early extended compositions, Ellington's earliest encounter with a bona fide symphony orchestra was at a July 25, 1949, concert with the Robin Hood Dell Orchestra. (The Robin Hood Dell Orchestra is the "pops" configuration of the Philadelphia Orchestra. The ensemble appears in an annual summer concert series held at Robin Hood Dell in Philadelphia's Fairmount Park.) For their solo performance in the first half of this concert, the Ellington orchestra resurrected several concert-style arrangements and extended compositions from the band's December 1947 and November 1948 Carnegie Hall appearances. For the second half of the concert, where the band appeared in conjunction with the Robin Hood Dell Orchestra, Ellington presented symphony-plus-jazz-band arrangements of his 1943 *New World A-Comin'*, a new, witty, blues-oriented work called *Grand Slam Jam*, and a "Medley of Ellington Hits." Ellington's next significant symphonic encounter occurred in 1950, when the conductor Arturo Toscanini asked the composer to write a musical portrait of Harlem for the NBC Symphony Orchestra. This commission was to be premiered on an NBC radio-television simulcast as one part of a larger, multicomposer suite entitled *Portrait of New York*.[3] This never-realized larger project was the origin of Ellington's *A Tone Parallel to Harlem*, a masterful twelve-minute composition that has also been known as *Harlem* or the *Harlem Suite*.[4]

That Ellington chose to designate *Harlem* a "tone parallel" rather than the more generically symphonic designation of "tone poem" is telling. Despite the honor of the prestigious commission from a major classical orchestra, Ellington's use of this subtitle epithet was likely meant to distinguish his concert work effort from the European symphonic tradition. Regardless, this specific designation has a longer history in his compositional history. Ellington first employed this personal genre designation in *Black, Brown and Beige*, which was more ambitiously subtitled *A Tone Parallel to the History of the Negro in America*. As the historian Harvey Cohen has observed, in the premiere of this latter work, "Ellington used the music business power at his disposal . . . to place the subjects of black achievement, pride, and history into the national consciousness."[5] These latter topics—and this social agenda—remain central to the programs of nearly all of Ellington's works for the concert hall during the 1940s and up to the 1950 *Harlem*.

The bandleader later described his annual Carnegie Hall concerts as "a series of social significance thrusts," by which he meant that they provided high-profile opportunities for social commentary both through music and his ensemble's very presence—as an African American big band—on the stage of the prestigious Carnegie Hall.[6] Ellington's social commentary largely resided in the descriptive written programs and titles of his extended works. For instance, in their *Deep South Suite* from 1946, Ellington and his longtime composition partner Billy Strayhorn sought to provide commentary on the complexities of African American life in the contemporary Deep South. In his autobiography, Ellington described one movement of this work as a "little parable in music."[7] This characterization could be extended to the entire work, and to the programmatic intent of most of Ellington's concert works of the 1940s and early 1950s. As Ellington recalled, William Morris Jr., his publicity agent, had encouraged the composer to create more "out-and-out protest" statements. But Ellington "felt it was good theatre to say it without saying it. That is the art."[8] In sum, at its core, these compositions have an innate consciousness-raising, didactic function. As in a symphonic tone poem, Ellington tells a story through descriptive music and the ideas suggested in an extramusical programmatic text (which was provided in both his concert programs and the imagery of composition titles). This dual programmatic and social premise—however subtle or overt in practice—is central to Ellington's conception of "tone parallels," and in turn his more generalized artistic conception of concert jazz. This final chapter broadly explores the idea of the "symphonic Ellington," Ellington's post–*Black, Brown and Beige* public image as "serious" concert music composer, and, finally, the formal and programmatic ideas behind his contemporaneous vision for concert jazz.

Ellington's near-annual concert hall performances during the 1940s closely resemble the 1924–38 concert series of Paul Whiteman. Ellington was personally familiar with the latter, as he was commissioned to write his *Blue Belles of Harlem* for the December 1938 concert. Each series included several jazz-styled concert work premieres. Each involved medleys and groupings of band hits, features that highlighted the artistry of the ensemble as a whole, and lighter, character-type (or even novelty-comedic) numbers. Both series likewise included solo features for star musicians. Lastly, like the Whiteman events, the Ellington Carnegie Hall concerts led into traveling tours on the national concert hall circuit. Ellington, however, expanded on this model in his frequent inclusion of a prominent, race-based social agenda, though some compositions were lighter in their social intent and commentary than others.

While the January 23, 1943, concert at Carnegie Hall was centrally a showcase for *Black, Brown and Beige*, this performance also featured Ellington's *Blue Belles of Harlem*, in a new arrangement by Billy Strayhorn. Beyond this second concert work and its light programmatic reference to the beautiful women of his community, the main political content of this larger event was found in the program for *Black, Brown and Beige* (see chapter 4).

Ellington's return to Carnegie Hall on December 11, 1943, again featured *Black, Brown and Beige*, although this performance reduced the work to a short collection of excerpts. The concert's major premiere was the quasi concerto for piano and jazz orchestra, *New World A-Comin'*. While this work avoided the detailed, elaborate program that Ellington had attached to *Black, Brown and Beige*, he nevertheless described it as a representation of the postwar racial optimism expressed in Roi Ottley's 1943 book, *New World A-Coming: Inside Black America*. This program—like the book—sought to portray the social and cultural riches of Harlem, which Ottley described as "the most complex of Negro communities" and "a sort of test in which the germs of Negro thought and action are isolated, examined, and held up to full glare to reflect Black America."[9]

The band's December 19, 1944, Carnegie Hall concert also included excerpts from *Black, Brown and Beige*, but the main focus was on two new Ellington-Strayhorn concert works, *Blutopia* and the *Perfume Suite*. As noted, *Blutopia* was originally premiered by Paul Whiteman's radio orchestra on November 21, 1944. As with the Whiteman-commissioned *Blue Belles*, Billy Strayhorn fashioned a new arrangement of this work for the Ellington band (though Strayhorn was not credited).[10] According to the concert's program, *Blutopia* "expresses, through the blues mood, the 'yearning of the people of the world for the Utopia of the brotherhood of man.'" *Perfume Suite* was the first concert work of the Carnegie Hall series that was credited to both Ellington and Strayhorn. While supposedly "inspired by the characters of women," the suite includes a number of programmatic references to nightclub life, including the second movement, "Strange Feeling," which "was first created as a mood number for a dance specialty . . . at the Hurricane Club on Broadway," and the third movement, titled "Dancers in Love."[11]

Beyond its inclusion of three excerpts from *Black, Brown and Beige*, the January 4, 1946, Carnegie Hall concert featured Ellington's three-part suite *A Tonal Group* and a newly expanded arrangement of *Diminuendo and Crescendo in Blue* entitled *Diminuendo in Blue/Transblucency/Crescendo in Blue*. Neither of these two extended works carried a programmatic social agenda or even a clear program.[12]

The absence of a social agenda in January 1946 concert was made up for in the November 23–24, 1946, Carnegie Hall concerts, which featured a major new Ellington-Strayhorn composition, *Deep South Suite*, which looks at the complex stereotypes of the black Deep South. The most detailed outline of the descriptive content in the suite is provided in Leonard Feather's program notes. The suite begins with a movement titled "Magnolias Just Dripping with Molasses," which means to present the surface themes of typical southern caricatures: "Here, as the first conception of the Deep South, . . . we find what might be called the Dixie Commerce dream picture, complete with beautiful blue skies, Creole gals with flashing eyes, fried chicken and watermelons—and those good old nostalgic memories." By contrast, the remaining three movements provide social commentary on real-life racial tensions. Ellington and Strayhorn specifically set this first movement's "Dixie Chamber of Commerce dream picture" against the programmatic themes of the second movement, "Hearsay," which evokes the tarnished reality behind the image of the first movement. The third movement, "There Was Nobody Looking," depicts the everyday positive interactions that occur between the races away from the public eye. The fourth movement, "Happy-Go-Lucky Local," is considerably lighter in its subject matter, depicting "a train that runs in the South" from the perspective of its dutiful "Negro fireman." This train-themed descriptive composition was regularly performed outside its original context in the suite.[13] This second 1946 concert also premiered the two-part suite *The Beautiful Indians*. While this short work carried no significant "social thrust," it notably featured both a wordless vocal by Kay Davis in its first movement ("Minnehaha") and a swing-oriented showcase for trumpeter Taft Jordan and tenor saxophonist Al Sears in the second movement ("Hiawatha").

Ellington's December 26–27, 1947, Carnegie concerts featured his new *Liberian Suite*, as well as a shorter concert-style work entitled *The Clothed Woman*. While the latter composition carried no program beyond its abstract title, the *Liberian Suite* was commissioned by the Liberian government in honor of the centennial of the founding of that nation by black Americans who had returned to their ancestral roots in Africa. The first movement, "I Like the Sunrise," is an optimistic song about "new hope." The remaining five movements are structured as five dances, which the program notes cryptically suggest "parallel . . . the four freedoms" and a "fifth that we hope for." These "freedoms" are never explicitly explained, however. (The "four freedoms" presumably refers to President Franklin D. Roosevelt's "Four Freedoms" speech, which was delivered to the United States Congress on January 6, 1941. Roosevelt proposed that "everywhere in the world" humans have the right to enjoy freedom of speech and expression, freedom of religion, freedom from want, and freedom from fear.) The first dance represents "the building of a nation," the second suggests "a gayer mood," the third is described as an "afromantique," the fourth is said to be "full of the velocity of celebration," and the fifth is simply characterized as "exotic."[14]

The band's April 13, 1948, Carnegie Hall concert was a benefit for the Booker T. Washington Birthplace Memorial fund. Despite its location, Ellington did not treat this concert as part of his annual performance series. Most notably, the event involved no premieres of Ellington concert works. Rather, Ellington acted as a master of ceremonies for an evening of diverse entertainment, of which his own band was only one act (albeit a headlining act) among several.[15]

The Ellington concert series formally returned to Carnegie Hall on November 13, 1948. For this performance, Ellington both resurrected *Reminiscing in Tempo* and introduced two new extended concert works, his *The Tattooed Bride*, and the two-part Ellington-Strayhorn suite, *Symphomaniac*. The latter two premieres involved much lighter programmatic ideas. Ellington described the comical *Tattooed Bride* as a "musical striptease" involving "a week-end honeymoon spent at a seaside resort by an energetic young man and his bride" during which the husband finds out "that his wife is tattooed."[16] *Symphomaniac*, a two-part Ellington-Strayhorn work, presented a similar sort of musico-comedic vaudeville routine in that the first movement was partly meant as a "musical satire" on the symphonic jazz dance bands of the late 1920s. The suite's second movement, "How You Sound," was meant to represent Ellington and Strayhorn's reflections on the "serious" jazz of bebop. Lastly, this November 13 performance also included an unusual, and rather loosely organized, concert-style arrangement of the band's theme song, *Take the A Train*. This Ellington-Strayhorn arrangement (mostly written by Strayhorn) was introduced under the title *Manhattan Murals*. This six-minute, quasi concert work features concert-style piano solos by Ellington, as well as both big band jazz and melodramatic concert-style episodes based on Strayhorn's song. In Ellington's spoken introduction, he describes the arrangement as "a look at Manhattan from the [windows of the] A Train, which of course is the obvious place from which we should look at Manhattan because it's our theme." The arrangement is said to "follow the regular route of the A Train" from "where [it] . . . starts up at Sugar Hill" in Harlem, to "the ending . . . where it goes right down to the East River."[17] In his autobiography, Ellington states that this arrangement was meant to be seen as a concert work, but he also anachronistically claims that it was dedicated to the New York mayor Vincent Impellitteri (who was mayor from 1950 to 1953).[18]

The final concert in the series was an NAACP benefit held at New York's Metropolitan Opera House on January 21, 1951. While Ellington continued to compose extended suites well beyond this concert, his autobiography positions this event as the conclusion of the 1940s concert series, noting that "by 1950 everybody was giving concerts, and even a concert at Carnegie Hall no longer had the prestige value it had in 1943, but our series there had helped establish a music that was new in both its extended forms and its social significance."[19] This concert featured three Ellington concert work premieres, including the two-part *Controversial Suite, Monolog/Duet/Threesome,* and—most importantly—Ellington's *Harlem*. While *Harlem* was designed as a musical travelogue of the Harlem community, the two-part *Controversial Suite* depicted the contemporary critical tensions between supporters of Dixieland and the proponents of progressive jazz. The three-part *Monolog/Duet/Threesome* suite depicted "a threesome of dancers" and "a parallel with the age-old triangle of love."[20]

13 THE SYMPHONIC ELLINGTON

It is with Ellington's Carnegie Hall series that the idea of concert jazz composition for big bands is fully formed. This development was a key influence on a new, postwar tradition of extended, concert-style jazz suites. Beginning with his July 25, 1949, concert with the Robin Hood Dell Orchestra, however, Ellington also regularly pursued opportunities to perform his concert works in hybrid arrangements for jazz musicians and symphony. Despite the indifference to the symphonic tradition expressed in the interview from 1945 cited earlier, Ellington regularly expressed pride in this new, post-1949 area of work. In his 1973 autobiography, Ellington provides a "partial list" of his appearances with thirty-eight international orchestras, adding that "some of them liked us well enough to invite us more than once."[21] Following his 1949 symphonic debut, however, it took Ellington fifteen years to release an album that included this performance repertory. The cover of this 1964 Reprise LP, *The Symphonic Ellington*, prominently displays added text that reads "Duke Ellington and his orchestra and 500 of Europe's finest [classical] musicians."[22] This LP includes performances of *Harlem*, the three-movement *Night Creature*, and *Non-Violent Integration* (NVI), each of which had been in Ellington's "symphonic" repertory for nearly a decade. *Night Creature* was composed for a March 16, 1955, Carnegie Hall concert at which the Ellington orchestra appeared in conjunction with the composer-conductor Don Gillis and the Symphony of the Air orchestra. (The Symphony of the

Air was an independent reconstitution of the NBC Symphony Orchestra. The ensemble was formed in mid-1954, after NBC had disbanded its radio orchestra when Toscanini retired in the spring of that year.) The event was billed under the title "Excursions in Jazz" (presumably this refers to the Symphony of the Air's dabbling in "jazz" through this concert). Ellington's half of the concert also featured jazz-band-plus-symphony performances of *Harlem* and *New World A-Comin'*. In the latter, Ellington conducted the symphony with the concert pianist Don Shirley performing as the soloist. Thanks to Carnegie Hall's regular practice of recording performances, this event actually marks the first known recording of Ellington's growing symphonic repertory and of the Ellington orchestra performing with a symphony, though these recordings were commercially released only in 1984.[23]

The complicated origins of *Non-Violent Integration (NVI)* suggest a number of points about the "symphonic Ellington." In his liner notes to *The Symphonic Ellington* album, Stanley Dance wrote that "in 1949, thrilled at the prospect of performing with the Philadelphia Orchestra in Robin Hood Dell, Duke Ellington wrote what he called a 'little thing,' which he hoped might interest the great musicians of that magnificent orchestra. . . . His [successful] experience with that particular type of 'tonal hybrid,' gave inspiration for the present day title: *Non-Violent Integration*."[24] This recollection tells part of the story: *Non-Violent Integration* is a later title for *Grand Slam Jam*, which was performed at Robin Hood Dell in 1949. As evidenced in score materials, however, the orchestral score was originally titled *Boogie Bop Blue*. The Ellington historian-archivist Annie Kuebler has noted that the arranger J. Calvin Jackson "was involved with Ellington in the late 1940s and claimed to have worked on an orchestration for *Boogie Bop Blue* to be performed at Robin Hood Dell."[25] Jackson is credited as the arranger on the undated, full-score, jazz-band-plus-symphony arrangement of *NVI*, but this later title is actually printed on a separate piece of paper that has been taped to the top of the first score page. The original title was clipped off this page, but a second copy of the score shows the original title: *Boogie Bop Blue*. This earlier title was also notably used on a band-only arrangement that was recorded in October 1947 as *Boogie Bop Blues*.[26]

The significant differences between the big band and symphonic

(a)

(b)

Example 6.1a. Excerpt from the big band arrangement for Duke Ellington's *Boogie Bop Blues* (1947)

Example 6.1b. Motive from Duke Ellington's *Non-Violent Integration* (1949)

Boogie Bop Blue[s] arrangements reveal a complicated relationship. The melody in the lower sax parts of example 6.1a shows the primary riff that defines the 1947 big band arrangement of *Boogie Bop Blues*. The number is a straightforward blues jam tune with an added twist: the basic, riff-based boogie-woogie frame of the first-chorus/out-chorus arrangement is juxtaposed against a busy, jagged bebop counter-melody set in the alto saxes—hence the number's name (which juxta-poses all these stylistic ingredients). In sum, the basic premise is a "non-violent integration" of bop, boogie woogie, and blues (though beyond the first and last choruses, Ellington's musicians stick largely to a swing-derived improvisational idiom).

At some point before the Robin Hood Dell appearance, Ellington wrote out an unusual eight-page short score that includes two titles: *Boogie-Bop-Blue* and *Basso-Mo-Thundo*.[27] The score includes names of musicians whose tenures with Ellington imply that the score was written between 1946 and 1949. What is most unusual about this Ellington-penned score is that it includes orchestration markings for both members of his band *and* various symphony orchestra sections.[28] This attempt at symphonic scoring was highly unusual for Ellington, as he largely relegated scoring for this larger orchestral palette to other arrangers in his future symphonic repertory. This sketch score may have been developed in several different sittings, as the chorus arrangements are haphazardly ordered. A comparison with Jackson's symphonic *NVI* orchestration, however, reveals that the sketch was closely followed in Jackson's orchestration. The connection to *Grand Slam Jam* is further reinforced in Ellington's sketch references to his musicians, which include Al Sears, a tenor saxophonist who permanently left the band in 1949.[29]

Ellington-Jackson's *NVI* orchestration is by no means a slavish translation of the original big-band arrangement of *Boogie Bop Blues*, and there are also major discrepancies between Jackson's *NVI* orchestration and the first recorded performance of *NVI* on the *Symphonic Ellington* LP. Ellington-Jackson's *NVI* orchestration largely features a new theme, which is shown in example 6.1b. This new theme is loosely derived from a repeated blues-based sax riff that appears in the background of the second chorus of the big band arrangement of *Boogie Bop Blues*. Jackson's *NVI* orchestration is built on twelve blues choruses, with the eleventh chorus being presented as an eight-bar truncated blues. It is only in the twelfth chorus—the climactic outchorus—that one hears a reorchestration of the original first chorus from the 1947 big band arrangement. In the symphonic arrangement of this passage, the original *Boogie Bop Blues* riff appears with the original bebop countermelody, which is now scored for strings (per the "add bop lick with strings" direction written in Ellington's sketch score). The woodwinds superimpose the new *NVI* theme on top of this original texture, while the symphonic brass and big band reed sections add two additional countermelodies to this dense texture. Many of the internal chorus backgrounds throughout Ellington-Jackson's *NVI* orchestration are indebted to ideas that were first presented in the 1947 big band arrangement, though there is a wealth of new material in this symphonic score. Nevertheless, Jackson's manuscript clearly indicates that the "symphonic" *NVI* was still intended to be performed as a Ellington-band jam number, as there are numerous references to wholly improvised chorus solos throughout the chart. The fundamental jazz-oriented basis of this orchestration is notably highlighted in the realization of this score on the *Symphonic Ellington* album.

Though the first-chorus statement of the *NVI* theme is written in unison for symphonic woodwinds and big band saxophones, the *Sym-*

phonic Ellington performance opens with Ellington's piano performing the theme backed only by rhythm section. This jazz-combo texture continues through another chorus statement (0:21). At the third chorus (0:43), an oboist from the Hamburg Symphony provides an able single-chorus solo. At the fourth chorus (1:04), the alto saxophonist Johnny Hodges takes over the solo duties. He is backed by the rhythm section and several loose big-band interjections that are unrelated to any of the extant score materials. This texture continues into chorus 5 (1:25), but within a few moments the woodwinds enter tenuously, almost as if they missed their cue by two or three bars. What they perform is the symphony's woodwind parts from the fourth chorus of the Ellington-Jackson *NVI* orchestration. It is in the sixth chorus of the performance that the Ellington-Jackson orchestration enters full swing, so to speak. While the symphony's woodwind and string sections perform the fifth chorus of the original orchestration, the trombonist Buster Cooper begins a typical Ellingtonian growl-and-plunger brass solo. This "integrated" texture continues into the next chorus (2:08). At the eighth chorus of the performance (2:30), the Ellington-Jackson orchestration is dropped to make room for the rhythm section and a solo by the Ellington clarinetist, Jimmy Hamilton. At the ninth chorus of the performance (2:51), the string section takes their original section solo from the Ellington-Jackson orchestration (chorus 8 in that score). The tenth and eleventh choruses (3:12 and 3:34) are based on the ninth chorus of the Ellington-Jackson orchestration (which is repeated once). Paul Gonsalves is given a two-chorus solo over this passage, and notably begins by quoting the second theme from Gershwin's *Rhapsody in Blue* (which begins at m. 11 in the Gershwin score). On top of the first chorus of the solo, there is also an improvised, florid flute obbligato part. The twelfth chorus of the performance (3:56) aligns with the tenth chorus of the Ellington-Jackson orchestration, and Jimmy Hamilton takes the improvised clarinet solo for that section. After this, Hamilton is given another interpolated solo chorus with just rhythm section (4:17). Chorus 14 (4:38) follows the eight-bar eleventh chorus of the Ellington-Jackson orchestration, though Ellington increases his own florid piano interjections and Hamilton continues his solo in response to the orchestral statements. The final out-chorus (4:52) is performed nearly as written, though the score is augmented with both the high-note trumpet work of Cat Anderson and a florid clarinet obbligato by Hamilton. The performance then concludes nearly as written.

As evidenced in this *Symphonic Ellington* performance, Ellington treated the *NVI* score as he might a typical big band arrangement or even a performance of a commercial stock arrangement, each of which could be quite mutable in conventional practice—with instrumental parts or sections dropped, doubled, or added, depending on the needs of a particular performance context. The symphonic *NVI* still functions quite ably as a blues-based jam number because of its entirely unclassical conception.

Unlike most of the Carnegie Hall extended works of the 1940s, *NVI* has little in the way of a program outside of its witty later title. At one level, this title refers to the "nonviolent integration" of a jazz band, symphony, and various instrumental idioms. As Maurice Peress has noted though, the post–Robin Hood Dell title of *NVI* is a rather "sly [racial] metaphor," as the Philadelphia Orchestra was entirely white in 1949—a fact that may explain the name change to the more subtle *Grand Slam Jam*, which also ably describes this glorified blues for big band and symphony. While it is by no means profound symphonic literature nor a top-flight Ellington orchestral jazz arrangement, *NVI* is nonetheless quite innovative. It displays a far more integral merging of African American jazz aesthetics with "symphonic" scoring than any manifestations of the Whiteman symphonic jazz model. Ellington's conception also repositions the idea of concert jazz closer to the jazz tradition than the symphonic tradition. This vision lies at odds with even James P. Johnson's more thoroughly symphonic conception of concert jazz, despite Johnson's significant attention to the aesthetics of African American popular music. In addition, if the Ellington-Jackson arrangement does indeed date to somewhere around 1946–49, then *NVI* also foreshadows key developments in the burgeoning jazz-with-strings trends of this era, including the influential Charlie Parker "with strings" recordings (1949 forward), Stan Kenton's bestringed vision for "progressive jazz" (late 1940s and early 1950s), the big-band-plus-strings vogue (the bands of Artie Shaw and Tommy Dorsey, 1940s radio orchestras, etc.), and the various jazz-plus-strings arrangements (including the strings-plus-soloist Ellington-Strayhorn charts of *Sono* and *Frustration*) on Norman Granz's landmark 1949 album (of 78 rpm recordings), *The Jazz Scene*.[30] While it is difficult to know exactly where *NVI* falls in this jazz-with-strings chronology, this unusual arrangement was prescient of tradition-expanding directions that jazz—and parallel symphonic "excursions in jazz"—would follow in the late 1940s and 1950s.

Despite the innovations of this "little" experiment, it was *Harlem* and *New World A-Comin'* that became Ellington's two most frequently performed concert works—both in their jazz ensemble and big-band-plus-symphony orchestrations—from the 1950s until his death in 1974. As such, these latter compositions ideally represent the central musical vision behind the post-1949 "symphonic Ellington" repertory. This more compositionally oriented vision significantly contrasts with the playful, improvisation-friendly "tonal hybrid" of Ellington's *NVI*. The later "tonal hybrid" aesthetic seen in the jazz-band-plus-symphony arrangements of *Harlem* and *New World A-Comin'* is actually quite indebted to the presymphonic big band orchestrations of these works. The three central compositions in Ellington's post-1949 symphonic repertory—*Harlem, Night Creature*, and *New World A-Comin'*—were all orchestrated by Luther Henderson Jr. The personal and professional relationships between Ellington and Henderson thus provide interesting perspectives on the "symphonic Ellington."

Originally from Kansas City, Missouri, Henderson's family moved to Harlem when he was four, and he subsequently became friends with Ellington's son, Mercer. Henderson recalled that he and Mercer "hung out together on the same street in Sugar Hill," and that Henderson "knew [Mercer's] dad from the time I was 13."[31] Though he had a life-long connection to jazz as an arranger, pianist, and bandleader, Henderson pursued classical music studies at the Juilliard School with an emphasis on orchestration and arranging (instead of composition or performance). He graduated in 1942. Ellington first hired Henderson as an orchestrator in 1946 for work on *Beggar's Holiday*, Ellington's only musical theater project to make it to Broadway (briefly). From this point on, Henderson made periodic contributions to the Ellington organization, including both orchestrations and occasional songs. From this impressive professional foundation, Henderson became a top-flight commercial orchestrator and arranger. Over the course of his sixty-year career, he worked on more than fifty Broadway musicals, many television shows, and was a first-call arranger for Richard

Rodgers, Jule Styne, and other celebrated Broadway and popular music luminaries.

The *New York Times* critic Ben Sisario said in 2003 that Henderson's "skill was in transforming the rhythm and texture of jazz written for small ensembles into the much larger—but less flexible—Broadway pit orchestra."[32] In some respects, this was the same skill he applied to orchestrating Ellington's concert works. His deft touch at jazz-derived Broadway orchestrations also underscores the unavoidable proximity of the "symphonic Ellington" to traditional "symphonic pops" repertories. Indeed, Henderson's first assignment as Ellington's symphonic orchestrator was his 1949 work on scoring *New World A-Comin'* for the Robin Hood Dell Orchestra. In fact, many of Ellington's subsequent symphonic appearances were at pops-oriented concerts, and most of these performances were billed as such. Ellington even acted as a New York radio "commentator for a . . . summer series of symphonic pop[s] works" at the exact same time that he premiered *Harlem* in June 1951.[33] This "pops" connection is important for an understanding of the cultural reception of these concert works. Even in 2000, after a Carnegie Hall performance of Henderson's Ellington arrangements, the *New York Times* critic Ben Ratliff remarked that this "symphonic" repertory was merely "Ellington redone in Mr. Henderson's métier: Broadway music."[34] Granted, this sort of reading has much to do with the close proximity of the technical skills required for the orchestral scoring of symphony and Broadway theater orchestras, but Ratliff's comment is also premised on a knowledge of the long-standing American tradition of symphonic pops concerts, events that have traditionally been devoted to "lighter" symphonic fare and quasi-symphonic, concert-style arrangements of beloved popular music melodies. While similar repertories were a staple of prewar radio orchestras and movie palace orchestras (like that of the Roxy Theatre in New York), many established American symphonic orchestras had long accommodated this lucrative market by forming secondary summer "pops" configurations.

As the historian Lawrence Levine discusses in *Highbrow/Lowbrow*, the roots of the "pops" tradition lay with late-nineteenth-century organizations like the Boston Symphony Orchestra, which founded the Boston Pops concerts (in 1885) for "popular orchestral concerts that would present 'light, bright, sentimental' music to those who craved it and thus presumably free classical concerts from this obligation." Their intent was to avoid "anything that diluted or detracted from the great masterworks."[35] Levine observes that this repertory segregation was a practice that allowed the parent symphony orchestras to "purify" their mainstay programs, filling them with "serious" and "worthy" traditional classical repertory.[36] Levine describes this late-nineteenth-century trend as an act of "sacralization," and this process was accompanied by extensive efforts to educate American concert audiences on appropriate concert etiquette, the modes of properly appreciating musical art, and the class-based distinctions between the cultural values of high-art music (classical music), sentimental and "light" parlor music, and lowly popular music. These trends led to the mid-twentieth-century popular view of American musical culture as a hierarchical pyramid of cultural and social privilege and aesthetic value, with European classical music ("good" music) forming the very pinnacle of this relationship, and the vast quantities of commercial Tin Pan Alley popular song and most jazz being thought of as the lowest musical idioms in this social order (even below "folk" music).

Ellington's career was built on circumventing these cultural prejudices, though he may have hit a symphonic pops glass ceiling with midcentury views on the artistic position of concert music based on popular music idioms. Nevertheless, these hierarchical cultural and racial negotiations, and particularly the desire for upward social mobility and high-culture privilege and recognition, lay at the heart of the Ellington-Henderson "symphonic" repertory. Ellington, Henderson recalled, "dubbed me his classical arm . . . I had my Juilliard training. And he wanted me to legitimize him in this society we call classical music . . . I didn't know that then. It's taken me 50 years to figure that out." Henderson described his contributions to these projects as an "attempt to give Ellington a 'classical' presence with a 'jazzical' sensibility."[37]

One difficult facet of the cultural aspirations behind this project lay in their division of labor between composition and orchestration in concert works that were intended to be received as "classical compositions." In classical music culture that was the legacy of Beethoven, the powerful romantic myth of artistic genius has made it a virtual prerequisite that true musical art be entirely written and orchestrated by the composer. Any deviations from this practice open a composer up to suspicions of charlatanism. This was Gershwin's artistic dilemma after the premiere of Ferde Grofé's orchestration of the *Rhapsody in Blue* in 1924. By contrast, in the conventional industry practice of Broadway and Hollywood film orchestration, composers rely upon a hand-picked group of orchestrators to create the requisite "Broadway sound" or "Hollywood sound." This role defined Henderson's highly successful career on Broadway, where there was special interest in his ability to translate jazz orchestration and phrasing into musical theater orchestration. This division of labor—and the artistically suspicious art and/or craft of the arranger—was also native to much of the middlebrow pops concert repertory, particularly popular music medleys that were arranged by crack Broadway orchestrators such as Robert Russell Bennett.

This team approach to the creative process was also very much the norm in big band jazz, where creative collaboration could include score contributions and refinements by band members, the individual improvisational components in a score, the contribution of improvised and paraphrased solos (where a player elaborated upon a precomposed passage in a score) that become set score materials over time, the unique instrumental voices in any given orchestra, and so on. This was Ellington's compositional milieu, and Henderson saw great value in this art. According to Henderson, "Ellington's genius . . . was knowing how to project himself through other people. . . . He heard things in others, collected their stories and retold them incorporated into himself, into his music. That's why his band and his bandsmen really were his instrument."[38]

When Ellington first approached the project of creating a symphonic *Non-Violent Integration,* he seems to have initially felt up to the task of attempting a symphonic orchestration. Somewhere between the work on his sketch score and the Robin Hood Dell engagement, his opinion changed. In hiring Henderson to score and arrange *Beggar's Holiday,* the division of labor between composition and orchestration was obviously industry practice. Even with many of the arrangements for his big band, Ellington often wrote short scores for his associates (Strayhorn, Juan Tizol, Tom Whaley, and others) to extrapolate into full orchestra arrangements, a process that invariably involved introductions of small and large musical details (all of which were subject to Ellington's approval). Ellington's request for the Jackson *NVI* orchestration may have been the result of a similar sort of thinking, but this arrangement likely involved a whole new set of issues beyond the time constraints of a busy bandleader.

The subject of these symphonic works arises several times in Ellington's extensive taped interviews with the journalist Carter Harman in 1956. At one point in their discussions, Ellington provides a sizable history of his symphonic encounters to that date. When Harman asks Ellington, "Do you like to do that kind of thing best . . . [the] big symphonic stuff?" the band leader's response is, "Well, I don't know that much about the symphony orchestra, frankly." Harman counters with the aside, "Well, as you said, it's not a terrible problem to you," to which Ellington responds, "Writing for the symphony orchestra is a technique, you know. And, rather than expose myself completely to all this shit, I mean, I just turn it over . . . I make a six-line score and give it to Luther [Henderson] and let him do it . . . with suggestions, you know. . . . I mean, the[se] things are good as they are."[39] Here, Ellington emphasizes that extended works like *Harlem* and *New World A-Comin'* were complete in their original big band orchestrations ("the[se] things are good as they are"), and irreverently refers to the skills of symphonic orchestration as merely a "technique" that he has little interest or time in learning.

This professed indifference to symphonic orchestration highlights the fact that these works were initially presented without public recognition of their arrangers, leaving the public to presume that Ellington had both composed and scored his orchestral works, just as any other "symphonic" composer would have done. This was the case, for example, at Ellington's 1955 Carnegie Hall debut as a symphonic composer (with the Symphony of the Air). Henderson recalled his shock at this lack of recognition for his extensive work:

> I wanted to be sure I got credit for what I'd done. And Duke, he said to me, "Yes, oh yes. Of course." But when I went down to Carnegie before the concert to see if my name was in the program, it was not. I had to have inserts printed up "Symphonic orchestrations by Luther Henderson." I didn't like him for that. Which was very hard on me. Because I loved the Duke.[40]

These comments are prefaced by Henderson's reflections on Ellington's relation to their mutual friend and associate Billy Strayhorn. As Henderson notes, "While Duke never ever took credit for '[Take the] A Train,' no one ever thought that it was written by anyone other than Ellington either." While Henderson's assumption that Ellington's ego was the primary catalyst for this oversight in recognition cannot be proved, the bandleader regularly treated his band members' contributions in the same way he treated Strayhorn and the "Take the A Train." Henderson's concerns were well-founded, as there were prominent precedents of this oversight. Like Jackson, Henderson's work was not publicly acknowledged in the Robin Hood Dell program. Nor, apparently, did he receive any recognition for his work when the Ellington orchestra performed his symphonic orchestrations of *New World A-Comin'* and *Harlem* at a June 1951 joint appearance of the Ellington orchestra and the NBC Symphony orchestra in Lewisohn Stadium. (This appearance is discussed more fully later.) (The six-thousand-seat Adolph Lewisohn Stadium of the City College of the City University of New York was a regular site for summer pops-oriented concerts until it was demolished in the 1970s.) Henderson began to receive regular recognition for his orchestrations following Ellington's fourth symphonic engagement, where the concert program prominently noted "Luther Henderson, *Orchestrator for Duke Ellington.*" This July 10, 1956, New Haven Pops Concert Series appearance featured Ellington as a solo artist with the New Haven Symphony Orchestra in performances of *New World A-Comin'* (with Ellington at the piano), *Harlem*, and *Night Creature*.[41]

𝄢 NEW WORLD A-COMIN'

From their inception through to 1974 (Ellington's death), *New World A-Comin'* and *Harlem* were regularly performed in their original jazz orchestra scoring (*Harlem* more often than *New World*), and with and without a big band in Ellington's symphonic appearances. During the 1960s and 1970s, Ellington even performed *New World A-Comin'* as a solo piano work on several occasions. Because of their rich programs, especially *Harlem*'s, these works illustrate the ways that Ellington sought to convey social concerns through both his Carnegie Hall concert series and the general relations between his extramusical texts and his extended compositions. While the following examinations of the compositional thinking behind *New World A-Comin'* and *Harlem* will briefly consider Henderson's later orchestrations, I tend to side with Ellington's candid view that "the[se] things are good as they are" in their original big band arrangements. This opinion is based first on the fact that, as Ellington noted, he wrote these types of "symphonic" works on a "six-line score" (a practice that—in truth—involved a sketch score based on four-stave systems) precisely as he would for a big band chart. Similarly, outside of *NVI*, the original short-score conceptions for both *New World* and *Harlem* reveal that these works were conceived expressly for his big band, thus confirming Ellington's view that "writing for the symphony orchestra" was a secondary "technique" that he need not "expose" himself to. That said, Hendersons' orchestrations are central to both the creation of the "symphonic Ellington" and—as Henderson noted—the desire to "legitimize" Ellington "in this society we call classical music."

Despite his creative intentions, most of Ellington's extended compositions bear only loose connections between music and program. Even in cases where there are extensive and detailed descriptive texts (especially those for *Harlem* and *Black, Brown and Beige*), Ellington's compositions are constructed with only the broadest brushstrokes of evocative stylistic and generic musical references to the topical ideas suggested in the given programmatic texts or titles of works. Beyond local stylistic details of rhythm, harmony, instrumentation, and characteristic musical gestures, these connections lie at the larger episodic or movement level, with the basic character of that passage functioning as a broad topical allusion to a programmatic theme (rather than conveying a detailed musico-dramatic portrayal of specific actions and narrative developments).

The potentially weak relations between music and program can be seen in the history of *New World*. While this work avoids the type of elaborate program Ellington had attached to *Black, Brown and Beige*, at its December 11, 1943, premiere at Carnegie Hall, he nevertheless describes the work as a representation of the postwar racial optimism expressed in Ottley's *New World A-Coming: Inside Black America*, published earlier in that year. Again, this program—like the book—sought to portray the social richness of Harlem.[42]

In his interview sessions with Carter Harman in 1956, Ellington performs a passionate, nine-minute, private solo piano rendition of *New World*. The interview that follows is unfortunately marred by ambient noise, but there is enough fidelity to reveal a number of further details about the history of *New World*. Harman asks, "Where did you get that name, *New World a Coming*?" Ellington replies,

> Oh, we borrowed it from a book written by Roi Ottley. It was done in . . . 1943 . . . And we did it originally, of course, just with our band and it was mostly a piano solo [composition] . . . *New World a Coming* was one of those ["suggestive" or "subversive"?] type books. I never read the book. . . . [inaudible] said, "Why don't you name it after the book [inaudible]" . . . with an idea that could explain why I named it *New World a Coming*. I explained that I hadn't read the book, but I did [inaudible] . . . It might not be in totally in keeping with the book, but the [inaudible] . . . during the war is that it was [wrapped up] with this new world coming where everything was [inaudible] . . .[43]

Despite its unintelligible moments, the fragmentary text reveals subtle details that were only hinted at in Ellington's Carnegie Hall introduction to the work. This candid moment reveals that Ellington had secondhand knowledge of the contents and themes of the book, and that the title was suggested by someone else. A likely candidate is William Morris, Ellington's publicity agent, who firmly supported both Ellington's Carnegie Hall appearances and the social awareness agenda they represented.

It is interesting that in his Carnegie Hall introduction Ellington distinguishes the program/composition connection in *New World* from his conception of "tone parallels," which he characterizes as musical "parallels" to a story or program where broad narrative themes, emotions, and cultural ideas are referenced through sequences of musical strains. Despite *Harlem*'s nature as a single-movement episodic composition, this personal conception of a "tone parallel" explains why this work is described as a suite. *Harlem* is built through a progressive sequence of contrasting musical topics and moods—or, rather, individual musical strains—that loosely suggest the musical narrative behind Ellington's supposed community tour (as described in concert program and album liner note texts). By contrast, as described in both the Carnegie Hall introduction and the Harman interview, *New World* represents a single, generalized mood represented in the title. This emotional and social theme is variously described as "optimistic," "anticipatory," and "contented." Each of these words expresses something about hoped-for improvements in postwar race relations, and—because of Ellington's multiple references to a loose connection between the idea of the work and the general themes of Ottley's book—suggests a postwar optimism for social and economic improvements in Harlem as a community. Ellington never read the Ottley book, yet he recalled that it was "suggestive" or "subversive." While the exact wording of this passage is mangled by ambient noise, this suggestive and subversive confusion (on my part) evinces two important qualities that he was likely attracted to in the idea of creating a conceptual association between his instrumental work and this text. This association is largely a matter of a juxtaposition of Ellington's new piano concerto and a number of social ideas that arose from a contemporary popular book that many of his audience members, and community members, could have been expected to know—hence Ottley's personal appearance at the concert and the audience's positive response at this news. Beyond aural and textual suggestion, the principal connections between program and actual composition are found in passages like the lush, lyrical primary theme, which evokes optimism and contentment.

The short score for *New World* reveals at least three different handwriting samples. One layer is Ellington's music notation. Added to this material are familiar markings from the band's longtime copyist, Tom Whaley. Whaley's contributions include measure numbers, the score title, and a number of instrumentation, score layout, and expression notes.[44] A third hand has added a few score expressions, apparently darkened Ellington's notation in a number of passages, and possibly expanded the original harmonies at certain points. Most notably, this third contributor added a number of indications for symphonic scoring details (such as references to strings, horns, woodwinds, etc.). This contributor even left an odd question of "swinging strings?!!" over one passage. The evidence of the handwriting indicates that this third contributor was not Strayhorn. Presumably it was Henderson, who subsequently scored the 1949 symphonic orchestration of *New World*.

Regardless, this score gives evidence for how the symphonic orchestration grew directly out of the original compositional materials for the big band chart.

New World is built from contrasting episodes "bound together by elaborate cadenzas for the piano," as one reviewer suggested.[45] As table 6.1 shows, the composition is constructed from varied statements of four song-style strains, a collection of transitional bridges and interludes, and several solo instrumental cadenzas. The number's exaggerated "rhapsodic" devices—melodramatic cadenzas, prominent textural

TABLE 6.1.   Formal outline of Duke Ellington's *New World a Comin'* (1943)

M.	Section	Length	Key	Texture
1	**Part I.** Strain A^1 (*orch exposition*)	8	C	orch
9	Strain A^2	8	C	orch
17	Strain A$^{var.1}$ (*solo exposition*)	18	C → mod.	piano
35	**Part II.** Interlude	9	A	orch/piano
44	Motive X^1	8	C	orch
52	Interlude (= Piano Cadenza 1)	8	mod.	piano
60	**Part III.** Motive X^2	12	A♭ → mod.	orch
72	Vamp^1	4^a	Fmin	piano/rhythm
76	Strain B^1 (piano solo) (a^{1}a^{2}a^{3}b+)	14		piano → orch
90	Strain extension	5		orch/piano
95	Vamp^2	4		piano/rhythm
99	Strain B^2 (a^{1}a^{2}a^{3}a)	16	Fmin → A♭	orch
115	Strain C^1 (piano solo) (a^{1}a^{2}a^{3}a^4)	16	C	piano/rhythm
131	Strain C^2 (piano solo) (a^{1}a^2)	8		piano/rhythm
139	Interlude A^1 (= Piano Cadenza 2)	14	Cmin/maj	piano
153	Vamp A^3 (var.)	4	G	orch/piano
157	Strain D^1 (a^{1}ba^2) (built on Motive Y)	14	G	piano/rhythm
171	Extension	5	mod. → F	piano/rhythm
176	**Part X.** Extension cont.	8	F	orch/piano
184	Strain A$^{var.2}$ (a^{1}ba^2)	22	F	orch/piano
206	**Part Y.** Extension (= Piano Cadenza 3 + Clar Cadenza)	15	mod.	piano → clar
221	Strain B^3 (piano in 3/4) (a^{1}a^{2}a^3)	12	Dmin	piano
233	Strain D^2 (incomplete) + Interlude/Extension with Motive X	14	mod.	orch
247	Interlude A^2 (= Piano Cadenza 4)	3	C	piano
250	Strain A$^{var.3}$ (*recapitulation*)	16	C → mod.	piano
266^b	Coda (Part 1) (with motivic refs)	26	mod.	orch/piano
292	Coda (Part 2)	5	F	piano → orch

^{a}In the 1943 premiere, this two-bar vamp is only performed one time. In all subsequent performances, it is performed twice (= four bars).

^{b}In the 1943 premiere, the band tentatively plays mm. 266–69 and then drop out. Ellington then adds another lengthy solo reiteration of various important themes before returning again to the band's m. 269 entrance and continuing. This interlude arrangement is not included in other performances (i.e., there is only one statement from m. 266 forward and no piano interlude), and so it has been omitted from this outline.

shifts, dramatic changes in tempo with frequent use of rubato phrasing, pseudo-Lisztian piano cadenza passages, and so forth—owe much to the earlier symphonic jazz tradition. That said, the compositional material and developmental thinking are far more Ellingtonian than Whitemanesque. Gone are the whole-tone, Tin Pan Alley modernist interludes and predictable sequence-based, quasi-developmental textures. Moreover, in place of the earlier, self-conscious motivic saturation technique seen in *Reminiscing in Tempo*, Ellington more subtly builds developmental qualities and a sense of unity by concentrating on more integrated (and less frequent) references to earlier themes. These recurrent materials include two prominent motives (labeled X and Y) that appear throughout the work in a variety of contexts.

The manuscript short score and original band charts show that Ellington conceived of the work in five sections that he labeled "I," "II," "III," "X," and "Y." In both the short score and charts, these sections are distinctly offset from each other, though in actual performance these labels function as no more than rehearsal numbers. In performance, these five large-scale episodes are separated by extended solo piano passages. While this simple formal description might loosely imply some sort of connection to a baroque ritornello-based concerto movement (where returning orchestral thematic statements alternate with solo instrumental episodes), Ellington's more complicated formal design bears greater relation to the nineteenth-century concerto.

Of all of Ellington's concert works, *New World* likely provides the greatest "classical" impression, hence its later centrality in the "symphonic Ellington" repertory. These "classical" qualities are most prominent in the melodramatic, virtuosic solo piano parts and their placement in a concerto-like structure. Granted, the work only emulates the typical formal model of the Classical-Romantic concerto in a broad gestural manner. While Ellington's composition does include an extended, exposition-like passage (mm. 1–34) that functions somewhat like a concerto orchestral exposition followed by a solo exposition, and while the work similarly includes a final recapitulation of the primary theme in the home key (though as a solo piano variation) before a triumphal extended coda, *New World* hardly follows the formal prescriptions of the Classical-Romantic concerto model. In place of a single- or double-theme first-movement sonata design with an exposition, development, and recapitulation—or a three-move-ment form or even a continuous concerto form that merges all three movements without pause—Ellington offers a decidedly personal variation on piano concerto formal design. This design seems to be Ellington's personal impression of how concerto form works, and this impression is integrated with the compositional lessons he learned from his earlier multistrain extended works, symphonic jazz, and pos-sibly even the multistrain concert jazz efforts of peers like James P. Johnson. These latter connections can be seen at all formal levels, from key relationships to motivic practices. I do not make these ob-servations to suggest that Ellington's composition is in some way deficient because it does not conform to a classical model or compo-sitional ideal. Rather, I want to underscore that Ellington's composi-tional thinking belongs to a formal tradition that is quite distinct from classical music. In fact, alongside Johnson's concert works, Ellington's extended compositions represent the artful height of the pre-1950 symphonic jazz and concert jazz repertories. Nevertheless, *New World*'s self-conscious emulation of concerto form and style raises an important question as to where Ellington may have gleaned his classical impressions.

Unlike James P. Johnson or Will Marion Cook, Ellington proudly avoided formal training in classical composition, harmony, and coun-terpoint. Ellington's many accounts of his youth emphasize his influ-ences from both trained and untrained musicians, and the balance of these influences with Ellington's internal, self-guided interests. In his autobiography, for example, Ellington notes that in his childhood in Washington he "used to spend nights listening to [the pianists] Doc Perry, Louis Brown, and Louis Thomas. They were schooled musi-cians who had been to the conservatory. But I listened to the un-schooled, too. There was a fusion, a borrowing of ideas, and they helped one another right in front of where I was standing, leaning over the piano, listening. Oh, I was a great listener!"[46] In both Wash-ington and New York, Ellington had the good fortune to circulate among respected Clef Club musicians (like Will Marion Cook) and "conservatory-trained" pianists (like Doc Perry) who saw great two-way educational value in interactions across these musical camps. This is clearly a social perspective that Ellington valued throughout his life, and it regularly informed his activities as a "great listener."

The roots of some of these cross-class and cross-genre listening and training habits lay in his own family home. This influence can partly be sensed in a 1964 interview with Carter Harman:

EKE: I heard all kinds of music [in my youth], because they had all kinds of music in the [Washington, D.C.] schools. We always had recitals and that at school, and high school, and my mother used to play piano by [reading] music. My father used to play by ear.

CH: What did your mother play? Did she play classics and things like that?

EKE: Yeah. What's that woman's name? Mary what's-its-name—all those comp . . . —she used to write songs. That was before your time. That's not Mary Rein- . . . Roberts . . . Reinhar- . . . Reinhar- . . . no, wait a . . . There was somebody, a woman who wrote all those beautiful piano pieces. They were beautiful. Every time I'd hear my mother play it, I'd cry. It was so pretty.

CH: Did she play it directly from the music or did she put a rhythm in it?

EKE: No, she played just the music. . . .

CH: You never wrote music like that. You never wanted to, right?

EKE: Oh, *yes!*

CH: Did you?

EKE: Oh yeah, I like that kind of music.

CH: Did you ever write any?

EKE: I write pretty music, yeah. . . . I would say that, for instance, things like "Little African Flower" [aka "Fleurette Africaine," 1963]—these are new things . . . Like "[A] Single Petal of a Rose" [from *The Queen's Suite*, 1959] has that quality. . . . They are probably just pianistic enough to be . . . [The interview is then interrupted.]

Ellington's emphasis on his broad cultural education in Washington, D.C., schools is important to bear in mind, as he was clearly exposed to certain facets of classical music culture and some degree of classical repertory.[47] As he also notes, his middle-class family home gave him significant contact with nonragtime musical traditions. In his autobiography, he provides a notable variation on the preceding account of music in his family home: "My mother used to play piano, pretty things like 'Meditation,' so pretty they'd make me cry. My father used to play too, but by ear, and all operatic stuff."[48] In quite a number of interviews, Ellington describes his father as a refined man who aspired toward upward social mobility despite the constraints of his race, professional pursuits, and income. Ellington's recollections of his father's fondness for opera clearly display one way in which his social aspirations were reflected in musical taste. In spite of his inability to clearly identify specific piano pieces that his mother played, the two reflections above underscore her predilection for—*and* Ellington's appreciation of—sentimental, turn-of-the-century parlor piano music of the kind that was widely circulated up through his youth. In many middle-class American homes, much of this repertory was commonly considered to be semiclassical or light concert music.

Beyond the promotional benefits of his late 1920s and 1930s critical comparisons to such modern classical composers as Frederick Delius, Maurice Ravel, and Igor Stravinsky, such upwardly mobile cultural attention likely encouraged Ellington to seek out recordings, scores, or performances of these composers. Even if he did not do this, he had some important exposure to areas of classical and light concert musical repertories in his youth. As a young adult in the 1920s and 1930s, he must have also been regularly exposed to some areas of classical and concert music repertories through radio, where classical performances by conductors like Toscanini and Stokowski where celebrated, popular events and weekly entertainment fare. Moreover, like most entertainment consumers of the 1920s and 1930s, Ellington must have attended the occasional prefilm orchestra concert in the era's deluxe movie palaces. I suggest that even without an interest in either obtaining a formal musical education or playing classical repertory, it would be nearly impossible for Ellington not to have had regular exposure—as an audience member, as a consumer of commercial records, as a musician circulating among a broad range of musicians, as a radio listener, and so on—to many popular areas of the classical repertory in his middle-class youth and early adulthood. That said, Ellington's friend, the concert pianist Don Shirley (who performed the piano part of *New World* in 1955), recalled that Ellington never showed any interest in discussing or exploring classical music when

Shirley and Strayhorn would read through classical scores or listen to new concert music recordings in Ellington's company.[49] In sum, Ellington's familiarity with classical repertory is surprisingly difficult to determine with any degree of accuracy.

Again, Ellington prided himself to be a "great listener" and—like in his Washington youth—his encounters with a wide variety of musicians regularly included "educational" discussions. After his many classical comparisons began to appear in the press from the late 1920s forward, the press also began to regularly report on Ellington's social encounters with classical musicians as well as big-name classical figures who attended Ellington performances.[50] One would assume that such encounters encouraged questions, dialogue, musical exchanges at a piano, and so forth. If such exchanges occurred, as a "great listener," Ellington likely absorbed a significant amount of musical knowledge, though this knowledge was likely more in the form of generalized impressions rather than precise formal information. In this respect, Ellington's casual absorption of the sound, character, and gestural rhetoric of the "classical" idiom is likely akin to James P. Johnson's early stride piano adaptations of the "orchestral effects" and the type of "abrupt change[s]" that he "heard Beethoven do in a sonata." Lastly, Ellington also undoubtedly had ready access to a well-trained, enthusiastic source of knowledge about classical music: his close friend and writing partner, Billy Strayhorn.

The above account offers a variety of likely sources for Ellington's impressions of the style and formal designs of the classical idiom. While he did proclaim that "if serious means European [classical] music, I'm not interested in that," Ellington's professed reservations about classical music do not preclude a desire for his compositions to be received in a manner that might parallel the privileged cultural reception of classical music. Unlike Whiteman, Johnson, or numerous other figures connected to symphonic jazz, Ellington initially saw no need to "expose himself" to orchestration beyond the intimate palette of his big band. This opinion was likely reinforced by the enthusiastic, classically biased jazz criticism—European and American—of the 1930s that sought to elevate the image of Ellington to the level of a "serious composer." Ellington publicly advanced this viewpoint even up to the 1951 Metropolitan Opera House premiere of *Harlem* in its big band orchestration, an event that notably occurred *after* his 1949

Robin Hood Dell premiere with a symphony orchestra, and after the original NBC Symphony Orchestra's commission of *Harlem*. Ellington's close friend and associate, the critic Leonard Feather, broached the subject of Ellington's seeming moves toward classical music in a January 1951 *Down Beat* interview with the bandleader:

> "Strings? Positively no! Out of the question!" . . .
> "What on earth would I want with strings?" the Duke continued heatedly. "What can anybody do with strings that hasn't been done wonderfully for hundreds of years? It wouldn't be any novelty anyway; Paul Whiteman used strings 30 years ago. No, we always want to play Ellington music—that's an accepted thing in itself.[51]

This response was notably made not so long after the successful—but critically controversial—1949 debut of Stan Kenton's massive Innovations in Modern Music orchestra. This ensemble had expanded the white bandleader's vision for "progressive jazz" into a huge orchestra that was built as a standard big band augmented by a sixteen-man string section, an expanded woodwinds section, French horns, and a harp. That Ellington may have sought to distance himself from such developments can be sensed in his added caveat, "I don't want to be controversial just for the sake of being controversial." (This may have been the meaning behind the mild parody of progressive jazz in Ellington's 1951 *Controversial Suite*.) An additional layer of the contemporary implications of crossing over from big band to symphony can be seen in the pretentious promotional copy of a 1950 Kenton concert program, which rhetorically asks, "Why the Strings?" The answer: Kenton had "grown into manhood—and with manhood comes . . . musical maturity."[52] While Ellington's manhood was certainly not in doubt, the implied sense of "musical maturity"—or "serious" musical expression versus the implied entertainment overtones of composing for the big band —was an important cultural marker that Ellington had long resisted the influence of, but one he ultimately embraced in his subsequent efforts to promote the "symphonic Ellington."

As seen in *Black, Brown and Beige* and other extended works up to and including *Harlem*, Ellington clearly felt that concert jazz—in order to be received as concert music and as "serious" composition—required elements that suggested the dramatic, "serious" structural

Example 6.2. Measures 9–22 (Strain A²) from Duke Ellington's *New World A-Comin'* (1943). Piano transcription and expression markings based on the big band parts in Maurice Peress's transcription of *New World A-Comin'* for G. Schirmer. *New World-A Comin'*. By Duke Ellington. Copyright © 1949 (renewed) by G. Schirmer, Inc. (ASCAP), Music Sales Corporation (ASCAP) and Tempo Music, Inc. All rights in the United States controlled by G. Schirmer, Inc. All rights outside of the United States controlled by Music Sales Corporation and Tempo Music, Inc. International copyright secured. All rights reserved. Reprinted by permission.

forms that evoked classical music, or at least light concert music. Example 6.2 shows mm. 9–22 of *New World*, a passage that includes the second orchestral statement of strain A and the opening of Ellington's solo piano variation on this same strain. This passage represents something like the end of an orchestral exposition and the opening of a solo exposition for a first movement of a solo concerto. The passage exemplifies a number of the work's strategies for integrating concert-style and big band textures.

In its instrumentation, mm. 9–16 show some very conventional big band arranging traits. The balladlike theme in the unison trumpets is supported by a saxophone choir that moves with the harmonic changes in a half-note rhythm. The saxes also interject short, harmonized responsorial phrases in quintessential Ellingtonian voicings (notice his predilection for moving Harry Carney's baritone saxophone into an inner voice across mm. 13–16). Despite the "optimistic" quality of the slow concerto theme, the passage swings like a period dance-band arrangement. In Luther Henderson's subsequent 1949 symphonic arrangement, these dance-band qualities are wholly sublimated under the new symphony-plus-big-band instrumentation. Gone is the swing of the rhythm section's original drum and bass parts. In their place are rolling timpani and a straight-eighths-based rhythmic sensibility. Henderson lushly rescored the strain A theme for full symphonic strings, and this part is performed in the native stylistic language of their instrument family. Across m. 11, Henderson introduces a new, Mahleresque horn section countermelody. Meanwhile, the band's sax section provides their original underscoring and responsorial phrases, though with slightly less swing. Measures 14–16 increase the self-consciously symphonic qualities of the passage through a grand, romantic tutti swell replete with cymbal crashes.

To an extent, Ellington's original orchestration for strain A recalls certain qualities found in a period "jazzed classics" arrangements like the John Kirby Orchestra's witty 1942 "Charlie's Prelude," which is a "little big band" reworking of Frédéric Chopin's popular Prelude in E Minor (op. 28, no. 4).[53] (Kirby's orchestra notably included the clarinetist and alto saxophonist Russell Procope, who was with Ellington from 1946 to 1974.) Ellington's eight-bar strain and Chopin's twelve-bar, songlike theme share a number of attributes. Both are slow, slightly melancholy themes that feature recurrent held notes connected by neighbor-note ornamentation that circles around the primary melodic note (as in mm. 9–11 in strain A). Both themes also feature supporting chord progressions in which harmonies subtly shift qualities by stepwise internal voice movements (see the saxes across mm. 9–12 and 14–16). And both themes involve an expansive concluding phrase that breaks away from the static melodic qualities of the primary melody of the theme. Granted, these are generalized traits that can be found in a wealth of classical and parlor prelude-style piano compositions. These are likely the same "pretty" qualities, however, that Ellington admired in the parlor piano pieces his mother favored (like the "Meditation" composition he cited).

Ellington's "solo exposition" of the strain A theme displays rhapsodic qualities that Ellington likely thought were "pianistic enough" to resemble the classical and parlor piano pieces he heard in his youth. With its "orchestral," expansive left- and right-hand parts, parallel-octave melodic voicings, regular arpeggiated runs in left- and right-hand parts (including harmonized melodic arpeggiations), Ellington's piano work strongly suggests the stylistic traits that can be heard in the rhapsodic piano work of Romantic composers like Franz Liszt or Sergei Rachmaninoff (particularly a popular classic like Rachmaninoff's 1893 Prelude in C-sharp Minor, op. 3, no. 2).

It should be noted, though, that very little—if any—of Ellington's piano part was written down by the composer. When Shirley performed this part at the 1955 concert, he was only given the equivalent of a lead sheet (i.e., a single-line score largely restricted to melodic material). At this performance, Shirley personally arranged his fully realized piano part from this lead sheet, his recollections of Ellington's solo piano performances of *New World* before big band rehearsals and smaller club engagements (where Shirley's trio was an opening act), and new material (particularly in Shirley's extended, penultimate solo cadenza and the final cadenza that closes the work).[54] Despite these recurrent "classical" qualities in *New World*, it should be noted both that Ellington's piano part references the jazz idiom as well (including stride-type solo textures), and that his solos in the 1943 premiere performance are frequently backed by the rhythm section. In comparing a significant number of Ellington's big-band, symphony-with-big-band, symphony-with-soloist, and solo-piano performances of *New World*, one sees that the composer viewed his piano part as a jazz pianist typically views his/her relation to any composition—that is, a performance context where a musician is expected to subject melodies to paraphrase improvisation, where bass lines and chord voicings are regularly subjected to improvisational alterations, and where various solo passages are also truncated and expanded at will (though all of these traits are less prominent than one might find in Ellington's more straight-ahead work as a jazz pianist). This attitude reflects how he left Shirley to approach the piano part, though Shirley's personal additions to the work's cadenzas notably reflect eighteenth- and nineteenth-century concerto practices. In general, however, these exaggerated, self-consciously rhapsodic textures gradually lost their prominence in Ellington's subsequent concert works, and these traits are largely absent in *Harlem*, a composition that is often regarded as Ellington's concert jazz masterwork.

13 *A TONE PARALLEL TO HARLEM*

Ellington's 1950 *Tone Parallel to Harlem* marks a high point in both Ellington's extended compositions and his lifelong celebration of the rich community of Harlem. *Harlem* was largely written in the spring of 1950, as the orchestra returned from a European tour on the ocean liner *Ile de France*. Despite its commission source, the work was premiered by the Ellington in its big band arrangement at a benefit concert for the National Association for the Advancement of Colored People (NAACP) that was held at Carnegie Hall Orchestra on Sunday, January 21,1951.

The work received its premiere performance with the NBC Symphony Orchestra at New York's Lewisohn Stadium on June 20, 1951. This latter event was promoted as a benefit concert for the Damon Runyan Memorial Fund for Cancer Research.[55] The first half of the concert was performed by the big band. The symphony joined the big band for the second half of the concert, which began with Henderson's arrangement of *New World*.

As a high-fidelity studio recording that followed on the heels of the work's premiere and the concert tour that featured this work, the richly expressive and hard-swinging December 1951 *Ellington Uptown* recording of *A Tone Parallel to Harlem (The Harlem Suite)*, as it was labeled on this album, offers a quintessential representation of mature Ellingtonian concert jazz and this composition's ideal performance.[56] Here we see a wholehearted expression of "serious American music" (and "serious" African American music) that is largely purged of classically evocative—or even rhapsodic—musical references. The album was released in 1952 on Columbia's prestigious Masterworks label, which had been previously reserved for classical performances and recordings of Broadway shows.

Harlem notably combines key structural elements from both *New World* and *Non-Violent Integration*, though *New World*'s rhapsodic concert music qualities are largely absent. In addition, without the flexible solo piano features of *New World*, *Harlem* is more regularly performed as written, though comparisons of the many recorded versions of the work reveal that Ellington's musicians regularly introduced smaller elements of paraphrase improvisation into the written solos.

As table 6.2 shows, *Harlem* is built from three strain-based sections that are connected by two extended interludes.[57] The middle section is built from a series of blues choruses that are inventively varied through stylistic shifts, a changing instrumentation palette, shifting chorus lengths, and key modulations. The larger composition is framed by an extended introduction and a ten-bar coda. As it is performed without pause or interruption, *Harlem* lacks the overt multimovement suite structure of many other extended Ellington compositions. Nevertheless, Ellington's characterization of this work as a suite describes the composition's sequential progression through

TABLE 6.2. Formal outline of Duke Ellington's *Harlem* (1950)

Section	M.	Design	Length	Key
Intro.	1	Intro., Parts A, B, C, and D	10 + 8 + 6	F
Section I	25	Strain A1 ($a^1a^2a^3b$)	8 + 9 + 11 + 10	
	63	Vamp	4	
	67	Vamp expansion	2	
	69	Strain A2 (a^1a^2)	8 + 8	
	85	Tenor cadenza	1	
	86	Strain A2 (b)	12	
Section II	98	Interlude 1, Parts A and B intro. to blues (rhumba)	8 + 4	
	110	Blues chorus 1 (= Strain B)	16	
	122	Interlude 2	4	
	126	Blues chorus 2 (swing)	12	
	138	Blues chorus 3 (rhumba)	12	
	150	Blues chorus 4 (swing)	12	
	162	Blues chorus 5	12	B♭
	174	Blues chorus 6	12	E♭
	186	Blues chorus 7	14	G
	200	Blues chorus 8	12	A♭
	212	Interlude 3, Parts A, B, and C	8 + 5 + 4	A♭ ⇒ F
	229	Interlude 3, Part D clarinet cadenza	6	A♭
Section III	235	Prestrain C, Parts 1 and 2	6 + 16	F
	257	Vamp 2	4	
	261	Strain C1 ($a^1a^2a^3b$) hymn	8 + 8 + 8 + 8	
	293	Strain C2 (a^1a^2b var.) big band texture	10	F ⇒ A♭
	319	Extension/Bridge	4	
		Interlude 4	17	
	340	Strain C3 (a^1)	8	
Coda	348	Coda	10	

three distinct strain-based episodes. Moreover, *Harlem* does not include a recapitulation-like return of the opening strain theme, a practice that he had followed in all of the nonsuite extended works that have been discussed in this book.

The work presents a rich vision of concert jazz written expressly in the vernacular, jazz-based voice of the Ellington orchestra. In its original big band orchestration, *Harlem* shows few self-consciously "classical" qualities beyond a more generalized interest in regularly changing tempi and a multistylistic palette. While these latter qualities are atypical in most dance-oriented big band arrangements, they are certainly not foreign to the secondary concert-oriented repertories (typically for theater, vaudeville, and broadcast engagements) of many big bands, dance bands, and radio orchestras of the 1940s. Ellington's *Harlem* presents a through-composed, "serious" concert jazz work that speaks almost exclusively through an extension of the characteristic voice of Ellington's big band and what critics from the 1930s called Ellington's "ten-inch record form."

Beyond the evidence of his commitment to using innovative blues chorus variations as a central building block in his vision for concert jazz, Ellington's *Harlem* is also full of exemplary passages that equally illustrate how expressive concert-style gestures and textures can be integrated into the indigenous compositional and arranging traditions of big band jazz. This integration is readily seen across the introduction and first chorus statement, an extended passage that employs concert-style expressive devices and phrasing to announce that this "tone parallel" is a "serious" composition that demands intensive listening. The work begins with a three-part, twenty-four-bar introduction in a slow, dramatic tempo. (All references to timings and musicians derive from the *Uptown Ellington* performance.) Ellington regularly described Ray Nance's opening, plunger-muted trumpet solo—which is built on a two-note, minor third motive—as a pronouncement of the word "Harlem." This gesture introduces the central "Harlem" motive that permeates the score. This concert-style, rubato-phrased trumpet solo is first backed by the reeds (across mm. 4–6). Next, Ellington introduces a call-and-response texture of descending shake glissandi between two solo trumpets. Part A ends (0:23, m. 7) with a concerted ensemble passage built on rising chords over melodramatic drum rolls. At part B (0:35, m. 11), the saxes re-

Example 6.3.   Theme A from Duke Ellington's *Harlem* (1950). *A Tone Parallel to Harlem*. By Duke Ellington. Copyright © 1952 (renewed) by G. Schirmer, Inc. (ASCAP). International copyright secured. All rights reserved. Reprinted by permission.

state the Harlem motive in call-and-response exchanges with the brass. Part C of the introduction (0:56, m. 19) begins with a growl-and-plunger trumpet cadenza (played by Ray Nance?) that is backed by spare accompanimental chord stabs. This passage is followed by Jimmy Hamilton's sultry clarinet solo, which leads directly into the first strain.

The opening of the first strain A statement (1:19, m. 25) is seen in example 6.3. Strain A is built in an a¹a²a³b song form with unusual phrase lengths. Hamilton's one-bar, solo clarinet cadenza/pickup leads directly into strain A's (a) phrase, which is built around varied statements of the Harlem motive. The (a¹) phrase closes with a responsorial, varied inversion of the two-note Harlem motive played by Harry Carney's baritone saxophone (1:37). These opening eight bars thus foreshadow the many forthcoming permutations of the two-note motive. The second (a) phrase statement (1:44, m. 33) harmonizes and simplifies the melodic materials that Hamilton previously played.

Here, lushly scored saxophone statements of the Harlem theme (based on the motive) are set in a call and response with the trombones, before the trumpets take over the melodic lead at the end of the phrase. The (a³) phrase (2:12) passes the melodic and responsorial materials from the full band, to the reeds, to a plunger-muted solo trombone, to a broad clarinet solo that ultimately segues into the (b) phrase of the strain. As with the (a) phrase, the (b) phrase (2:38) is built with a number of internal references to the Harlem motive. Likewise, melodic material is divided among various shifting instrumental call-and-answer textures, first between the divided reeds, and then, after the trumpets take the lead, the phrase is extended and subsequently arrives at a held cadence.

A similar attention to a balance between a faithfulness to a merging of bona fide jazz textures and jazz-centered, concert-style expressive devices can be seen in the opening strains of the stirring third section of the work. Jimmy Hamilton's florid, solo-clarinet cadenza (7:17, m. 229) leads into a seductive, slow introduction to the third major section of *Harlem* (7:31, m. 235). The first six bars of this introductory passage are for solo clarinet and bass alone. At m. 241 (7:50), this dirgelike texture builds in four four-bar sections with minor-key, descending ostinato bass figures in the reeds and a melodic lament above. Sewn throughout are varied Harlem motive statements. This introductory passage builds in intensity with additions of a wailing clarinet trio, the "wah-wahs" of Ellington's plunger-muted brass, and melodic foreshadowings of strain C. A bass drum (or timpani) part accents beats 1 and 2 and rests on beats 3 and 4. The effect is somewhat like a shuffling march. After a tutti orchestral swell, the texture suddenly thins to an ominous, solo bass clarinet vamp.

Strain C first takes on the character of a hymn played during the first part of a New Orleans jazz funeral (8:57, m. 261). (The first part of the jazz funeral tradition involves a march to the cemetery with family and friends of the deceased and a brass band performing somber hymns or dirges.) Again, this passage is song-form based (a¹a²a³b). The bass drum shuffle is reintroduced with the bass doubling this pattern. The bass clarinet continues its ostinato part, while a plaintive muted trumpet performs the lyrical hymn melody. The second (a) phrase (9:24, m. 269) shifts the theme to clarinet, as the bass clarinet—with trombone doubling—moves to an ornamented countermelody. The

Example 6.4.   Theme C1 (a3), mm. 277–86, from Duke Ellington's *Harlem* (1950).
A Tone Parallel to Harlem. By Duke Ellington. Copyright © 1952 (renewed) by
G. Schirmer, Inc. (ASCAP). International copyright secured. All rights reserved.
Reprinted by permission.

third (a) phrase (9:50, m. 277) reaches a full New Orleans polyphonic
jazz texture, with clarinet on top, and three- and four-part interlocked
melodic textures that also involve a tenor sax, a trumpet, a trombone,
and another clarinet. (See example 6.4.) The (b) phrase (10:16, m. 285)
returns the work to another hard-swinging, blaring-brass and riff-
based-horns big band texture—one that almost sounds like the climax
of a heated, burlesque bump-and-grind striptease act. This passage
builds in intensity to a sudden, dramatic cadential chord. A baritone
saxophone cadenza leads into a more subdued second statement of
strain C (10:43, m. 293). This strain C2 setting features a richly voiced
sax ensemble on the harmonized melody. (There is also a brief solo
trumpet responsorial fill that is oddly borrowed from *Black, Brown and*

Beige.) The second (a) phrase modulates and drops the rhythm section, thereby leaving a hymnlike texture of a lyrical solo trumpet on the theme and a countermelody scored for muted trombones and baritone sax (11:13, m. 303). This passage is followed by a variation on the (b) phrase rather than the third (a) phrase of strain C2 (11:40, m. 311). Here, the trumpet solo continues and is backed with an arpeggiated bass part, shuffling brush work on the snare drum, and a four-part reed accompaniment. The full band enters at the (b) phrase turnaround, and the texture builds to an interlude that opens with a recollection of the concerted ensemble passage from the introduction. From here, Ellington reintroduces a swinging, full ensemble of blaring brass and wailing saxophones on varied statements of the Harlem motive.

As evidenced in the preceding overviews of these two extended passages, one potential remaining "symphonic" trait in *Harlem* can be seen in Ellington's building compositional unity through recurrent permutations of a single, simplified motive across the work. While such a design may indeed have distant roots in classical formal ideology, *Harlem* displays a far more integrated motivic technique than the earlier, self-conscious motivic saturation textures that were seen in *Reminiscing in Tempo* or *Black, Brown and Beige*. In *Harlem*, these recurrent two-note Harlem motive variations flow quite naturally from the melodic material of each strain (as well as the accompaniment textures of each strain). This approach somewhat resembles a master jazz musician's use of recurrent motivic materials to build coherence and developmental qualities into solo improvisations. This latter practice is by no means driven by classical influence, and I believe the same can be said for the motive manipulations in *Harlem*. What is surprisingly missing from this vision for concert jazz is unrestrained room for extended improvisation. This latter quality increasingly found its way into some later Ellington suites—to varying degrees—in the coming two decades after *Harlem*. Similarly, the extended jazz suite model that became popular in certain jazz circles during the 1950s and 1960s (and beyond) left far more room for improvisational contributions. Nevertheless, as I have noted, the long history of the Ellington orchestra's performances of *Harlem* suggest that the composer must have encouraged paraphrase-based improvisational contributions to the solos within the work, though obviously there was more improvisational leeway built into the designs of *Non-Violent Integration* and *New World A-Comin'*.

Harlem displays a highly individual vision for concert jazz, one that embraces the blues, that speaks of "serious" musical matters through the rich idioms of historic African American musical genres, and that Ellington believed was purely American in its musical voice and programmatic social concerns. While Luther Henderson's later orchestral arrangements transpose Ellington's vision to a new symphonic tonal palette, this new high-end clothing does not fundamentally change the basic structural and idiomatic elements that I have described. Indeed, Henderson's arrangement of *Harlem* introduces far fewer orchestration liberties than were seen in *New World*.

In a 1956 interview with Carter Harman, Ellington described the symphonic arrangement of *Harlem* as "more or less a *concerto grosso*" that featured the big band in alternating episodic statements "with the symphony," and passages where the symphony also provided a more basic "supporting" role for the big band.[58] As implied in this characterization, both the big band and the original big band orchestration remain central to the aural identity of the work. For example, nearly all of the solos remain in the distinctive voices of Ellington's musicians. In general, Henderson created something akin to a symphonic version of an old-time, utilitarian stock orchestration, particularly in his heavy use of cross-scoring (instrument doubling). For instance, many areas of the orchestration directly transfer saxophone parts to the strings or have the strings simply double the still-present saxophone section, which remains the foregrounded instrumental color. Likewise, there are various passages where original backing colors have been replaced by near-equivalent symphonic sonorities, but in these instances, an original Ellington soloist remains the central voice. This can be seen, for example, in the first section's vamp and the second statement of strain A (m. 63ff.). As heard in the *Symphonic Ellington* performance (3:05ff.), this passage features the quintessential Ellingtonian voice of Harry Carney's lush baritone saxophone. The original pizzicato bass, staccato clarinet trio, and high-hat-with-brushes texture is replaced with a pizzicato scoring for full string section (along with the original high-hat-with-brushes part).

The central performance roles of Ellington's musicians make this symphonic *Harlem* something quite distinct from the typical middle-brow symphonic pops repertory, as one foot—and the full body weight—of the composition rests firmly on the idiomatic soil of the performance voices, stylistic idioms, and formal language of authentic jazz. This jazz voice remains in the foreground despite the outward aural and performance presentation appearances of the symphonic instrumental tuxedo that clothes this version of the work. The orchestration may have gained Ellington entry into—and some degree of "legitimacy" in the eyes of—symphonic culture, but he retains his Harlem voice once he is allowed to join this highbrow, "serious" company.

13 RHAPSODIZING ABOUT HARLEM

Beyond the *Harlem Suite*'s 1951 premiere, Ellington and his publicists continued to refine and expand on the work's extramusical program. While Leonard Feather's concert notes for the work's premiere describe an experience of Harlem from a static perspective (i.e., listening "through a Harlem airshaft window"), later references to the program describe a rich "tour of this place called Harlem," as Ellington characterized the suite in his autobiography.[59] By 1974, near the end of his life, *Harlem*'s program had evolved to the following form:

> When you arrive in Harlem, . . . you discover first that there are more churches than cabarets, and when you really get to know Harlem, you know that it's like any other community in the world, . . . with people, some plain and some fancy, some living luxuriously, others not so luxuriously, some urbane, some sub-suburban, laughing, crying, and experiencing a million different kinds of ups and downs. So the piece of music goes like this: (1) Pronunciation of the word "Harlem," itemizing its many facets from downtown to uptown, true and false; (2) 110th Street, heading north through the Spanish neighborhood; (3) Intersection further uptown—cats shucking and stiffing; (4) Upbeat parade; (5) Jazz spoken in a thousand languages; (6) Floor show; (7) Girls out of step, but kicking like crazy; (8) Fanfare for a Sunday; (9) On the way to church; (10) Church—we're even represented in Congress by our man of the church; (11) The sermon; (12) Funeral; (13) Counterpoint of tears; (14) Chic chick; (15) Stopping traffic; (16) After church promenade; (17) Agreement *a cappella*; (18) Civil Rights demandments [*sic*]; (19) March onward and upward; (20) Summary—contributions coda.[60]

With the stylistic overview of the work I have provided in mind, it should be clear that this detailed program connects to the music in only a few concrete—or even merely suggestive—ways. For example, the introduction and the many motivic variations in the first strain A statement could be roughly mapped onto the ideas of a "pronunciation of the word 'Harlem,'" and a presentation of the "many facets" of Harlem (the motive) "from downtown to uptown." The topics of the "Spanish neighborhood" and "cats shucking and stiffing" can be plausibly tied to first and second (maybe even third and fourth) chorus rhumba and swing stylistic juxtapositions in section 2. Quite possibly Ellington meant to tie the remaining blues choruses of this section to the ideas of an "upbeat parade," "jazz spoken in a thousand languages," and a "floor show" with "girls out of step," but there is no real means of connecting these ideas to the music other than through this loosely programmatic suggestion. Similarly, while a "fanfare for a Sunday," travel to church, a church "sermon," and a "funeral" with a "counterpoint of tears" can be comfortably tied to the stylistic topics that progress across section 3 up through the first statement of strain C, and while the ideas "chic chick" and a beautiful woman "stopping traffic" might conform to the cultural coding inherent in the swinging, burlesque-type scoring of the (b) phrase of strain C1, it becomes a bit more tenuous to map an "after church promenade," "agreement *a cappella*" (whatever that means), "Civil Rights demandments," and a "march onward and upward" onto the remainder of section 3.

Irrespective of the real-life social and grave economic ills of mid-century Harlem, and even in spite of the intended social lessons embedded in the program for the *Harlem Suite*, this tourist introduction to Harlem bears traces of what the Mark Tucker has called Ellington's "familiar smiling mask of diplomacy." As Tucker has rightly noted, Ellington rarely "air[ed] . . . negative opinions publicly."[61] Ellington's positive portrayal of Harlem in this concert work is no different. His musical and programmatic characterizations of Harlem strongly underscore both the community's historic reputation as the celebrated heart of African American success and culture, and the community's great pride in its entertainers and its popular entertainment traditions and institutions. Above all, Harlem is portrayed in a self-consciously positive, tourist-friendly light. Ellington clearly felt it was more artful—and likely more diplomatic—to avoid direct statements about the political and social concerns that he hoped to express in his concert works. This covert approach to cross-race social education through music and acts of accomplishment (like his appearances at Carnegie Hall) was seen earlier in the history of *Black, Brown and Beige*. While the public program for this 1943 work was broadly discussed in chapter 4, this final chapter's opening quotation from the "Beige" section of a contemporary Ellington script for *Black, Brown and Beige* reveals a far more complex, private side of this artistic vision. Here, Ellington again displays his great pride in the art, romance, racial pride, and commercial success of "Hot Harlem." But there is a new double-sided vision here, one that also recognizes the painful social travesty that a venue like the Cotton Club represented.

In the case of the extramusical program to the *Harlem Suite*, there were similarly important views that Ellington regularly left out of the printed concert programs for the work. Some of the added private associations that he tied to the *Harlem Suite* are noted in his autobiography's page-long description of the work. Here, he expands the discussion of his personal pride in Adam Clayton Powell's "social demands," including the senator-minister's success in breaking the earlier ban on African American employment in the shops on 125th Street (the main business thoroughfare in Harlem). Ellington likewise discusses the social victories of the NAACP and its president, Walter White. Even with this expanded discussion of his pride in Harlem, however, Ellington approaches the underlying subject of race relations indirectly, even though this topic lies at the heart of the didactic "tourism" project he attached to *Harlem*. At its core, this project hoped to peel away the veneer of the widely celebrated—and, by 1951, long outdated—image of Harlem as a jazz-drunk nightclub paradise where black culture was put on display for voyeuristic white audiences. Ellington hoped to reveal a diverse, vibrant, sober community that represented the highest achievements and ideals of both American and African American culture. The 1951 public image of Harlem as a dangerous ghetto slum greatly contrasted with the social optimism of the program to Ellington's *Harlem*, but this contrast is not surprising since the artistic roots of Ellington's *Harlem Suite* predate this work's composition by a decade or more.

Ellington's reference to Harlem as a community of "more churches than cabarets" actually dates back to the formative plans for the 1943

Black, Brown and Beige. A more in-depth and private understanding of the program to that work can be seen in the aforementioned, thirty-three-page, early 1940s typescript with the title *"Black, Brown and Beige* by Duke Ellington."[62] In "Beige," the third "movement" of the script, the story of Boola vanishes and the poetic voices shifts from a third-person narrative to a first-person poetic voice—presumably Ellington's voice—in conversation with Harlem. Maurice Peress notes that this section marks a shift "from the metaphoric world of Boola to Harlem, from the mythical to the autobiographical."[63] Peress further observes that the poem contains a mixture of "anger and pride" in Harlem's—and African Americans'—social history.[64] For instance, Ellington asks Harlem whether its jazz-delirious image ever really revealed to the white world "what you *really* are." He asks, "Did it [Harlem entertainment] say to them / The joy I'm giving / Is the foil I use to lose my blues / And make myself an honest living?" He describes the nightclub management as "knaves and robbers" that "came to prostitute your [Harlem's] art" and "outraged your honor / for their gain." He continues this thread for several more stanzas before reaching a climax at "Who brought the dope / And made a rope / Of it, to hang you / In your misery?" and "Why did they need to spread their fear / And discount every good thing here?" He caps this passage with an optimistic turn:

Ah, yes! But Harlem
You are strong.
You've stood the test
and *they* are wrong!

You've dodged the snare of subjugation
And ripped the bars with education,
And now you stand prepared to lead
Your brothers [African Americans nationwide] from the wilderness
Of hopelessness and need.

TAKE HEART!

In these passages, Ellington's reveals a far more passionate and personal view on the racial dynamics of Harlem entertainment and his community's difficult decline into a ghettoization after its proud accomplishments of the 1920s. With his turn toward optimism in the final page and a half of the poem, Ellington suggests social themes that soon informed his 1943 quasi piano concerto, *New World A-Comin'*. As seen in the programs to *Black, Brown and Beige*, *New World A-Comin'*, and the *Harlem Suite*, Ellington's expansive, complex, romantic vision of Harlem was remarkably consistent across the related themes—and didactic social intent—of these concert works.

Ellington's interviews with Carter Harman provide further candid reflections on his relation to Harlem, and the distance between fact, opinion, and his idealized renderings of this community in *New World* and the *Harlem Suite*. Harman's and Ellington's various Harlem discussions in these 1956 and 1964 interview sessions reveal similar tensions between the public and private reflections of the bandleader-composer.[65] In this commentary, Ellington again provides a tourist-friendly, glowing image of Harlem as an ordinary community of hardworking, devout, socially responsible American citizens. There is a significant emphasis on cultural accomplishments and respectable professionalism (from lawyers and doctors to nightclub dancers). When Harman and Ellington return to this subject a short while later, Ellington lowers his diplomatic guard in more candid reflections on the reputation and myths that trouble his community. Ellington's eleven-minute soliloquy on this subject forms one of the most extended topical discussions in the Harman interviews. Here he notes that "as far back as I can remember, it has always been a place that was thought of, spoke of, imagined, and considered a place of great extremes." He rhetorically acknowledges that "Harlem, of course, has many facets, and all of them are extremes," but he stresses "that you never hear anything about Harlem in the middle like, say, for instance, it's a place where—well, nice quiet people live, and they live a very conservative life, or anything." He seems particularly concerned that the American public never hears "any middle rumor[s] about Harlem." For Ellington, these negative "rumors" of Harlem life seem to be the most troubling facet of Harlem's "extreme" image. As Ellington continues his ruminations, he meanders into a discussion of the celebrated "tourism" image of the "great nightlife in Harlem" during his youth in the 1920s. This discussion soon drifts to his recollection of the downfall of the Harlem entertainment renaissance: "Somebody started a rumor that . . . [you shouldn't] go to

Harlem because people get . . . mugged and robbed in Harlem. And so they did a good propaganda job. And so the business slid, and went further downtown, and it's more or less stayed downtown ever since." Ellington sadly reflects that because of this entertainment shift, "Harlem has retired into a place which is reputed to be full of gangs."[66] Ellington's late-life reflections on the downfall of his beloved Harlem reveal variations on the social themes that he sought to highlight both twenty years earlier in *Black, Brown and Beige* and in subsequent programmatic works such as *New World A-Comin'* and the *Tone Parallel to Harlem*. These subjects thus formed the inspirational core of Ellington's lifelong, intertwined social and artistic concerns.

13 CONCLUSION

The Legacy of Harlem's Concert Jazz

While the midcentury racial and class politics that motivated the concert music aspirations of Ellington and Johnson have greatly diminished in twenty-first-century America, the concert works of these two Harlem composers still speak volumes about the intertwined nature of American race relations, cultural hierarchies, and the marketplace. Indeed, despite their historical importance, intelligence, and beauty, these truly hybrid compositions have yet to find the sustained support of an American performance tradition. Even with occasional performances and regular CD and MP3 reissues of Ellington's concert works, they remain largely lost as living repertory works in the cultural no-man's land between the "art music" canons of authentic jazz and classical music. This situation partly reflects the declining public interest in both classical music and jazz, but the lowered presence of both these traditions underscores the fact that the long-standing perception of high and low musical cultures has become more difficult to maintain as these two traditions have struggled to remain relevant and visible in modern American society. With post-1960s popular music saturating every corner of American (and Western) musical life, the middlebrow cultural trends of the

1930s through 1950s—trends that sought to bridge art, entertainment, and commerce—are at one and the same time antiquated and the forebears of the twenty-first-century view that classical music is just one art, and by no means the dominant art, among many forms of musical expression. Nevertheless, following the touchstone aesthetics of Paul Whiteman's early 1920s symphonic jazz, American popular music has continued to glorify itself with visual and instrumental references to the classical tradition, and with particular fondness for the symbolism of merging popular music performers with tuxedo-clad string sections. This long history of "glorified pop" efforts range from early-twentieth-century movie palace prologue revues, to interwar radio orchestras, to production numbers in stage and film musicals from the late 1920s to the early 1950s, to Hollywood "crime jazz" underscoring of the 1940s to 1960s, to the jazz-with-strings vogue of the 1950s and 1960s, to the now venerated orchestral jazz-pop of the "Great American Songbook" tradition. Nonjazz postwar popular music that carried on this tradition includes the "teenage symphonies" and Brill Building adult pop of the early 1960s (i.e., the music of Phil Spector, Motown, Burt Bacharach, etc.), early 1970s soul and blaxploitation film scores, areas of psychedelic and progressive rock, a chamber-music-minded singer-songwriter tradition (which extends from the Beatles' 1965 "Yesterday," to the late 1960s' "baroque pop" of artists like Nick Drake, to numerous acts performing today), 1960s and 1970s orchestral-pop film soundtracks, the string textures of disco, various heavy-metal-meets-symphony events, and even recent hip-hop adoptions of live string sections (especially by Kanye West and Jay-Z), among other trends. These "glorified pop" manifestations are most certainly part of the legacy of the cultural ideas and musical trends that produced Ellington's and Johnson's hybrid concert works. That said, many of the post-1960 orchestral pop efforts operate far outside the middle-culture and racial-uplift concerns that shaped these midcentury notions of concert jazz.

Unlike much of the glorified pop tradition, Johnson and Ellington strove for classical legitimization through the composition and symphonic performances of their concert works. These compositions were meant to be heard as "serious" art music rather than sophisticated popular entertainment, although—following Ellington's cultural arguments—they were intended to be read as "serious *American music*" (where "American music" is defined as African American jazz and popular music) rather than direct extensions of the European classical tradition. Despite this lofty ambition, even in their respective performance histories with Ellington and Johnson, these compositions have long been relegated to the less esteemed symphonic pops repertory (if they are performed at all). This situation is not necessarily a bad thing, as this orchestral tradition can help to ensure continued performances and an audience. For most defenders of classical music, however, the typical symphonic pops fare is second-class, glorified popular music rather than Art with a capital *A*, and thus this secondary performance context is hardly the venue for a composition to attain classical legitimization. For a hybrid, middle-ground art form like concert jazz, the symphonic pops tradition can function something like a cultural purgatory where this music's "sinful" social origins in "popular" jazz might bar a composition from attaining an equal footing with the classical canon. Likewise, this music's symphonic aspirations have removed such hybrid compositions from the parallel canon of the jazz tradition, despite the undisputed canonical standing of composers like Johnson and Ellington.

The idea of concert jazz has taken many different forms since Ellington's *Harlem*. Beyond the self-consciously "serious" hybrid jazz-classical compositions of so-called progressive and third-stream jazz efforts of the 1950s and 1960s, improvised, small-group jazz has also long been accepted as a "serious" concert music idiom. In addition, Ellington's extended suites inspired—and continue to inspire—a wealth of concert-oriented extended jazz works that balance both compositional and improvisational concerns. However, few of these later works address Johnson's and Ellington's fundamental concerns for finding common ground—and points of contact, real or imagined—that might allow African American music and Euro-American concert music to engage in dialogue. This quest was fueled by period aspirations for racial uplift and a historically specific desire for artistic recognition and equality.

Even though Ellington ultimately commissioned and performed symphonic reorchestrations of his concert works, he seems to have sensed that there were significant aesthetic differences between his concert works and the extended compositions of James P. Johnson.

Ellington located this difference in the influence of the "conservatory." In his 1964 interviews with Harman, Ellington discusses his great admiration for Johnson in his youth, but then he reflects on Johnson's post-1930 career:

> He went to the conservatory, and uh, I don't know—it, uh, I, I certainly couldn't say that the conservatory did him any harm. But as far as his uh, uh, *popular* audience was concerned, now what, uh— well, *me*, I consider myself a popular audience as far as James P. is concerned. And, uh, as far as I am concerned, it slowed him down. He had already written a Broadway show. You know, he wrote, uh, the Miller and Lyles show. The thing, the show that the "Charleston" came out of. That was his, the "Charleston." [CH: And he was a real composer then.] . . . Yeah, he was already there, you know. And what obviously the conservatory had done, it changed his perspective, and it . . . made him *careful*, which is a *reeeal* funny thing, you know, when you get careful. And then there's a certain blandness, that, you know, you don't go beyond the, uh, the outer limits or something.

In these rather blunt, off-the-cuff reflections, Ellington seems to imply that Johnson's original voice as a popular, jazz-based composer and performer had somehow become too conventional, and possibly too "classical." He notes somewhat later that "people sort of held him above his old image" after Johnson "had simmered down to being a very serious composer. And, you know, they just didn't expect, or invite, or encourage him to do the things he did originally . . . when he was such a beautiful, such a colorful musician."[1] Ellington seems to imply that Johnson's concert jazz lost sight of the pianist's colorful jazz voice and individualism. This sentiment echoes Will Marion Cook's admonition to Johnson in 1936 that he not be "influenced by *anybody*— no matter how great, how popular." That said, in his discussion of his younger friend's concert works, Cook also told Johnson that "your rhythms are magnificent and are your own." This brief bit of praise reinforces the earlier point that—when compared to Ellington—Johnson's mature vision for concert jazz more closely reflected the musical-theater-derived symphonic aspirations of Cook's generation.

That Ellington faulted Johnson for a supposed "conservatory" blandness may partly reflect Ellington's lifelong compositional explorations at the forefront of big band jazz, while Johnson had long expressed his orchestral interests through the medium of musical theater. Like many musicians of the 1920s, Johnson seems to have seen no real musical boundary between his performances and compositions in straight-ahead jazz and his work in musical theater. While Ellington may have had a lifelong ambition to succeed on Broadway, and while Luther Henderson subsequently became a major Broadway arranger, this musical tradition had little formal influence on Ellington's vision for concert jazz after *Black, Brown and Beige* (though Ellington continued to toy with the idea of turning that work into a stage presentation well into the 1960s). The diluted "jazz" of the Broadway musical tradition, at least when held up to the vitality of the Ellington orchestra, may partly explain Ellington's characterizations of Johnson's "serious" music as "bland," a personal opinion that hardly does justice to the rich, inspired music in these concert works.

Similar negative characterizations have been leveled at the "symphonic Ellington" repertory, particularly by stalwart Ellington enthusiasts and jazz aficionados. A typical response can be seen in the two *New York Times* reviews of Luther Henderson's "Classic Ellington" concert at Carnegie Hall in 2000. The jazz and popular music critic Ben Ratliff called Henderson's efforts "a strangely naive project, unconscious of its shortcomings," in which Henderson's symphonic arrangements "washed out most of Ellington's more biting original harmonies." Similarly, the *Times* classical critic, Bernard Holland, argued that "pure Ellington . . . got lost in the demonstration. Listen to the Ellington band on records, and be lifted up by the sharpness and energy, an edge and a bite that a symphony orchestra can only dilute and weaken."[2] Holland's comments unintentionally point to another major issue in the current repertory problems of these concert jazz works: the historical loss of a middle-ground theater, radio, and studio orchestra tradition that knows how to perform and phrase jazz- and swing-based idioms. These orchestras thrived from the 1920s until Frank Sinatra's famous 1950s orchestral pop catalog with the arrangers Nelson Riddle and Billy May (where Capitol Records employed a studio orchestra that still included several players whose careers dated back to Paul Whiteman in the 1920s). Beyond their expanded stylistic capacities, the instrumental makeup and sectional proportions of these hybrid orchestras was significantly different from the traditional symphony orchestra. These two problems generally impose an overly European, lush, straight-jacketed, romantic performance style on top of music that requires swing and African American–derived musical phrasing and articulation. This major discrepancy can be heard in comparisons of more recent "symphonic" performances of Johnson's and Ellington's concert works with the period musical evidence of documents like the Vitaphone *Yamekraw* film soundtrack, Johnson's solo piano renditions of his concert works, the extant acetate transcription recordings for Johnson's original performances of the *Harlem Symphony,* and the 1940s and 1950s concert and studio recordings of the Ellington big band performing his extended works. In some respects this ahistorical, modern symphonic performance practice reflects the similar aesthetic insensitivity that critics find in the conducting of Arturo Toscanini, the so-called "Rhodes of rhapsodic music," who indiscriminately applied the same lush interpretive style—and a full nineteenth-century symphonic orchestra—to the music of such different composers as Johann Sebastian Bach, Franz Joseph Haydn, and Richard Wagner.[3] In sum, as in good jazz, a stylistically sensitive performance is central to bringing out the brilliance, vitality, and art of these hybrid concert jazz compositions, and much is lost if this jazz-based script is performed with a thick, Old World, European, symphonic accent. As with humor, too much of the original meaning and inherent humanity and wit can be lost in insensitive, cross-genre translation.

The studies of this book have demonstrated the emergence and growth of the idea of jazz composition from the 1920s through the early 1950s. Alain Locke's hierarchical categories of the "worthwhile" traditions of "jazz composition" emphasized the arts of jazz orchestration and composition in their own right within the big band tradition. Locke's categorical account of black music, however, still hoped for a "higher" cultural mediation—what he called "classical jazz"—between this big band tradition and the ideals of Euro-American classical music. This latter aspiration, based on the schism between the cultivated and vernacular music traditions, had a long life in American culture and even in the bona fide jazz tradition. Ellington's concert jazz efforts were central to how Locke's "classical jazz" ideology evolved up through the 1960s. Moreover, in the late 1950s to late 1960s, in the wake of a wave of so-called third-stream jazz compositions by the Modern Jazz Quartet, Charles Mingus, and others, jazz scholars such as Gunther Schuller and A. J. Bishop began to acknowledge Ellington's role behind this latter vogue's ideal for "serious" extended jazz composition. As noted, Schuller and his peers argued for the idea that jazz was "a music to be *listened* to" and that extended jazz compositions needed to evolve "out of the material itself" and from "within . . . [the] domain forms [that were] much more indigenous to its own essential nature."[4] This model was exemplified in Ellingtonian extended jazz composition, and indeed—despite period cultural politics and residual highbrow grievances about populist applications of the word *composer*— Ellington clearly was at the forefront of efforts to convince critics and audiences that the African American jazz tradition could be a "serious" art form and a viable foundation for a new hybrid genre of artful concert music, while still closely adhering to its "indigenous" and "domain forms." In this latter project, beyond their reflection of Harlem entertainment strategies of cultural uplift, Ellington's concert works also exemplify interwar "Afro-modernism," as uniquely artful expressions of black urbanity and black modernity with rich juxtapositions of black and white vernacular and cultivated music traditions.

While Johnson's orchestral works are grounded on the same principle, that African American jazz could be a basis for a "serious" art form and that a composer could use this idiom's "indigenous" and "domain forms" as the basis for concert music, he ultimately arrived at a different artistic vision for concert jazz. Ellington's sense that these works were too indebted to either the conservatory or the classical tradition proper is considerably off the mark, however. For Johnson's slightly older generation, beyond the improvisation-based, instrumental jazz tradition that was later elevated to the center of the jazz canon, the vernacular jazz idiom—at least as this generation understood this idiom—was also deeply embedded in black popular song, the stride piano tradition, and the music and orchestral sounds of black musical theater. Like Cook before him, Johnson saw black musical theater orchestration and its "indigenous" arranging traditions as the most direct bridge to translating Harlem popular music into concert music. In his translation and self-conscious elevation of this music, and in the fact that his works would likely not be performed by the same African American musicians who inhabited the pit orchestras of black musical theater, there is a regrettable loss of inherent expressive qualities that were likely meant to be part of his concert music. Similarly, the unique qualities of Johnson's voice as a jazz pianist are seemingly lost on the notated page, but these qualities were vibrantly brought to life in Johnson's solo piano performances of his concert works.[5] This unique facet of orchestral jazz—that is, the desire to unite a collection of unique instrumental voices—was obviously central to the compositional vision of Ellington, and Johnson's works certainly have the potential for enriched vitality if the jazz performance conception and actual jazz musicians are used to bring this music to life.

Throughout this book, I have stressed that the concert works of Ellington and Johnson reflect key interwar cultural discourses concerning race, Afro-modernism, art and entertainment, and American high, middle, and low subcultures. I have attempted to illustrate that the symphonic jazz concert work and arranging traditions are significant for our understanding of American musical culture, the place of concert music in American society, and music in modern media. The middle-culture topics explored in this book have the potential to open new perspectives on interwar musical traditions, from jazz and syncopated dance music, to the arranging and production number traditions of Tin Pan Alley, the deluxe movie palace orchestras, musical theater and nightclub entertainments, and areas of interwar radio and film scoring. While a few of these subjects have acquired a modest scholarly literature, other areas have almost been entirely neglected.

The subject of black symphonic jazz has also been useful for articulating the larger background and cultural context of certain orchestral jazz trends of the postwar era. These trends include the progressive and third stream jazz movements of the later 1940s to 1960s, and Hollywood's late 1940s and 1950s vogue for a new jazz-classical hybrid score style that was influenced by the soundtracks to *A Streetcar Named Desire* (Warner Bros., 1951), *On the Waterfront* (Columbia, 1954), and *The Man with the Golden Arm* (United Artists, 1955). A thread that connected many of these concert-style, orchestral jazz efforts was the influence of Duke Ellington's extended compositions. This connection is particularly apparent in the influence of Ellington on the early concert-jazz compositions of Charles Mingus, John

Lewis, Mary Lou Williams, Ralph Burns, and a number of other pre–third stream jazz composers and arrangers of the late 1940s and early 1950s. In the manner of the relationship between the Whiteman "Experiment" concerts and Ellington's annual Carnegie Hall appearances of the 1940s, Ellington's Carnegie events in turn provided an important program model for similar concerts in the middle to late 1940s by Mary Lou Williams, Count Basie, Stan Kenton, Woody Herman, and Dizzy Gillespie, among others. These latter concerts frequently included pre–third stream concert jazz works, many of which were modeled after, or meant to rival, Ellington's suites. Most jazz histories forget that these concert jazz compositions of the 1940s only represent the "authentic" jazz contribution to a much larger musical trend. Because of our culture's continued interest in the "authentic" jazz legacy, many of the recordings of these specific events and concert works have remained in our present-day marketplace and cultural memory. This continued visibility and the lingering influence of the aesthetic priorities of most post-1930 jazz criticism have perpetuated a somewhat distorted historical narrative that has lost sight of the cultural trends that led up to and informed postwar concert jazz. The connections between "authentic" jazz and the jazz-derived entertainments of the interwar era are readily visible, however, if one examines the diverse entertainment landscape that "authentic" jazz thrived in between the wars. In the contemporary music journalism of such magazines as *Down Beat*, *Metronome*, and *Variety*, for example, it is apparent that a figure like Duke Ellington pursued a much broader entertainment career than is usually represented in post-1930 jazz histories. Ellington's connection to Whitemanesque symphonic jazz is one of these near-forgotten facets of his professional activities.

In examining the symphonic jazz connections between "authentic" jazz and jazz-derived entertainment, I was invariably drawn to a rich and contradictory body of American cultural criticism. Such figures as Winthrop Sargeant, Roger Pryor Dodge, Gilbert Seldes, Henry Osgood, Constant Lambert, and Olin Downes were important eyewitnesses to the emergence of both modern entertainment and media and American musical middlebrowism. This diverse body of criticism both condemned and celebrated these democratic cultural trends. In many ways, the prejudices and passions of these 1920s and 1930s critics laid the ground for a new breed of postwar American intelligentsia who made great efforts to convince the public that middlebrowism posed a significant cultural threat. When considered together, the opinions of these interwar and postwar critics reveal a tapestry of views that converged in the middlebrow tendencies of symphonic jazz activities like those by Johnson and Ellington. While symphonic jazz turned out not to be the major cause of the postwar erosion of highbrow cultural authority that many critics thought it would be, it certainly was a vital early contributor to this twentieth-century trend.

In this first decade of the twenty-first century, "culture" and "art" are broader and more inclusive concepts than they were at midcentury. America's once-sacred concert halls are likewise far more ecumenical now in the spectrum of their performers, musical repertories, and cultural functions. This development has largely been the result of pressures for both economic survival and the quest for cultural relevance. Similarly, many of the resident symphonic orchestras of these institutions have been forced to seek out new ways of expanding their audiences and of making their concert offerings relevant to a pluralistic, modern American society. These conditions suggest a favorable environment for reevaluating and appreciating the interwar middlebrow trends that first sought to bridge the social chasm between mass and highbrow musical cultures in the interwar era.

𝄢 NOTES

The notes to each chapter provide extensive bibliographic and discographical information on important correspondence, recordings, published scores, concert
programs, taped interviews, interview transcripts, professional scrapbook clippings, and other manuscript sources.

ABBREVIATIONS

BRTC   Billy Rose Theatre Collection, New York Public Library for the Per-
        forming Arts, New York, N.Y.

DEC   Duke Ellington Collection, Archives Center of the Smithsonian Insti-
        tution's National Museum of American History, Washington, D.C.

DER   Tucker, Mark, ed., *The Duke Ellington Reader* (New York: Oxford Uni-
        versity Press, 1993).

JPJC   James P. Johnson Collection, Institute of Jazz Studies, John Cotton
        Dana Library, Rutgers University, Newark, N.J.

JRDD   Jerome Robbins Dance Division of the New York Public Library for
        the Performing Arts, New York, N.Y.

JWJC   James Weldon Johnson Collection in the Yale Collection of American
        Literature, Beinecke Rare Book and Manuscript Library, Yale Univer-
        sity Library, New Haven, Conn.

PWC   Paul Whiteman Collection, Williams College Archives and Special
        Collections, Williamstown, Mass.

SCRBC   Schomburg Center for Research in Black Culture, New York Public
        Library, New York, N.Y.

1. Louis Alter, *Manhattan Serenade* (New York: Robbins Music, 1928) and *Side Street in Gotham* (New York: Robbins Music, 1938); Vernon Duke, *New York Nocturne: A Modern Composition for Piano* (New York: Robbins Music, 1939) and *Lake Shore Drive* (New York: Robbins Music, 1939); and Ferde Grofé, *Broadway at Night: A Musical Kaleidoscope* (New York: Robbins Music, 1944), and *Metropolis* (New York: Robbins Music, 1928). For more information, see John Howland, "Between the Muses and the Masses: Symphonic Jazz, 'Glorified' Entertainment, and the Rise of the American Musical Middlebrow, 1920–1944," Ph.D. diss., Stanford University, 2002.

2. These extensive scrapbooks of career-related clippings and other White-man memorabilia were donated to the Williams College Archives in Williams-town, Mass., by the bandleader and his staff in the 1930s and 1940s.

3. Emphasis added. See H. L. Mencken, "The Colored Brother," *New York Tribune*, July 17, 1927, n.p. This clipping and additional copies of this essay are in the scrapbooks of the PWC.

4. For more on this topic, see Ted Merwin, *In Their Own Image: New York Jews in Jazz Age Popular Culture* (New Brunswick, N.J.: Rutgers University Press, 2006); and Michael Rogin, *Blackface, White Noise: Jewish Immigrants in the Hollywood Melting Pot* (Berkeley and Los Angeles: University of California Press, 1998).

1. Gilbert Osofsky, *Harlem: The Making of a Ghetto* (New York: Harper Torchbooks, 1966), 128.

2. Alain Locke, "Harlem: Dark Weather-Vane," *Survey Graphic*, August 1936, 457. Online at http://newdeal.feri.org/survey/36457.htm (accessed March 12, 2007).

3. "Police Ease Curbs with Harlem Quiet," *New York Times*, August 5, 1943, 28.

4. Ibid., 17.

5. Duke Ellington, *Music Is My Mistress* (New York: Doubleday, 1973; reprint, New York: Da Capo, n.d.), 94.

6. Ibid., 35–36.

7. One of the best accounts of these sites can be found in the extended liner-note booklet to *The Sound of Harlem*, vol. 3, *Jazz Odyssey*, ed. Frank Driggs, Columbia C3L33, n.d., LP. Also see Jim Haskins, *The Cotton Club* (New York: Random House, 1977).

8. Johnson, "Making of Harlem," *Survey Graphic*, March 1925, 635. Online at http://etext.lib.virginia.edu/harlem/JohMakiF.html (accessed 6 June 2007).

9. Thomas Riis, *Just before Jazz: Black Musical Theater in New York, 1890–1915* (Washington, D.C.: Smithsonian Institution Press, 1989), 4.

10. Ibid., 13.

11. James Weldon Johnson, *Black Manhattan* (New York: Knopf, 1930), 95.

12. Tim Brooks, *Lost Sounds: Blacks and the Birth of the Recording Industry, 1890–1919* (Urbana: University of Illinois Press, 2004), 105.

13. Maurice Peress, *Dvořák to Duke Ellington: A Conductor Explores America's Music and Its African American Roots* (New York: Oxford University Press, 2004), 55.

14. W. E. B. DuBois, *The Souls of Black Folk*, reprinted in *Three Negro Classics* (New York: Avon, 1965), 215. For a broad understanding of the impact of black double consciousness, also see Paul Gilroy, *The Black Atlantic: Modernity and Double Consciousness* (Cambridge: Harvard University Press, 1994).

15. Johnson, *Black Manhattan*, 120.

16. Reid Badger, *A Life in Ragtime: A Biography of James Reese Europe* (New York: Oxford University Press, 1995), 30–31.

17. David Levering Lewis, *When Harlem Was in Vogue* (New York: Penguin, 1997), 25.

18. Thomas L. Morgan, "Gotham-Attucks," http://www.jass.com/gattuck .html (accessed July 21, 2006). On Gotham-Attucks, also see Wayne D. Shirley, "The House of Melody: A List of Publications of the Gotham-Attucks Company at the Library of Congress," *Black Perspectives of Music* 15 (Spring 1987): 79–112; and Elliott S. Hurwitt, "W. C. Handy as Music Publisher: Career and Reputation," Ph.D. diss., City of New York University, 2000, 57–58.

19. Badger, *A Life in Ragtime*, 37.

20. Peress, *Dvořák to Duke Ellington*, 13.

21. Badger, *A Life in Ragtime*, 54.

22. See Brooks, *Lost Sounds*, 299–320.

23. *New York Age*, October 5, 1911, 6.

24. The photograph can be seen in Badger, *A Life in Ragtime*, on the bottom of p. 10 of the photograph folios between pp. 150 and 151.

25. Badger, *A Life in Ragtime*, 59.

26. Rudolf Fisher, "The Caucasian Storms Harlem," *American Mercury*, August 1927, 324.

27. Ibid., 393.

28. Ibid., 397.

29. Ibid., 396.

30. Ibid., 398.

31. Tom Davin, "Conversations with James P. Johnson": part 1, *Jazz Review*, June 1959, 14–17; part 2, *Jazz Review*, July 1959, 10–13; part 3, *Jazz Review*, August 1959, 13–15; part 4, *Jazz Review*, September 1959, 26–27; and part 5, *Jazz Review*, March–April 1960, 11–13. Additional biographical information on Johnson can be found in Scott E. Brown, *James P. Johnson: A Case of Mistaken Identity* (Metuchen, N.J.: Scarecrow Press, 1982), and Scott E. Brown, "Johnson, James P(rice)," *International Dictionary of Black Composers*, ed. Samuel A. Floyd Jr. (Chicago: Fitzroy Dearborn, 1999), 639–49.

32. Conservatory of Musical Art, New York, "Certificate of Award," June 28, 1921, JPJC.

33. Davin, "Conversations with Johnson," part 2, 11.

34. Hurwitt, *W. C. Handy*, 57.

35. Brown, *James P. Johnson*, 84.

36. Davin, "Conversations with Johnson," part 5, 7.

37. Ibid., part 4, 26.

38. Fisher, "The Caucasian Storms Harlem," 394.

39. Ibid., 395.

40. Haskins, *The Cotton Club*, 11.

41. Mamie Smith and Her Jazz Hounds, "Crazy Blues" (Okeh 4169; rec. August 1920); reissued on Mamie Smith, *Mamie Smith: Complete Recorded Works in Chronological Order*, vol. 1, Document DOCD-5357, 1995, compact disc.

42. See the Williams and Bradford overviews in David A. Jasen and Gene Jones, *Spreadin' Rhythm Around: Black Popular Songwriters, 1880–1930* (New York: Schirmer Books, 1998), 255–307.

43. Rex Stewart, *Boy Meets Horn*, ed. Claire P. Gordon (Ann Arbor: University of Michigan Press, 1991), 90–91.

44. See "Jazz Age Chicago: Urban Leisure from 1893 to 1945: Vendome Theatre," http://chicago.urban-history.org/ven/ths/vendome.shtml (accessed April 12, 2007).

45. Sidney Bechet, *Treat It Gentle: An Autobiography* (London: Cassell, 1960; reprint New York: Da Capo, 1978), 140 and 142.

46. Ellington, *Music Is My Mistress*, 71.

47. See chapter 2 in Jeffrey Magee, *The Uncrowned King of Swing: Fletcher Henderson and Big Band Jazz* (New York: Oxford University Press, 2005).

48. Ibid., 36.

49. Mark Tucker, "The Renaissance Education of Duke Ellington," in *Black Music in the Harlem Renaissance: A Collection of Essays*, ed. Samuel A. Floyd Jr. (Knoxville: University of Tennessee Press, 1990), 111–27, and "The Genesis of *Black, Brown and Beige*," *Black Music Research Journal* 13 (Fall 1993): 67–86.

50. John Hasse, *Beyond Category: The Life and Genius of Duke Ellington* (New York: Simon and Schuster, 1993; reprint, New York: Da Capo, 1995), 55.

51. See Ellington, *Music Is My Mistress*, 34–35.

52. Mark Tucker, *Ellington: The Early Years* (Urbana: University of Illinois Press, 1995), 92.

53. See ibid., 196–98.

54. Mercer Ellington with Stanley Dance, *Duke Ellington in Person* (New York: Da Capo, 1979), 34.

55. See Mark Tucker's essays "In Search of Will Vodery," *Black Music Research Journal* 16 (Spring 1996): 123–82; and "Vodery, William Henry Bennett ("Will")," in Floyd, *International Dictionary*, 1166–68.

56. "Duke Ellington on Arrangers," *Metronome*, October 1943, 35.

57. See the spring 1938 Cotton Club Parade Program in the collection of the SCRBC.

58. Tucker, "In Search of Vodery," 169.

59. Ibid., 168–69.

60. Ibid., 169–70.

61. Ibid., 170.

62. Richard O. Boyer, "The Hot Bach," part 3, *New Yorker* (July 8, 1944), 29, reprinted in DER, 241.

63. Ellington, *Music Is My Mistress*, 97.

64. Letter from Will Marion Cook to James P. Johnson dated November 25, 1936, JPJC.

CHAPTER TWO

1. DuBose Heyward, "Porgy and Bess Return on the Wings of Song," *Stage*, October 1935, reprinted in *Gershwin in His Time: A Biographical Scrapbook, 1919–1937*, ed. Gregory R. Suriano (New York: Gramercy Books, 1999), 105.

2. December 6, 1926, program for *George White's Scandals*.

3. See Bernard L. Peterson Jr., *A Century of Musicals in Black and White: An Encyclopedia of Musical Stage Works by, about, or Involving African Americans* (Westport, Conn.: Greenwood Press, 1993), 39–40 and 291–92.

4. "Van Grona, Resume/Chronology," Von Grona Collection, JRDD.

5. W. C. Handy, *Father of the Blues: An Autobiography* (New York: Da Capo, 1941), 212.

6. James P. Johnson, *Yamekraw: Negro Rhapsody* (New York: Perry Bradford, 1927); *Yamekraw (A Negro Rhapsody)*, arr. William Grant Still (New York: Alfred & Co., 1928); and *Yamekraw: An Original Composition by James P. Johnson* (Folkways Records FJ 2842, 1962); and *Yamekraw*, Vitaphone 1009 (Warner Bros., 1930).

7. Foreword to Johnson, *Yamekraw: Negro Rhapsody*.

8. James P. Johnson and Perry Bradford, *Dixieland Echoes: A Collection of Five Descriptive Negro Songs* (New York: Perry Bradford, 1928), back cover.

9. Alex Belledna and Marion Dickerson, "It's Right Here for You (If You Don't Get It—Tain't No Fault o' Mine)" (New York: Perry Bradford, 1920).

10. Okeh Records advertisement, *Talking Machine Journal*, August 1923, 1.

11. Liner notes to *Yamekraw*, Folkways.

12. See Wayne D. Shirley, "Religion in Rhythm: William Grant Still's Orchestrations for Willard Robison's *Deep River Hour*," *Black Music Research Journal* 19 (Spring 1999): 1–42.

13. See Henry Jenkins, *What Made Pistachio Nuts? Early Sound Comedy and the Vaudeville Aesthetic* (New York: Columbia University Press, 1992); and Robert W. Snyder, *The Voice of the City: Vaudeville and Popular Culture in New York* (Chicago: Ivan R. Dee, 2000).

14. John F. Szwed, *Jazz 101: A Complete Guide to Learning and Loving Jazz* (New York: Hyperion, 2000), 6–10.

15. Scott DeVeaux, "Constructing the Jazz Tradition: Jazz Historiography," *Black American Literature Forum* 25 (Fall 1991): 525.

16. Ann Douglas, *Terrible Honesty: Mongrel Manhattan in the 1920s* (New York: Farrar, Straus and Giroux, 1995), 4.

17. Cab Calloway, *Of Minnie the Moocher and Me* (New York: Thomas Y. Crowell, 1976), 105–6.

18. Eubie Blake, quoted in *Voices from the Harlem Renaissance*, ed. Nathan Irvin Huggins (New York: Oxford University Press, 1976), 339–40.

19. Samuel A. Floyd Jr., *The Power of Black Music: Interpreting Its History from Africa to the United States* (New York: Oxford University Press, 1995), 134.

20. John Graziano, "Black Musical Theater and the Harlem Renaissance Movement," in Floyd, *Black Music in the Harlem Renaissance*, 108 and 86, respectively.

21. Allen Woll, *Black Musical Theatre: From "Coontown" to "Dreamgirls"* (New York: Da Capo, 1989), 111.

22. Alain Locke, *The Negro and His Music and Negro Art: Past and Present* (1936; reprint, New York: Arno Press, 1969), 133. For a fascinating, broad-range discussion of related black musical stereotypes in American music and culture, see Ronald Radano, "Hot Fantasies: American Modernism and the Idea of Black Rhythm," in *Music and the Racial Imagination*, ed. Ronald Radano and Philip V. Bohlman (Chicago: University of Chicago Press, 2000), 459–80.

23. A reproduction of this letter appears in Howland, "Between the Muses," 632.

24. Locke, *Negro and His Music*, 94.

25. Ibid., 94 and 98, respectively.

26. Ibid., 96.

27. Floyd, *Power of Black Music*, 134.

28. See Peress, *Dvořák to Duke Ellington*, 22–27, 206 n. 24.

29. Ibid., 49.

30. James Weldon Johnson, "Go Down Death! A Funeral Sermon," *American Mercury*, April 1927, 394–95.

31. James Weldon Johnson, *God's Trombones: Seven Negro Sermons in Verse* (1927; New York: Viking, 1945), 9.

32. See James Weldon Johnson, *The Autobiography of an Ex–Colored Man*, in *Three Negro Classics* (New York: Avon, 1965), 441–49 and 453–61.

33. Noble Sissle, foreword to *Yamekraw*, Folkways.

34. Perry Bradford, "YAMEKRAW," *Yamekraw*, Folkways. Bradford's idiosyncratic uses of punctuation have been regularized in this quotation. Both Bradford and Sissle refer to *Yamekraw* in terms of "movements." The 1927 score, Still's arrangement, and the Vitaphone film short all display the same continuous formal structure shown in example 1. The misnomer of "movements" arose in part from the technological necessity of dividing the work into three- to four-minute segments that could accommodate the time constraints of 78 rpm recording technology. Folkways' engineers spliced together the recordings in their remastering of the original acetate sides for the LP format.

35. From both the side B label to the LP and the information provided on the back side of the album's liner jacket. *Yamekraw*, Folkways.

36. Davin, "Conversations with Johnson," part 2, 12–13. See also Davin, "Conversations with Johnson," part 1, 17.

37. See Samuel A. Floyd's definition of African American musical signifying traditions in Floyd, *Power of Black Music*, 8.

38. Davin, "Conversations with Johnson," part 5, 11.

39. For an account of publications in the Robbins Modern American Music score series, see appendices 1 and 2 in Howland, "Between the Muses," 599–611.

40. The score is prefaced by two pages of working sketches on an in-house manuscript paper from Irving Berlin, Inc. The presence of this office address suggests that the work was composed/arranged between 1922 and 1933. The evidence of the stock score manuscript papers used on the full score—as well as the arrangement's 1920s theater orchestra instrumentation—suggest that the work was composed in the mid-1920s. The *Symphonic Dance* may be related to the 1923 orchestral *Carolina Shout* arrangement that was used as the overture to Johnson's *Plantation Days* revue. This show is the only point in Johnson's career at which this type of orchestration could have been performed, though the arrange-

ment seems a bit too sophisticated for 1923. This early date would also place the work before Gershwin's *Rhapsody in Blue*, but after Gershwin's *Blue Monday Blues* of 1922. The *Symphonic Dance* differs stylistically from Johnson's 1940s symphonic reorchestrations of early works from the second decade of the century.

41. Davin, "Conversations with Johnson," part 4, 26.

42. Ibid., 142.

43. *Carolina Shout*, Jimmie Johnson's Jazz Boys, Arto 9096, 1921, reissued on *James P. Johnson: Harlem Stride Piano, 1921/1929*, Jazz Archives, CD No. 111, 1997.

44. Leonard Bernstein, *The Joy of Music* (New York: Simon and Schuster, 1954), 52–53.

45. George Antheil, "Jazz Is Music," *The Forum*, July 1928, 64.

46. David Schiff, *Gershwin: Rhapsody in Blue* (New York: Cambridge University Press, 1997), 12–29.

47. Willie "the Lion" Smith, *Music on My Mind* (New York: Da Capo, 1964), 225–26.

48. Mamie Smith and Her Jazz Hounds, "Old Time Blues," Okeh 4296 (rec. February 1921).

49. King Oliver's Dixie Syncopaters, "(Hello Central Get Me) Doctor Jazz," Vocalion 1113 (rec. April 1927). Brian Priestley kindly pointed out this association.

50. *Caprice Rag*, Metro Art 203176 (rec. May 1917).

51. Also see Johnson's *Caprice Rag*, Blue Note 26 (rec. December 15, 1943).

52. Eubie Blake, *The Charleston Rag* (New York: M. Witmark & Sons, 1917), initially recorded as a piano roll played by the composer, Ampico 54174-E (August 1917). The first use of the title "Sounds of Africa" was on Eubie Blake's 1921 solo piano recording, "Sounds of Africa—One Step," Emerson 10434 and Paramount 14004 (rec. July 1921). (Thanks to Brian Priestley for making this observation.)

53. From the performance of "Charleston Rag" on Eubie Blake's *The Eighty-Six Years of Eubie Blake*, Columbia C2S847, 1968–69, LP.

54. This observation was made by Bob Pinsker, e-mail correspondence with the author, December 14, 2004.

55. The connection of this number to *Yamekraw* was first brought to my attention by Bob Pinsker. See James P. Johnson, *Stop It*, piano roll performance, Universal 203205 (rec. August 1917); William Farrell and James P. Johnson, "Stop It" (New York: F. B. Haviland, 1917); James P. Johnson (piano and vocals), "Stop It, Joe," an unissued interview by Alan Lomax recorded for the Library of Congress (rec. December 1938), 2490-B-2; and Rosetta Crawford with James P. Johnson's Hep Cats, "Stop It, Joe," Decca 7567 (rec. February 1939).

56. James P. Johnson, *Yamekraw Blues* (New York: Alfred Music, 1930) and *Hot Curves (Fox Trot)* (New York: Alfred Music, 1931), both arranged by Ken Macomber. The *Hot Curves* connection was made by Bob Pinsker.

57. The role of improvisation in the 1920s-era performance tradition of stride cutting-contest works is surprisingly limited. See Henry Martin, "Balancing Composition and Improvisation in James P. Johnson's *Carolina Shout*," *Journal of Music Theory* 49 (Fall 2005; forthcoming).

58. The Asch recording includes several audible page turns.

59. H. L. Mencken, *The American Language: An Inquiry into the Development of English in the United States*, 3rd ed. (1919; New York: Knopf, 1923), 30–34.

60. From a reproduction of the concert program published in Maurice Peress, *The Birth of the Rhapsody in Blue: Paul Whiteman's Historic Aeolian Hall Concert of 1924*, Music Masters LP MMD20113x/14T, 1986, LP.

61. George Gottlieb, "Psychology of the American Vaudeville Show from the Manager's Point of View," in *American Vaudeville as Seen by Its Contemporaries*, ed. Charles W. Stein (New York: Knopf, 1984), 179.

62. Ibid.

63. Ibid.

64. From the reproduction of the concert program in Peress, *Birth*.

65. Gottlieb, "Psychology of Vaudeville," 179.

66. Ibid., 179–80.

67. Ibid., 180.

68. Ibid., 180–81.

69. Ibid., 181.

70. Ibid.

71. Olin Downes, "Whiteman's Jazz," *New York Times*, October 8, 1928, 27; emphasis added.

72. Winthrop Sargeant, *Jazz: Hot and Hybrid* (New York: E. P. Dutton, 1946), 231–32.

73. Arnold Shaw, *The Jazz Age: Popular Music in the 1920s* (New York: Oxford University Press, 1987), 154.

74. Ibid., 151 and 155. See also Vincent Lopez, *Lopez Speaking: An Autobiography* (New York: Citadel Press, 1960), 179–88; Henry Osgood, *So This Is Jazz* (Boston: Little, Brown, 1926), 158–59; and Handy, *Father of the Blues*, 218.

75. Osgood, *So This Is Jazz*, 160–61; Handy, *Father of the Blues*, 218–19; and cover text to Albert Chiaffarelli, *"Blue Destiny," Scherzo from Symphony Blue Destiny* (New York: Handy Brothers Music, 1945).

76. Handy, *Father of the Blues*, 212.

77. Donald Friede, *The Mechanical Angel* (New York: Knopf, 1948), 49.

78. Handy, *Father of the Blues*, 297–98.

79. Legal agreement between James P. Johnson, Perry Bradford, and Lewis Warner, dated February 18, 1930, 2, JPJC. Johnson and Bradford may have also licensed the score to Pathé Studios, as documents in the JPJC suggest.

80. The U.S.C. Warner Bros. Archives possess several legal documents for this production. These include a July 12, 1930, Warner Bros./Vitagraph inter-office communication from Mr. Murphy to Mr. Attenberg; a March 22, 1932, letter from William P. Siegfried to Mr. Arthur S. Boucher, Music Publishers Holding Corp.; a March 23, 1932, letter from V. Blau to Mr. M. Spiero of Thomas & Friedman, New York City; an October 26, 1932, notary public statement by Michel Hoffman; and an October 27, 1932, legal agreement between Michel Hoffman and Albert Warner.

81. Vitaphone Release Index, undated, Academy of Motion Picture Arts and Sciences Library, 170.

82. See Char., "Yamekrow" [*sic*], *Variety*, April 30, 1930, 17.

83. Donald Bogle, *Toms, Coons, Mulattoes, Mammies, and Bucks: An Interpretive History of Blacks in American Films* (New York: Continuum, 1996).

84. Mamie Smith and Her Jazz Hounds, *The Road Is Rocky*, 7589-C-Phonola 4194 (rec. September 1920).

85. Dwight Macdonald, "Masscult and Midcult," part 2, *Partisan Review* 27 (Fall 1960): 610.

86. Donald Crafton, *The Talkies: American Cinema's Transition to Sound, 1926–1931*, ed. Charles Harpole, *History of the American Cinema*, vol. 4 (Berkeley and Los Angeles: University of California Press, 1997), 63.

87. Ibid., 88.

CHAPTER THREE

1. The one obvious exception to this blanket statement can be found in the significant (and growing) body of literature on Ellington's *Black, Brown and Beige*. See the notes to chapter 4 for relevant citations.

2. Barry Ulanov, *Duke Ellington* (New York: Creative Age Press, 1946), 161.

3. Gunther Schuller, *The Swing Era: The Development of Jazz, 1930–1945* (New York: Oxford University Press, 1989), 72.

4. Sargeant, *Jazz: Hot and Hybrid*, 231–32.

5. Kevin K. Gaines, *Uplifting the Race: Black Leadership, Politics, and Culture in the Twentieth Century* (Chapel Hill: University of North Carolina Press, 1996), 2–3.

6. On the relationship between Cook and Douglass, see Peress, *Dvořák to Duke Ellington*, 32, 49, and 55.

7. Ray Allen and George P. Cunningham, "Cultural Uplift and Double-Consciousness: African-American Responses to the 1935 Opera *Porgy and Bess*," *Musical Quarterly* 88 (Fall 2005): 346.

8. Ibid.

9. See Magee, *Uncrowned King of Swing*, 28–33.

10. Lewis A. Erenberg, *Swingin' the Dream: Big Band Jazz and the Rebirth of American Culture* (Chicago: University of Chicago Press, 1999), 101.

11. Langston Hughes, "The Negro Artist and the Racial Mountain," *The Nation*, 1926, online at http://www.english.uiuc.edu/maps/poets/g_l/hughes/mountain.htm (accessed November 4, 2006).

12. On Cook's music and career, see especially Marva Griffin Carter, "The Life and Music of Will Marion Cook," Ph.D. diss., University of Illinois, 1988; and Will Marion Cook, *The Music and Scripts of "In Dahomey,"* ed. Thomas L. Riis (Madison: American Musicological Society, 1996).

13. Ernst Ansermet, "Sur un orchestra nègre," reprinted in *Reading Jazz: A Gathering of Autobiography, Reportage, and Criticism from 1919 to Now*, ed. Robert Gottlieb (New York: Pantheon, 1996), 745. Also see Edward S. Walker, "The Southern Syncopated Orchestra," *Storyville*, August–September 1972, 204–8.

14. This program was discovered among the film-related collections of Cambria Master Recordings and Archives in Lomita, California.

15. See the following concert programs: "F. C. Coppicus Presents Paul Whiteman and His Orchestra of Twenty-Five in Their First Transcontinental Concert Tour, Season 1924–1925"; "F. C. Coppicus Presents Paul Whiteman and His Greater Concert Orchestra in Their Second Transcontinental Concert Tour, Season 1925–1926"; and "F. C. Coppicus Presents Paul Whiteman and

His Greater Concert Orchestra in Their Third Transcontinental Concert Tour, Season 1928–1929," PWC.

16. C. A. Parker, New York, to Edmund Jenkins, London, June 1, 1923, Edmund T. Jenkins Collection, SCRBC.

17. See Howland, "Between the Muses," 352–55, for an overview of the extant revue scores at the Will Mercer Cook Papers, Moorland-Springarn Research Center of Howard University, Washington, D.C.

18. Tucker, "Genesis," 69. Also see Tucker, *Ellington: Early Years*, 7–8.

19. Jenkins, *What Made Pistachio Nuts?*, 63.

20. See the April 10, 2004, Associated Press and *Telegraph* obituary clippings for Reed at "American Dance Legends: Leonard Reed," http://www.theatredance .com/legends/reed.html (accessed January 6, 2007).

21. Transcript to "Interview with Leonard Reed," *MGZMT 3-2098 (transcript), 72, JRDD.

22. Ibid., 73.

23. Dan Healy, in Edward Jablonski, *Harold Arlen: Happy with the Blues* (New York: Da Capo, 1985), 55.

24. Reed, "Interview with Leonard Reed," 73.

25. Ibid., 71.

26. Ibid., 46.

27. Leonard Ratner, *Classic Music: Expressions, Form, and Style* (New York: Schirmer Books, 1980), 9.

28. Originally Robert S. Hatten, *Interpreting Musical Gestures, Topics, and Tropes: Mozart, Beethoven, Schubert* (Bloomington: Indiana University Press, 2004), 2. See also Jeffrey Magee, "'Everybody Step': Irving Berlin, Jazz, and Broadway in the 1920s," *Journal of the American Musicological Society* 59 (Fall 2006), 700–701 and n. 18.

29. Arthur Lange, *Arranging for the Modern Dance Orchestra* (New York: Arthur Lange, 1926), 190.

30. Ibid., 214.

31. Tom Bennett, "Arranging for Radio," in *Music in Radio Broadcasting*, ed. Gilbert Chase (New York: McGraw-Hill, 1946), 79.

32. Ibid., 86.

33. See, for example, James Agee, "Pseudo-Folk," *Partisan Review*, Spring 1944, reprinted in *Agee on Film: Criticism and Comment on the Movies*, ed. Martin Scorsese (New York: Modern Library, 2000), 431–37; and Willis Laurence James, *Stars in de Elements: A Study of Negro Folk Music*, ed. Jon Michael Spencer, *Black Sacred Music* 9 (1995): 195–200.

34. "Moan, You Moaners!," in *Joe Davis Folio of Paul Whiteman's Favorite Modern Rhythmic Spirituals as Featured by Mildred Bailey* (New York: Joe Davis, 1932), 12–14.

35. Bessie Smith accompanied by James P. Johnson and the Bessemer Singers, *Moan, You Moaners!*, Columbia 14538-D (New York, 1930), reissued on *The Chronological Bessie Smith, 1929–1933*, Classics (France) 977, 1998, compact disc.

36. From the JPJC. Programs and reviews exist in the collections of the JPJC and the BRTC.

37. The *St. Louis Blues* short has been reissued on *Hollywood Rhythm, the Paramount Musical Shorts: The Best of Jazz and Blues*, vol. 1, Kino Video, 2001, DVD.

For a partial account of the evidence for this arrangement's possible stage origins, see Howland, "Between the Muses," 452 n. 108.

38. These materials are found in the JPJC and the DEC.

39. All materials are in the JPJC. The meaning of "Intro 1, 4, Last ending 4/4" is unclear here, and there is no obvious relation to music in the extant parts. The actual ending for this number is also unclear, as this information is missing in the extant part materials. In addition, this typescript outline vaguely notes only that the number should end with "Break stop," a description that does not convey a clear structural meaning. As indicated in table 3.2, I have assumed that Johnson intended that the orchestra jump from the "Boston" chorus statement to that number's earlier coda (thereby jumping over a stop-time chorus arrangement). One trumpet part seems to indicate this form through a player's handwritten note of a few bars from this coda.

40. This claim is based on the evidence of both 1938 Ellington orchestra recordings from Cotton Club broadcasts, and similar April 1931 broadcast recordings for Cab Calloway's orchestra. The best commercial collection of these recordings for both Calloway and Ellington is *Live from the Cotton Club*, Bear Family Records BCD 16340 BL, 2003, compact disc.

41. Another ideal example of this can be found in J. Rosamond Johnson's "Rhapsody in Blue" choral arrangement that was the first-act finale for Leslie's 1931 revue, *Rhapsody in Black: A Symphony of Blue Notes and Black Rhythm*. See a discussion of this number in John Howland, "'The Blues Get Glorified': Harlem Entertainment, *Negro Nuances*, and Black Symphonic Jazz," *Musical Quarterly* 90 (Spring 2007; forthcoming).

42. Peter De Rose, Harry Richman, and Jo Trent, "Muddy Waters: A Mississippi Moan" (New York: Broadway Music Corp., 1926).

43. Joe Turner and His Memphis Men (aka Duke Ellington and His Orchestra), "Mississippi Moan," Columbia 1813-D (rec. April 4, 1929), 78 rpm. This has been reissued on *The Okeh Ellington*, Columbia C2K-46177, 1991, compact disc.

44. April 22, 1929, program (opening night) to *Messin' Around*, Hudson Theatre, New York, BRTC.

45. Perry Bradford, "YAMEKRAW," in the liner notes to *Yamekraw*, Folkways.

46. Richard Watts Jr., "*Messin' Around* Not as Bad as It Seems; New Negro Show On," *New York Herald Tribune*, April 23, 1929, 22.

47. William G. King, "*Messin' Around*: Louis Isquith's Negro Revue Arrives at the Hudson Theatre," *New York Evening Post*, April 23, 1929, 14.

48. L. W., "Again from Harlem: *Messin' Around*," *World*, April 23, 1929, n.p.

49. John C. Fitzgerald, "*Messin' Around*," *Evening World*, April 23, 1929, n.p.

50. M. W., "Song Saves a Show: With That Exception *Messin' Around* Is Ordinary," *New York Sun*, April 23, 1929, 22.

51. Program to "First Concert of Symphonic Works by James P. Johnson," Brooklyn Civic Orchestra directed by Dr. Paul Kosok, Heckscher Theatre, New York City, March 8, 1942, JPJC. Johnson's truncated piano performance of this score has been released on James P. Johnson, "Jungle Drums," *The Original James P. Johnson, 1942–1945: Piano Solos*, Smithsonian Folkways SF CD 40812, 1996, compact disc. The orchestral score has been recorded by Marin Alsop and the Concordia Orchestra, *Victory Stride: The Symphonic Music of James P. Johnson*, MusicMasters 01612-67140-2, 1994, compact disc.

52. Langston Hughes, typescript lyrics to "Can't You Hear Those Jungle Drums?," JPJC.

53. See, for example, the full orchestral score and instrumental part scores to the composition, as well as the following letter: Charles Handy, New York, to James P. Johnson and Andy Razaf, New York, February 4, 1938. All from the JPJC.

54. Abel Green, "Night Club Reviews: Connie's Inn, N.Y.," *Variety*, May 27, 1932, 58.

55. See Marshall Stearns's often-repeated account of a similar Ellington performance in *The Story of Jazz* (New York: Oxford University Press, 1956), 184.

56. Ibid., 183.

57. See Tucker, "Genesis," and Peress, *Dvořák to Duke Ellington*, 11–12 and 180–88.

58. See the program entitled "*The Plantation Revue*, first edition featuring William Bryant and Barrington Guy in 'Doin' the King Kong'" in the SCRBC.

59. Woll, *Black Musical Theatre*, 111.

60. Ibid., 110.

61. Blake, quoted in Huggins, *Voices from Harlem Renaissance*, 339–40.

62. See Klaus Stratemann, *Duke Ellington: Day by Day and Film by Film* (Copenhagen: JazzMedia, 1992), 119.

63. Ibid., 120.

64. *New Theater*, December 1935, 6, Jerry Valburn Duke Ellington collection, Box 1, Library of Congress, Washington, D.C., reprinted in Stuart Nicholson, *A Portrait of Duke Ellington* (London: Pan Books, 2000), 173.

65. Jeffrey Magee, "Kinds of Blue: Miles Davis, Afro-Modernism, and the Blues," *Jazz Perspectives* 1 (May 2007): 4.

66. Guthrie P. Ramsey Jr., *Race Music: Black Cultures from Bebop to Hip-Hop* (Berkeley and Los Angeles: University of California Press; Chicago: Center for Black Music Research, 2003), 28–29.

67. Ibid., 111.

68. Magee, "Kinds of Blue," 4. See also Ramsey, *Race Music*, 44–51.

69. Ramsey, *Race Music*, 45. See also Floyd, *Power of Black Music*.

CHAPTER FOUR

1. Tucker, "Genesis."

2. Sargeant, *Jazz: Hot and Hybrid*, 246.

3. Dodge, "Negro Jazz," in *Hot Jazz and Jazz Dance: Roger Pryor, Collected Writings, 1929–1964*, ed. Pryor Dodge (New York: Oxford University Press, 1995), 3–8. The 1925 origins of this essay are outlined by Dodge's son, Pryor Dodge, on p. ix of the preface.

4. See, for example, W. F., "Arts and Letters," *New York Sun*, February 15, 2005, 18. This review considers Joshua Berrett's *Louis Armstrong and Paul Whiteman: Two Kings of Jazz* (New Haven: Yale University Press, 2004). Additional new Whiteman research can be seen in Don Rayno, *Paul Whiteman: Pioneer in American Music*, vol. 1, *1890–1930* (Lanham, Md.: Scarecrow Press, 2003).

5. Charles Hamm, "Towards a New Reading of Gershwin," in *The Gershwin Style: New Looks at the Music of George Gershwin*, ed. Wayne Schneider (New York: Oxford University Press, 1999), 6. Also see Kathy J. Ogren, *The Jazz Revolution:*

Twenties America and the Meaning of Jazz (New York: Oxford University Press, 1989).

6. See DeVeaux, "Constructing the Jazz Tradition"; and Bernard Gendron, "'Moldy Figs' and Modernists: Jazz at War (1942–1946)," in *Jazz among the Discourses*, ed. Krin Gabbard (Durham, N.C.: Duke University Press, 1995), 31–56.

7. Scott DeVeaux, from the abstract to his paper entitled "Core and Boundaries," 2005 Leeds International Jazz Conference, Leeds, March 11, 2005.

8. See Tucker, "Genesis"; and Lisa Barg, "Race, Narrative, and Nation in Duke Ellington's *Black, Brown and Beige*," in "National Voices/Modernist Histories: Race, Performance and Remembrance in American Music, 1927–1943," Ph.D. diss., State University of New York at Stony Brook, 2001, 166–238.

9. Ellington, *Music Is My Mistress*, 103. This Whiteman performance can be heard on Paul Whiteman, *Paul Whiteman: Carnegie Hall Concert, December 25, 1938*, Nostalgia Arts 3033-3025, 2005, compact disc.

10. Duke Ellington, "Duke Becomes a Critic," *Down Beat*, July 1939, 8, 35, reprinted in DER, 95–96.

11. DER, 132.

12. A 1933 advertising manual from Ellington's association with Mills Artists can be seen in Nicholson, *Portrait of Duke Ellington*, 152–59. The DEC contains numerous advertising manuals from Ellington's association with the William Morris Agency in the late 1930s and early 1940s. Also see H. T., "Music in Review: Paul Whiteman Brings the Broadway Spirit to the Classic Reaches of the Stadium," *New York Times*, August 5, 1933, 9.

13. There is some confusion over the title of this series in both Whiteman- and Ellington-related sources. See "New Music Works in Radio Concerts: 13 Composers Named by Paul Whiteman Represented on Weekly Broadcast Series," *New York Times*, September 6, 1944, 17; Thomas A. DeLong, *Pops: Paul Whiteman, King of Jazz* (Piscataway, N.J.: New Century Publishers, 1983), 268; Leonard Feather, program notes to Duke Ellington and His Orchestra, Carnegie Hall, New York, December 19, 1944, n.p., DEC; and sample listings in "Radio Today," *New York Times*, September 5, 1944, 31 (the premiere program) and "Radio Today," *New York Times*, October 17, 1944, 37. I have listened to two broadcasts of this program (September 19, 1944, and October 17, 1945), and neither refers to the show as "Music Out of the Blue." From the author's personal collection, no additional information known.

14. DeLong, *Pops*, 268.

15. *Decca Presents an Album of Modern American Music Played by Meredith Willson and His Concert Orchestra*, Decca Album 219, 1941, 78 rpm (3 discs). Duke Ellington, *American Lullaby* (New York: Robbins Music, 1942).

16. "Six Composers to Collaborate on NYC Portrait," *Down Beat*, October 20, 1950, 3.

17. Leonard Feather, "Duke Readies New Works for Met Opera House Bow," *Down Beat*, January 26, 1951, 1; Ellington, *Duke Ellington in Person*, 96–97; and James Lincoln Collier, *Duke Ellington* (New York: Oxford University Press, 1987), 283.

18. Zez Confrey, *Kitten on the Keys* (New York: Jack Mills, 1921).

19. Louis Alter, *Manhattan Serenade* (New York: Robbins Music, 1928). This work was published both as a piano solo and as a concert orchestra arrangement

(by Domenico Savino). Recordings include Nathaniel Shilkret and the Victor Salon Orchestra, *Manhattan Serenade*, Victor 35914 (rec. 1928; arr. Savino); and Whiteman's later recording (arr. Leeman) in his *Album of Manhattan: Metropolitan Impressions by Louis Alter,* Paul Whiteman and His Concert Orchestra, Decca Album no. 116, 1940, 78 rpm (3 discs).

20. Lange, *Arranging,* 212.

21. Ferde Grofé, *Metropolis: A Fantasie in Blue* (New York: Robbins Music, 1928).

22. For examples of this trend in Ellington criticism, see R. D. Darrell, *Phonograph Monthly,* July 1928, reprinted in DER, 35; R. D. Darrell, *Phonograph Monthly,* January 1931, reprinted in DER, 38–39; R. D. Darrell, "Black Beauty"; Dodge, "Negro Jazz"; Roger Pryor Dodge, "Harpsichords and Jazz Trumpets," *Hound and Horn* (July–September 1934), 602–6, reprinted in Dodge, *Hot Jazz,* 12–26; Constant Lambert, *Music Ho! A Study of Music in Decline* (London: Faber and Faber, 1941), 155–64; and Constant Lambert, "Gramophone Notes," *New Statesman and Nation,* August 1, 1931, 150.

23. Lambert, *Music Ho!,* 156.

24. The William Morris Agency, *Manual for Advertising,* ca. 1938, for Duke Ellington and His Orchestra, from the first page entitled "Advertising Manual." Assembled on loose pages without numbers, DEC.

25. Ibid., "Ellington's Ability as Composer Given Serious Approval," from a page entitled "Press Stories."

26. See Ellington, *Duke Ellington in Person,* 34.

27. Ellington, *Music Is My Mistress,* 73.

28. Tucker, *Ellington: Early Years,* 266.

29. *Orchestra World,* January 1927, 21. See Tucker, *Ellington: Early Years,* 199 and 303 n. 18.

30. For a reproduction of this undated, mid-1920s lead sheet of *Rhapsody Jr.,* see Erik Wiedemann, "Duke Ellington: The Composer," *Annual Review of Jazz Studies* 5 (Metuchen, N.J.: Institute of Jazz Studies and Scarecrow Press, 1991), 41 and 60–61. Wiedemann notes that Mercer Ellington had the impression that the lead sheet was not in the handwriting of his father.

31. Arrangements of both *Bird of Paradise* and *Rhapsody Jr.* were recorded by the Jimmie Lunceford Orchestra in 1935. These performances can be heard on Jimmie Lunceford, *The Jimmie Lunceford Orchestra: Stomp It Off,* vol. 1 (1934–35), GRP 1001694, 1992, compact disc. Both recordings were made on May 29, 1935, and were issued together on Decca 639. For each chart, arranging credits were given to Edwin Wilcox and Eddie Durham (both members of the Lunceford orchestra).

32. Leroy Smith and His Orchestra, *Rhapsody in Blue,* Victor 21328 (rec. February 23, 1928).

33. Felix Mendelssohn, "Spring Song," op. 62, no. 6 (from *Songs Without Words,* 1842).

34. The 1926 score's conclusion on the D strain is not entirely verifiable, in that on the undated, mid-1920s lead sheet this strain closes with a *sectional* double bar line, rather than a *final* double bar line. According to the standards of stride and novelty composition in 1926, it is likely that the composition returned to a final A strain statement.

35. Ellington, *Music Is My Mistress*, 73.

36. Billy Strayhorn, "The Ellington Effect," *Down Beat*, November 5, 1952, 2.

37. This performance can be heard on Duke Ellington, *The Duke Ellington Carnegie Hall Concerts: January 1943*, Prestige 2PCD-34004-2, 1991, compact disc. The December 1938 Whiteman performance can be heard on Paul Whiteman, *Paul Whiteman: Carnegie Hall Concert, December 25, 1938*, Nostalgia Arts 303 3025, 2005, compact disc.

38. Duke Ellington and His Orchestra, *Creole Rhapsody*, Brunswick 6093 (rec. January 1931), and Victor 36049 (rec. June 1931). For early examples of this literature, see A. J. Bishop, "Duke's *Creole Rhapsody*," *Jazz Monthly*, November 1963, 12; reprinted in DER, 347; Robert D. Crowley, "*Black, Brown and Beige* after 16 Years," *Jazz* 2 (1959): 98–104, reprinted in DER, 180; Max Harrison, "Some Reflections on Ellington's Longer Works," *Jazz Monthly*, January 1964, 12–16, reprinted in DER, 387–94; Gunther Schuller, "The Future of Form in Jazz," *Saturday Review of Literature*, January 12, 1957, 561, reprinted in Gunther Schuller, *Musings: The Musical Worlds of Gunther Schuller* (New York: Oxford University Press, 1986), 18–25; and Gunther Schuller, *Early Jazz: Its Roots and Musical Development* (New York: Oxford University Press, 1968), 353–54.

39. Ellington, *Music Is My Mistress*, 82.

40. Crowley, "*Black* after 16 Years," 183.

41. Schuller, "Future of Form," 561, and *Early Jazz*, 353–54.

42. Ibid., 18–19.

43. Ibid., 19.

44. See, for instance, Schuller's concert notes to a Whiteman tribute concert, in Schuller, *Musings*, 44–46.

45. Bishop, "Duke's *Creole Rhapsody*," 347.

46. Schuller, *Swing Era*, 76–79.

47. Enzo Archetti, "In Defense of Ellington and His *Reminiscing in Tempo*," *American Music Lover* 1 (April 1936): 359–60, 364, reprinted in DER, 122.

48. These *Reminiscing in Tempo* performances can be heard on the following releases: Duke Ellington, *Duke Ellington and His Orchestra: The Treasury Shows*, vol. 8, Storyville Records 6395484, 2003, compact disc; Duke Ellington, *Duke Ellington: Carnegie Hall, 11/13/48*, Vintage Jazz Classics 1024, 1991, compact disc; and Duke Ellington, *Duke Ellington: Cornell University Concert*, MusicMasters Jazz 01612-65114-2, 1996, compact disc.

49. Paul Lopes, *The Rise of a Jazz Art World* (Cambridge: Harvard University Press, 2002), 12.

50. See Lawrence Levine, *Highbrow/Lowbrow: The Emergence of Cultural Hierarchy* (Cambridge: Harvard University Press, 1988).

51. H. Wiley Hitchcock, *Music in the United States: A Historical Introduction*, 3rd ed. (Englewood Cliffs, N.J.: Prentice Hall, 1988), 54–55.

52. See Shirley's biography at "Don Shirley: Biography," at http://www.donshirley.com/bio.html (accessed December 10, 2007).

53. Donald Shirley, interview by the author, December 8, 2007.

54. Locke, *Negro and His Music*, 94 and 98, respectively.

55. Ibid., 96.

56. DER, 104; emphasis added. Originally Warren W. Scholl, "Duke Ellington—a Unique Personality," *Music Lover's Guide*, February 1934, 169–70, 176.

57. Howard Taubman, "The 'Duke' Invades Carnegie Hall," *New York Times Magazine*, January 17, 1943, 10, 30, reprinted in DER, 159; emphasis added.

58. Jess Krueger, "Duke Ellington Plans Symphony: Orchestra Director Humming Parts of Composition," *American* (Chicago), January 2, 1935, Ellington Scrapbooks of the DEC.

59. Doron K. Antrim, "After Jazz—What? Is American Music Stymied or Are We Going Somewhere?" *Metronome*, December 1933, 22–23, 31.

60. Ibid., 22.

61. Ibid., 23.

62. "Program for the First Carnegie Hall Concert," DER, 162.

63. See Tucker, "Genesis," and Barg, "Race, Narrative, and Nation."

64. Johnson, *Black Manhattan*, 4.

65. On musical "signification," see Floyd, *Power of Black Music*, 8. See also Henry Louis Gates Jr., *The Signifying Monkey: A Theory of African-American Literary Criticism* (New York: Oxford University Press, 1988).

66. Tucker, "Genesis," 69. *BB&B*'s Dixie-to-Harlem narrative was only the latter half of a larger story that Ellington had composed for his incomplete opera, *Boola*. Two working texts have surfaced for this opera. The first is an untitled, twenty-nine-page manuscript in Ellington's hand. The second, titled "*Black, Brown and Beige* by Duke Ellington," is a thirty-three-page typescript. See Tucker, "Genesis," 76–77. See also Peress, *Dvořák to Duke Ellington*, 11–12 and 180–88. Maurice Peress kindly provided me with copies of both texts.

67. John Pittman, "The Duke Will Stay on Top!" (August or September 1941), DER, 148.

68. See Brian Priestley and Alan Cohen, "Black, Brown & Beige," *Composer* 51 (Spring 1974): 33–37; 52 (Summer 1974): 29–32; and 53 (Winter 1974–75): 29–32; reprinted in DER, 185–204. Priestley and Cohen did not have access to the transcription recording of the 1943 Carnegie Hall concert, which was commercially released on LP in 1977 (*The Duke Ellington Carnegie Hall Concerts, The Duke Ellington Carnegie Hall Concerts, No. 1, January 1943*, Prestige P-34004 [Berkeley, 1977], rereleased on CD as Prestige 2PCD-34004-2). See also Schuller, *Swing Era*, 141–49; and Tucker, "Genesis."

69. For an account of the performance history of this work, see Andrew Homzy, "*Black, Brown and Beige* in Duke Ellington's Repertoire, 1943–1973," *Black Music Research Journal* 13 (Fall 1993): 87–110.

70. The Ellington centennial's plethora of journalistic commentary on this work is too extensive to mention here. For academic criticism, see the essays by Mark Tucker, Andrew Homzy, Kurt Dietrich, Scott DeVeaux, and Maurice Peress in *Black Music Research Journal* 13 (Fall 1993). See also the reprints of contemporary *BB&B* criticism in DER. For more recent academic discussions of *BB&B*, see Graham Lock, *Blutopia* (Durham, N.C.: Duke University Press, 1999), 107–18; and Barg, "Race, Narrative, and Nation."

71. Antheil, "Jazz Is Music," 64.

72. Walter van de Leur has observed that *Beige* involved a number of compositional and arranging contributions from Billy Strayhorn. See Walter van de Leur, *Something to Live For: The Music of Billy Strayhorn* (New York: Oxford University Press, 2002), 87–89, and 203.

73. Schuller, *Swing Era*, 141 and 144.

74. Priestley and Cohen, "Black, Brown and Beige."

75. Lange, *Arranging*, 212.

76. Cohen and Priestley were the first to note the importance of this two-beat rhythmic figure. See Cohen and Priestley's "Black, Brown and Beige," 188–89.

77. Sargeant, *Jazz: Hot and Hybrid*, 246.

78. I employ the term *intermusical* here as a correlate to *intertextual*. For a similar use of this term, see Ingrid Monson, *Saying Something: Jazz Improvisation and Interaction* (Chicago: University of Chicago Press, 1996), 127–28.

79. For an extended discussion of Whiteman's "Experiment in Modern Music" concert series, see chapter 4 and appendix 4 in Howland, "Between the Muses."

80. This performance can be heard on Duke Ellington, *Duke Ellington: Live at Carnegie Hall, Dec. 11, 1943*, Storyville 1038341, 2001, compact disc.

CHAPTER FIVE

1. A detailed list of James P. Johnson's extant concert works can be found in appendix 7 of Howland, "Between the Muses," 623–28. Also see Brown, "Johnson, James P(rice)."

2. Henry Allen Moe, Secretary for the John Simon Guggenheim Memorial Foundation, New York, to James P. Johnson, Jamaica, N.Y., March 16, 1937, typescript letter; Henry Allen Moe, Secretary for the John Simon Guggenheim Memorial Foundation, New York, to James P. Johnson, Jamaica, N.Y., December 2, 1937; James P. Johnson, "Accomplishment," untitled and undated typescript application for a fellowship from the John Simon Guggenheim Memorial Foundation, ca. 1942 (henceforth "Guggenheim"; no date is given, but his composition lists include works up to 1942 and a reference to a forthcoming 1943 film score adaptation). All from the JPJC.

3. James P. Johnson, Jamaica, N.Y., to James Weldon Johnson, New York City, undated, transcript in the hand of James P. Johnson, JPJC.

4. James Weldon Johnson, New York City, to James P. Johnson, Jamaica, N.Y., November 11, 1936, transcript in the hand of James Weldon Johnson, JWJC.

5. Peress, *Dvořák to Duke Ellington*, 42.

6. Guggenheim, "Creative Work: Accomplishments," 4.

7. A listing of Guggenheim fellows by year can be found at the website for the Guggenheim Fellowship, http://www.gf.org/year.html (accessed March 22, 2006).

8. Guggenheim, "Creative Work: Accomplishments," 2. Percy Goetschius, *The Theory and Practice of Tone-Relations: An Elementary Course of Harmony with Emphasis upon the Element of Melody* (Boston: New England Conservatory of Music, 1892; this text was regularly reissued in new editions up until at least 1931).

9. Percy Goetschius, *The Homophonic Forms of Musical Composition: An Exhaustive Treatise on the Structure and Development of Musical Forms from the Simple Phrase to the Song-Form with Trio* (New York: G. Schirmer, 1898; republished in numerous later editions); Percy Goetschius, *Counterpoint Applied in the Invention,*

Fugue, Canon and Other Polyphonic Forms: An Exhaustive Treatise on the Structural and Formal Details of the Polyphonic or Contrapuntal Forms of Music, for the Use of General and Special Students of Music (New York: G. Schirmer, 1902; republished in numerous later editions); Percy Goetschius, *The Larger Forms of Musical Composition: An Exhaustive Explanation of the Variations, Rondos, and Sonata Designs, for the General Student of Musical Analysis, and for the Special Student of Structural Composition* (New York: G. Schirmer, 1915; republished in numerous later editions); Ebenezer Prout, *Instrumentation* (London: Novello, 1877).

10. Guggenheim, "Creative Work: Accomplishments," 4. Ernst Friedrich Richter, *Manual of Harmony* (New York: G. Schirmer, 1912); Ebenezer Prout, *Counterpoint: Strict and Free* (London: Augener, 1890).

11. Guggenheim, "Plan of Work," 1.

12. See especially the typescript "First American Ballet," in the Von Grona Collection, JRDD.

13. See for example, "Symphony Music," photo, caption, and text without attribution, from the Von Grona Collection, JRDD.

14. "American Negro Ballet Premieres: Von Grona's Troupe at Lafayette Theatre," *New York Amsterdam News*, November 20, 1937, from the JPJC scrapbooks.

15. "American Negro Ballet Gives Initial Program: Group Dances to Music of Bach and Ellington," *Herald Tribune*, November 22, 1937, from the Von Grona Collection, JRDD. Also see concert program, presumably opening night, "The American Negro Ballet under the Direction of Von Grona, New York Negro Symphony Orchestra, Wen Talbert, Conductor"; and I. K., "Negro Ballet Has Performance: Large Audiences See New Dance Group," no source or date given. Both from the Von Grona Collection, JRDD.

16. Fred M. Harmon of the Transradio Press Service, New York, to James P. Johnson, Jamaica, N.Y., December 7, 1937, typescript letter, JPJC. Also see "From: News Desk, Radio Station WNEW, 501 Madison Avenue, New York," typescript, JPJC.

17. "Black, Black," *Time*, November 29, 1937, 15, from the Von Grona Collection, JRDD.

18. The American Negro Ballet, performance program, n.d. (presumably from the November 21, 1937, premiere), JPJC.

19. Program to the "Fourth Concert of the Schubert Festival by the Brooklyn Civic Orchestra," March 11, 1939, from the JPJC.

20. "Hughes' Libretto Is Set to Music" and "Music Notes: Symphony Played in Brooklyn," both without source, pages, or dates (though ca. 1939), newspaper clippings in scrapbook, JPJC.

21. This fragile transcription disc is located in the JPJC. It includes the performances of all four movements. Digital archival copies of this recording are in the possession of the author and the JPJC.

22. Concert program to "American Society of Composers, Authors and Publishers, Festival of American Music," October 2, 1939, JPJC.

23. "Turns from Popular Field to the Classics." I have been unable to locate a program for this performance. Johnson's biographer, Scott Brown, also cites a 1940 Brooklyn Academy of Music performance of the symphony by Kosok and the Brooklyn Symphony Orchestra. Brown, "Johnson, James P(rice)," 648. The

date of "April 31" is given without a year in an undated article in Johnson's scrapbooks. See "Turns from Popular Field to the Classics." Lastly, Johnson's composition performance list in his 1942 application for a Guggenheim Fellowship includes a 1940 performance of the symphony.

24. Paul Kosok, Lima, to James P. Johnson, Jamaica, N.Y., n.d., transcript in the hand of Paul Kosok, JPJC.

25. Friends of James P. Johnson, n.d., typescript form letter, JPJC. A second January 21, 1942, letter from the organization states that the first letter was sent a month earlier.

26. "First Concert of Symphonic Works by James P. Johnson," March 8, 1942, concert program, JPJC.

27. O. V. Clyde, "James Johnson Tries Jazz Style Symphony," March 12, 1942, no source, n.p., JPJC.

28. "G. W. Lattimore Announces the 1945 (Series No. 1) Jazzfest and 'Pop' Concert," JPJC.

29. Carnegie Hall "'Jazzfest' and 'Pop' Concert," May 4, 1945, JPJC.

30. Brown, "Johnson, James P(rice)," 648.

31. Goetschius, *Homophonic*, 210.

32. Goetschius, *Larger Forms*, 230.

33. While this passage can be heard in the 1939 radio transcription, this eight-bar episode is not included on Marin Alsop's recorded performance of the symphony (Concordia Orchestra, *Victory Stride*). Alsop originally loaned me her copy of the manuscript score, which was missing these two pages—and the music still works well without this initial "train" episode.

34. This number exists in both extant manuscript materials and a commercial piano-vocal arrangement. Jimmy Johnson and Jo Trent, "Yes, I Love You, Honey" (New York: Harms, 1931).

35. "Walk with Me," arr. Edward Boatner, in *Spirituals Triumphant, Old and New* (Nashville: Sunday School Publishing Board, 1927), no. 40.

36. Magee, "Kinds of Blue," 4.

37. Floyd, *Power of Black Music*, 134.

38. Joseph Horowitz, *Understanding Toscanini: How He Became an American Culture-God and Helped Create a New Audience for Old Music* (New York: Knopf, 1987).

39. Levine, *Highbrow/Lowbrow*. Also see Levine's essay "Jazz and American Culture," in *The Unpredictable Past: Explorations of Cultural Hierarchy in America* (New York: Oxford University Press, 1993), 172–88.

40. Joan Shelley Rubin, *The Making of Middlebrow Culture* (Chapel Hill: University of North Carolina Press, 1992). In addition, with specific regard to race- and class-mediations in Western music, see Richard Middleton, "Musical Belongings: Western Music and Its Low-Other," in *Western Music and Its Others: Difference, Representation, and Appropriation in Music*, ed. Georgina Born and David Hesmondhalgh (Berkeley and Los Angeles: University of California Press, 2000), 59–85. Among other topics, Middleton's essay suggests how the music of Duke Ellington contributed to a "politics of reappropriation" in challenging the symphonic jazz concert works of white composers like George Gershwin.

41. Ibid., xi.

42. Horowitz, *Understanding Toscanini*, 243. A wonderful document of this

critical legacy is the anthology *Mass Culture: The Popular Arts in America*, ed. Bernard Rosenberg and David Manning White (Glencoe, Ill.: Free Press, 1957).

43. Dwight Macdonald, "Masscult and Midcult," part 1, *Partisan Review* 27 (Spring 1960): 211.

44. Horowitz, *Understanding Toscanini*, 262.

45. Hughes, "Negro Artist."

46. James Weldon Johnson, preface to Sterling Brown, *Southern Road* (New York: Harcourt Brace, 1932), online at http://www.english.uiuc.edu/maps/poets/a_f/brown/johnson.htm (accessed February 13, 2007).

47. Langston Hughes, Cleveland, to James P. Johnson, Jamaica, Queens, N.Y., January 24, 1937. Also, James P. Johnson, Jamaica, Queens, N.Y., to Langston Hughes, undated, JWJC.

48. Sterling Brown, Washington, D.C., to James P. Johnson, Jamaica, Queens, N.Y., May 4, 1937, JPJC.

CHAPTER SIX

1. Excerpts from the text for the "Third Movement" (aka "Beige") of Duke Ellington's unpublished typescript copy of the poem *Black, Brown and Beige*, 1 and 3. Maurice Peress kindly provided me with a copy of the poem. Peress discusses the poem in his book *Dvořák to Duke Ellington*, 179–88. The manuscript is now in the DEC.

2. "Why Duke Ellington Avoided Music Schools," no source, n.p., December 9, 1945, from the microfilmed Duke Ellington scrapbooks of the DEC.

3. See, for instance, "Six Composers to Collaborate on NYC Portrait," *Down Beat*, October 20, 1950, 3.

4. Walter van de Leur notes that Strayhorn contributed ten uncredited measures to the composition and/or arrangement of *Harlem*. See van de Leur, *Something to Live For*, 115 and 250.

5. Harvey G. Cohen, "Duke Ellington and *Black, Brown and Beige*: The Composer as Historian at Carnegie Hall," *American Quarterly* 56 (December 2004): 1003.

6. Ellington, *Music Is My Mistress*, 183.

7. Ibid., 184.

8. Ibid., 185.

9. Ottley, *New World*, v.

10. Van de Leur, *Something to Live For*, 115.

11. Program notes to Duke Ellington's December 19, 1944, concert at Carnegie Hall, New York City, DEC.

12. Program notes to Duke Ellington's January 4, 1946, concert at Carnegie Hall, New York City, DEC.

13. Leonard Feather, concert notes to Duke Ellington's November 23–24, 1946, Carnegie Hall performance, DEC.

14. Program notes to Duke Ellington's December 26–27, 1947, concerts at Carnegie Hall, New York City, DEC.

15. Program notes to Duke Ellington's April 13, 1948, concert at Carnegie Hall, New York City, DEC.

16. Ellington, *Music Is My Mistress*, 187.

17. From Duke Ellington's introductory and postperformance remarks on *Manhattan Murals*. Duke Ellington and His Orchestra, *Carnegie Hall, November 13, 1948*, Vintage Jazz Classics VJC-1024/25-2, 1991, compact disc.

18. Ellington, *Music Is My Mistress*, 190.

19. Ibid.

20. Program notes to Duke Ellington's January 21, 1951, benefit concert for the NAACP at the Metropolitan Opera House, New York City, DEC.

21. Ellington, *Music Is My Mistress*, 475.

22. Duke Ellington, *The Symphonic Ellington*, Reprise R6097, 1964, LP. Reissued as *The Symphonic Ellington*, Collectables COL-CD-6731, 2005, compact disc.

23. Concert program, "The Symphony Foundation of America, Inc., Presents the Symphony of the Air in 'Excursions in Jazz,'" Carnegie Hall, March 16, 1955, DEC. The Carnegie Hall transcription recording was first released on the album *Duke Ellington: Le Suites "Sinfoniche,"* Musica Jazz (Italy) 1021, n.d., LP.

24. Stanley Dance, liner notes to Ellington, *The Symphonic Ellington*.

25. My thanks to Annie Kuebler for our conversations about *Non-Violent Integration, Grand Slam Jam*, and *Boogie Bop Blues*. An extended discussion on the connections between these Ellington titles can be seen in *The International Duke Ellington Music Society Bulletin*, December 2005–March 2006, online at http://www.depanorama.net/dems/053b.htm (accessed May 22, 2007).

26. Reissued on Duke Ellington, *The Chronological Duke Ellington and His Orchestra: 1947*, Classics (France) 1086, 2000, compact disc.

27. *Boogie-Bop-Blue/Basso-Mo-Thundo*, DEC.

28. Annie Kuebler was the first to point out the unusual hybrid/symphonic nature of this sketch. See *The International Duke Ellington Music Society Bulletin* vol. 5, no. 3 (December 2005–March 2006), viewed online at http://www.depanorama .net/dems/053b.htm (accessed May 22, 2007).

29. In the *Duke Ellington Music Society Bulletin*'s article on the connections between *Non-Violent Integration, Grand Slam Jam*, and *Boogie Bop Blues*, Annie Kuebler and Stanley Slome note that Luther Henderson claimed to have orchestrated *Grand Slam Jam*. G. Schirmer owns and circulates a Luther Henderson jazz-band-with-symphony arrangement of *Grand Slam Jam*, which was copyrighted in 1975 under Ellington's name. According to Chuck Dotas, this later score references the names of the trumpeter Shorty Baker, trombonist Tyree Glenn, and clarinetist Jimmy Hamilton. All of these musicians were in the Ellington band in 1949, but they were also together in the band at later periods in the 1950s and 1960s. Baker and Glenn are not referenced as key soloists in the sketch score. These facts, as well as the close relation between the Jackson score and the sketch score, lead me to surmise that this Henderson arrangement—which is reported to be quite different from the *Non-Violent Integration* arrangement heard on *The Symphonic Ellington*—must be from a later date and was not the arrangement heard at Robin Hood Dell (even if Henderson had arranged *New World A-Comin'* for that same concert).

30. *The Jazz Scene*, Verve 314 521 661-2/EV01, 1994, compact disc.

31. Barry Singer, "Bridging the Worlds of Broadway and Jazz, Outside the Limelight," *New York Times*, September 24, 2000, AR29.

32. Ben Sisario, "Luther Henderson, 84; Arranged Broadway Music," *New York Times*, August 1, 2003, C11.

33. Sidney Lohman, "News and Notes from the Studios," *New York Times*, June 17, 1951, X11. Also see "Radio-TV Notes," *New York Times*, June 13, 1951, 51.

34. Ben Ratliff, "Seeing Jazz as a Folk Art Awaiting Fusion with the Classical," *New York Times*, September 30, 2000, B10.

35. Levine, *Highbrow/Lowbrow*, 122.

36. Ibid., 127.

37. Singer, "Bridging the Worlds," AR29.

38. Ibid., AR31.

39. Carter Harman, Duke Ellington interview, 1956, tape 1 (1 of 3), side A, DEC.

40. Singer, "Bridging the Worlds," AR29.

41. Concert program, "Pops 1956 with the New Haven Symphony Orchestra," DEC.

42. Ottley, *New World*, v.

43. Carter Harman, Duke Ellington interview, 1956, tape 1 (3 of 3), side A, DEC.

44. See Van de Leur, *Something to Live For*, 185–93, for a useful account of handwriting evidence in the Ellington band charts.

45. N. S., "Ellington's Fans Applaud Concert," *New York Times*, December 12, 1943, 62.

46. Ellington, *Music Is My Mistress*, 26.

47. On Ellington's Washington, D.C., cultural education, see Tucker, "Renaissance Education."

48. Ellington, *Music Is My Mistress*, 20.

49. Shirley, interview by the author.

50. See, for example, "Duke Ellington Guest of Leopold Stokowski," *The Call* (Kansas City, Mo.), May 7, 1937, n.p.; Ellington scrapbooks, DEC.

51. Feather, "Duke Readies New Works."

52. Concert program, "Stan Kenton and His Orchestra in Concert: Innovations in Modern Music for 1950," n.d., n.p., collection of the author.

53. John Kirby and His Orchestra, "Charlie's Prelude," *John Kirby and His Orchestra, 1941–1942*, Circle CCD-14, 1992, compact disc.

54. Shirley, interview by the author. On the *New World* recording on *Le Suites* "Sinfoniche," Shirley's additions can be heard from 10:14 forward, and from 12:49 to the final tutti cadence.

55. See C. H., "Ellington Group in Benefit Concert," *New York Times*, June 21, 1951, 25.

56. Duke Ellington and His Orchestra, *Ellington Uptown*, Columbia ML 463, 1952, LP. Reissued as Sony Jazz 5129172, 2004, compact disc.

57. Walter van de Leur (*Something to Live For*, 25) has noted that the final ten measures of the work were contributed by Billy Strayhorn.

58. Carter Harman, Duke Ellington interview, 1956, tape 1 (1 of 3), side A, DEC.

59. Leonard Feather, program notes for Duke Ellington's January 21, 1951, Metropolitan Opera House concert, DEC; Ellington, *Music Is My Mistress*, 189.

60. Stanley Dance, liner notes to Duke Ellington, *Ellington for Always: The Duke with Full Symphony Orchestra*, Stanyan Records, 10105, 1974, LP.

61. DER, 132.

62. See Tucker, "Genesis," especially 77 and 77 n.11. On the larger cultural politics of *BB&B*, see Kevin Gaines, "Duke Ellington, *Black, Brown, and Beige*, and the Cultural Politics of Race," in *Music and the Racial Imagination*, 585–602.

63. Peress, *Dvořák to Duke Ellington*, 186.

64. Ibid., 187.

65. Carter Harman, Duke Ellington interview, 1964, tape 3 (2 of 2), side A, DEC.

66. Ibid.

CONCLUSION

1. Carter Harman, Duke Ellington interview, 1964, tape 6 (1 of 2), side A, DEC.

2. Ratliff, "Seeing Jazz."

3. Quote from "Toscanini a 'Bring-Down' to American Composers," *Down Beat*, November 1937, 13.

4. Schuller, "Future of Form," 19.

5. See *The Original James P. Johnson, 1942–1945: Piano Solos*, compact disc.

𝄢 INDEX

Fisher, Rudolf, 23, 27
Fleurette Africaine (Ellington), 273
Floyd, Samuel A., Jr., 53–54, 56, 141
Folkways Records, 48, 58–59, 69, 71, 82
42nd Street, 106
Foster, Stephen, 127–28
Fowler, Billy, 31–32
Frankfurt School, 242
Frogs, The, 19–20
Frustration (Ellington, Strayhorn), 260

Gaines, Kevin, 108
George White Scandals, 40, 46
"Georgia's Always on My Mind" (Bradford, Johnson), 59, 73–74
Gershwin, George, 1, 4, 8, 40, 46–49, 55, 59, 64, 66–67, 84, 86–88, 90, 100, 103, 106, 123, 153, 158–62, 205, 207–8, 259, 264; "Gershwinesque" scoring traits, 69, 244; James P. Johnson and, 65, 69; Mencken, H. L., on, 4, 117. *See also, Blue Monday*; Concerto in F; *Lady Be Good!*; and *Rhapsody in Blue*
Giannini, Bruto, 208
Gilbert, Mercedes, 216
Gillespie, Dizzy, 302
Gillis, Don, 10, 255
Glorified entertainment, 21
Glover, Barry, x, 202
"Go Down Death!, A Funeral Sermon," 57
"Go Down Moses," 238
God's Trombones, Seven Negro Sermons in Verse (J. W. Johnson), 57, 82, 111
Goetschius, Percy, 208–9, 224–25, 229–31, 233–34
Goldberg, Isaac, 90
Gonsalves, Paul, 259
Gotham & Attucks Music Company, 19, 25
Gottlieb, George, 83–87, 117
Grainger, Percy, 158
Grand Slam Jam (aka *Non-Violent Integration*) (Ellington), *See Non-Violent Integration*
Granz, Norman, 260

Graziano, John, 54
Greenberg, Clement, 242
Greer, Sonny, 37
Grieg, Edvard, 60
Grofé, Ferde, 2, 48, 65, 67–69, 84, 86, 99, 151, 154, 158, 161, 165, 167, 171–72, 187, 190, 264
Grona, Eugene Von, 211, 213, 235
Gruenberg, Louis, 1

Hallelujah (Vidor), 98
Hamilton, Jimmy, 194, 259–60, 283–84
Hamm, Charles, 146
Hammerstein, Oscar, 104, 106
Hammond, John, 217
Handy, W. C., 6, 29, 40, 58; Carnegie Hall concert of, 40, 45, 47–48, 51, 83, 88–90, 117, 200
Hansen, Miriam, 141
Harlem (Ellington), aka *A Tone Parallel to Harlem* and *Harlem Suite*, 8, 10–11, 150, 193, 199, 249–50, 255–56, 261, 265–67, 275–76, 280–88; formal design of, 268–69, 281–88; program of, 10–11, 267–69, 288–89
Harlem entertainment community, 7, 11, 15, 17; castes, 30; cultural achievements, 45; defined, 6; differences from New Negro agenda and aesthetics, 53–55, 80, 101, 103–4, 109–11; Ellington, Duke, relation to, 13–14; Johnson, James P., relation to, 13; mentoring relationships in, 26
Harlem entertainment renaissance. *See* Harlem entertainment community
Harlem Hotcha (Johnson, Razaf), 132
Harlem race riots, 11–13
Harlem Renaissance in art and literature. *See* New Negro movement
Harlem Suite (Ellington). *See Harlem*
Harlem Symphony, aka *Harlem Suite* (Johnson), 8, 11, 65, 200–202, 212–13, 240, 299; formal design, 220–39; performance history, 211–20. *See also April in Harlem*

Harlem Symphony Orchestra (aka New York Negro Symphony Orchestra, Negro Symphony Orchestra, and American Symphony Orchestra), 211–12

Harman, Carter, 265, 268–69, 273, 287, 292, 297

Harris, Roy, 206

Haskins, Jim, 28

Hasse, John, ix, 37

Hatten, Robert, 119

Haydn, Franz Joseph, 209, 225, 299

Healy, Dan, 118

Hearts in Dixie, 98

Henderson, Fletcher, 26, 30, 32, 35, 51, 87, 121

Henderson, Luther, 177–78, 261–67, 269, 278, 280, 287, 298, 325n29

Henderson, Skitch, 10

Herbert, Victor, 86

Herman, Woody, 302

Heyward, DuBose, 57, 131

Heywood, Donald, 135

Hickman, Art, 27, 111

Highbrow/Lowbrow (Levine), 242, 262

Hindemith, Paul, 1

Hitchcock, H. Wiley, 176

Hocky, Milton, 137

Hodges, Johnny, 139, 194–95, 259

Hogan, Ernest, 15, 17–18

Holiday, Billy, 139–40

Holland, Bernard, 298

Hollywood Club, 33, 38

Horowitz, Joseph, 241–43

Hot Chocolates, 91

Hot Curves (Fox Trot) (Johnson), 78

Huggins, Nathan, 53

Hughes, Langston, 53, 56, 111, 132, 201, 217, 243–44

Hunter, Alberta, 114

Huxley, Carroll, 149

"I Want Jesus to Walk with Me," 237

Ink Spots, 120

Innovation (Johnson), 222

"It's Right Here for You (If You Don't Get It—Tain't No Fault of Mine)" (Bradford), 50

Jackson, E. A., 208–9

Jackson, J. Calvin, 256, 258–60, 265–66

Jackson, Mahalia, 195

Jay-Z, 295

Jazz Scene, The, 260

Jazz Symphony (Antheil), 88

"Jazz" (jazz-related music) in the 1920s and 1930s, 51–52

Jazzmania, 38

Jenkins, Henry, 117, 119

Joe Davis Folio of Paul Whiteman's Favorite Modern Rhythmic Spirituals, 120

Johnson, Hall, 121

Johnson, J. Rosamond, 15, 17, 45, 48, 121, 123, 125, 203–4, 214, 315n39

Johnson, Jack, 11, 28

Johnson, James P., Bechet, Sidney, on, 33–34; career overview, 6, 24–29; concert work performances, post–1930, 13, 40, 142, 202, 212–21, 239; classical performance/scoring effects and, 60–64, 210; Clef Club connections, 26; compositional legacy of, 9, 200; Cook, Will Marion, relation with, 43–45, 111, 136, 140–41, 244, 297, 300; diversity of concert compositions, 6; Ellington, Duke, relation with, 37, 148, 245, 260, 272, 275, 297–98, 300–301; formal training of, 205–6, 208–10, 243; Gershwin, George, relation with, 65, 69; Guggenheim applications of, 201–2, 204–11, 221, 244; Harlem entertainment circle, relation to, 13, 40, 43–45; *Negro Nuances*, role in, 114–15; opera, ambitions in, 203, 244–45; Whitemanesque symphonic jazz, relation to, 6, 105. *See also, American Symphonic Suite* (aka *Symphonic Suite on "St. Louis Blues"*); *April in Harlem*; "Boston"; "Brothers"; "Can't You Hear Those Drums"; *Caprice Rag; Carolina Shout*; "The Charleston"; *Concerto Jazz a Mine* (aka *Jazzamine Concerto*); *Dixieland*

Text design by Jillian Downey
Typesetting by Huron Valley Graphics, Ann Arbor, Michigan
Text font: Janson
Display font: Scala Sans

Although designed by the Hungarian Nicholas Kis in about 1690, the model for Janson Text was mistakenly attributed to the Dutch printer Anton Janson. Kis' original matrices were found in Germany and acquired by the Stempel foundry in 1919. This version of Janson comes from the Stempel foundry and was designed from the original type; it was issued by Linotype in digital form in 1985.

—courtesy www.adobe.com

Scala Sans was designed by Martin Majoor in 1990 and published by www.FontFont.com.

—courtesy www.identifont.com